Nurturing Natures

This book provides an indispensable account of current understandings of children's emotional development. Integrating the latest research findings from areas such as attachment theory, neuroscience and developmental psychology, it weaves these into a readable and easy to digest text. It will leave the reader confident that they have grasped the important issues about psychological and social development.

It provides a tour of the most significant influences on the developing child, always bearing in mind the family and social context. It looks at key developmental stages, from life in the womb to the pre-school years and right up until adolescence, whilst also examining how we develop key capacities such as language, play or memory. Issues of nature and nurture are addressed and the effects of different kinds of early experiences are unpicked, looking at both individual children and larger-scale longitudinal studies. Psychological ideas and research are carefully integrated with those from neurobiology and understandings from other cultures to create a coherent and balanced view of the developing child in its context.

Nurturing Natures integrates a wide array of complex academic research from different disciplines to create a book that is not only highly readable but also scientifically trustworthy. Full of fascinating findings, it provides answers to many of the questions people really want to ask about the human journey from conception into adulthood.

Graham Music is a Consultant Child Psychotherapist and Associate Clinical Director at the Tavistock Clinic in London. His main clinical interests are in developing services in community settings such as schools, and in working with children who are Looked After or adopted, and the adults in their lives. He teaches on many courses and trainings in Britain, and abroad, is on the editorial board of the Journal of Child Psychotherapy and has published particularly on the interface of developmental research and therapeutic practice. He is also an adult psychotherapist working in private practice.

D1145653

Nurturing Natures

Attachment and children's emotional, sociocultural, and brain development

Graham Music

Psychology Press
Taylor & Francis Group

HOVE AND NEW YORK

Published in 2011
by Psychology Press
27 Church Road, Hove, East Sussex, BN3 2FA

Simultaneously published in the USA and Canada
by Psychology Press
711 Third Avenue, New York, NY 10017

*Psychology Press is an imprint
of the Taylor & Francis Group,
an Informa business*

Copyright © 2011 Psychology Press

Typeset in Futura and Century Old Style by
RefineCatch Limited, Bungay, Suffolk
Printed and bound in Great Britain by
TJ International Ltd, Padstow, Cornwall
Paperback cover design by Lisa Dynan

This publication has been produced with paper
manufactured to strict environmental standards
and with pulp derived from sustainable forests.

British Library Cataloguing in Publication Data
A catalogue record for this book is available from
the British Library

*Library of Congress Cataloging in
Publication Data*
Music, Graham, 1957–
   Nurturing natures : attachment and children's
   emotional, sociocultural, and brain development
   / Graham Music.
      p. cm.
   Includes bibliographical references and index.
   ISBN 978–1–84872–052–7 (hb : alk. paper)
   1. Emotions in children. 2. Attachment behavior
   in children. 3. Nature and nurture. I. Title.
   BF723.E6M87 2010
   155.4′124 – dc22   2010007722

ISBN: 978–1–84872–052–7 (Hbk)
ISBN: 978–1–84872–057–2 (Pbk)

This book is dedicated to my dad,
who I loved deeply and miss dearly.

Contents

CONTENTS

Part II

CONTENTS

List of figures

Acknowledgements

A book such as this inevitably owes its existence to a vast array of people. Maybe the greatest debt is to all those inspirational writers, researchers, and teachers who have led the field and paved the way, the many great innovators who I hope are sufficiently formally acknowledged in the text.

Many individuals have helped me with this book, particularly in reading sections and giving their thoughts. I would like to thank John Cape, Colin Campbell, Geraldine Crehan, Darren Cutinha, Hilary Dawson, Paul Gordon, Sally Hodges, Rob Jones, Britt Krause, Penelope Leach, Tony Lee, Andy Metcalf, Nick Midgely, Asha Phillips, Margaret Rustin, Sara Rance, Danny Sofer, Margot Waddell, and Helen Wright. A special thanks also to Teresa Robertson whose illustrations bring alive the neuroscience chapter.

I am also very grateful to all the students of Tavistock child development courses who have forced me to get my thinking straight and who have been so inspiring in sharing enthusiasm for this area of work. I also thank the many clients I have worked with over the years who have helped me to give these academic ideas a place to come alive and become meaningful in direct work.

Particular thanks too to the editorial team at Psychology Press, in particular Lucy Kennedy and Sharla Plant.

Last but the very opposite of least I am most grateful to Sue and Rose, for putting up with me and my foibles, and for still being there after my too frequent and lengthy disappearances into the land of computers, cyberspace, and heavy tomes.

A note on the text

In case some words and concepts are not familiar to readers, I have included a glossary at the back of the book. Words that appear in the glossary are written in bold when they are first used. Also, for want of finding a better term, I have used the word 'Western' a lot throughout the text to denote the social, cultural, and economic influences derived primarily from European and American societies, as well as the intellectual traditions within which most academic thinking, such as in psychology, has been situated. I am very aware that this word cannot do the huge job asked of it.

Introduction: the blind men and the elephant

This is a book about how a human baby, that tiny bundle of biological inheritances, develops into a psychological, emotional, and social being. I describe many of the increasingly rigorous yet exciting research findings of recent years. This is a big and complex subject, and our understanding of how people develop from infancy into adulthood, and how early beginnings affect later functioning, has grown beyond all measure. Although there is so much written on the subject, this is mainly scattered in a vast array of scholarly books, chapters, and journal articles, and hopefully much of this research is distilled here into a digestible form that can provide a sound knowledge base, and also a jumping off point for further exploration.

Nature and nurture

The question of the relative importance of nature or nurture is a theme that runs throughout this book. Whether people arrive with ready-formed personalities, or are more influenced by the experiences they have, has been hotly debated as far back as the Ancient Greeks. In the post-war period many argued that humans are 'blank slates' who could be moulded by parental and other influences (Pinker, 2002). An opposing view, increasingly made by those who argue that genetic influences are primary, is that parents have little influence on children's development (Harris, 2009). Both views are too simplistic and we now know that neither nature nor nurture is dominant. Children are all born with different **temperaments** and genetic endowments, and if 100 children are subjected to similar influences then each will respond in different ways. Yet we will still see common patterns emerge. For example, children reared in poor-quality orphanages who receive little human contact are less likely than most to develop good language skills, to build secure attachments to adults, or to have a strong understanding of the minds and emotions of others.

Throughout this book I keep in the foreground the fact that humans always develop within a context. The psychoanalyst Donald Winnicott (1996) famously stated that 'there is no such thing as a baby', by which he meant that we can only ever understand a baby in relation to the minds and behaviours of those around it. Similarly systemic thinkers have long argued that an individual is only understandable in relation to his or her context (Bateson, 1972). I try to bear in mind the way human development needs to be understood from a bioecological perspective (Bronfenbrenner, 2004), taking account of how individuals are always influenced by their biological inheritance, but also by the various systems they are nested in, whether the microsystems around the child such as family, school or neighbourhood, or larger societal macrosystems.

We are increasingly aware of the complexity of contexts and the non-linear ways in which development takes place. From the moment of sexual intercourse, and indeed before, there are trains of influences. At conception there is straight away a genetic inheritance from both parties. The newly conceived foetus carries all kinds of biological predispositions but is interacting with its environment, and influencing and being influenced by it, always in a bidirectional way. Depending on one's culture the developing foetus will hear and remember different sounds *in utero*, will imbibe different smells, and be subject to different rhythms. Some foetuses share the womb with a twin, which again is a different experience to most foetuses. If the mother's state of mind is highly anxious then stress hormones cross the placenta and affect the unborn baby. Genetic inheritances combined with prenatal influences might lead some babies to be very fragile and hard to sooth at birth, and others to be more robust or calm. Parents too can be more or less fragile, and live in more or less stable or supportive environments, and the meeting of each mother–baby pair results in unique relationship patterns and potentials.

This book will examine what makes personality development understandable and even predictable. So much can influence later outcomes. Are there older siblings in place who affect an infant's development? Is the baby raised in a culture where there are constantly many adults around, like in some hunter–gatherer societies, or at home with an isolated, inexperienced, and unhappy mother? Is this baby born into a culture that believes that infants should be carried all the time, or one that believes that babies should be placed at the end of the garden in a pram? Is the baby long awaited and desired, or the result of an accident? If the mother is not very confident then is there an experienced father, or friend or grandparent around? Are the parents relatively affluent, or on the poverty line, and do they live in a prosperous area or in inner city ghetto where violence is rife?

In recent years our understanding of such trajectories has increased hugely. However trajectories rarely follow a linear path where X always causes Y, and research these days often follows a more 'fuzzy' logic (Kosko, 1993). One can no longer straightforwardly ask, for example, if childcare is a good thing for young children. We have to ask what kind of childcare (whether nurseries, nannies or childminders), of what quality, for what kind of children, from which kinds of background, at what age, and also whether a form of childcare affects either cognitive or emotional development. Each factor added into the equation adds further complexity but aids more accurate understanding.

In terms of nature and nurture we will see that genes are important but that experiences turn genetic potentials on or off. To take one example, one of two variants of a particular gene predisposes people to be more novelty seeking and increases the likelihood of a child developing **attention-deficit hyperactivity disorder (ADHD)** (Belsky, Bakermans-Kranenburg, & van IJzendoorn, 2007a). Thus biological inheritance is extremely influential, but it does not hold all the cards. If one has this variant of the gene and receives insensitive rather than sensitive parenting then one is much more likely to develop ADHD than if one receives sensitive parenting. Genetic inheritance increases the likelihood of ADHD but the form of parenting determines whether particular genetic potentials become a reality. We will see how experience and genes interact to produce very specific results.

Multiple perspectives

Partly because of the many perspectives that are now needed to understand human development, this subject reminds me of the ancient Indian fable of the blind men and the elephant. In this, each blind man touched a different part of the elephant's body, such as the tusk, trunk or leg, and each disagreed about what the elephant was *really* like. One blind man felt the elephant's leg and insisted that the elephant *is* like a pillar, while another felt its ear and *knew* that the elephant was like a hand fan. The same can happen when thinking about children's development. We now understand much more about neuroscience and how different experiences affect brain development. Yet this knowledge is only one small part of the story. Anthropologists and historians can teach us how childrearing varies across cultures and epochs, and other vital perspectives such as attachment theory, developmental and social psychology, mother–infant interaction, psychoanalytic and systemic theory, behavioural and cognitive science, genetics and evolutionary theory, all illuminate other aspects of the mythical elephant.

I also at times cite research on animals such as rats or monkeys. Because something is true of another animal does not mean that it is also true for humans. Typical is the misinterpretation of research about bonding; grey-lag geese might bond with the first creature they see after birth but humans do not. Yet I do quote animal research if I think it illuminates human development, such as that the response to stress in the part of the brain called the **amygdala** is very similar in humans and most mammals (e.g., LeDoux, 1998).

Lack of space stops me describing in detail the various research methods used in the studies I quote. I hope it will become clear how researchers use extraordinary ingenuity to devise experiments, and for those interested in the detail of research methodology I would point to more specialist texts (e.g., Breakwell, Hamond, Fife-Schaw, & Smith, 2006; Coolican, 2009). For example, even though babies cannot speak, researchers can work out what infants prefer, such as that they favour human faces, and we learn this by watching which pictures babies look at most, or by physiological tests such as measuring heart rates. Some kinds of research look at the fine grain of childhood experiences, such as examining the physical response in babies who unexpectedly lose their mother's attention. Much of this is **qualitative**, looking at people's experience, using observation and interpreting meanings. Other research is more 'macro' and **quantitative**, often examining huge samples of data using complex calculations in longitudinal studies, such as to work out the particular effects of earlier experiences, maybe using experimental models or statistical designs.

Some research is in naturalistic settings, such as seeing how language develops in family homes, while other research is undertaken via artificial experiments in laboratories, such as looking at what parts of the brain light up when people are shown alarming pictures. Each form of knowledge can add something extra to the overall picture. We can try to understand particular experiences, such as that most 1-year-olds cry when their mothers leave them on their own. We also need to understand how this links to broader understandings, such as why it is that not all 1-year-olds cry when left. We might find that some babies are born temperamentally prone to cry more than others, but also that some babies become used to being alone and learn not to cry out. From here one can look at samples, say of the non-crying babies, and find out if similar early experiences generally have a similar long-term effect. Each kind of research has its strengths and flaws. Some think that microstudies are too small to generalise from, and others that huge meta-analyses of factors, such as the effect of emotional neglect across different cultures, do not really compare like-for-like phenomena. I have relied heavily on published **peer reviewed** articles, some of which no doubt could be critically 'deconstructed' methodologically, while others might in time be superseded or regarded from different angles. Hopefully on balance the research quoted in this book is meaningful, of use and is as reliable as possible.

Expectations and unconscious biases of researchers can also influence results. A classic example is how experimenters who were told (wrongly) that the rats they were using for experiments were bred to be good with mazes. These rats in supposedly objective tests ended up navigating mazes far better than those whose experimenters were told the opposite (Rosenthal & Fode, 1963). The observer often affects the observed, especially when the observed is alive and sentient. Another early experiment (Rosenthal & Jacobson, 1968) exemplifies this point: teachers were told that the children in their class had been tested and some children were predicted to have a learning spurt. In fact there was no truth to this ascription and the children had been randomly labelled. The labelling had such an effect on the teachers' nonconscious expectations that these particular children showed a huge rise in their achievement levels. Because such subtle biases can creep into research practice, a degree of caution is always sensible.

It is also possible to do research using the wrong assumptions. A good example was early research in America in the 1950s which supposedly 'proved' that having a father present in a boy's life made them more masculine (Leichty, 1978). The evidence seemed to be there. Researchers developed a measure for masculinity and found that sons whose fathers spent time with them had more of these masculine traits. These days boys whose fathers spend more time with them are often more socially skilled and take on less rigid gender roles (Barker, Nascimento, Segundo, & Pulerwitz, 2004). Children of course like to emulate those they love and admire, which in America in the 1950s was often a model of tough masculinity that has less purchase today. The original researchers maybe answered the question as best they could but used the wrong assumptions. Erica Burman (2007) in particular has helpfully urged a critical approach to developmental research and has cautioned against a use of research that has normative and moral assumptions hidden in it. Ideas about what is 'normal' all too often hide cultural and other biases.

It is never helpful to uncritically accept research methodologies and I would always encourage reading with a critical eye. I take it for granted that beliefs about what is true can change over time and that scientists might only be able see one version of reality (Kuhn, 1970), often a culturally dominant one (Feyerabend, 1993). I also agree with Popper's (2002) idea that we 'should' always be testing our ideas and that good scientists are always prepared to be proven wrong. I work on the assumption that one can honestly seek to get nearer what seems truer, according to the definitions of truth we currently use. Our knowledge is always provisional; we are all like the blind men groping in the dark. However, my main interest is in seeing what we *can* learn from the research rather than primarily deconstructing all the findings. Nowadays we have more information from different fields that helps us grope for an increasingly realistic view with more assurance.

There are areas I have inevitably had to leave out of this book. I do not describe, except peripherally, children's cognitive development, as space would not permit this, and I believe that this area is more than adequately dealt with in most traditional developmental psychology texts. Similarly, this book is not about physical development, and other areas also might have had more attention, such as maybe moral development. I have attempted to keep the emphasis primarily on emotional, social, and psychobiological issues.

Un-nurtured children, feral children, and the lack of human input

From conception the developing human is influenced by and is influencing its environment. Some children receive loving, attuned care, while others suffer violence or abuse, and a few other children receive little human input and are left much to their own devices. Humans have partly survived so successfully through their extraordinary versatility in adapting to different environments. Just as people thrive in Arctic snow, in oxygen deprived high altitudes and in Saharan deserts, so too can humans survive and develop while receiving loving, empathic care, or strict and regimented care, or even abuse or neglect. The developing brain will grow differently in each of these situations. This is called **experience dependence**, which suggests that brain development differs depending on the kinds of experiences one has.

There is also something called **experience expectance**, which refers to input that humans are primed to expect, and without which they do not thrive. Food, water, and oxygen are the obvious physiological examples. A kitten needs light for its visual capacities to come on-stream and if blindfolded at a critical time in its development it will never see normally (Hubel & Wiesel, 1970). Human infants similarly need certain experiences in order for capacities like language to come fully online. This did not happen for some children who have been studied in depth who tragically lived in the worst institutional orphanages (Rutter et al., 2007). I will later describe research showing how only some of these 'caught up' with their peers, while others fell behind in language, social abilities, and physical development. Often these children had been left alone for most of their young lives, and film footage showed shocking pictures of infants staring into space and rocking themselves.

This suggests that particular experiences are needed to make people 'properly' human, and challenges beliefs that there can be 'noble savages' (Rousseau, 1985) who thrive untainted by the influences of civilisation. The absence of expected human contact can have devastating consequences. Many such children are described as wild or 'feral', which often means something like 'having no civilising influence' or 'like animals'. Such children lack what most experience from the first moments of life, such as basic care and actively learning from close relationships. Children imbibe and become part of cultural rules and ways of being, what the social theorist Bourdieu (1977) calls the habitus. However, some children have less, or very little, human life to adapt to and learn from.

Over the centuries descriptions have abounded of 'wild' children, supposedly reared without human input, some reportedly even living alongside animals. Although such stories are more anecdotal than scientific, there are enough of them to put together some consistent themes. A typical example is Peter the Wild Boy, found in woods near Hanover in 1725. Descriptions of him were rife with statements about whether he was 'human or beast'. He climbed trees, gorged himself on meat with bare hands, had no sense of morality, no ability to speak and no capacity to take seriously another's point of view. Similarly Kamala and Amala were purportedly found living in a wolves' den in India, and other famous accounts include Caspar Hauser, or Viktor the Wild Boy of Aveyron, who was described as 'a disgusting, slovenly boy, affected with spasmodic, and frequently with convulsive motions . . . indifferent to everybody, and paying no regard to anything' (Itard, 1802, p. 17). Although the accuracy of each and every one of these stories cannot be guaranteed, putting them together with recent carefully investigated accounts and evidence from deprived orphans and other neglected children suggests that there is a consistent effect when children do not receive the experience expectant inputs needed to develop into cultural and social beings. Such children often never use language fully, despite huge efforts on the part of educators, and have only a rudimentary sense of their own and other people's feelings. Many steal and are quite without remorse. Such stories reveal that human development can take many forms, but that without certain kinds of experiences children fail to thrive. Exactly what is 'necessary' for someone to become human is controversial, and much that people assert is 'necessary' can be based on cultural beliefs or prejudice. Such questions will be at the heart of this book.

These findings raise another central theme of this book. To become a 'person', with what is often called a sense of self, requires large amounts of input from other people early in life, and an experience of ourselves as reflected back through the eyes and minds of those around us. Thus ironically a person's sense of self arises from the experience of being in the minds of others, without which it simply does not develop. Central to this book is the idea, illustrated by much of the research that I will describe, that one's sense of self is socially and co-constructed. Phillip Rochat puts it well when he writes (2009, p. 8) 'if there is such a thing as a self, it is not just interior to the individual but rather also at the intersection of the individual as he or she transacts with others'. Many of the following chapters will tease out this central idea in more detail.

The chapters

The first few chapters each describe key elements in early development. Our journey begins with prenatal life, and the birth process. We will see what an active being a foetus is, learning and interacting, already a character forming, but also affected by the mother's state of mind. I next describe the newborn's pre-wired abilities to relate to other human beings, adapting and responding to the particular emotional environment it arrives in, whether loving or cold, happy or depressed. In Chapter 4 I describe the strategies even young infants must resort to when coping with difficult experiences such as neglect, using defensive states that can sometimes become character traits. We see that such strategies always occur within relational two-way processes, that different parenting affects children in different ways but similarly the kind of child one is can affect the parenting one receives. Then Chapter 5 describes how empathy and the capacity to understand other minds develop, what helps and hinders this, and particularly how having a carer interested in one's feelings and thoughts affects how a child makes sense of their own and other's emotions.

The next three chapters each take a subject which provides a lens through which much of the research in this book can be viewed. First in Chapter 6 attachment theory is described and in particular how different kinds of parental sensitivity give rise to children who form different kinds of attachments. Next, in Chapter 7 culture is given attention, and like attachment, an understanding of cultural differences needs attention in its own right but also is central in thinking about most topics. I examine the huge variation in childrearing practices across societies, and in particular between cultures that expect a socially intertwined as opposed to more individualistic ways of living. In Chapter 8 the third area of theory, neuroscience is considered; a body of thought that has exploded in recent years, and here I focus in particular on how the brain's development is affected by experience, and the impact of trauma and **stress** on neuronal architecture and hormonal programming.

The next chapters each describe a further fundamental aspect of development. Chapter 9 focuses on language and how it is intertwined with emotional and social development. I outline the precursors of speech in the musicality of mother–infant communications, and how language acquisition and **Theory of mind** skills are closely connected. In Chapter 10 I look at how the past affects later experiences, and in particular I examine different kinds of memories, those that can be consciously recalled and others that are habitual ways of being that are learnt from past experiences. The controversial question of repressed memories also gets attention, and how memory can be notoriously unreliable. I look at children's play in Chapter 11 and what the capacity to play signifies about a child's development, as well as how playing also spurs development. I discuss the role of **symbolism** as well as the place of enjoyment and 'fun', and examine how the content of play reveals much about a child's psychological states. The final chapter in this section takes up another somewhat contentious area, that of gender differences. Here I tease out the relative roles of biological and social influences in determining gender identity, and the ways that boys and girls develop both similarly and differently.

There is a danger in a book like this that mothers are focused on too much, particularly as so much research about children focuses on how mothers interact with their infants. This can lead to blaming of mothers and criticism of parenting. Chapters 13–16 redress this balance by focusing on people other than mothers who are important in children's development. Attention is paid to how humans evolved to rear children in groups, with **alloparents** such as grandparents and adolescent girls supporting biological mothers. The impact of different kinds of childcare such as nurseries is also assessed. Next, in Chapter 14, I describe how children are influenced by peers and siblings, particularly as they move into middle childhood, as well as showing how humans are group animals, hugely influenced by those around them. Chapter 15 again stays away from mothers and discusses the roles that fathers play, describing cultural variations in fathering and considering whether there is anything distinctive that a father offers to a child's development, and what is lost when a father is not present. Adolescence is considered next, again a time when parents generally are becoming less central in a child's life. We see how adolescence relates to earlier childhood as well as being a distinctive phase, and I cast an eye on how the adolescent brain is developing fast and furiously.

As the book nears its end, I ask what impact early experiences really have on later life trajectories. Chapter 17 takes on the less pleasant topic of how traumatised and neglected children are affected by their experiences and what this means for their later development. A distinction between trauma and neglect is outlined, and some variants, such as **disorganised attachment**, are focused on. Chapter 18 then moves on to examine **resilience**, and the role that good experiences play in fostering emotional well-being. Chapter 19 looks at exciting recent research about the relative roles of genes and environment, before I sum up and revisit the question of the longer-term effects of early experiences in the final chapter.

Reporting research is central to my task, and so this book needs to be accurate and reliable. However, the research I examine can rarely be read neutrally. Thinking about infancy, early childhood, parenting, or the birth process means raising issues that evoke intense passions and strong opinions, which stir up memories, wishes, regrets, and hurts, and inevitably makes it harder to read about these subjects purely factually. I try not to take sides about what are good or correct practices. This is less out of a belief in scientific neutrality and more from understanding how transient and fleeting scientific and moral certainties can be. I rather hope that the findings discussed here can illustrate the huge range of potential psychological and emotional development that an infant and child is capable of.

The questions posed in this book are not just academic ones. When politicians argue, for example, that fathers should spend more time with their children and that single parent families are not a good idea, we can examine the data and see whether such ideas have solid foundations. Similarly, research can illuminate the effects of childcare practices, or ways of interacting with children, which can then inform parents and professionals. Although this is not a 'how to' book, and does not give direct advice, I hope that the research will inform people's work with children and families, and in how services for them are organised. My place of work is the Tavistock Clinic in London, which for many decades has combined high-quality psychotherapy services with research and training for thousands of professionals. John Bowlby founded and developed attachment theory there, and it was a place that first developed trainings in child psychotherapy and family therapy in Britain. The kind of research quoted in this book fundamentally informs how professionals like myself approach our work.

Strong feelings are an inevitable part of learning about these aspects of human development. We have all been treated in a variety of ways by parents or caregivers, have all suffered upsets, disappointments, and in some cases, terrible losses or horrible experiences. Many readers are parents, some whose own emotional histories have affected how they have acted with their own and others' children. Some come across this learning when it feels 'too late', wishing wholeheartedly that this knowledge was available when they were being parents, or being parented, wistfully wondering how different things might have been.

Neuroscience and psychology research teaches us that we absorb things best when we are neither over- nor underaroused, and my hope is that the reader will be sufficiently emotionally stimulated to be interested to learn, and neither be stirred up too little or too much. I have aimed to give as clear a picture as I can of the findings available that can help us in our lives and work. Such understanding can change how we interact with, respond to and think about children and families. Research can also fuel discussion about the practices and policies we adopt, areas where passions and strong feelings can have an outlet. My aim is to convey an understanding of recent research that has illuminated how the human child develops in its context. In the end all I would hope for is that the reader feels they have learnt something important and helpful which might inspire them to look at children and family life a little differently.

Part I

Beginnings of emotional and social development

Life begins: from conception to birth

Many aspects of life before birth, of processes that might seem purely physiological, can also be thought about from a psychological and social, or at least psycho-biological, perspective. The growth of the human from an embryo into a foetus, and the journey until birth is a complex, almost miraculous process. After a successful conception the fertilised egg, at this stage called an embryo, moves slowly down the fallopian tube and settles in the lining of the mother's womb, constantly dividing and growing. By 7 weeks the embryo is only 10 mm long but already the heart, lungs, and brain are taking shape and a face is forming. We start to call it a foetus, literally meaning 'young one', by about 8 weeks. By 14 weeks it has a strong heart beat, its internal organs are formed and we start to see hair, eye lashes, and other details. Each foetus is subject to myriad influences; each develops inside a particular mother, has specific genetic inheritances, and is living in a unique intrauterine environment. Across the placenta nutrients and oxygen pass into the foetus' bloodstream via the umbilical cord, as can drugs, alcohol, and various hormones. This chapter tries to unravel some prebirth influences that begin to affect the growing child.

The foetus is its own being, with its own rhythms, urges, and biological expect-ations. Its arrival transforms the mother's body into an effective host, and once plugged into the uterine wall it basically fiddles with its mother's control mechanisms, leading some to liken it to a cosmonaut in charge of a spacecraft. The foetus deter-mines which way it will lie in pregnancy, the timing of the birth, and which way it will present for the birth. It has feeling, responds to painful stimuli by turning away (Goodlin & Schmidt, 1972) and has demonstrated a surprisingly clear capacity for choice. As early as 1937 experiments (Bradley & Mistretta, 1975) showed that after adding saccharin to the amniotic fluid foetuses swallowed more, whereas foetal drink-ing rates crashed after the injection of bitter substances. The foetus can learn to get used to initially unnerving stimuli, and for example the first time it encounters a vibrating stimulus it might move, but on subsequent occasions it pays less attention (van Heteren, Boekkooi, Schiphorst, Jongsma, & Nijhuis, 2001). By 8 to 10 weeks it is moving its limbs, and rather than being an inert cell collection blissfully bathing in amniotic fluid, it is active and responsive.

It is nonetheless profoundly influenced by its milieu. A foetus responds to musical signals, moving in synchrony to a rhythm and even continuing moving after the music has stopped (Sallenbach, 1993). As early as the first trimester the foetus will jump if touched by an amniocentesis needle, turn away from the light of a doctor's foetal stethoscope (Goodlin & Schmidt, 1972), and foetal heart rates increase when pregnant mothers smoke cigarettes. Recent ultrasound video research has shown foetuses responding to both cigarette smoking and loud noises by what seems like crying (Gingras, Mitchell, & Grattan, 2005). Already we see nature–nurture inter-action; the foetus is its own being but also is being socialised. It learns to recognise sounds that it later prefers after birth, while culturally influenced tastes are also being picked up, so that for example, if the mother eats garlic during pregnancy, the newborn will show less aversion to it (Mennella, Jagnow, & Beauchamp, 2001).

A mother's state of mind influences the prenatal environment via the release of hormones. When a small acoustic/vibrational sound stimulus was administered, ultrasounds revealed that foetuses of depressed and non-depressed mothers reacted differently. Heart rates of the foetuses of depressed mothers were higher than the norm anyway, and after the stimulus they took 3.5 times as long to return to their normal baseline. Foetuses of the non-depressed group reacted more responsively, and also calmed down more quickly (Dieter et al., 2001). This is uncannily like chronically anxious or stressed older children and adults who tend to recover more slowly from alarming stimuli. Field and colleagues presented research that showed not only that foetal movement is higher when a mother is depressed, but also that a foetus moves differently *in utero* depending on the form of the mother's depression (Field, Diego, & Hernandez-Reif, 2006). The foetuses of mothers whose depression resulted in more intrusive behaviours moved around less than those of mothers who had a more withdrawn form of depression.

Neither foetuses nor children are primed to live in a world of perfect mother–infant harmony. Conflict is engrained in human nature and, as psychoanalysts and evolutionary psychologists (Trivers, 2002) argue, parents and children, who share only 50 per cent of their genes, have conflicting as well as common interests. As Trivers illustrated, it is in the interest of the foetus, not the mother, to transfer as many nutrients as possible across the placenta. The foetus sends hormones into the mother's blood stream that can raise maternal blood pressure, sometimes giving rise to symptoms ranging in seriousness from swollen calves to preeclampsia, all to increase its own supply of nutrients. The foetus re-models the mother's arteries so that she can no longer constrict the vessels that supply the embryo without starving herself. In effect the foetus establishes control of the territory and can then start to grow. The mother's body develops its own response to foetal demands, so that a complex mutually regulating balance occurs. This works well unless the fine balance is disturbed, as sometimes seen, for example, when pregnant women contract diabetes after placental hormones increase glucose (Hrdy, 1999). The relationship between foetus and the maternal body is replete with such fine-balanced 'tugs-of-war'.

The foetus itself is the locus of innumerable conflicts, maybe the best documented of which is that between the male and female genome. Haig (2004) studied genetic imprinting, whereby the same gene will express itself differently depending on which parent it comes from. In an extraordinary experiment with mice the paternal and maternal instructions were alternately rendered inactive, and researchers ensured that only one parent's genome was 'in charge' of a foetus. In foetuses where the mother's genome ruled, babies were born smaller but with larger brains, especially the parts to do with intelligence and complex emotional responses, whereas those born by rule of the father's genome were brawny and less clever. Even in pregnancy conflicting interests are engrained in our very genes and cell structure.

Observing the unborn baby

With the advent of ultrasound technology we have gained a window on the previously private lives of foetuses. Ultrasound films have shown foetuses yawn, get comfortable by moving about, grimace with pain, undergo rapid eye movement (REM) sleep, and male foetuses having erections. By 12 weeks a foetus will grasp when its palm is stroked, will suck when its lips are stimulated, and squint when its eyelids are touched.

Scans and careful observations of twins have allowed observers to witness what looks like personalities forming *in utero*. For example, one might see a twin kick another, and the other flinch and move away, or in some pairs the other twin will instead retaliate and push back. There have been several examples of such twins showing similar personality traits well into postnatal life, with for example a seemingly more placid and conciliatory twin *in utero* showing similar behaviour with their more aggressive twin in later childhood. Best known for such research is the psychoanalyst Allessandra Piontelli (1992) in Italy, who adapted a method of detailed infant observation originally developed at the Tavistock Clinic in London in the 1940s by Esther Bick. Piontelli observed foetuses through ultrasound equipment rather than infants in the flesh. She found that the intrauterine environment is quite different for each twin in a pair, one often claiming more space and resources, and seeming to grow almost at the other's expense. This might cast doubt on studies that suggest that twins have identical environments before birth. She found that some twins recoiled from contact, others barely noticed it and still others actively sought it out. She documents one set of affectionate twins who stroked each other's head through a membrane, and after birth they were seen stroking each other in a similar fashion using a curtain as the membrane. Such accounts may seem more anecdotal and open to interpretation but they raise important questions and suggest that at least some aspects of personality are developing in the womb. Another example was of twins who were violent in the womb, seeming to hit out and punch each other, interaction patterns that persevered as they grew older. As ever, nature and nurture, physiology and psychology, are hard to disentangle. It is possible that in such cases a mother's emotional states, such as of stress and anger, might have physiological effects on the developing foetuses via the accompanying release of hormones that cross the placenta.

Piontelli's work asks questions about memories seemingly developed before birth. She even suggests in one example that the behaviour of an 18-month-old was linked to the death of his twin 2 weeks before birth. This infant seemed to forever be looking for something he had lost, shaking objects in the room as if bringing them to life, and becoming anxious whenever he made a developmental leap. This interesting, but speculative, clinical example might not count as scientific 'evidence' of personality development influenced by prenatal life. However Piontelli's work, with clear video footage of prenatal life, certainly provides observational confirmation of the kinds of interactive capacities one sees in the foetus, and suggests a degree of continuity between pre- and postnatal life.

Where does parental influence start? The meeting of biology and psychology

A central theme throughout this book is how carers affect a child's psychological and emotional development. Knowledge of a pregnant mother's states of mind can predict an infant's behaviours a year or more after birth. In a fascinating experiment undertaken by Howard and Miriam Steele (Fonagy, Steele, & Steele, 1991), pregnant first-time mothers were given the **Adult Attachment Interview (AAI)**. This asks about parent's own childhood memories. Their interviews predicted with surprising accuracy the future attachment status of their as yet unborn child. Such interviews reveal less about a mother's actual childhood and more about her ability to reflect on her own emotional experiences. Typically an adult who produces a coherent narrative and self-reflective story tends to have a child who at a year is classified as securely attached. Mothers whose stories are more chaotic or inconsistent, or who are emotionally cut-off, tend to have insecurely attached children. Thus, extraordinarily, the psychological capacities of a pregnant mother predict how their unborn child will react to stressful situations such as separation a year after birth. It is a mother's sensitivity to emotional life, her own and others, that seems to lead to this effect.

Such findings imply that people who are sensitive to and reflective about emotions might also be sensitive to their baby's psychological states, and also that there is likely to be continuity between a mother's states of mind during and after pregnancy.

However, prenatal experiences have lasting influences in themselves, irrespective of a mother's state of mind after birth. A well-known example comes from the Second World War in Holland where a cohort of mothers did not have enough food to eat; many were starving and even resorted to eating tulips (Lumey et al., 2007). The foetuses of the starving mothers grew into children and adults with 'thrifty' metabolisms who stored more fat, despite the food shortage disappearing after birth. Such research describes what is called 'foetal programming', whereby unborn babies learn lessons to prepare for life later. In this case, such thrifty metabolisms led to difficulties such as heart disease and diabetes, as well as higher rates of psychiatric illness, in many of the starved babies who grew into adults living in a more plentiful world.

Factors such as birthweight are a predictor of illness decades later. Records of over 13,000 men born in Yorkshire showed that those with lower birthweight were more likely to suffer from conditions such as strokes, diabetes, and heart disease as far ahead as 50 years of age (Barker, Forsén, Uutela, Osmonds, & Eriksson, 2001). Indeed, if born less than 2.5 kg (5.5 lbs), they had a 50 per cent higher chance of developing heart disease, even accounting for socioeconomic circumstances.

However, even such seemingly purely physiological matters as birthweight often have psychological as well as physiological elements. There is consistent evidence that high stress levels in pregnancy increases the likelihood of both birth complications and low-birthweight (Wadhwa, 2005), as well as affecting a foetus' capacities for memory and **habituation**, and that such effects persist after birth. **Cortisol**, may be the best-known stress hormone, crosses the placental wall and affects the foetus and seems to play a central role, and there are correlations between maternal and foetal cortisol levels (Glover & O'Connor, 2002). When a mother becomes fearful her heartbeat alters, often leading to reduced oxygen flow to the foetus (Monk, Fifer, Myers, Sloan, Trien, & Hurtado, 2000), speeding up its heart rate.

Other known and less surprising dangers to the foetus include maternal use of alcohol and drugs. Some babies are born addicted to drugs such as crack cocaine, or have foetal alcohol syndrome. Clinicians who have worked with heroin addicted newborns have described how their jerky desperate movements make excruciating viewing (Emanuel, 1996). The effect of maternal stress on foetal development has been shown to hold up even when other factors such as social class, diet, or smoking are screened out. Once again it seems there is a nature–nurture interplay, as was cleverly shown in one recent research study. In this the effects of prenatal stress were examined in mothers who were either pregnant with their own genetic child or one conceived via *in vitro* fertilisation (IVF) that did not carry her genes (Rice, Harold, Boivin, van den Bree, Hay, & Thapar, 2010). Here prenatal stress had a clear effect, but had a greater effect on later behavioural problems when the child was the mother's genetic child. In other words, at least some of the later behaviour was influenced by the child's genetic inheritance, but only some, and once again genes and environment both play a role.

However, because maternal stress leads to low birthweight and other issues, we can on no account blame stressed mothers for the physical and emotional health of their offspring. This research takes us far beyond the responsibilities of the individual mother. Stress, anxiety, depression, and other psychological issues do not occur by chance; such stress is more likely if one is socially and economically marginalised, particularly if one is poor in an unequal society (Wilkinson, 2005), or has low social status (e.g., the victim of racism), or if one is the victim of domestic violence or abuse, or socially isolated. There are exceptions to this, such as otherwise ordinarily well-functioning pregnant women who happened to be present at the World Trade Centre on 9/11, who later showed post-traumatic stress symptoms, and also had children with altered stress responses and cortisol levels (Yehuda, Engel, Brand, Seckl, Marcus, & Berkowitz, 2005). Generally though ongoing social causes of stress such as poverty or interpersonal trauma are the most prevalent, and one can argue that maternal stress levels are a signifier of social, political, economic, and cultural deprivation. If responsibility lies anywhere it is with society as a whole rather than individuals.

Lasting effects, social effects

Although it is important not to place blame on mothers, if we want to alter trajectories then we cannot downplay what the research finds. Maternal stress and anxiety not only influence birthweight, but are a precipitating factor in birth complications and prematurity. High stress levels can alter the foetus' brain structure and functioning, and contribute to later mood and anxiety disorders (Talge, Neal, & Glover, 2007). The foetus is programmed by such early prenatal experiences, as if the unborn baby is trying to work out what kind of world to prepare for. Low-birthweight babies born to very anxious mothers are likely to have higher cortisol levels throughout their lifespan and a permanently altered stress response system (Phillips, 2007). Adults who at birth are of low-birthweight are more susceptible to the physiological effects of stress caused by factors such as poverty and unemployment (Barker et al., 2001).

Severe antenatal stress affects levels of hormones that regulate mood, such as **dopamine**, and **serotonin** and has been increasingly linked to a range of childhood emotional and behavioural problems such as ADHD, the effects of which remain present at least into early adolescence. Such influences hold firm after screening out factors such as gender, parental educational level, smoking in pregnancy, birthweight, and postnatal maternal anxiety. The impact on later behavioural problems particularly holds up if the mothers are anxious between 12 and 22 weeks of pregnancy, but less so when the anxiety is between 32 and 40 weeks (van den Bergh, Van Calster, Smits, Van Huffel, & Lagae, 2007). This suggests a programming effect of stress hormones during particular moments of foetal development. Prenatal stress affects neuronal development and can lead to infants with smaller head circumference (Obel, Hedegaard, Henriksen, Secher, & Olsen, 2003). Of course, the impact of prenatal stress can be increased by living with equally stressed parents later on, but stress in pregnancy has its own impact. Such research might aid arguments for providing psychological and social support for pregnant mothers.

Some stress can derive from one-off rather than chronic experiences, such as a mother experiencing bereavement during pregnancy, and then if good support is available the impact on the infant will be lessened by later positive influences. More tragic are overdetermined causative factors such as a highly stressed mother born into poverty, who is the victim of violence, and has little social support. She might be more likely to have a low-birthweight baby, have birth complications, which in turn can lead to difficulties in bonding. If one then adds the likelihood of intrusive medical attention, a decreased likelihood of breastfeeding, less attuned interaction, poor housing, little support, then a baby's prognosis exponentially worsens.

Social forces, biology, and psychology surprisingly interlink, an example being the case of teenage pregnancy. In teenage girls one is more likely to reach puberty earlier, and indeed to become pregnant, if one has a stressful early life, or lives with marital discord (Ellis & Essex, 2007), while a close relationship with one's father delays puberty (Maestripieri, Roney, Debias, Durante, & Spaepen, 2004). Belsky and colleagues influenced by evolutionary theories, believe that a stressful upbringing, where conditions are tough and infant survival is doubtful, leads females to breed early and often, rather than wait in the hope that there would be more stable circumstances later (Belsky, Steinberg, & Draper, 1991). In other animals such as rhesus monkeys early stress also leads to earlier pregnancies. The forces that lead us to act as we do are often hidden from our view.

Being born

While this chapter primarily focuses on prenatal life, aspects of the birth process also are fundamentally linked with psychological processes. Human birth is more hazardous and painful than in most species, due to a combination of the relatively large size of our brains, and the small pelvises that appear to have developed several million years ago when our forebears became bipeds (LaVelle, 1995). It is probably in response to this that human infants are born so relatively immature.

Cultural practices concerning birthing differ, and those thought of as 'natural' in one era might seem alien in another. Until recently the use of stirrups for birthing was *de rigeur*, in Western hospitals, and nowadays across the Western world caesarean section is on the increase, while many women also espouse natural births, often with fathers present (until recently males attending births were almost unknown). Ideas about what birth means vary hugely across cultures and historical eras, as anthropology particularly shows. For example, the Beng of West Africa (Gottlieb, 2004) believe that babies come from a place of spirits called *wrugbe*, and are reincarnations of ancestors. Gottleib described a Beng woman having a difficult childbirth who summoned a diviner who stated that the baby would only come out when she called the particular name the baby had had in *wrugbe*. When the mother did this, the anthropologist witnessed that the birth proceeded speedily. This might seem inexplicable to us, and I do not want to make such ideas out to be primitive or exotic, but simply to point out that odd practices in one culture can seem normal in another. Although throughout this book I use what I think of as the latest research to understand children's development, I also aim to be very aware of cultural difference and bias. What we think of as cutting-edge knowledge today can tomorrow seem a quaint superstition, and cultural differences are a particular challenge to us in these respects.

Psychological factors such as stress have an impact on the quality of a birth as well as on a pregnancy. The presence of a supportive empathic, and experienced person can ease births and reduce the risks of complications (Hodnett, Gates, Hofmeyr, & Sakala, 2005). Klaus and Kennel as early as the 1970s in maternity hospitals in Guatemala piloted schemes in which supportive women stayed with the mother throughout the birth, and the result was quicker births and less complications (Klaus, Kennell, & Klaus, 1993). In a later study 240 first-time mothers were randomly assigned either to a control group whose births were managed 'as normal', and another group who were assigned to a continuous supportive companion called a 'doula' (Klaus et al., 1993). The supported mothers had babies with less caesarean sections, less muconium staining or foetal distress, and who were less likely to be hospitalised in their first 6 months. A similar impact on the length of labour was seen elsewhere when a personal nurse was guaranteed for each mother, and labour times were so reduced that no increase in staff numbers was needed (O'Driscoll, Foley, & MacDonald, 1984). Research with very large samples has confirmed the impact of support in labour (Hodnett et al., 2005). Women with continuous focused support are much less likely to have a caesarean section, to give birth with vacuum extraction or forceps, to need drugs or to be dissatisfied with their birth experience. The importance of psychological support begins very early.

A huge chemical cocktail is released during the birth process. **Oxytocin** is probably the best known, a hormone released when we feel good, make love and also in high levels during labour, in both the mother and baby. It enhances immune responses and protects against physical pain and is released in greater doses when one feels supported and cared for. Oxytocin is also artificially given in pregnancy, and can speed up a labour, but this has less effect on pain and feelings of well-being as artificially given oxytocin does not cross the blood–brain barrier. Many other chemicals are also naturally released such as adrenaline and noradrenalin, and beta-endorphins, all of which protect against pain and make the process more manageable.

The quality of the experience of birth can have a knock-on effect on mother–child relationships, as research on post-traumatic stress symptoms following birth testifies (Olde, van der Hart, Kleber, & van Son, 2006). Traumatised mothers often feel rejecting of their babies and the mother–infant relationship can struggle to recover (Ayers, Eagle, & Waring, 2006). Some research suggests that later adult mental health problems, such as the use of drugs in adolescence, can be influenced by having had a difficult birth (Jacobson & Bygdeman, 1998). It is clear though that companionship and support for mothers can smooth the birth process, as well as reducing the risk of postnatal depression in mothers, leading them to feel closer to their infants (Wolman, Chalmers, Hofmeyr, & Nikodem, 1993). Of course sometimes bad luck intrudes and there are physiological complications. However, generally the research suggests that psychological, social, and biological factors interact; reducing stress levels through emotional support leads, on average at least, to easier labours, less birth complications and hence better outcomes generally. As in much of this book, the research in this chapter demonstrates the importance of psychological and emotional support, and also suggests that there is much that can be done to make the experience of pregnancy and giving birth better for mothers and babies.

Summary

This chapter has demonstrated how psychological life begins before physical birth. A swathe of influences affects the foetus' physiological, psychobiological, and psychic being, and appear to have a role in programming it in preparation for the world it is likely to encounter. The foetus is also an active being from the start, responding to stimuli but also actively initiating events. The experience of the foetus is directly affected by the psychological state of its mother. Not only do stress hormones and other chemicals such as alcohol cross the placenta and affect the developing foetus, but also the mother's capacity to process emotional experience predicts what her unborn baby's attachment status will be a year later. Emotional support for mothers makes pregnancy easier but can also make the birth process considerably smoother, again showing the importance of psychological well-being from the very beginning of the life cycle.

Born to relate

Immaturity

The human infant is born extremely immature and can do little unaided in its first months. Its survival requires reasonably constant physical and emotional care. In this chapter I look at how babies are nonetheless pre-wired with wide-ranging capacities for social interaction. They try to elicit the human responses they need, and have an impressive ability to respond to the social environments they find themselves in. Babies arrive with varied temperamental and genetic potential, while the ways in which adults respond to babies also varies enormously. A human life develops from the delicate interplay of nature and nurture, the meeting of a bundle of inherited potentials and the cultural, social, and personal influences of the adults in an infant's life.

Potentially such two-way meetings can begin immediately after birth. Marshall Klaus (1998, p. 1244) described the newborn's astonishing capacity, moments after birth, to crawl towards its mother's breast, and find the nipple, inching slowly forward with its legs, pushing on its mother's abdomen, and eventually coming 'close to the nipple, he opens his mouth widely and, after several attempts, makes a perfect placement on the areola of the nipple'. Most babies can do this if they are not washed after birth nor born with too much medical intervention. Smell is central; if one washes the right breast then infants crawl to the left one, and vice versa, and if both breasts are cleaned, the infant will choose one with the mother's amniotic fluid on it.

Babies are born primed to recognise their mother's smell. In one experiment newborns were placed in cots, and the scent of their mothers' breast milk was blown through breast pads on their left side while the scent from another mother was blown through the right side of the cot. The babies turned and strained towards the side from which their own mother's scent was coming, and when the breast pads were swapped over, then their efforts were re-directed in the new direction (Macfarlane, 1975).

Such instinctual movements are not simply reflex, but illustrate the young infant's ability to adapt and its active desire to stay close to its mother. In skin-to-skin contact a mother's body maintains an unclothed baby at just the right temperature, forming a two-person homeostatic system. When mothers breastfeed, oxytocin is released, a hormone that induces feelings of elation and love, helping bonds form, and also enabling higher pain thresholds. Encouraging more contact between mothers and babies reduces the risk of abandonment. In mothers who are at risk of parenting disorders, just increasing the time babies spend with their mothers by a few hours a day can lead to a fivefold reduction in abandonment, abuse or neglect (O'Connor, Vietze, Sherrod, Sandler, & Altemeier, 1980). For some parents bonding is not straightforward, and a helpful nudge makes quite a difference, as seen in hospitals across the world where mother–infant bonding has been actively supported (Buranasin, 1991). Swedish researchers noted that if an infant's lips touched its mother's nipple in the first hour of life, it increased the time mothers kept her infant with her by 100 minutes every day (Widström et al., 1990). Physical closeness and breastfeeding triggers the release of hormones like **vasopressin** and oxytocin, thus leading to better feelings for the baby, and also better feelings in the baby.

Bonding: humans are not grey-lag geese

Some believe that mothers and babies *should* bond at birth or else grave consequences ensue, an idea popularised in animal studies by ethologists. They described for example how geese bond with and follow around the first creature of any species that they see, and sheep imprint on their lambs' smells and reject wooing from lambs without the right scent. Humans are different though and do not have a critical period just post-birth when bonding must occur. Humans have the potential to bond with most babies, not just their own, and such bonding rarely happens immediately. John Bowlby, the founder of attachment theory, found that it is consistent care and closeness over time which gives rise to what he termed 'affectional bonds' (Bowlby, 1969). There has been a misconception that bonding must occur immediately or irrevocable damage is done.

Maternal commitment is by no means certain and bonding is a two-way and gradual process, and unlike in other species, need not be immediate and can be helped along. It begins in pregnancy when mothers often immediately become more committed to their babies after seeing scans (Ji et al., 2005) and particularly after tests showing that the babies are normal and likely to survive. Babies increase their chances of survival by being primed to gain attention from carers. Neonates are often born with startling features designed to be attractive. The mitered leaf monkey infant, for example, is born dazzlingly white with a dark stripe from head to toe. Most of us think human babies are adorable, and these feelings can extend to other baby-like creatures, such as seals with big wide eyes.

Breastfeeding facilitates bonding and lowers women's reactivity to psychological stressors, probably partly through oxytocin release (Carter & Keverne, 2002). It also provides many immunological benefits for the baby, particularly from collostrum, the rich fluid that arrives before ordinary milk. Of course birth mothers are not the only ones who breastfeed. In aristocratic medieval Europe survival rates for infants fed by **wet nurses** were as good as with maternal nursing, and facilitated both increased fertility and infant survival, and in France particularly wet nursing was endemic across all classes by the mid-eighteenth century (Fildes, 1988), and remains a common practice across the world.

Breastfeeding gives rise to the release of other helpful hormones, such as **prolactin** that increases protective feelings and attentiveness. Prolactin levels even increase in fathers before and after birth as well as mothers (Storey, Walsh, Quinton, & Wynne-Edwards, 2000). Oxytocin is present only in mammals, and is released in pleasurable moments such as when breastfeeding, receiving a massage, when we fall in love, or have sex. It is found more in monogamous mammals, as it helps attachments form, even inducing positive feelings that can blind us to the faults of another and making us too trusting. Pregnant women with higher levels of oxytocin bond better with their babies (Leng, Meddle, & Douglas, 2008), and show more positive gaze and affectionate touch. The common, almost obsessive kind of love that mothers often have for their babies has been shown by scientists such as James Leckman (Leckman et al., 1994) to have similar features not only to falling in love, but also to obsessive–compulsive symptoms, with a similarly high level of oxytocin being found in both obsessive–compulsive patients and new mothers. He suggests that the vigilant checking a mother might do, such as constantly scrutinising the cot to ensure their infant is

25

still breathing, has similarities with how obsessive–compulsive patients might check whether the oven is left on. There is even a link between high anxiety, oxytocin, and what is often called 'love-sickness' (Marazziti, Akiskal, Rossi, Cassano, 1999). Generally though oxytocin facilitates good feelings, not anxiety, and high levels in infancy leads to more oxytocin receptors, programming the body to produce more of it later in life.

Time spent with an infant after birth stimulates closeness and strong feelings of mutual affection. Some mothers of course struggle to form affectional bonds, whether for social reasons, such as living in extreme poverty, or psychological ones, such as being depressed, or being a victim of violence. In an experiment in mid-nineteenth-century France mothers who gave birth near a hospice where one could leave babies were abandoning many of their infants. Reformers came up with a plan, almost forcing mothers to stay with their babies for 8 days, and the result was that abandonment rates decreased from 24 per cent to 10 per cent (Hrdy, 1999). Affectional bonds developed, but over several days, not immediately after birth. Something akin to bonding does occur in humans, but it takes time rather than being instant, and can be helped along when there is a risk of it not occurring.

Wired to relate

Babies actively elicit 'bonding' reactions in adults, and are primed to relate to people and faces. Not so long ago people believed that infants were born blind, but babies visually discriminate between all kinds of things, like colours, and many of an infant's earliest perceptual abilities are geared to becoming social beings. Several decades ago Tronick & Brazelton (1980) showed how babies are pre-wired to relate differently to humans and inanimate objects. Infants were filmed as a toy monkey moved almost within reach and then away, suspended on a wire. Babies responded to the toys with excitement, but as something to explore, touch, and grasp, using rather jagged movements. However, they responded to their mothers totally differently, as a person to interact with, looking for a response, smiling, looking back and away. Infants generally show preference for looking at faces over inanimate objects. In the first minutes of life their attention can be drawn to a black and white drawing of a face, but not to fuzzier less distinct variants. Mothers and babies often seek out each other's eyes after birth, and newborns prefer pictures of their own mother's face to a stranger's. They also prefer looking at pictures of faces with eyes open rather than closed (Field, Cohen, Garcia, & Greenberg, 1984) and distinguish face-like shapes, such as lines resembling eyes, mouth, and a nose. Recognising faces can elicit positive responses and enhance bonding.

Such capacities for facial recognition are innate, and indeed babies prefer conventionally attractive faces, looking longer at the same faces that adults find attractive, something that cannot have been culturally learnt (Slater, Quinn, Hayes, & Brown, 2000). Yet such innate capacities allow early social learning. If you show babies pictures of lots of faces, and then later show them pictures of faces they had already seen and also one they had not seen before but which is the nearest to an 'average' of the previously seen faces, they are most interested in that 'average' one (Walton & Bower, 1993). Such skills can be actively used in making sense of who is known, or safe, or enjoyable to be with.

Newborns also show clear preferences for their own mother's voice. Foetal heart rates change when hearing tapes of their mother's voice as opposed to a stranger's voice, demonstrating early capacities to learn (Kisilevsky et al., 2009). A baby's brain waves are different when listening to their mother's voice as opposed to another female voice, babies being far more interested in their own mother's voice, even if outsiders can barely distinguish between them. Field, though, suggests that such capacities are dimmed in both foetuses and neonates of depressed mothers, who show inferior performance in face and speech discrimination tests (Field et al., 1984). Thus some experiences can turn these capacities on or off.

In one fascinating experiment De Casper and Spence (1986) worked out infants' normal sucking rates, as babies characteristically suck at different rates. They then piped recordings of their mother's voice through a speaker, but only when babies were sucking at a lower rate than usual. When sucking at their usual rate they heard another woman's voice. Sure enough these almost newborns could deliberately suck on the teats at speeds that brought alive their own mother's voices. They could equally well suck at a faster rate than usual to hear her voice, changing their behaviour to be closer to their mothers. The babies were even able to discriminate between their mother reading a Dr. Seuss story, 'The Cat in the Hat', that they had heard in the womb, and another Dr. Seuss story with similar style and rhythm, but different words, The babies learnt to manipulate their sucking to get the story they knew piped through to them. They not only recognised the difference between the stories, but could change their behaviour to get the story they wanted. Such skills might well play a role in infant survival, helping to locate mothers and elicit interactions, which in turn might reinforce her desire to interact.

Infants who are only weeks old have highly developed capacities to learn. They can translate experiences received in one sensory modality (such as sight) into another (such as touch). For example, blindfolded babies were given pacifiers with differently shaped nipples, some with spherical shapes and others with protruding nubs. Babies got to know them, via the touch and feel in their mouths, and then the blindfolds were removed. Incredibly the infants looked longer at the nipple they had just sucked, which means they recognised something using sight that they had only previously experienced through a different sense, touch and sucking (Meltzoff & Borton, 1979). Something similar is seen with other sensory modalities, such as sound and light, allowing audiovisual cross-modal matching. Such capacities aid infants in integrating different experiences, allowing the new to be linked with the old, so making life predictable and understandable. Unlike early accounts by some psychological theorists, the infant knows that the thing seen is different from the thing that is felt, that the 'sucked breast' and the 'seen breast' are not different.

Infant imitation and contingency

Infants are born with many potential social skills, but for these to develop they need to interact with others. One skill that facilitates this is imitation, and infants can imitate adults as early as 20 minutes after birth (Meltzoff, 2007). In experiments parents stick out their tongue and babies watch carefully and after a lot of effort stick out their own tongue. A 20-minute-old baby does not know it has a thing called a tongue, but is somehow translating what it sees into a physical gesture. Babies only 2 days old can imitate a range of facial expressions such as smiling, frowning, or showing surprise (Field, 2007).

Infants are definitely communicating when they imitate. They do not imitate involuntary movements such as sneezes. Heart rates increase as they imitate adult gestures, and interestingly, when they provoke an adult to imitate them, then their heart rates slow, suggesting a different intent (Trevarthen & Aitken, 2001). Soon babies can also imitate sounds and gestures. Slow-motion films of babies show how their limbs move in time to adult sing-song baby-talk, and through this what we call entrainment develops, whereby babies and mothers acclimatise to each other's rhythms. This becomes a form of mutual resonance, with each party a sounding board of the other, but also a facilitator of the next exchange. Thus, an infant experiences physiological and emotional regulation as well as learning about the interpersonal world they live in. Some babies of course have parents who cannot attune to them but all are learning quickly what they can or cannot expect of the adults in their lives.

Such imitative skills are more than reflex reactions or superficial copying. Babies engage in conversational cooing exchanges within weeks, feeding off the rhythm of the other. One might say that infants are learning who they are through the gestures and eyes of the other. Mothers respond to their infant's gestures as quickly as in a sixth of a second, and the infant in turn within a third of a second (Beebe, Lachmann, & Jaffe 1997), more like one interactive system than two separate individuals. Infants produce more speech-like sounds when their mother is smiling, especially when the smile is of a genuine kind, sometimes called a **Duchenne smile** (Hsu, Fogel, & Messinger, 2001). Although such capacities are present in the first months, much initial energy is geared to physiological regulation, sleeping a lot for example, and it is at between 2 and 6 months that infant sociability increases fast, with more vocalisations and interactive gazing.

Through imitation and having their signals responded to infants learn that they can have an effect on others, and they start to develop a sense of their agency. Making things happen is enjoyable. A 2-month-old kicks more when their kicks have an effect, such as making a mobile move, but do not do kick so much when the mobile moves but it is not of their doing (Ramey & Watson, 1972). Similarly, when their acts have been responded to contingently but then this stops, infants protest, and they develop a growing perception of the contingent relationship between their actions and its effects.

Early on babies prefer almost perfect **contingency** (Fonagy, 2002); they might stick their tongue out and another might do the same and they are happy. Imitation is perhaps not the best word as both parties always slightly vary their pitch, tone, and expression. By about 3 months they like less perfect contingency, and become increasingly attracted to novel interactions that provide high but less perfect synchrony. A father might make a sound that the infant responds to, and the father then slightly varies the pitch and this becomes a game. People are enjoyed as interactive partners and this is the start of mutual 'dances'; which leads to the capacity to tease and muck about later in the first year. Vasuveddi Reddy (1991) describes 6-month-old infants teasing, offering something and then withdrawing it and bursting out laughing, or just not going along with another's expectations for fun. Babies need an attuned interactive partner in order to fully develop these complex interpersonal skills.

Attunement, affect regulation, and marking

In many early experiences, from nappy-changing to being fed or bathed to being calmed in readiness for sleep, parents try to understand their child's emotional and physiological states and communicate that understanding. Parents read an infant's cues and respond to these, often verbally (e.g., 'oh now you seem a bit twitchy, I wonder what's wrong'). Infants who are quickly responded to, without too much parental anxiety, learn to trust that the world is a safe, reliable place. The young baby needs an adult to comfort and regulate it, and those who receive this soon expect such external regulation.

When a baby is upset a carer often empathically shows they understand by making noises rather like the infant's. Gergely and Watson (1999) have called this **marking**, which is a slightly exaggerated reflection of an infant's feelings, not quite hamming it up but not quite real, conveying a sense of an emotionally attuned mind alongside them, bearing their feelings and reflecting them back. This can be central also in therapeutic work with children (Music, 2005). Marking conveys that the emotional state, such as anger or sadness, has not been overwhelming, something that the psychoanalyst Bion (1977) called emotional **containment**. In empathy or marking we might pout in the way a distressed baby is pouting, making sounds that match theirs, moving in time to their gestures. This is not just **mirroring**, as just having one's distress reflected straight back would make a baby feel worse rather than better. However, when one's distress is understood and managed by another, it becomes less frightening.

Distressed babies who are picked up and soothed in their first year cry less than others after a year (Ainsworth & Bell, 1977). They experience their emotions being managed, contained, and modulated, and learn not to be overwhelmed by experiences. They also learn to manage their own feelings, as if a parental capacity has been internalised. Such early experiences, of being understood by another, facilitate the development of self-understanding. Subjectivity and self-awareness first requires another to be aware of one. Some never receive this, such as the tragic examples of severely neglected children who often do not develop many self-reflective or inter-personal abilities. Many of the children who show up on the worry-lists of profes-sionals have lacked the kinds of interpersonal experiences described here.

Maternal instinct questioned: abandonment and infanticide

It is important not to be sentimental over what is called maternal instinct. In most primate species parents, particularly mothers, have to take tough decisions about whether to invest the huge amount of time, energy and devotion that bringing up a child requires. Hrdy (1999) reports many examples of primate and human females sacrificing their own offspring. Coroner reports for 5 years in nineteenth-century England listed 3900 deaths, mostly newborns, and over 1100 at inquest were deemed to be murder. This is a difficult area, as our values define such acts as immoral. Yet Hrdy is convinced that infanticide has been a common and even adaptive behaviour. In hunter–gatherer societies where conditions might only support one birth every 3 or 4 years, infants born too quickly were often killed, as were one of twins. An !Kung San mother has only one child at a time as they have to be carried everywhere they go. Hrdy writes 'many millions of infant deaths can be attributed directly or indirectly to maternal tactics to mitigate the high cost of rearing them' (p. 297), and this has varied from leaving them in foundling homes to other forms of disinvestment.

In one foundling hospital in fifteenth-century Florence about 90 babies a year on average were abandoned, but in the year of famine 961 babies were left. Survival rates are rarely good in such homes. In Russia over 1000 were admitted in 1767 and 91 per cent failed to survive the year. Scheper-Hughes (1992) studied Brazilian shanty towns with high infant mortality, disease, and dire economic conditions, and observed mothers distancing themselves from babies who were unlikely to survive. Mothers described some babies as 'strong' and others as lacking the will to live. The latter were often allowed to die in a way that might seem cruel to Western eyes.

Timing is often crucial; human and other primate mothers can abandon a child when the circumstances are wrong, and yet can lovingly and devotedly care for another child born in more propitious times. Younger mothers in poor circumstances are more likely to abandon offspring, perhaps feeling confident that they will have other chances, while older mothers tend to abandon less (Wilson, Daly, & Weghorst, 2008).

Hrdy's point is that most mothers in human history have not had the luxury of loving every child that is born. Some evolutionary theorists (Hagen, 1999) have even argued that the propensity for postnatal depression, with its particular hormonal release, is nature's way of allowing a mother to step back from her bonding with this particular infant at this particular time. There might be good reasons to invest in children only when resources or support systems are better or when there is less danger. This idea is a very challenging one for people working with parents and children.

Entrainment, culture, and becoming one of us

Biological potentials interact with cultural and family expectations to give rise to different interaction patterns. Infant crying is a typical area where the biological and social are inextricably linked. Crying is an inbuilt signalling capacity but crying babies depend on having a sensitive listener. Babies might not know what they are distressed about, and carers often need to work out whether a cry is due to teething, hunger, or an appeal to be picked up, for example. Parents try to learn about their particular baby and babies also learn to adjust to their parents. Babies who are securely attached cry when they are distressed and want help, and learn to expect such a response. Others learn that crying does not bring a comforting parental response, and so learn not to cry.

Crying might be a common primate signal, but it also can be unbearable and send some parents into despair. In the West babies are often diagnosed with colic. Looking at babies who either did or did not have colic, Barr, Hopkins, and Green (2000) found little difference in the amount of crying, but more variation in the impact of crying on a parent and on their capacity to soothe a baby. Protective factors against colic include having a supportive partner, less stress during pregnancy, and less social isolation. When mothers increase the amount of time they hold their infants after feeding this reduces crying considerably, compared with control group babies who cry the same amount. Colic is rarer in nonWestern societies (Lee, 2000), and cross-cultural research suggests that babies begin to cry in similar proportions, whether Dutch, American or !Kung San, but what differs is how long they cry for and how quickly they are responded to. Mary Ainsworth, a pioneer of attachment research, found that American carers were likely to ignore about 46 per cent of infant crying episodes in the first 3 months of life, whereas in some cultures babies are put to the breast within 15 seconds of starting to cry (Ainsworth & Bell, 1977). This is typical of how culture interacts with biology.

Crying evolved for infants to communicate distress and is mostly biologically adaptive, but not when it drives a parent away. Temperament plays a role, and some babies are born fussier and harder to sooth. Crying evokes different responses depending on cultural expectations and parental states of mind. Many adults prefer 'good' calm babies, but that is not always the case. In a period of bad drought in the 1970s some Maasai babies were labelled either 'difficult' or 'easy', based on how adaptable, calm, or manageable they were (Wermke & Friederici, 2005). A researcher identified the ten easiest and most difficult babies, but when he returned 3 months later the drought had worsened. He re-found 13 infants and of these 7 already malnourished ones died in the coming months, but interestingly only 1 of the 7 was in the 'difficult' group. The fretful crying babies maybe got more attention, or more milk, and showed more fight. In the study by Scheper-Hughes (1992) of Brazilian Shanty towns with high infant mortality rates, it was the babies labelled as 'fighters' who received the attention and they were the ones who lived. Hrdy (1999) similarly narrates an anthropological account from the Eipo people in New Guinea, a culture that has used infanticide as one means to keep the population down. One mother had stated that she would not accept another girl, and prepared herself to abandon her newborn. She wrapped her in fern leaves laced with a rope, while the infant screamed. The mother left, but did not throw the bundle into the bush as would be usual. Two hours later she returned, cut the umbilical cord and took the baby with her, apparently explaining that her daughter was 'too strong'. Sometimes it makes sense to cry and such signalling is typical of how infants are active, communicative, and social beings from birth onwards.

Summary

This chapter has given examples of how infants adapt to their environment, learning both what to expect from it and how to actively influence it. Bonding is gradual and not guaranteed, and newborns maximise their attractiveness to survive. Many features of 'babyness', such as large heads, big eyes, round faces, prominent foreheads, induce positive and protective feelings and deter aggression.

Some infants receive attuned attention and contingent responses, but by no means all. Babies in the earliest weeks and months are acclimatising and adapting to the world they find themselves in. They learn quickly to adjust to the day–night cycle of their parents and entrain their heart rates and breathing to the adults around them. Infants separated from their mothers for a few days and then returned still quickly entrain to their mothers' sleep–wake cycle within days, although in fact boys take longer (Sander, 2007). Babies are able to recognise faces, smells, and sounds and are getting used to their own culture. They are better than adults at seeing the differences between faces of people from different racial backgrounds. Babies become acculturated, whether to the rhythms of an African hunter–gatherer tribe or a Western European middle-class family. A baby can be like a sponge for emotional, psychological, or cultural atmospheres. When mothers show expressions of joy and pleasure, their infants often do too, and when they show more sad expressions infants become subdued and begin to self-sooth (Haviland & Lelwica, 1987).

Infants are wired to relate, and to recognise and actively respond to their mother's smells, voice, and face from birth onwards. They 'entrain' to the rhythms of their environment, and in microsecond encounters are learning expectable behaviour patterns. Whether their environment is a highly interactive one, or a more socially withdrawn one, whether or not infants have a carer who responds to emotional cues, all infants are learning to survive and thrive in the particular world in which they find themselves, using the hugely varied stock of responses with which evolution has endowed them.

Chapter 4

Infant coping mechanisms, mismatches, and repairs in relating

Infants are very sensitive to the moods and intentions of their interactive partners. Beebe and Lachmann's research (2002) has shown that a mother can respond to an infant's gesture just a sixth of a second after the infant has begun to make the gesture, and an infant similarly responds within about a third of a second. This is too fast to even see in real time, requiring slowing down video footage to fractions of a second. Tronick (2007) described such interactive 'dances' in terms of a mutual regulation model in which both parties actively regulate each other. I now discuss research that demonstrates the fine-grained manoeuvres an infant resorts to in order to maintain its equilibrium in the face of stressors.

Infants have limited repertoires for self-regulation and resort to clear coping mechanisms when distressed. One well-known method for observing this is the 'still-face' procedure, developed by Tronick and since replicated all over the world. In this a mother is asked to interact ordinarily with her infant, who is normally between 3 and 6 months old. Then the mother is signalled to hold a still and expressionless face for up to 2 minutes. An infant's expectations are disrupted by this sudden change. They become surprised and perplexed, with a sense that 'this is not what is meant to happen'. Some infants work hard to try to re-initiate the interaction, others display more negative expressions, such as grimacing, and still others use both kinds together. Many babies manage by looking away, cutting off or self-soothing.

In such circumstances infants generally try to regulate themselves by getting the other person to interact with them. Ordinarily if a parent suddenly becomes preoccupied an infant might frown to communicate dissatisfaction or smile broadly to regain the attention. If such interactive ploys fail then they often focus inwards, turning away from relationships temporarily, and 'holding themselves together'. Some will avert their gaze or focus on objects around them, and distressed infants often self-soothe, maybe stroking themselves or clasping their hands together. These are all attempts to self-regulate in response to a stressful situation and can become standard responses so that when in a similar situation again they tend to react similarly.

The first examples, such as smiling beseechingly or crying out, are signalling manoeuvres, attempts to remain in communication with the other in order to feel regulated, whereas the self-soothing strategies are more a 'giving up on the other for now' and trying to self-regulate instead. The 'still-face' places infants in situations that they have to cope with anyway in ordinary life. Tronick (2007) has shown that even the best mother–infant dyads are matched only about 30 per cent of the time, and in every relationship there is mismatching and mis-cueing. More sensitive mothers have babies with higher expectations of being responded to, who are more likely to actively signal and less likely to show distress or turn away when their mother puts on a still-face. If a baby's signals are habitually not responded to, then what starts as a momentary coping mechanism, something that all infants have to manage, can turn into an ongoing defensive strategy. Such infants might automatically turn away from even friendly and empathic adults. Infants are aiming to avoid negative and uncomfortable experiences and optimise their chances of experiencing regulation of their **affects** (Music, 2001) and emotions.

It takes two to tango: blind babies, premature babies, and sensitive babies

Interactive mismatches and awkward relationships are by no means just due to maternal insensitivity. Babies are not all born the same, and parents might not always understand the actual baby they have. A classic example comes from the work of Fraiberg (1974) in the 1970s when she worked with blind babies and their sighted mothers. She found that some blind babies developed normally while others seemed cut-off and asocial. When these mothers used their natural ways of communicating, such as smiling at their babies, they did not receive the feedback they expected or yearned for. The babies' eyes did not light up in response to their mother's presence, and some mothers felt rejected or inadequate. Fraiberg noticed how some then detached themselves from their blind babies, interacted less, and the babies then withdrew into themselves more, employing coping strategies such as turning in on themselves. This could become a vicious circle, whereby the mothers felt even more helpless, interacted even less, and the babies had no choice but to withdraw further. Such patterns were broken, Fraiberg noted, when mothers vocalised and in response to these vocalisations their babies' toes or hands moved in an expressive way, with a movement here or an excited rhythmic retort there. When this was pointed out the mothers gained confidence that their babies were responding to them, and also felt they were being effective and were important to their babies. They then responded with more energy and life and interactive dialogues and affective matching could begin. These mother–infant pairs were hauled back from unrewarding relationships that otherwise could lead to a serious stymieing of their babies' development.

This work with blind babies provides an important lesson. Parents must adjust to the baby they actually have and vice versa, and there are all kinds of babies and mothers, with all kinds of predispositions and temperaments. Another interesting example comes from studies of postnatal depression. Lynne Murray and colleagues of Reading University (Murray, Stanley, Hooper, King, & Fiori-Cowley, 1996) recruited a large cohort of mothers who were at risk of becoming depressed. Babies at birth were assessed using the Brazelton Neonatal Behaviorial Assessment Scale (Brazelton & Nugent, 1995) to work out how sensitive, irritable or hard to soothe they were. The results were startling as, despite the sample being only of healthy babies with no neurological problems, those mothers who had given birth to more irritable babies were over three times more likely to become depressed than other mothers in the study. Having a baby who is harder to cope with seems to act as a 'final straw' and push some mothers into a depression they might otherwise avoid. If babies were a bit sluggish then the chance of this happening increased even more. This effect was found irrespective of whether the babies were 'perceived' as difficult by their mothers, and was a result of the interaction between objectively measurable factors (infant temperament) and maternal mood. Luckily if help was offered early then a recovery was likely but otherwise a downward spiral could ensue. Other studies have shown similar results (Sutter-Dallay, Murray, Glatigny-Dally, & Verdoux, 2003), particularly that an infant's ability to 'orientate' and be attentive makes a difference, suggesting that a difficult to engage baby makes its mother more vulnerable. These are clear examples of the two-way nature of interactions, and how the kind of baby one has makes a big difference to a parent's ability to cope.

Premature babies are another group who often find themselves in uneasy inter-actions. Partly because of improvements in medical care many more premature babies are surviving nowadays, often not much older than 20 weeks after conception. Pre-maturity can give rise to difficulties, the more so the more premature the infant. By school age premature babies are likely to show more behavioural problems, have lower IQs and there is a greater likelihood of learning difficulties (Delobel-Ayoub et al., 2009), and as late as adolescence they have more emotional, attentional, and peer problems (Gardner et al., 2004). As babies they tend to be more distractible, harder to soothe and more demanding. Again a parent who might cope perfectly well with an average newborn can struggle with a premature one. Mothers of premature babies often show less confidence and more anxiety, maybe not surprisingly, given that they are so often physically separated from their infants at birth. Mothers find premature infants' cries harder to understand, and are more likely to withdraw from them than from the cries of full-term newborns (Stallings, Fleming, Corter, Worthman, & Steiner, 2001). The human infant is not biologically primed to communicate via crying before birth. Preterm babies are also less able to recognise their mothers' voices after birth (Therien, Worwa, Mattia, & deRegnier, 2004), potentially compounding communication difficulties.

Despite this, the quality of the parent–child relationship and of family function-ing counts for a lot, and for example predicts the likelihood of later behavioural problems (Minde, 2000). Interestingly Field (2007, p. 51) showed that preterm infants who were rated by nurses as more physically attractive were more likely to thrive in neonatal intensive care units, gaining more weight and leaving hospital earlier, again suggesting that both the particular qualities of babies and the interpersonal dynamics between babies and adults affect outcomes. Children born with a disability might then be even more at risk, as parents can, despite themselves, struggle to engage lovingly with a baby they had not expected, and on top of that, babies and children with disabilities require considerably more emotional, social, and financial resources (Reichman, Corman, & Noonan, 2008).

As with other relationships, the more time a mother spends with their pre-mature infant the better the relationship that develops, and the level of engagement with premature babies in hospital predicts how frequently mothers interact with their babies on returning home. Such research has implications for intervention. Premature babies in special units might have excellent medical care but suffer conditions inimical to social and emotional development, such as constant bright lighting, intrusive, pain-ful medical interventions, and constant changes of nursing staff. Understanding this has led to changes in systems of care, such as by providing soothing sounds and lower lighting, and organising environments to minimise discomfort. Parents of premature babies also have less control and must defer more to medical specialists, which might lower confidence.

One well-researched intervention is 'kangaroo care', in which premature infants are carried upright under their mother's clothes, which has been shown to stabilise heart rate, temperature, and breathing, to increase weight gain, decrease crying, and improve sleep (Feldman, Eidelman, Sirota, & Weller, 2002). Mother–infant interactions are more positive after such care, with better adaptation to infant cues, more touch and better mutual **attunement**. Preterm infants gesture and vocalise less and their mothers also tend to gesture and vocalise less. Premature infants can seem less responsive but in fact are very sensitive, so it is easy for mothers to mis-read cues and excessively stimulate infants who then withdraw or become dysregulated. Mothers who are controlling or less attuned might not affect more robust infants but with preterm babies this can lead to worse social and emotional development when compared with more 'cooperative' mothering (Forcada-Guex, Pierrehumbert, Borghini, Moessinger, & Muller-Nix, 2006).

Such matters are always overdetermined. Prematurity is linked with high stress levels in pregnancy, and mothers who are highly stressed during pregnancy might also be stressed after the birth and less able to interact easily with their babies. Other factors also have an effect. Minde (2000) reports that mothers' fantasies about their newborn tend to become very rich from roughly 4 months and then become vaguer after about 7 months, allowing a child to be born into an atmosphere where there are less predetermined expectations, a shift that prematurely born babies do not receive the benefit of.

The research around prematurity echoes other research emphasising the importance of attuned sensitivity to the psychological state of the other. The quality of interaction between mothers and premature infants is better when family relationships are good, and results are better when parents of premature babies are well supported (Browne, 2003). Good relationships seem to breed good relationships. Yet even taking this into account, the more ill the infant, the less attuned and positive were the interactions between mothers and babies, irrespective of these other factors. While good relationships might generally breed good relationships, it is not so easy to have a good relationship with a baby we do not understand, or did not quite expect, such as a blind or very physically disabled one, a very sensitive one, or one that arrives before we were expecting it.

Early emotional defences

Selma Fraiberg, whose work with blind babies I described above, was also one of the first to understand infants' responses to painful or unmanageable situations (Fraiberg, 1982). Her work showed that under stressful situations infants develop exaggerated coping mechanisms that can become entrenched and habitual patterns of behaviour, used even when situations seem not to require this. Fraiberg's sample was of children of about 18 months who were referred after ongoing neglect or abuse. The effects of their early experiences were clear. These babies rarely sought eye contact or exchanged gazes with their mothers, rarely smiled in response to mother's voice or face, nor crawled in the direction of their mothers.

Their most obvious strategy was avoidance, and they avoided their mothers at all costs, such as by turning their bodies away. Yet interestingly they did not necessarily avoid other, more friendly adults. This was an extreme group, suffering particularly bad experiences, but such avoidance to a lesser extent is something that all infants resort to at times. If a parent comes too close, or shouts too loudly, then infants will turn their heads or bodies away. This only becomes a pattern if this happens repeatedly and in a more forceful way.

Another common response to fear is freezing. Like all mammals, humans resort to primitive fight, flight, and freeze mechanisms to aid survival. Fraiberg (1982, p. 622) described 'complete immobilization, a freezing of posture, of motility, of articulation' in babies as young as 5 months old. Many infants who have witnessed violence tend to adopt such freezing **defences** as a way of coping.

The children in Fraiberg's sample suffered an unusual degree of deprivation and poor early care. By the end of their second year the 'fight' response had been added to their range of responses, and they were often described as 'stubborn' or 'monsters'. These children were not simply 'naughty' or lacking discipline, but resorting to desperate measures to manage fear, upset, and high anxiety. They had no one reliable to turn to or capable of helping them to regulate themselves. As such children grow older their aggression tends to be either focused outwards in what are seen as aggressive and antisocial acts, or alternatively re-directed towards the self, such as in self-hitting or head-banging.

Other defences that Fraiberg discussed included how infants manage painful affects by turning them into something positive. One baby was hungry but its mother excruciatingly 'teased' him by putting a bottle into his mouth and then removing it, and allowing drops of the milk he craved to fall into her own mouth. This baby looked perplexed and upset initially, but then seemed to change his response into pleasure, by starting to kick and laugh, in effect indulging in almost sadomasochistic actions. This at least allowed the baby to remain in contact with the mother who was so needed. Fraiberg's observational work allowed people to see how early such defensive patterns develop, and also allowed important intervention work to take place. Fraiberg's clinical accounts suggest that she had great success in helping such worrying mother–infant pairs find a way of getting more healthily 'on-track' together.

Mismatches and dodges

Even when things are going very well, mutual synchrony and attunement is by no means ever perfect. Beebe and Lachmann (2002) found that mothers and babies rarely matched each other's moods and states exactly and when things were going well, both parties were moving 'in the same affective direction'; when excitement is rising in one party, the other will respond but not exactly in sync. Both parties match each other's bodily rhythms and affects, but not perfectly, which is much as happens with adults. Adult strangers who match each other's rhythms tend to like each other more (Siegman & Feldstein, 1987) and feeling attuned with others and having similar rhythms to them is a 'feel-good' factor. As Tronick found, the best functioning mother–infant pairs were in an attuned state less than one might expect, from 28 per cent of the time at 3 months to 34 per cent of the time at 9 months. This might reassure parents who believe they should be 'perfect' rather than 'good enough'.

There is a lesson here. Mismatches do induce stress in infants who in response often resort to a variety of coping mechanisms. In much everyday mother–infant interaction the infant is attempting to get an interaction back 'on-track', or in other words to repair a mismatch. Typical is the infant in the still-face experiment who smiles charmingly to regain its mother's attention. An infant thus learns that a bit of mis-cueing between people can be repaired and is not disastrous. In Tronick's samples 34 per cent of initial mismatches were repaired to a matched state by the next phase of the interaction, and 36 per cent of the remaining mismatches were then repaired by a second step. For example, a baby who wants to be picked up might sigh, but its mother might be momentarily preoccupied and this might lead the baby to feel disheartened and look away, this being a first mismatch. A mother then might try to regain the baby's attention but come too close too quickly, and the baby might look aside and place its thumb in its mouth, this being a second mismatch. The mother, realising what has occurred might delicately take the thumb out of the baby's mouth, talk soothingly while stepping back to a manageable distance, and the baby might then look into its mother's face and smile. This would be a mismatch repaired on the third attempt. Such 'dances' are subtle and leave plenty of scope for repair, but also for things to go even more wrong. Through such experiences infants develop coping mechanisms, a sense of agency, and learn that they can actively change an interaction for the better. Importantly they develop an internal representation of relationships as ordinarily characterised by mismatches followed by repairs.

Daniel Stern, another early pioneer of infancy research, examined mother–infant attunement using video analysis, in particular looking at mis-cues, mis-timings, and what he evocatively termed 'missteps in the dance' (Stern, 1977, p. 133). He found that mothers and infants are exquisitely sensitive to each other, and ironically when mothers were most controlling and intrusive then, counter-intuitively, both partners were even more aware of the other. Any baby will occasionally find the intensity of an interaction too much to bear, and will need some respite, maybe through turning its head away to the side. Research by Field found that an infant's heart rate increases about 5 seconds before it turns away, its body signalling a need to take a break from contact (Field, 1981). If a carer is sensitive enough to notice this, they too take a step back from the interaction, allowing the infant its moments of respite, and the infant will in its own time return to the interaction and its heart rate returns to normal. Stern (1977, p. 136) described interactions he called 'chase and dodge', effectively cases of 'mother-chase and infant-dodge', in which mothers did not manage such sensitivity, and seemed threatened or even rejected when their infants turned away. These mothers then came up close to their babies to force a response, and the babies in turn used whatever resources they could muster to escape this overstimulation and to regulate themselves.

When an infant's mood shifts, from being relatively happy to suddenly seeming upset, this too can be taken as a signal to 'back-off', but more controlling or intrusive parents tend then to escalate the intensity and almost force the infant to attend to them. This might regain the infant's attention, but at the cost of heightening the infant's distress. A major loss for such infants is in not learning to be interactive partners who can regulate themselves through signalling to the other. With regular experiences of this, entrenched interactive patterns can take root. Such infants do not learn to trust their own bodily signs of discomfort, such as their increased heart rates, and begin to override them.

Paradoxically to be intrusive and controlling you have to be sensitive, as it is necessary to pick up signs of another's wish to withdraw, and it is then that such parents tend to 'up the ante'. There is an increased likelihood of 'chase and dodge' with premature babies, who are very sensitive and whose mothers often want to 'haul' back into interactions, which can give their infants insufficient 'pause' time. When parents are taught to imitate their infants and so adjust to their rhythms, infants look for longer at their mothers, and with more positive affect (Cusson & Lee, 1994). In effect such parents learn about the real-life baby they have in front of them, not the imaginary baby they might have hoped for.

There can be a misconception that perfect attunement is possible or even necessary. Researchers such as Beebe argue (Beebe & Lachmann, 2002) that in good mother–infant interactions there is a 'mid-range' mutual attunement; mothers are aware of their infants but not 'overaware' and both parties give each other space. However, when there is a likelihood of danger, as seen in children who have been traumatised or regularly intruded upon, then children can become hypervigilantly attuned, needing to pay extreme attention to what might happen next.

Stern (1977) describes interactions between a mother and her twins that illustrate this. The mother found things easier with one twin, Mark, who she felt was more like herself, and she had less rapport with the other twin, Fred. Through video analysis Stern discovered that, although things were not as easy between mother and Fred, the two of them moved in almost perfect synchrony with each other. The pattern was that when mother approached Fred he then withdrew, and when Fred approached, mother withdrew. Ironically they were more sensitive to each other than the other dyad of mother and Mark, who could move in and out of synchrony without worrying about the other, a looser thread joining them. Fred was always monitoring his mother, even when he was seemingly not even looking at her. Mother was more likely to allow Mark to avert gaze without reacting, but when Fred averted his gaze, she would move closer to him, as if to force contact. Paradoxically Fred and mother never really got together much, spending little time being close, yet in another way they were indivisible, keeping a very close eye on each other.

Intrusive interactions are not based on reciprocity, and when interactive rules are not jointly set and one party consistently violates the other's wishes, then Tronick (2007) has argued that an infant experiences a form of 'learnt helplessness' in which their physiological regulatory systems become overwhelmed. In many cases Tronick noted effects such as infants who 'turn away, had dull looking eyes, lost postural control, orally self-comforted, rocked and self clasped' (p. 171).

An infant's determination to regain its mother's attention in still-face experiments demonstrates just what strong expectations some 3-month-old babies have built up about how other people are likely to respond. It is the challenge to their already formed expectations, not the silence that disconcerts them. Other forms of perturbation do not have such a dramatic effect. A related experiment asks mothers to interact with their infants, and then the interaction is disrupted by a stranger who comes and talks to the mother (Murray, 1998). In these cases the infants' positive affect lessens and they become quiet, but they do not protest, as in the still-face, and they continue looking at her. Such interactions are disrupted but in an understandable and expectable way.

In another kind of perturbation experiment designed by Murray (1998) infants and mothers interacted via video link. Surprisingly this worked fairly smoothly, with both able to engage fluently, albeit with the infant watching its mother's face carefully. This changed when a slight time-lag was artificially introduced between the mother's actions and what the infant saw on the screen, so that the mother seemed out of sync with the infant's communications. The infants then tended to get disconcerted, looking away and back at the screen in an anxious way, frowning, grimacing, and self-soothing by touching their clothes and bodies. There was less protest than in the still-face experiments, and Murray suggests that these infants were more puzzled and confused than anything.

As one might expect, the kind of parenting an infant has had will alter how they react to such experiments. Infants who have been responded to less sensitively also recover less quickly from such experiments. They show more negative affect and turn away from their mothers more. When heart rates were monitored in 6-month-olds during the still-face, infants of more responsive mothers showed more ability to regulate their heart rates and manage negative affect (Haley & Stansbury, 2003). Field used the still-face with depressed mothers and their infants, and what was striking was that these infants reacted less than other babies, seemingly because they were accustomed to a flatter response, having less expectation that they would be responded to contingently. Generally in still-face experiments infants of depressed mothers are fussier, less regulated, and show more negative affect (Field, 2002). They already have an idea of what they can and cannot expect from relationships.

The effect of maternal depression and other mental health problems

The mental health of parents impacts on the psychological development of even very newborn babies. This is not to blame mothers or parents, especially those already beset by often crippling psychological worries, these in turn often compounded by issues such as poverty or domestic violence. The risk of blaming mothers is not helped by the fact that the research is nearly all about mothers and babies, leaving out not only fathers, but also the impact of factors such as social position. Nonetheless this research remains relevant, not least in thinking about how to target help. For example, the research by Murray on the effects of maternal depression on infants also showed that screening for this, and putting appropriate therapeutic help in place made a huge difference to mother–infant pairs, and to how these infants developed into early and middle childhood and adolescence (Murray & Cooper, 1999).

Researchers such as Murray ask about the impact on infants of being in the company of a depressed adult for many hours a day. Being with someone flat and cut-off is very different from being with someone who is attuned and sensitive, and that again is different from spending days in the presence of someone who is intrusive and unpredictable. Babies of depressed mothers score worse than the norm on many tests, and have an increased risk of insecure attachment (Martins & Gaffan, 2000). Depression in the 6 months after birth has the most impact, and its effects are seen well after a mother recovers. At 2 years of age children have more sleep problems, temper tantrums, and separation issues (Stein, Gath, Bucher, Bond, Day & Cooper, 1991). On starting school they have more problems in peer relationships, and maybe most strikingly, they have a more passive sense of themselves, and show less belief in being able to influence events and boys particularly are more likely to have behavioural problems. Some of Murray's initial cohort of infants are now well into adolescence and there are high levels of depression and anxiety disorders in the girls.

Studies of mothers and babies can help to make sense of how such later patterns take root. Mothers who are depressed are less able to read their baby's signals and can be unresponsive. Their babies can respond by cutting off, dulling themselves down and self-regulating. In most still-face experiments infants are trying to reinstate normal interactions, but infants of depressed mothers expect less from interactions. This is mirrored in the physiology, brains and bodies of mother–infant pairs, with both depressed mothers and their infants showing lower dopamine levels at a month and higher cortisol levels. Infants of depressed mothers have been shown to act rather flat and depressed not only with their mothers but also with attuned and responsive adults as they reach the end of their first year (Field et al., 1988), taking their expectations into later relationships.

Different kinds of depression have different effects. Field and colleagues' research (2006) distinguishes between mothers whose form of depression was more intrusive (for example mothers who might poke or come too close to their babies), as opposed to depressed mothers whose interactive patterns were more withdrawn. Of the two groups, Field found that the infants of the withdrawn, less interactive mothers did worse. As newborns they had lower dopamine levels and serotonin levels and by only a month they had more activation in the prefrontal right sides of their brains, an area dominant for negative feelings, and this remained in follow-up research for up to 3 years.

Infants of intrusive mothers spent 55 per cent of their time watching their mothers, whereas those of withdrawn mothers watched their mothers less than 5 per cent of the time, spending much time staring into space. There is little point looking at someone who is not going to respond, but if someone is unpredictable and intrusive it makes sense to keep a close eye on them. Such adaptations can quickly become character traits. By one year in Field's sample infants of withdrawn depressed parents were less exploratory than their intruded upon counterparts, by 3 years old they were showing little empathy, had more **internalising** behaviours and were more passive and withdrawn, different to the aggressive lack of empathy seen in children suffering intrusive parenting. The intruded upon infants even did better cognitively, and perhaps inconsistent and intrusive stimulation is at least stimulating.

Maternal depression is just one psychological condition that can impact on infants, and others include anxiety disorders, **borderline personality disorders** and eating disorders. A common feature in all of these is less parental attunement to an infant's pace and wishes. Alan Stein, working at the Tavistock Clinic in London and subsequently at Oxford University, researched mothers with eating disorders interacting with their infants at mealtimes, in play and other settings (Stein et al., 2006). He found that they were generally more controlling of their infants at a year, using strong forms of verbal control particularly. Maybe not surprisingly this was most evident at mealtimes, when there was more conflict than in other samples. Interestingly there was also more marital conflict in these families, suggesting again that mothers are not the 'sole cause' of these matters.

Understanding these issues can help make a difference, and Stein has had success helping mothers with eating disorders with interventions using video-feedback. When mothers in his sample realised the impact of their interactions on their infants then the relationships improved, and the infants became more confident and autonomous.

Peter Hobson and colleagues at the Tavistock Clinic undertook similar research with mothers with borderline personality disorder (Hobson, Patrick, Crandell, García-Pérez, & Lee, 2005). They interviewed them, videotaped interactions with their infants and used the still-face experiment, and also the Adult Attachment Interview, which measured the mothers' capacity to reflect on their own experiences. These mothers were more intrusive and insensitive than control groups, had more trauma in their backgrounds and were less aware of their infants' mental states. Not surprisingly, the infants showed signs of disturbance such as not recovering well from stressful situations, being more cut-off in still-face experiments, being less positive with strangers, and were far more likely than the control groups to be insecurely attached. This makes sense in terms of the themes of this book. These mothers showed enmeshed/preoccupied thinking about their early relationships, their thought processes showed troubled features, they often had symptoms of self-harm and they struggled generally with relationships. It is hard to imagine that this would not impact on how they interacted moment-by-moment with their infants. The impact of their unresolved and troubled early lives remained powerfully alive in the way they approached relationships, and without understanding such processes and intervening, it is likely that such patterns would get passed on to the next generation.

Such patterns can be handed down in subtle ways. Murray has been researching mothers with social phobia and their infants. Most interactions between them seem ordinary enough when just mother and infant and no one else is present. However, when a stranger comes on the scene the mothers become fearful and phobic, and this anxiety is transmitted strongly to their infants. These infants learn that strangers are to be distrusted and avoided, a learning that they then take into other situations (Murray, Cooper, Creswell, Schofield, & Sack, 2007). Infants born more sensitive were even less likely to interact positively with strangers, but learning from their mothers had the biggest effect. Other studies of mothers with severe anxiety disorders demonstrate similar interactive styles, often including ill-timed responses, intrusiveness, overprotection, and insensitivity (Kaitz & Maytal, 2005). Once again the importance of parental sensitivity and attunement emerges. Infants of anxious mothers are less interactive in their mother's presence, recover less well from disruptions, and show physiological effects such as disturbed sleep and higher cortisol levels. Their experience of life is less satisfying and more anxious, and they develop less confidence that their emotions will be regulated by others, or that they can safely explore and make sense of the world.

Summary

This chapter has described how infants are active partners in interactive exchanges, and when things are going well it is often infants who make and break contact. They may have few resources at their disposal, but they can look away, avoid contact, gesture, and elicit interest. Infants are born different. They might be blind, drug addicted, more or less sensitive and born with different genetic endowments. Parents too have different capacities and people live in different social niches with different pressures and advantages. All these factors influence the emotional and social interactions an infant experiences.

Some infants are born with more capacity to self-regulate, and this is seen as early as in pregnancy when a foetus can regulate its level of arousal. However, an infant needs an adult carer to really regulate it. As Sander (2007) showed, babies self-regulate better when they have been regulated by another. Perfect parental attunement is neither possible nor desirable, and in interactions there is a constant sequence of matching, mismatching and repairing. When a parent is able to be sensitive to an infant's states of mind then infants learn to be active interactive partners. When interactions go a little wrong then infants can play a part in repairing them. The world feels less frightening if children (or adults) know they can effectively get interactions back on track. This is very different to being left to one's own devices, or being intruded upon.

I have described some of the strategies infants use to manage difficult experiences. These include avoidance, self-soothing, staring at objects, as well as more hopeful communicative strategies such as drawing their mothers back into contact with big smiles. I have elucidated the development of some early coping defences against overwhelming or painful experience, but have not wanted to cast blame anywhere, particularly at mothers. Psychiatric disorders such as postnatal depression are far more common if one lives in deprived areas, has had bad early experiences, has suffered a trauma, or has less social support. It can help, however to really understand what happens in the fine detail of moment-by-moment interactions between infants and their carers, however painful, as then it is possible to intervene and find ways to break potentially damaging intergenerational cycles.

Empathy, self, and other minds

This chapter will focus on the ability to empathise and understand other minds. I have discussed how the human infant is born prepared for social interaction with abilities such as being able to imitate at birth, recognise their mother's voice, and preferring human faces. I will now explain how more sophisticated interpersonal skills develop from this, and how the young child builds on these early experiences to become increasingly aware of their own and other people's minds. Although there has historically been much theorising about these matters by developmental psychologists, there has though been a sea change in recent years with more emphasis on the role of emotion rather than just cognition in understanding mental states. I will describe the processes whereby the ability to empathise with and make sense of the feelings and thoughts of other people develop from the first months of life through to 4 or 5 years old, when the capacities, often denoted by the term theory of mind, are normally in place.

Early precursors of understanding other minds

From birth children are learning about the intentions, feelings, and expectations of people around them. Interactive gestures such as imitating are not simply copying behaviours, but show a rudimentary yet definite awareness of another person's feeling states and intentions. Infants resonate and respond to those around them, smiling broadly in response to laughter, or looking sad when others are upset.

Infants are constantly appraising the social world and its subtle nuances. When an infant makes a gesture, such as a startled judder or a sad cry, then if a parent responds to this by 'marking' the infant gesture, by for example saying 'oh what a huge shock that was, that big door slamming', then not only has the infant's affect been regulated, but he or she has been pulled into a world of meaning by another person. This is what Meins et al. (2003) has called **mind-mindedness**, describing a parent's acknowledgement of a child's mental states. Parents who are mind-minded have children who develop skills in empathy and understanding other minds sooner than others, as do infants who are securely attached at a year. Having siblings also makes a difference, and singletons and oldest children develop theory of mind skills more slowly on average than those with older siblings (McAlister & Peterson, 2006), presumably because they have fewer minds to practise interacting with.

Such marking has links with what is often called affect regulation, which describes how a child's emotional and physiological states are regulated by an adult attuned to them. Trevarthen and Aitken rightly cautions that the concept of regulation privileges difficult emotions and underestimates positive social interactions. Parents not only regulate an infant's affects, such as monitoring the amount of excitement, but are also what Trevarthen and Aitken (2001) have called a companion in meaning making. Attunement describes someone being in touch with both positive and negative mental states, and leads to trusting that one's feelings and thoughts can be accepted and understood. One can think of affect mirroring as a form of biosocial feedback (Gergely & Watson, 1996). If a crying infant's state of mind is understood, and he or she calms down following soothing input, then we might surmise that its affect state has been regulated. But over and above this the infant has gained an understanding through the eyes of the other of what they were feeling, and their state of discomfort is thus given meaning by another. This in turn leads to the development of an internal representation of oneself as seen through other's eyes, which also enhances the ability to regulate one's own emotional states and to develop capacities for **executive functioning** (Carlson, 2009).

Some babies and children have an experience that is rather like looking into a kind of fairground version of a distorted mirror, and see and hear reflected back something which might increase their difficult feelings and leave them with no way to process them. This can give rise to distorted self-understandings, such as when a child shows fear on hearing a loud noise and his or her father shouts 'don't be such a wimp, just pull yourself together'. In such a situation the child probably will struggle to make sense of such feelings in themselves, or to be sympathetic to such scared feelings in anyone else.

Yet empathy is more than just having one's feelings reflected back at one. If an infant cries and an adult responds with a pretend cry which is too much like the baby's cry, that infant might feel that there is no escape from their upset, or that there are just two people feeling the same thing. A good example is given by Peter Fonagy (2002). Babies were taken for their first injections by their mothers. The babies who recovered best were those who had mothers who empathised with them, but also knew just when to distract them. The mothers who tried to distract the babies too soon did not soothe their babies, but nor did those who seemed too empathic, as the babies then just had their own emotions of terror and upset reflected back at them rather graphically. This again is what Bion (1977) describes as the containment of emotions, in which another person, often the mother, takes in the emotional experience of the baby, modulates it inside themselves, and conveys understanding of these emotions in a 'digested' form. Contained or marked emotions are no longer so dangerous, one can say they are 'detoxified', and need not be overwhelming.

By 2 months one can see rhythmic **proto-conversations** between infants and parents, both as active partners, each watching the other 'thoughtfully' and working out how to respond. These are sophisticated skills that help infants negotiate with other infants by only 6 months. Positive mutual affect is central here. Being with someone one loves and cares about gives rise to release of the hormone oxytocin, and higher oxytocin levels have recently been found to increase the ability to understand other minds (Domes, Heinrichs, Michel, Berger, & Herpertz, 2007). Indeed, artificially giving adults doses of oxytocin leads to them paying more attention to the eye regions of those around them (Guastella, Mitchell, & Dadds, 2008).

In these early months babies can already be aware that they are the object of another's attention (Reddy, 2008), and this soon transforms into more sophisticated awareness of being attended to. Such awareness is 'experienced' rather than known in a cognitive sense, but is certainly 'known' emotionally. The 2-month-old can smile with pleasure when they know an adult is looking at them, or be uncomfortable and turn away, but they fully know the difference between an attentive adult and one who is not attending. By 3 months infants are able to 'call' an adult, not just when they are in distress but also to share positive feelings. Infants both know that they are being attended to, and also what it is in them that is being attended to, such as a deliberately funny face. Psychological and emotional understanding about oneself in relation to others develops apace through such processes.

By 3 months many infants are becoming interested in objects not just to look at but also to play with, touch, and explore, and they can 'lead' their 'companion in meaning-making' towards areas of interest. By 6 months many infants are capable of complex game playing, including what Reddy (1991) has described as teasing and mucking about. An infant might offer something and as its partner makes a grab for it, the infant might take it away and smile at the fun of this game. Such episodes show sophisticated understanding of other people's wishes and intentions. By 6 months an infant can clown about and show off, and to 'clown' a baby needs to make sense of how they are perceived by others. They can also by this age show self-consciousness or coyness when they know they are the focus of attention, and indeed Reddy has detected this as early as 2 months. Later in the first year babies begin to get interested in seeing themselves in mirrors, and can be seen experimenting by mimicking, and playing to their reflection. They are starting to seek praise and beginning to know how to get others to react as they wish, all requiring some understanding of another's mind.

Such research challenges those who argue that there cannot be self-consciousness in the early years, that is, before people traditionally thought there was something one could call a self. It seems that self-awareness is available and active much earlier, and can be viewed as an emotional not a cognitive skill, an emotion linked with awareness of oneself as seen through another's eyes. Infants generally love the mutual understanding seen in musical play and 'tricky' games in which one needs to predict timings and the gestures of others. This requires skills and capacities that are precursors of later 'fully-blown' theory of mind skills.

Developmental leaps from nine months and onwards

At around 8 or 9 months infants generally become able to do many new things. They move around, explore, become aware of danger, and want to get close to an attachment figure if a stranger comes close. By this age infants have become sufficiently sophisticated to be able to check out whether their caregiver thinks a situation is safe by reading their facial expressions. A famous test which demonstrated this is the 'visual cliff' experiment (Sorce, Emde, Campos, & Klinnert, 1985).

In this a sheet of clear plexiglass is placed over some fabric in such a way that the fabric appears to form a drop that an infant might fall down. In one version mothers are on the other side of a 'bridge', and are trained to pull faces, such as sadness, anger, joy, or interest. As the infant crawls along the plexiglass and reaches what appears to be a drop, the mother is told which face to pull. The infants look up at and 'reference' their mothers, and if the mother shows pleasure or interest, then they tend to cross and if a mother shows fear or anger they generally remain where they are. This shows how acutely aware infants are of the emotions and wishes of others and how carefully these are interpreted as cues. One might say that the world is being interpreted through the eyes of the mother, and an infant's world changes in response to their mother's communications. Infants are particularly responsive to negative emotions (such as anger), and pay more heed to these in moments of uncertainty. Such negative associations between a situation and the accompanying emotion are quickly inscribed in brain pathways for future reference (Carver & Vaccaro, 2007). For example mothers with severe social phobia give signals that severely inhibit their baby's desire to interact with others.

Figure 5.1 Visual cliff experiment (adapted from Gibson & Walk, 1960)

To read such signals infants must already be adept at recognising states of mind like happiness or worry, and also understand what the state of mind is about. For example, a fearful expression in the partner might refer to a snake nearby or a hazardous drop. Infants are generally capable of this kind of shared attention by about 9 months. If a child points at a toy in the presence of an adult who then fetches it, then the infant knows it can get the adult to pay attention to a third object. This is called **proto-imperative pointing**. There is also a more sophisticated capacity also developing at this time called **proto-declarative pointing**. This is more than just pointing and requires what Trevarthen and Aitken (2001) calls **secondary intersubjectivity**. This describes how an infant might see something they find interesting, such as a colourful flower, and point to this with an expectation that the other person will also appreciate what they are seeing. In such **joint attention** both parties know that both themselves and the other person have the same object in their minds at the same time. Such joint attention is more likely to be accompanied by mutual pleasure, unlike the visual cliff and other **social referencing** experiments, which are more likely to be triggered by fear or danger. Both require some understanding of what is in another's mind. This is a central developmental milestone that most children achieve in the latter part of their first year.

Toddlers who do not manage joint attention or to point proto-declaratively are likely to struggle with understanding and empathising with others. Children with autism are particularly likely to show deficits in joint attention skills from an early age. The leaps in understanding at this age are huge. At 8 months an infant can work out another's emotion but is not able to infer a person's next action on the basis of the direction of their gaze or their emotional expression, but by a year they can often do this (Phillips, Wellman, & Spelke, 2002). Developments continue apace in the next few years. Generally during the latter part of the second year infants show increasing awareness of mental states. Many infants can show some empathy for another's distress by about 10 to 14 months, but it is not until about 18 months that they can exhibit altruistic behaviour, such as approaching others in distress and showing sympathy. Not all children will do this, and one is more likely to exhibit empathy if one has been empathised with oneself (Radke-Yarrow & Zahn-Waxler, 1984).

Infants aged 18 months can infer someone's underlying intention even by watching them *failing* to manage a task (Meltzoff, 1988). They will later be able to succeed in the same task they watched someone failing at by combining imitation with inferences about the person's intentions. Interestingly they do not infer any such intentions when the same action is attempted by a robot, which says something about the human predisposition to learn from live other minds. By about 2 years infants can work out what another person had *intended* to do, even if the person did not actually carry out the intention. Similarly at around this age children start to use language that refers more to mental states, starting to talk about themselves and others as having wants and desires. A classic example is that 18-month-olds were asked to give an experimenter some food, and they worked out what the experimenter liked, this being inferred by clear signals such as lip smacking and other gestures. More egotistical and immature 14-month-olds just gave the experimenter foods that *they* themselves like, such as sweets (Repacholi & Gopnik, 1997)!

Such mind-reading skills do not just automatically develop, but depend on having other minds attuned with one's own. Children who suffer neglect and receive little attuned attention can be less able to make sense of another's mental states. Others who experience more abusive rather than neglectful parenting can develop a skewed understanding of others. They might not have been sensitively attuned to, yet need to pick up the intentions of others for self-protection, albeit with far less genuine appreciation of the other's point of view. Such mental-state understanding tends to be superficial, watching for behavioural signs and consequences, rather than genuinely or empathically understanding the other.

Mind-reading skills are also enhanced by becoming able to use complex language that includes words referring to mental states. For example in a study of deaf Nicaraguans, some had been taught a rudimentary form of sign language and others a form of sign language that contained many more mental state words (like 'know' or 'think'). It was the latter group who were more likely to develop theory of mind skills (Pyers & Senghas, 2009).

By the latter part of the second year infant language is often developing fast. It is also when children start to properly recognise themselves in mirrors, and by this age when they see rouge on their reflected nose they often remove the mark. This stage is often seen as the start of autobiographical memory. From such developments children can begin to develop a sense of themselves as existing over time with specific characteristics and histories. Three-year-olds still struggle to recognise themselves in video footage and when a sticker is placed on their head, and they are shown a video of this minutes later, children say things like 'it's on *his* head' (Povinelli, Landau, & Perilloux, 1996). This gets easier by around the age of 4 or 5 when they can hold multiple versions of themselves and others in their minds, and work out that that sticker on the head of the person (them) in the video might in fact be on their own head now.

Theory of mind

The capacities I have just described, such as beginning to make sense of other people's emotions and mental states from the earliest months, are all precursors of a capacity that is often called theory of mind. This is a term that some psychologists have used to describe the capacity to take the perspective of another. The idea of children having a 'theory' about minds is a cumbersome and possibly not very helpful description of knowledge that intuitively develops from the emotional hurly-burly of day-to-day interactions in the first few years. Having this capacity means stepping outside ourselves, understanding the intentions, beliefs, and feelings of others, and distinguishing these from our own. This is an important ability, yet one that some develop more fully than others. For example, mothers with borderline personality disorder tend to be less in tune with their infant's emotional states, and might ascribe all kinds of thoughts and feelings to their children that reveal more about them than their infants (Hobson, 2002). Piaget (1976) had argued that young children are 'ego-centric' and assume that everyone sees the world as they do. If I watch a child who is about to grab what he thinks is a full packet of sweets but I know that the packet is really empty, I assume that the child has a different belief and sense of anticipation from mine, and that when he finds the box he might be disappointed. Such thoughts require what is called theory of mind. There is a classic experiment which tests whether children have developed these abilities, generally called the False Belief Test, and the best known of these, the Sally–Anne Test, has the following stages.

- A child is told that Sally puts a marble in a basket and then goes out to play.
- While Sally is playing Anne gets the marble from the basket and hides it in a box.
- The child is asked 'When Sally comes back, where will she look for the marble?'

Up until the age of 4 or 5 children tend not to get the right answer. They are not able to take the other's point of view, and are likely to say that Sally thinks the marble is in the box (Astington & Gopnik, 1991).

Some theorists have argued that theory of mind is something that automatically comes 'online' at a certain time, and that those who do not achieve this must have some kind of neurological deficit. However, recent findings suggest otherwise. Family background has an effect on achieving theory of mind skills, and children with many siblings close in age (Dunn & Brophy, 2005), or with parents who are more mind-minded (Meins et al., 2003), develop it sooner. It is possible to give children training that improves such skills, so children on the cusp of this capacity, or who have not been given the right input but have the potential, can be helped to achieve it (Cutting & Dunn, 1999). Theory of mind does not necessarily just happen, and particular experiences speed its arrival. There are also differences between under-standing another's thoughts and understanding their emotions. For example using the Little Red Riding Hood story children work out what the other feels ('when she goes into grandma's house, she is not scared'), rather than what she thinks ('that it is a wolf in the bed') (Bradmetz & Schneider, 1999). Such tests have shown that children come to understand emotional aspects of theory of mind ('was she afraid?') earlier than the cognitive ones. Much current research focuses on emotional deficits that some have in making sense of their own and other's mental states. One of the findings from studies of borderline personality disorder, for example, is that sufferers are likely to have impaired capacities for **mentalisation**, or in other words for reflecting on their own and others' mental states (Bateman & Fonagy, 2004). The research on attachment and mind-mindedness suggests that being able to reflect on mental states is a crucial capacity, the lack of which affects psychological functioning, even if it is a capacity that is differently valued and develops at different ages in different cultures. Furthermore, the capacity to use words and concepts to process experience has been shown to be fundamentally linked to capacities such as for self-regulation and what is often called executive functioning (Winsler, Fernyhough, & Montero, 2009).

Exceptions: the case of the autistic child

Maybe autistic children and adults cannot manage some tasks that others take for granted. In particular they often struggle to understand the world from another's perspective, and are more likely to fail False Belief tests like the Sally–Anne experiment. They are unlikely to manage the joint-attention and social-referencing tasks at which most children become proficient at around a year. Similarly autistic children do not easily understand the emotions of others, or indeed their own. Generally when people tell stories about other's feelings, brain circuits to do with empathy are used, but autistic children do not necessarily use these same circuits when reading such stories (Castelli, Frith, Happé, & Frith, 2002). Some people will be familiar with the triad of symptoms often identified as typical of autism, and these include the following.

- Severe social impairment, which includes not understanding others' feelings, or social rules, not seeking comfort when distressed, preferring to play alone.
- Verbal and non-verbal communication difficulties. Words might have a very concrete meaning for them, with little comprehension of shared assumptions about meaning.
- The absence of imaginary play, and the frequent use of repetitive rituals. One might see hand flapping or rocking in less high-functioning individuals, or an obsessional interest in a narrow range of activities, such as maths in higher functioning children.

Examining exceptions to more usual development, as in autism, can help understand more typical development. Some understand the lack of joint-attention skills at a year as primarily a cognitive deficit (Meltzoff, Tager-Flusberg, & Cohen, 1993), while others more recently have been emphasising the emotional nature of the deficit. Joint attention is generally accompanied by positive affect and enjoyment of the interaction, and such pleasure in the mutuality of joint activity is often lacking in autistic children (Kasari, Sigman, Mundy, & Yirmiya, 1990). The 12-month-old who engages in joint attention already recognises another as having their own attitudes and feeling states, and is able to somehow *identify* with their attitudes. The autistic child struggles with this.

Some interesting experiments by Peter Hobson and Tony Lee at the Tavistock Clinic in London illustrate these issues (Hobson, 2002). Children with autism were compared with a control group to see how well they could make a match between pictures and accompanying sounds. The pictures included neutral subjects, such as garden tools, types of birds, and vehicles, but also emotionally expressive faces showing fear, sadness, or puzzlement. As one might expect, the autistic children did just as well as the control group in matching pictures and sounds referring to nonemotional subjects, but they struggled to recognise or name the emotions on faces.

In another test, autistic children were shown videos of shapes of people who were in darkness and silhouetted with lights attached to them, so that their movements were distinguishable and recognisable. The movements were either emotionally neutral, like kicking a ball or digging, or movements expressing an emotion, such as jumping back in fear, or stamping in rage. Once again the autistic children did as well as the others in recognising emotionally neutral actions such as digging, but could not describe emotional gestures such as stamping in rage. A striking recent finding by neuroscientists is that whereas most people use different parts of the brain when looking at faces to looking at nonhuman objects, children with autism use the same brain regions in processing faces and objects (Schultz, 2005).

Another experiment illustrates the lack of emotional resonance often seen in autism (Hobson, 2002). In this Hobson's colleague Tony Lee asked children to watch him as he performed tasks, including putting a pipe rack on his shoulder and drawing a stick across it three times with gusto, as if playing an instrument. Then the children, both autistic and a control group, were asked to repeat the actions. The autistic children could repeat the stages of the actions in order (stroke a pipe cleaner with a stick) and hold it in roughly the same position, but their actions completely lacked the 'brio' of the original act. They had not understood the emotional feel and appeared very wooden. Autistic children struggle to imitate and identify, to 'feel with' another person, or put themselves in another's shoes. Life is very different if one cannot understand other people's minds or emotions.

The days when parents of autistic children were blamed for being emotionally cold 'refrigerator mothers' are long gone. Autism is now generally acknowledged to be a neurobiological disorder. Some professionals argue that autistic children they work with have both autistic and nonautistic aspects to their personalities, and that it is possible in careful therapeutic work to help build up 'nonautistic', more social and interactive parts of their personalities (Alvarez, 1992). Autistic-like symptoms, if not autism 'proper', can develop for various reasons, and interestingly a link has been made between autistic symptoms and low levels of oxytocin and vasopressin; hormones associated with social affiliation (Carter, 2007).

Although researchers tend to agree that autism has a physiological and neurological basis, some nonautistic children have also been found to develop some very similar symptoms as a result of very depriving early experiences. For example a large proportion of children adopted from depriving Eastern European orphanages showed symptoms that were strikingly like autism (Rutter et al., 1999). The symptoms included self-stimulating behaviours, rocking, and an inability to manage change, as well as having limited verbal ability, little desire to be close to others, to seek comfort, nor to understand their own and other's emotions. Unlike in organic variants some of the symptoms did improve when children were adopted into caring families, particularly when this happened when they were 2 years old or less.

This kind of research, albeit of a very tragic sample, has given us clear evidence of the effect of emotional neglect and the lack of mind-minded attention early in life. This might be viewed alongside other research that argues that the ability to understand other minds is developed through interaction with sensitive and attuned minds. Unless there is an organic disorder, the capacity for empathy seems to be dependent on being empathised with. Some people are more empathic than others, and those who are less empathic also show less activity in the appropriate brain circuits. For most children, capacities for empathy are not set in stone and can increase or decrease. For example, more experienced doctors have less activation in their empathy circuits than less experienced ones when watching needles being inserted into patients (Cheng et al., 2007). Thoughtful, empathic attention from an adult, particularly a parent, seems though to help most children grow emotionally resonant and affect regulating circuits of the brain, although of course some children cannot be thus helped to the same degree for neurological reasons, such as autistic children.

Empathy, mirror neurons, and Rizzolati's monkeys

Recently scientists discovered 'mirror neurons', about which the neuroscientist Ramachandran wrote 'I predict that mirror neurons will do for psychology what DNA did for biology' (Ramachandran, 2000, p. 1). The discovery was made by Italian neuroscientists (Rizzolatti, 2005) who were looking at single cells in the brains of macaque monkeys that fire in grasping. The monkeys were wired so that when they grasped something, a **neuron** in their wired-up brain fired. Scientists chanced upon an astonishing eureka moment when one of them reached for some food and was shocked to note that the machinery registered the same neuronal firing when *he* grasped his lunchtime snack; in other words the monkey's neuron for grasping also fired up when *he* grasped. Researchers soon discovered a complex mirror neuron system in humans too. If I see you inadvertently walk into a glass door, I might wince sympathetically, and here the corresponding neurons are firing in my brain too. The circuits in the brain for imitation, language and empathy in humans are closely linked (Iacoboni, 2005). Mirror neurons fire when seeing someone actively grasp an object, but not just at the sight of the object, nor at a pretend grasp. These neurons respond to intentions, which is how many actions are learnt, by watching them and then later replicating them. This is also partly how we learn about emotions, and similar areas of the limbic system, a brain area which is central to emotional functioning, are activated in both the imitation and the observation of emotions. Mirror neurons provide evidence of the human capacity to form powerful connections between people, as they allow one person to understand from the inside what another is experiencing, explaining how common, mutual understandings develop. They are found in Broca's area in humans, a region central to language development in the left hemisphere, and may form the basis of language development in humans.

Scientists (Oberman, Hubbard, McCleery, Altschuler, Ramachandran, & Pineda, 2005) have found evidence that autistic people have a deficit in their mirror-neuron functioning, which makes sense given that so much of what mirror neurons facilitate is lacking in individuals with autistism. One might also speculate about the impact of severe institutional neglect and lack of social contact on a developing mirror-neuron system, given that so many children adopted from emotionally depriving situations lack a capacity to be in touch with their own and other people's minds and emotions.

Summary: understanding minds

This chapter has suggested that there is a clear developmental line from the very early interpersonal understandings of the first weeks of life, to skills developed towards the end of the first year such as proto-declarative pointing, joint attention and social referencing, to the communicative capacities that develop via speech and gesture in the next few years, and eventually to the abilities to understand other minds that are seen in the classic False Belief tests, such as the Sally–Anne experiment, at 4 or 5 years of age. In short, children who receive 'mind-minded' attention are more able to reflect on their own and other's emotions. The child's mind literally grows and develops through being thought about.

Some children expect to be understood emotionally and can communicate openly about their distress, having learnt that their feelings can be understood, regulated, and thought about by another mind. Such infants recognise their own emotions, learning that their mental states are of interest to others, and they also are more able to recognise the emotions of others. For example, a securely attached child is likely to show empathy when a peer cries in nursery, while an insecurely attached child might well not (Lieberman, Padron, van Horn, & Harris, 2005). Other children have had less attuned experiences and are less able to be in touch with their own and others' mental states.

We cannot assume that empathy or the capacity to reflect on emotions is in any way 'natural'; rather it is acquired through interpersonal experience. Some cultures value this capacity more than others, and some kinds of families place a higher value on it than others. In some situations these skills barely develop at all, whether for organic reasons, as in the case of autism, or due to severe neglect. Some children have had to watch unpredictable parents carefully, and so develop a vigilant awareness of other minds, which is a very different form of understanding from one derived from more benign and enjoyable forms of joint attention seen in secure children. Tuning in to someone out of anxiety or a desperate need to know is very different to being genuinely interested in someone.

I have described how some children have difficulties in understanding other minds, such as children whose parents have borderline personality disorder, depression, eating, or anxiety disorders, as well as some children who are traumatised, abused, or neglected. Some people have had more experience than others of input that has variously been described as affect regulation, mentalisation, mind-mindedness or attunement. To develop empathy and attunement, to be able to regulate one's emotions and to understand one's own and others' psychological states requires the kinds of experiences that foster such capacities. Such understanding of thoughts and feelings, what Homer (Pope, 1867, Book XVIII, line 269) described as how '. . . taught by time, my heart has learned to glow for other's good, and melt at other's woe' this ability to not just understand another's mind but to feel with them, is something that many of us value. However, not everyone is lucky enough to be given the seedbeds from which this grows.

Part II

Overarching bodies of ideas

Attachment

Attachment is a term increasingly in circulation, with lots of colloquial uses, such as describing people as strongly or weakly attached. 'Attachment theory' though describes a field of scientific research originated by John Bowlby (1969) and expanded by many of his successors into one of the most influential bodies of thought in the field. In this chapter I focus on this latter body of research, giving an initial overview that will be expanded on in later chapters.

Bowlby was a psychoanalyst and psychiatrist who founded the child psychotherapy training at the Tavistock Clinic in London in the 1940s, and discovered that he needed a new theoretical lens to understand the kind of children he was coming across. The main influences on attachment theory, apart from psychoanalysis and psychiatry, were evolutionary theory and ethology, which is the study of how animals behave in their contexts. Bowlby learnt that infants of many species raised without maternal care were badly scarred. He was influenced by Harry Harlow (Blum, 2002) whose research compared monkeys reared by their mothers to those reared in isolation. The latter displayed shocking symptoms such as fearfulness of other monkeys, acting bizarrely, and an inability to interact or play. Harlow famously found that infant monkeys reared in isolation, when given a choice between two 'wire' monkeys, clung to one covered in a soft terry-cloth, and ignored the hard metal monkey holding a bottle of milk, only going to the bottle when hungry. Comfort, whether maternal or as near to it as they could get, was more important than food. Another researcher, Hinde (1970) showed that primates removed from their mothers at first protested, then later showed despair, and eventually became cut-off. These findings echoed Bowlby's, who argued that human infants too have a biological need for a protective attachment figure, and that the continued absence of such a person causes psychological difficulties to a growing child.

Bowlby also studied young criminals and found that most had suffered separations from parents, as well as inconsistent parenting, violence, and neglect. Bowlby argued that mothers were centrally important for children and he was unpopular with some who thought he encouraged mothers to stay at home rather than go out to work. Despite this many of his ideas have stood up to scrutiny over time.

He was one of the first psychologists to highlight the importance of evolution, realising that the felt need of human infants to be close to their mother had changed little over an evolutionary past shared with other primates. Bowlby was struck by how separated monkeys clung to their mothers when reunited, and even a year later continued being more clingy and fearful, and less exploratory and curious. Bowlby and his colleagues found similar patterns in humans. In the 1960s James and Joyce Robertson, who worked at the Anna Freud Centre in London, filmed young children being separated from their parents, such as in a child's separation experiences in a hospital stay (Robertson, 1971). These films shocked audiences, and continue to do so when shown today, as they graphically reveal the extraordinary stress a young child experiences when separated from its attachment figures. Indeed, hospital practice was changed as a result of these films, and mothers were often thereafter allowed to stay overnight with their hospitalised children. The children studied showed similar patterns to primates. They started off relatively composed, expecting to have their attachment needs met, but soon protested, crying and screaming, and later slowly but painfully sunk into a despairing state, and eventually into a very cut-off one.

Attachment theory at this stage was a kind of 'spatial' theory in which the closer the attachment figure, then the more happy and at ease the infant. An attachment figure becomes a secure base to return to when anxious, and the presence of this secure base gives confidence to explore and be more outgoing in the world. Such early research stressed the importance of physical closeness and the impact of separations from attachment figures, as well as the infant's tremendous vulnerability after birth, and the crucial nature of early experiences. He described the ties that develop between parents and children as affectional bonds, social bonds accompanied by powerful emotional involvement, building over time and long lasting. Such ideas were radical at the time, and did not fit with many prevailing views about babies' needs. Bowlby did though overestimate the importance of one-to-one infant–mother relationships and underestimated the importance of other attachment figures. Contemporary versions of the family, such as a nuclear family with a stay-at-home isolated mother, is very unlike that in which infants and children have been raised in most of human history, what Bowlby called the environment of evolutionary adaptedness.

Attachment theory's second phase: Mary Ainsworth and the Strange Situation Test

The next phase of attachment theory increased its range and subtlety. Added to the spatial theory was the idea that not all parents offered the same kind of secure base experience, and that different parenting styles influenced children to have different patterns of relating. A fairly simple empirical test was at the centre of this shift, which gave attachment theory a new scientific rigour. The **Strange Situation Test** was devised by Mary Ainsworth (1978) an early follower of Bowlby who worked in various contexts, including rural Uganda. She was struck by how at about 8 months infants begin to be fearful of strangers, and swiftly seek out attachment figures when near an unknown person. Stranger anxiety might derive from an inbuilt fear of predators, as Bowlby thought, or from fear of unknown humans. Stranger anxiety provided the basis for an experiment which was to profoundly alter attachment theory. This test, devised in 1963, is a straightforward 20-minute procedure, although it is not emotionally straightforward to witness.

- First there is a mother and a child of about a year old in a room with some toys, and the child is allowed to explore freely.
- Next a stranger enters the room and talks to the mother and then tries to interact with the child.
- The parent unobtrusively leaves the room, and the stranger adapts their behaviour to the child.
- Then the mother returns and comforts the infant, but then leaves again, and this time the stranger leaves and the infant is left alone.
- Then the mother returns again and tries to comfort the infant.

What is particularly fascinating about this experiment is the different reactions babies have to it. Some cry, scream, and crawl towards the door, but when their mother returns are quickly calmed and resume interest in their surroundings. Others seem to barely notice that their mothers have left the room, and carry on as before, and still others seem very preoccupied with their mothers before and after the separations and cannot settle. As a result of these distinct reactions Ainsworth categorised the behaviours into three main types, which she described as securely attached, and two types of insecure attachment, now mostly called **avoidant** and **ambivalent** attachment. Words like 'secure' and 'insecure' imply a judgement about whether such forms of attachment are good or bad, and although I prefer to avoid such judgements I will stick to the words as used in the research literature to avoid confusion. The babies who came to be classified as securely attached were those who cried when their mother left, but who greeted their mother with relief, and sometimes delight, on her return and then quickly settled back into a more relaxed state. The avoidant infants were those who seemed not to notice when their mothers left the room. I say 'seemed' because research has shown that when their mothers left their heart rates and other physiological stress symptoms increase in the same way as the securely attached children, despite seeming to not care (Sroufe & Waters, 1977). Interestingly in the early days many people thought it was the avoidant children, those who did not cry, who were doing best, something few think today. Ambivalently attached infants were preoccupied and clingy with their mother before she left, and when their mother returned they could not leave her easily, nor settle down again to play.

Ainsworth found a remarkable consistency between parental interactive styles and an infant's reactions in the Strange Situation Test, a link that has been replicated all over the world. Secure infants had parents who seemed sensitive to them, who responded to their distress, and who were consistently available. Generally parents of insecure children were less responsive to their children's emotional needs. Parents of avoidantly attached children tended not to respond to signals such as crying, and were less aware of a child's distress. For avoidant children there is little point crying if no one notices, or worse, if your attachment figure withdraws or gets cross when you do display upset. Ambivalently attached children tend to have parents who are more inconsistent. They might be very available at one moment, and then seem withdrawn or preoccupied, and so these children have to keep quite a close eye on their carers. Ambivalently attached children explore less, as if they do not trust that there is a consistent safe base to return to, and they are more clingy, enmeshed, and less at ease. It is important to remember that children in all three of these groups are attached to their carers, and their attachment styles are all successful strategies for staying close to their carers.

Some years later researchers found that there was a group of children who did not fit into Ainsworth's original categories. These were children who often had been subjected to unpredictable and traumatising parenting, and had failed to develop a coherent and consistent strategy to deal with these frightening experiences. They might, for example, wander up to a parent, then move aside, bang their heads on a wall, freeze or indulge in bizarre behaviours. The parent, who should provide solace or comfort when distressed, was for these children often the person causing the distress, such as by being violent, and so these children could not find a way of getting their attachment needs met. This group was classified as disorganised (Hesse & Main, 2000), and comprises children who often cause great concern to professionals as they grow up. Many of the children originally classified as ambivalent were later reclassified as disorganised, and the two categories have a large crossover, both often having parents who are inconsistent and unpredictable, generally more so when children are categorised as disorganised.

The Strange Situation Test only measures attachment at a year, and of course the building blocks for personality traits are being put in place much earlier. Beatrice Beebe and colleagues (1997) showed that mothers whose responses were attuned to and contingent with their infant's behaviours in the early months tended to have securely attached children at a year, and at 2 their toddlers looked at their mothers more, and showed more positive affect. Using videos of infants interacting at 4 months she predicted attachment classification at a year by examining the degree of mutual coordination between mother and baby. Interestingly, the infant's degree of contingency *with a stranger* at 4 months is also predictive of attachment status at a year, which means that infants are taking their expectations of interactive styles into other relationships, and even eliciting similar reactions in strangers. Infants who at a year are classified as avoidantly attached are already by 4 months looking at their mothers less frequently, and only manage this if at the same time they sooth themselves by, for example self-stroking. It is as if these avoidant infants are overwhelmed by looking at their mothers, and as Beebe describes, they have their 'heads cocked for escape'. This is unlike those who become secure who look straight at their mothers and smile. Infants develop very different regulatory strategies to survive. Avoidant infants need to self-soothe and self-regulate much more, as they have learnt there is little chance of emotional regulation from the outside. Ambivalently attached infants monitor adults very carefully, as they do not know what is coming next, and concentrate more on the outside world than on themselves. Secure infants expect and can rely on their mothers to regulate them when they need this.

These attachment styles are testament to a child's ability to adapt to their environment. Their best chance of survival comes from working out how to behave to stay close to attachment figures. The avoidant child learns to limit its emotional expressiveness, the ambivalently attached child learns to watch its unpredictable parent closely, and the secure child can explore knowing that it can rely on its attachment figure when needed. These become nonconscious behavioural templates. Children internalise an idea of what relationships are likely to be like, and this becomes a nonconscious model in their minds, an internal representation of themselves in relation to others. Bowlby used the concept of **internal working models** to describe this, and I will expand on this next. It is possible to have two or more attachment relationships that are different in style. One might behave in a securely attached way with one's mother and an avoidant way with one's father, both appropriate ways of maintaining proximity to different carers, and so children can learn several different attachment styles.

Attachment inside us

Attachment theory initially concentrated a lot on behaviours and seemed to have moved away from psychoanalysis' preoccupation with the psychological world. Bowlby's concept of internal working models kept this mental component alive. An internal working model is a kind of cognitive map, a way in which people learn to predict others' responses and develop a picture of how relationships are likely to go.

These models are not static, and are influenced by new experiences, although new experiences are also 'read' in the light of previous expectations.

The next leap forward in attachment theory occurred with the development of a tool called the Adult Attachment Interview (AAI), which brought this world of minds, ideas, and representations centrally back into the theory and began a host of new research. The tool was developed by Mary Main to measure adult thought processes (Main, Kaplan, & Cassidy, 1985). This research has demonstrated the links between adult states of minds measured in the AAI and the child's attachment as measured in the Strange Situation Test. This has been a revolutionary discovery, demonstrating that how parents think about their own lives impacts on their child's development.

The AAI is a semi-structured interview that takes about an hour to complete. It aims to 'surprise the unconscious', revealing important features of the representational world that relate to attachment. For example, one is asked for five adjectives that describe relationships with both parents, and then to supply some memories which explain these. Other questions include giving examples of when one was upset as a child, and what happened in these instances, or of memories of a first separation, and also specific questions about losses of important figures and about any traumatic experiences. Such questions tend to stir up strong emotional responses. The interview is painstakingly transcribed and analysed in accordance with scales that measure, interestingly, not what actually happened in the childhoods described, but rather the manner in which the questions are answered, and in particular the internal coherence, consistency, and reflectiveness of the narrative.

Some adults are classified as 'secure-autonomous' and these tend to produce narratives that are consistent and not muddled or contradictory. They have an ability to reflect on their lives, and develop a coherent story about their histories that takes account of emotional experience. They are also able to reflect on how significant others might have experienced events. These are the adults who are more likely to have securely attached children.

Adults who score 'preoccupied' tend to give answers that are quite angry in places, confused in others, and when asked to describe an event they can talk as if catapulted back into the moment the event took place, such as having an argument with their parent. They speak in longer, more jumbled sentences, giving answers full of detail but low on self-reflection. They are most likely to be parents of children with ambivalent attachments.

The adult category that tends to correspond with having avoidant children is termed 'dismissing'. These tend to give positive but very brief descriptions of their childhoods, but are not able to back up these positive views with actual examples. Their memories are generally fairly restricted, and when they do unearth stories they often contradict the original rosy picture. For example, an adult might say that his parents were very caring and then tell a story about getting lost in a strange wood and no one noticing for hours. Being in touch with emotions, particularly negative emotions, does not come easily to this group.

The 'unresolved-disorganised' is the fourth group. Their narratives lack coherence and show poor reasoning and bizarre thinking when asked about abuse or trauma. Their stories often show up unresolved trauma and loss. These are parents who tend to be both 'frightened and frightening' and are most likely to have children classified as disorganised.

It is striking that these findings, which have been consistently replicated, show how the reflective capacity of the adult predicts the attachment status of the child, with an accuracy level that seems to be fairly stable and as high as 75 per cent when the measures are simply between secure and insecure. Importantly it is not the kind of childhood the adults have that is predictive, but rather the ability to reflect on it. One is more likely to be secure-autonomous if one has had positive childhood experiences, but it is not inevitable. What makes the difference, even if one has had negative experiences, is the ability to mentalise, to reflect on one's experience, to be able to make peace with the past to some extent, and the capacity for what is called **reflective self-functioning**. Main coined the term 'earned security' for adults who scored secure despite having had difficult childhoods, her idea being that somehow this had been gained by some other protective factor, such as later good experiences with other adults (Roisman, Padrón, Sroufe, & Egeland, 2002). These findings have given hope to researchers and professionals that later on one can help to develop self-reflective capacities in both children and parents.

Transmission of attachment

We now have a clearer sense of the psychological worlds of children with different attachment styles. Children who are secure expect positive interactions with others, have confidence to explore, tend to have more flexibility and capacity to play, more ability to empathise with and get on with other children, are more able to regulate their emotions, and be in touch with their own and other's emotional needs. They develop hopeful internal representation of themselves in relationship with others. Such children generally have more confidence and they know that when they are in need they can expect help.

Thus being secure seemingly confers various advantages in our society. However, displaying secure behaviours could backfire if one's parents were abusive or cut-off, and so the children of such parents need to develop other strategies. The avoidant child for example dampens down feelings of need in order to remain in their carer's good books. Avoidant children screen out painful affects in themselves and do not recognise these in others. They also have less rich representational worlds, are less able to process the same range of emotional complexity as a secure child, depicting themselves as strong and independent. In contrast the ambivalent child can be so anxious that they make endless demands to avoid abandonment, but are less able to learn to regulate their own emotional needs.

Disorganised children however, are in the most parlous state. They have little strategy for getting their attachment needs met. The person who would usually make a child feel safe, a parent, is often unpredictable and likely to be the one to inflict hurt and upset. For them there is nowhere safe to turn. These children lack a coherent strategy other than to avoid danger in the next few seconds, and they can be unpredictable, although paradoxically this lack of organisation generally turns into a personality with very controlling characteristics as they get older. Often in relationships they tend to be inflexible as well as unpredictable. The world generally does not feel safe unless they are in charge, and attempts to control significant others comes in various forms, such as through aggressive behaviours, through compulsive caregiving, or via a rather desperate level of self-reliance.

It is not obvious to researchers by exactly what mechanism parents' states of mind have such an impact on the attachment status of their children. The most common theory is that adults who score secure-autonomous are more sensitive parents, and various measures of parental sensitivity have been devised as well as measures for parental reflective functioning (Slade, 2006). There is still something of a 'transmission gap' in explaining exactly how parental states of mind affect infant attachment. The concept of mind-mindedness developed by Elizabeth Meins measures how much parents make mind-related comments to their children, and seems to predict whether a child will be securely attached (Meins, Fernyhough, Fradley, & Tuckey, 2001). Parents who show mind-minded skills tend to focus on their children's subjective states, on what they are feeling, thinking, and experiencing. Such parents treat their children as having minds and feelings, rather than focusing more on physical needs or external behaviours. If a preverbal infant shows distress then the mind-minded parent might speculate aloud about why they are upset, maybe saying 'oh yes you have missed mummy' or 'well that was a frightening loud noise'. Meins showed that repeated experience of one's mental states being reflected upon helps children become aware of their own and other people's mental states and processes. Mothers of avoidantly attached children tend to make relatively few mind-minded comments whereas mothers of securely attached children make many more, and mothers of ambivalent children might make some mental state statements but these are often an inaccurate reading of the child's internal state.

Thus the ability to understand a child's state of mind are central. The number of maternal mind-minded comments about a child at 6 months predicts attachment security at a year (Bernier & Dozier, 2003), mentalising capacities at 48 months (Meins et al., 2003), as well as verbal and narrative skills at 5 years old. The findings about the importance of parental states of mind are exciting, not least because if we have learnt what 'transmits' attachment, then we can then begin to intervene and help parents develop mind-minded or self-reflective capacities.

A concept with much in common with mind-mindedness is mentalisation, developed by Peter Fonagy and Mary Target of the Anna Freud Centre, which describes the ability to make sense of one's own and others' mental states and reflect on these, and to realise that people's behaviour is driven by psychological and emotional factors. Here again one sees a range of concepts from slightly different traditions that describe very similar things. Mentalisation is increasingly being used in new mentalisation-based treatments (Fonagy & Target, 1998). Affect regulation, mind-mindedness, reflective functioning, and mentalisation are seen as linked concepts by Fonagy and colleagues who argue that they are central to attachment (Fonagy, 2002). Other concepts such as executive functioning and theory of mind describe different but clearly linked psychological abilities (Sabbagh, Xu, Carlson, Moses, & Lee, 2006) that are also related to capacities such as mentalisation.

There is a slight irony that needs teasing out. Secure attachment is linked with mentalising capacity. However, when we are securely attached to someone then some of our mentalising capacities go into abeyance in relation to that person (Bartels & Zeki, 2004), partly because the whole point of an attachment figure is that one trusts them. The more discriminating aspects of our judgement can shut down when we love someone, and we tend to give our loved ones more benefit of the doubt.

Attachment theory describes the effects of particular experiences on children. I described earlier how the Adult Attachment Interview of a pregnant woman predicted the unborn child's attachment status at a year (Fonagy et al., 1991). This was an incredible result, but the research was all done with first children. It is less certain that subsequent children will necessarily all have the same attachment style. An important recent study cast light on this (van IJzendoorn, Moran, Belsky, Pederson, Bakermans-Kranenburg, & Kneppers, 2000). Looking at a large international sample of sibling pairs, it was found that there is a link between maternal sensitivity and attachment status; such sensitivity predicts whether or not a child will be securely or insecurely attached, but not nearly so well what kind of insecure attachment a child shows, such as whether avoidant or ambivalent. We still have some way to go before we fully understand the exact mechanisms for the intergenerational transmission of attachment.

Finally, I have not mentioned biological temperament as a causal factor as few links have been found between this and a child's attachment status. Infants born more sensitive and less able to self-regulate seem not to be at more risk of insecure attachment generally (Nachmias, Gunnar, Mangelsdorf, Parritz, & Buss, 1996). The relationship between biological inheritance and attachment is also weakened by evidence that both therapeutic interventions and changes in a family's circumstances can alter a child's attachment status. Twin studies have similarly shown little link between inherited temperament and attachment status, and seem to show that parental sensitivity is more important than inherited temperament (Fearon, van IJzendoorn, Fonagy, Bakermans-Kranenburg, Schuengel, & Bokhorst, 2006). However, there is evidence that a combination of some genetic inheritance and very bad parenting can increase the likelihood of disorganised attachment (Lakatos et al., 2002). Overall genes and biological inheritance seem not to play a large role in the transmission of attachment. Parental reflective capacities do though and are the best predictor we have as yet of the eventual attachment status of a child.

Attachment theory and culture

It is argued that attachment theory is a universal biological system, and yet like all theories it developed in a particular time and within a specific cultural framework. It is important to ask whether attachment theory can usefully also be applied to other cultures, or whether there is a bias in the research towards parenting styles valued in the West.

It is certainly possible to apply the concepts of attachment theory across cultures. Doing so reveals that secure attachment is the most common form of attachment, although there are definite cultural variations. For example the Grossmans found that in a German sample, in North German but not the South German children, avoidant attachment was most common (Grossmann, Grossmann, & Waters, 2005). Similarly in Israeli Kibbutz children with communal sleeping arrangements ambivalent patterns were predominant (Sagi et al., 1995) for children not sleeping with their mothers. Some cultures simply do not seem to have children who fall into certain categories. For example in the Dogon people in Mali (True, Pisani, & Oumar, 2001), where the mother is the main attachment figure and sleeps with her infants, 87 per cent of the children were categorised as secure, and none at all as avoidant or ambivalent, while about 13 per cent were disorganised. The mother's constant presence and responsiveness meant that avoidance did not develop, although a disorganised response was seen when mothers were frightened or frightening. Attachment categories themselves are relatively broad, which is a strength, as they can be so widely applied, but also a weakness in understanding more subtle nuances. All secure children are not the same. For example Japanese secure children cry less when leaving their mother's arms than secure German children, yet both groups of children have the same secure classification.

We can ask not only if attachment concepts can be applied across cultures, but also if the very concepts of attachment theory contain cultural biases. Concepts like 'timely responsiveness' or 'maternal sensitivity' might mean something different in different cultures. Rothbaum and colleagues have argued that there is cultural bias in how attachment theory values autonomy, exploration, and independence, capacities more prized in the West (Rothbaum & Morelli, 2005). Puerto Rican mothers, for example, are on average more concerned with calm, respectful attentiveness than autonomy. Physical control of children might be associated with insecurity in American families but with security in Puerto Rican families (Carlson & Harwood, 2003). Similarly maternal interference predicts attachment insecurity in America but not in Colombia where the opposite is true (Posada & Jacobs, 2001). I discuss in more depth in the next chapter how cultures differently value independence or social responsibility. In many cultures it is the ability to anticipate the infant's needs that is prized. Attachment research does not measure this, but measures a child's response to an anxiety-inducing situation that has already occurred rather than an anticipated one.

Nonetheless there is compelling evidence for a universal attachment system in human infants, and also in other primates. There is also now some evidence from cultures as unrelated as Colombia, Mali, Chile, and others showing that maternal sensitivity is linked to attachment security, with scores being examined by raters from different cultures. Even in societies where children are reared in a more communal way and are often passed between carers, such as the Efe studied by Tronick and colleagues, children tend to have a primary attachment with their mothers (Tronick, Morelli, & Ivey, 1992). Likewise Hausa infants in Northern Nigeria form several attachment relationships including with their fathers, but even there they tend to form one primary attachment relationship (Marvin, VanDevender, Iwanaga, LeVine, & LeVine, 1977). While the nuances of attachment relationships might differ across cultures, and some attachment concepts might have some cultural bias, overall attachment theory appears to have significant applicability across cultures.

Attachment and disorders

Not all insecurely attached children have a bad prognosis, but at a year disorganised attachment, the most worrying kind, is a good predictor of psychopathology at 17 years old (Sroufe, 2005). Disorganised attachment often occurs alongside other risk factors, such as poverty, single parenthood, violence, drug and alcohol use, and poor neighbourhoods. The disorganised child is likely to suffer from high stress levels, a hyperalert way of being, show 'helpless' and/or 'hostile' behaviours, and the care they receive is often inconsistent, confusing, frightening and leaves them feeling dysregulated. Such children fail to find a strategy to cope, as both approach and withdrawal can induce fear. Many traumatised children displaying such behaviours, show poorly developed capacities for executive functioning, can seem hyperactive and even present in ways that seem very like children diagnosed with ADHD. They can be out of control but also become increasingly controlling as they grow older. The world for them is frightening and not to be trusted, and the unexpected is rarely something to look forward to, and so they can avoid change and control events as much as possible. Many children adopted from abusive backgrounds show such patterns, and this can make parenting very difficult for even the most sensitive and attuned carer.

Such children often have to deactivate attachment behaviours to survive, cutting themselves off from what is going on inside them, using extreme defences, such as flight, fight or **dissociation**. When something frightening happens there is no one to make sense of such experiences. These children often suddenly cut-off from a thought process, their minds can jump around and they do not stay consistently on a single mental track, something often also seen in their parents' confused reports in the AAI. They end up with deficits in cognitive capacities, in the ability to manage relationships, in the capacity to regulate their own emotions, and in developing consistent interpersonal strategies. Many fail at school, and advance along worrying trajectories, such as into the criminal justice system, psychiatric, or other services.

These days there is much talk of **attachment disorders** and it is important to be clear that disorganised attachment is a research category. **Reactive attachment disorder** is different to disorganised attachment, being an official psychiatric classification describing children who have been chronically neglected (such as some children brought up in depriving orphanages) or who have suffered massive abuse, a lack of care and have never developed an attachment to a particular caregiver. Officially there are both inhibited and disinhibited variants of reactive attachment disorder, according to the official classification systems, although these differences do not always hold up in practice. Caution is needed as there is a scientific and psychiatric discourse about reactive attachment disorder, but as Prior and Glaser note (2006), there is also a large industry of people offering popularised attachment therapies and using this diagnosis in a way that bears little resemblance to official psychiatric ones. Most controversial are probably the so-called holding therapies, which attempt to enhance interactions by forms of enforced contact between adults and children and have been critiqued by many (Simmonds, 2007), and actually found to be dangerous, even leading to fatalities (Lilienfeld, 2007). Some children who have a disorganised attachment might also be diagnosed with reactive attachment disorder but these categories are not coterminous. What is clear nonetheless is that the long-term implications for children with a disorganised attachment, and for those with a reactive attachment disorder, are not good.

Summary

This chapter has given an overview of attachment theory, although many of these ideas make further appearances throughout the book. Attachment research has travelled a long way since Bowlby and has developed a host of tools that have increasing empirical validity. The theory began as a spatial and behavioural one, highlighting the importance of children having proximity to a secure base. Later it became increasingly sensitive not just to whether a parent was nearby, but to the quality of parental presence, to the different ways a parent acts with their child. Later research increasingly emphasised the state of mind of the carer and the relationship of this to the attachment status of the child, and so psychological and representational aspects of attachment returned to the fore.

A child who is secure at a year is likely to have advantages in most cultures studied, such as being less likely to fight with peers, being more able to play creatively, having good skills at understanding their own and other minds, having a better developed sense of their own agency, and being better able to regulate their own emotions. The avoidant child, by contrast, maintains closeness to their carer at a cost; they learn to deny or cut-off from emotional life, and in particular from their feelings of neediness, dependency, or hurt, as showing such feelings risks rejection by the parent. They develop less rich stories about themselves, are less flexible, and less able to get on well with other children, whose minds they read less well. The ambivalent child needs to monitor their preoccupied parent fairly constantly, and often loses touch with their own needs in the process. To stay safe they need to work out their parents' rather changeable state of mind in any moment and pre-empt their actions. Such children tend to have less sense of agency and are more dysregulated. Secure children tend to rely on a flexible assortment of both affect and cognition, whereas avoidant children tend to rely on cognition more, and ambivalent children more on affect.

Attachment theory seems to have cross-cultural relevance, even if some of its concepts might have a Eurocentric bias. There are other discourses related to attachment theory, which are linked but different, such as seen in the psychiatric classification of reactive attachment disorders or the various therapeutic interventions that claim a link to understanding attachment. There remains some controversy as to how influential early attachments are across the lifespan, as well as exactly how attachment is transmitted from parent to child. However, we know that mind-mindedness and having someone around who can make sense of one's feelings, hopes and intentions makes a big difference. Only some infants are born into families where there is mind-mindedness, but fortunately the human infant is sufficiently adaptable to be able to survive in a range of emotional climates. The attachment style an infant develops is generally an appropriate response to the specific environment it finds itself in and children develop internal working models that ensure survival in these varied emotional cultures. Attachment styles are also not set in stone and as I describe later, they can change with new experiences and new relationships, which should give hope to professionals and parents.

The importance
of culture

Different cultures raise their children very differently, and people in most societies have strong beliefs about how to rear children. Sufficient cultural understanding is necessary to understand the various practices we come across, especially for those living and working in multicultural communities. Some aspects of children's development are almost universal to the species while others are culturally specific and all people are only understandable as cultural beings. It is challenging to think about how much one can even make sense of concepts that derive from very different cultures to one's own. Here is an example from the Pacific Bimin–Kuskusmin people, who have a complex cosmological belief system (White & Kirkpatrick, 1985). Although the ideas are different, one might be tempted to translate them into our own understandings. One of their central ideas is that of a 'finiik', which might loosely be translated as spirit or lifeforce.

Box 7.1   The finiik of the Bimin–Kuskusmin people

An infant's finiik is small, weak and fragile, and can easily escape. The finiik is present from conception, drawn from ancestral spirits who guide its development, and one's finiik might even give rise to foetal movements, although ritual acts can strengthen it. However, after birth it is weak, and will only be strengthened by the infant being embedded in the moral, social, and ritual community. At birth the infant is in a highly polluted state, and fragments of the finiik escape, through coughing, shrieks, and other movements. The mother can calm the infant with cradling, warming, nursing, and speaking to it, and all this prevents the finiik from escaping by reducing the infant's 'thinking feeling' and motor movements. A father has a key role, through his presence and ritual activities, in helping firm up the finiik but an abusive or neglectful mother severely threatens the child's future as the finiik or parts of it can come loose or escape.

We each might have our own explanations of what is going on, using our own ideas and preconceptions. An unanswerable question is how possible it really is to translate beliefs and values from one culture into those of another.

In utero we imbibe the tastes and sounds of the culture we are likely to live in, and from birth onwards an infant responds to a bath of culturally influenced movements, rhythms, and ways of being. Indeed, recent research has suggested that newborn's cries are influenced by cultural learning, seemingly before birth, with French newborns producing cries with rising melody contours, as oppose to German babies who straight after birth cry using falling contours (Mampe, Friederici, Christophe, & Wermke, 2009). To grow into a socially competent adult, people must learn the expectations of their cultural context. The sociological concept of a habitus (Bourdieu, 1977) describes how external cultural and social arrangements and influences become lived through the subjective life of an individual, mostly nonconsciously.

Most of us feel challenged by practices different to our own. Our language is replete with words implying that which is different is foreign or alien. For a long time Western thought has been suffused with ideas about 'civilised' people being different to 'savages', sometimes simplistically grafting evolutionary ideas onto beliefs about the superiority of its way of life. Most societies think their ways of looking after children are best. Rural Cameroonian mothers when shown videos of European mothers leaving their babies to cry, asked if they could come and teach them to do it better (Keller, 2007). People from one culture are often perplexed by values that others take for granted. This is a particular issue in societies where there is a lot of immigration.

Beliefs vary widely cross-culturally about many aspects of children's lives, such as how we care for babies, feed them, keep them safe, or communicate with them. I hope to flag up the extraordinary diversity of ways that humans bring up children, a diversity that challenges any ideas that 'our' ways of bringing up children are right. In doing so I give examples of practices that might seem unusual, and in this I certainly do not wish to portray any practices as in any way 'exotic'. However, the opposite danger, of taking our own beliefs and practices as 'natural', seems to me more risky. I also want in this chapter to outline an important distinction between societies that are more interdependent as opposed to being more autonomous, sometimes described as **sociocentric** as opposed to **egocentric** societies (Markus & Kitayama, 1991). More interdependent cultures are geared to ensuring that a child grows up much more aware of being embedded in its community and as part of a social context. More egocentric cultures value autonomy and individuality more, as often seen in Western industrial societies, where the development of the child as an separate individual is highly prized.

Some differences

Ideas about what a baby is or represents differ hugely. In some belief systems a baby is born full of sin, and needs to be civilised, while some Balinese babies are seen as reincarnated ancestors to be treated with reverence. Practices are performed to ensure that one is warding off 'the evil eye' in many cultures, such as Turkey or Nepal, and we all probably have our own beliefs that could be viewed as superstitions. Many newly pregnant European mothers often do not tell the wider world of their pregnancy until about 3 months as it is otherwise 'tempting fate' whereas in some societies people disclose pregnancies earlier.

Societies have very different practices and ways of conceptualising life events. For example, most cultures privilege particular moments in the lifespan as important transitional points. In the West many transitions are taken for granted that might make no sense elsewhere, such as starting or leaving school, even birthdays. In many cultures people do not know how long they have been alive, let alone on what day they were born. The rituals of a society tend to indicate something very central about the culture's core values. In the Hindu upanayana ceremony, boys become full members of the religious community; they undergo a ritual that includes spending a night all alone, often for younger ones the first night without their mother, and from then they will eat only with male members of the family (Friedlmeier, Chakkarath, & Schwarz, 2005). For the Navajo there is the 'first laugh' ceremony, celebrated by a major feast that is given by the first person to make the baby laugh, and ensures that the baby will be generous and happy (Chisholm, 1996). This is when a Navajo baby is thought of as becoming a person.

Such customs cannot really be understood in isolation from a culture as a whole, but to many of us they are 'interesting'. Some other beliefs and practices are more threatening than interesting. For example, most parents in most cultures worry about safety, but the nature of these worries varies across cultures. In some settings the worry might be about lions and other predators, and in other societies concerns might be about cars or paedophiles. Some cultures worry about dangers that might surprise us. Some Fulani mothers roll their babies in cow dung to try to fool the spirits into thinking their children are not worth taking. Ideas about what is appropriate and safe also vary hugely. In the USA and Europe children are normally not allowed to play with knives until at least 5 years old. Western parents or social workers might be aghast that young Congolese Efe children regularly use machetes safely, Fore infants in New Guinea use fire by the time they are walking (Sorenson, 1979), and Aka children in central Africa safely learn by 10 months how to throw spears and use axes (Rogoff, 2003).

A more controversial nonWestern example of very different childrearing comes from the Sambia of New Guinea (Herdt, 1994), whose practices provide a huge challenge to our assumptions. Inhabiting longhouses where the genders are segregated, in order to become men boys must move into the longhouse where initiation rituals include being 'inseminated' by older men so that they will become 'big and strong'. Masculinity is passed on through a ritual of 'fellatio', and the continuation of the masculine world depends on imbibing semen. Despite undergoing years of practices that most of us would describe as abusive, the males emerge seemingly unscathed into adult life. Practices that challenge our core values so drastically are rare, but many other ways of treating children seen in other cultures fly in the face of contemporary Western belief systems. A few examples many readers and practitioners come across include polygamy, marriage of girls before adolescence, or female circumcision. Other cultural differences such as arranged marriages also often cause controversy and are not always well understood, being often confused with forced marriages. Some such traditional practices, such as arranged marriages, can give rise to tensions between members of the same family and community, as often seen in second generation Asian young women in Britain (Uddin, 2006).

Practices also change over time from being deemed acceptable to unacceptable within a single culture. In pre-industrial and industrial Britain children took a full role in economic and work life, in factories, in the fields, and even notoriously up chimneys. The British childcare guru Truby King influenced a whole generation by devising a childcare system partly derived from rearing cattle. This included a fixed 4 hours between feeds, no picking up and cuddling or 'spoiling' between feeds, plenty of time alone in a pram at the end of the garden for 'fresh air', with crying seen as 'good for the lungs' (King, 1932). Practices that seem fine for one generation can seem barbaric to the next.

Our own values easily intervene when thinking about other cultures. The example I described earlier of Brazilian shanty towns is typical (Scheper-Hughes, 1992). Here mothers show what might seem like harsh indifference to babies seen as weak and unlikely to survive. They say 'if a baby wants to die, it will die', and actively discourage any attempt to save a baby that they think will not survive, as Scheper-Hughes, the researcher, herself found when rather naïvely trying to help a child who was seen as 'weak'. All of us are to an extent prisoner to our own cultural value systems.

Sociocentric and egocentric, dyads and groups

The distinction between cultures that are primarily egocentric or sociocentric is a central one, even if the distinction describes a spectrum rather than any absolute differentiation (Geertz, 2000). A central Western assumption is that the development of an 'autonomous self' is natural, an assumption not shared in all cultures. Caudill and Weinstein (1969, p. 27) write 'In Japan the infant is seen more as a separate biological organism who, from the beginning, in order to develop, needs to be drawn into increasingly interdependent relations with others. In America, the infant is seen more as a dependent biological organism who in order to develop, needs to be made increasingly independent of others.' Indeed, the Japanese have a concept, 'amae', which is not really translatable into Western languages but loosely describes an expectation of being loved, cared for, and looked after.

A typical example of how sociocentric or egocentric practices are expressed is in infant sleeping arrangements. Practices such as sleep training regimes teach babies to expect no comfort when they cry while in most societies in human history infant survival might well have depended on babies and mothers sleeping together. Research (e.g., Morelli, Rogoff, Oppenheim, & Goldsmith, 1992) shows that few babies in the USA sleep with their mothers, although some sleep nearby, whereas in many South American cultures it is unthinkable for babies to sleep separately. Many Japanese believe that co-sleeping aids children's transformation from separate beings to being members of the wider community (Caudill & Plath, 1966). The language we use is telling. Western parents often talk of the need to train infants to be 'self-reliant', 'independent', and worry about 'dependency', while mothers in more sociocentric cultures emphasise qualities of 'interdependence'. Where we think a child should sleep is linked to our most central views about being human. Co-sleeping possibly does not work so well in a Western industrial world where mothers often have to leave the home to do paid work, and too much infant dependence might interfere with economic survival.

Babies in cultures that value either independence or interdependence have very different experiences. In Heidi Keller's (2007) studies 3-month-old German babies spent 40 per cent of their time out of physical reach of their mothers, whereas infants in interdependent farming communities were never alone. In Western families the mother often does the lion's share of childcare, and maybe only a few other adults help, whereas in rural African and Indian cultures many other adults and young people were at hand to participate in childcare. A Nso (rural Cameroonian) saying is 'A child belongs to a single person when in the womb, but after birth he or she belongs to everybody' (Keller, 2007, p. 105), and in such more interdependent cultures social adaptation is highly valued, but not independence and autonomy. Immediate bodily comfort of infants, primarily via breastfeeding, is seen as 'obviously' what is needed. Nso mothers watching videos of German mothers trying to comfort their children without breastfeeding could barely believe what they saw, and several wondered if German mothers were forbidden to hold their babies, even questioning whether they were really watching the actual mothers.

Close bodily contact is taken for granted in more interdependent cultures, whereas there is more distal, face-to-face communication between Western mothers and babies. Similar differences are also seen in language use, with more vocalising with infants in egocentric cultures, where infants in turn generally become more vocal. Mothers with more interdependent values tend to use less language, and use it differently, less to encourage autonomy and more to support social and moral codes. In sociocentric practices it is also common for mothers to indulge in quite rigorous bodily stimulation and massage. German mothers watching such practices on video suggested that these mothers were being intrusive and insensitive in not matching the infants' own tempo.

In much of Europe and America the assumption is that dyadic, mother–child relationships are 'natural', and many theories have developed about the importance of the father being an external presence who helps to 'break up' a symbiotic mother–infant bond by facilitating a more triadic form of interaction. In many cultures though interaction is based on complex group dynamics and not dyadic ones, and webs of social bonds are more valued.

In some Guatemalan Mayan communities social organisation consists of a group interacting in a circle (Chavajay & Rogoff, 2002), and toddlers fit into the flow of group processes rather than expecting to gain someone's sole attention. To take an example using older children, in schools in Alaska teachers have by tradition tended to facilitate *group* processes and communal rather than individual learning, with students helping each other to build knowledge and teachers fostering group speaking. However, in one instance a supply teacher caused disarray when, on arrival, she turned all the desks to face her, insisting that all speaking was directed through her (Lipka, 1994). The usual culturally sanctioned practices, such as openly helping each other in lessons, were seen as insubordination and 'wrong'.

Yet even within Western societies, different cultural groups value cooperation and group goals more highly; for example Korean American pre-school children respond to other children more cooperatively than their Anglo–American counterparts (Kim & Lee, 1995). This can lead to judgement of the parenting styles of parents from other cultures. In Britain many have argued (Butt & Box, 1998) that the parenting styles and methods encouraged by many professionals, and in official government documents, are not culturally appropriate for parents from African–Caribbean or Asian backgrounds, for example. This might include too much emphasis on mothers and too little on the extended family, and too little appreciation of beliefs about parenting that differ from the cultural mainstream.

As Rothbaum and Morelli show (2005) in Western cultures autonomy, self-esteem and self-assertion are particularly valued. Yet from some Asian perspectives an 'assertive, autonomous ... person is immature and uncultivated' (Kitayama, Markus, Matsumoto, & Norasakkunkit, 1997). Sociocentric practices emphasise parental control, social cohesion, interdependence, and community expectations. A Cameroonian Nso mother will normally respond very quickly to an infant's signs of distress, whereas a German mother will respond more to positive signals (Keller, 2007). Gusi mothers do not amplify interactive excitement, but rather turn away from excited infants to calm them down, as they do not want to produce individualistic or expressive children. Such differences are not about one way being 'better', nor about some parents loving their children more or less. One study comparing Korean and German mothers even specifically tested this, and found no difference in how much the mothers loved or accepted their children overall, but that Korean mothers encouraged more group-oriented and social, rather than individual activities, more obedience, and less independence (Schwarz & Trommsdorff, 2005).

'Control' is highly valued in sociocentric cultures yet has quite negative connotations for many American or Western European parents. Many rural Chinese mothers actively discourage individuality in their children and encourage compliance, co-cooperativeness and interdependent ways of behaving (Chen, Hastings, Rubin, Chen, Cen, & Stewart, 1998).

As the influence of education, industrial development and urban life increases across the world then parenting has tended to move to a more independent 'egocentric' model and recent research (Hofstede, 2001) examining cultural attributes in 50 countries, showed that the USA, Australia, Britain, and Canada ranked highest in individualism. Even within contemporary European societies such as Germany, within a few decades parenting has become more individualistic and egocentric. Keller and Lamm (2005) looked at free-play scenarios with mothers and children in the 1970s and again in 2000. Mothers gave less bodily contact in the later examples, responded quicker to positive signals rather than signs of distress, and encouraged more face-to-face, distal contact, with more use of object manipulation and toys and more use of language that supported autonomy and personal expression. All this was change within just one culture in just a few decades. Generally cultures seem to be moving in more individualistic and egocentric directions, although it is as yet uncertain whether this will be the direction of travel in cultures such as China where industrialisation is growing apace but within distinct cultural patterns.

What is universal and biologically natural? Breastfeeding and emotions

As there are such large cultural variations, one can ask whether there are practices that humans are 'naturally' adapted for, given that for 99 per cent of our history humans have been hunter–gatherers. One seeming constant is the prolonged relationship between mothers and infants, even if the form of this relationship varies, from infants primarily being cared for by mothers to the Efe foragers of Zaire (Tronick et al., 1992) whose infants have simultaneous relationships with many carers, being handed from adult to adult, even if the mother remains the primary carer.

Breastfeeding is obviously something that human mothers are biologically primed to do and so is a good candidate for being considered a 'natural' practice. Human mothers produce a more diluted milk than some species, with smaller amounts of proteins and fats, fitting species where breastfeeding follows a 'little but very often' pattern. At birth mothers produce colostrum, a thick creamy milk with recognised immunity boosting capacities, being full of antibodies. During periods when doctors discouraged mothers from breastfeeding immediately after birth then infant mortality rates shot up (Hrdy, 1999) and in most societies, breast milk has been the only means of infant nourishment and survival.

A danger though of arguing that breastfeeding is natural, is that such thinking can slide into moral ideas such that not breastfeeding is 'unnatural'. There is also the opposite danger and mothers in some parts of Europe are discouraged from breastfeeding for too long, or in public, as this is considered 'unsavoury'. The human species adapts to its environmental conditions, and it is hard to argue that one adaptation is more 'natural' than another, particularly as we can only ever judge from our own moral codes.

Academics debate whether some emotions are universal to all cultures. Anthropologists have stressed cultural differences, but research by the psychologist Paul Ekman and colleagues (1987) suggested that there are basic emotions common to all cultures. He identified these as happiness, surprise, disgust, contempt, anger, fear, and sadness. In order to rule out the influence of culture he visited a tribe in New Guinea, the Fore, which had hitherto had no exposure to other cultures. He showed pictures of emotions as expressed in a photograph of white Western faces. He also asked what might have happened to the person just before the picture was taken. Generally the Fore people had no difficulty recognising the emotions, suggesting that such emotional signals were universally recognisable, although there was some difficulty differentiating between fear and surprise. These results were replicated by others, and showed that the levels of recognition of emotions, while above chance, still left room for some cultural misunderstandings. More recently similar studies with the Mafa ethnic group in the Cameroons found that they recognised the emotions in samples of Western music, despite never having been exposed to such music (Fritz et al., 2009). Interestingly babies born blind seem to express emotions using the same muscle movements as sighted people, despite never having seen them, again suggesting something that is evolutionarily inherited (Ekman, 1989). A recent study showed that the smiles of athletes at the Olympics were the same, irrespective of whether the athletes were congenitally blind, noncongenitally blind, or sighted athletes. For example, those who lost in the final of a fight all wore the same 'social smile', irrespective of whether they had ever seen anyone else's face, and their smiles were very different from the winners who wore broad Duchenne smiles. This suggests a high degree of species wide inherited wiring for emotional expressions (Matsumoto & Willingham, 2009).

Some have tried to disprove Ekman's views. Argyle (1988) looked at how well Japanese, Italian, and English people recognised each other's emotions. All groups were able to recognise each other's signals, with the exception that the Japanese faces were harder to read. This was taken to prove that emotional expression might be culturally specific. However, this was challenged when Japanese and American subjects were filmed watching TV programmes. The Japanese subjects expressed few recognisable emotions in the presence of the experimenter, but when watching films alone their emotional expressivity was as recognisable as that of the Americans. This implies a cultural rule about hiding emotional expressions in public rather than a different way of showing emotion.

There are many other cultural rules that can lead professionals and others to make mistakes in understanding the people they deal with. For example, in most Western societies looking someone in the eye is a sign of straightforwardness and honesty yet in some African countries it is seen as rude or disrespectful, while in some Arab cultures not looking at someone can be rude. One African mother I worked with was clear that misunderstandings about this with a social worker increased the risk of her parenting being judged inadequate, and that she was being judged as being 'evasive' whereas in her culture looking directly at people who had authority was a sign of disrespect.

Cultural values even impact on when emotions are deemed appropriate to express. As Barbara Rogoff showed (2003, p. 27), Hausa mothers in Nigeria do not show affection to their babies in public, which might confound European infancy researchers, or even social workers. Once again we find that there are no winners in the nature–nurture debate. The research is complicated by the fact that in some cultures, as David Matsumoto found (2002), there might be cultural rules about whether it is appropriate to even acknowledge recognition of another's emotions. Some research (Elfenbein & Ambady, 2003) suggests that there are advantages in recognising emotions of people in one's own group, and that people are better at recognising the emotion of another if the observer and the observed are of the same culture. There might well be a universal range of emotions, but their expression might be like different dialects in one language, rather than entirely separate languages, with cross-cultural nuances that are only picked up by members of one's own cultural subgroup. These issues are and will continue to be hotly debated, and in many ways might come down to a question of emphasis; it seems possible to delineate emotions that one might consider universal, but also to discover fascinating and significant cultural differences in emotional expression.

Cultural variations in development

Most psychology texts suggest a version of developmental 'stages' which 'should' be achieved at clearly defined ages, and children are often judged as being either 'behind' or 'ahead' in relation to these milestones. Often parents are understandably anxious about whether their child's behaviour is behind or 'on-track', and the Western competitive analogy implies a clearly defined developmental sequence.

However, age-specific expected developmental stages differ across cultures too. In parts of India children learn their left from their right far earlier than in most European children, and for good reason; their right hand is the 'clean' hand, used for eating, or shaking hands, while the left is used for cleaning oneself after defecation. Children as young as one and a half know this. In many societies physical skills, for example to do with hunting or setting fires, would be learnt very early, while the kind of learning valued in the Western school system might never occur.

There are large cultural variations in the ages that children manage many achievements cited in child development texts. For example there are cultural differences in the age when children recognise themselves when looking in a mirror after rouge is placed on their face, something that many textbooks suggest children should manage at between 15 and 18 months (Keller, Yovsi, Borke, Kärtner, Jensen, & Papaligoura, 2004). Keller shows that cultures differ in when several such milestones are reached, differences linked to the 'interdependent–independent' continuum. Children in cultures that value more sociocentric ways tend to achieve self-recognition later than their Western counterparts. Children who recognise themselves earlier are those who had received less bodily contact in early infancy and more face-to-face interaction and more encouragement in object manipulation. The more egocentric the culture, the earlier this skill develops.

Yet when it comes to self-regulation the opposite is true. Cultures that value close bodily contact and quick response to signals of distress, and where there are clear imperatives for children to abide by rules, are also the cultures where self-regulation develops earlier and more fully. Children in more interdependent cultures are also quicker to respond to adult requests and to develop skills in compliance.

Autobiographical memory is another example. This is highly prized in Western cultures, and beliefs in its importance are central to attachment theory. Western parents with good autobiographical skills are likely to have children who are securely attached; these parents tend to use more elaborative styles of talking about their own and their children's lives, spinning narratives about what has or might happen. Western children can develop such skills as much as 16 months earlier than some other children, and for example Nso Cameroonian children's first memories are of considerably later experiences than those of Western children. Similarly the ability to understand what is in someone else's mind, and to know that another person might perceive things differently from oneself, often called theory of mind (see Chapter 5), also comes on stream at different ages depending on which culture one is raised in (Chasiotis, Kiessling, Hofer, & Campos, 2006). It would be too easy to judge the parenting of someone brought up in another cultural belief system who did not value the elaborated autobiographical discourses that lead to early development of theory of mind skills.

As well as cultural differences in stages of development, there are also differences in how 'disorders' or problems are conceptualised. For example, toddler tantrums and the 'terrible twos', the bane in the life of many Western parents, seems not to exist in some cultures where there are different beliefs about children and childcare practices (Mosier & Rogoff, 2003). There also exist culturally specific mental health disorders, many of which have recently been included in official psychiatric classifications. These include *latah*, seen in Southeast Asia and marked by sudden startle reactions, loss of control, profanity, and mimicking of others, *koro*, seen in parts of Africa, where people fear that their sexual organs are shrinking or disappearing, and *Amok*, seen in Malaysia, in which males respond to slights by brooding and then are involved in frenzied, uncontrolled violence, giving rise to the term 'running amok' that has passed into everyday parlance (Lilienfeld & Arkowitz, 2009). *Taijin kyofusho*, seen in Japan, is a disorder marked by a terrible fear of upsetting others, such as via one's body odours, and such problems are especially seen in more sociocentric cultures where how one is perceived by others has huge importance.

Given the cultural variations in practices and what are seen as disorders, it is all too easy to see how any of us can inadvertently be prejudiced against other people's ideas, practices, or parenting by our own cultural beliefs.

Cultures frame our thoughts and very physiology and brains

The next chapter, on neuroscience, describes how experience changes the very structures and connections in our brains. Different cultures provide different experiences which in turn lead to different brain development. A typical example comes from the Moken society, often called sea gypsies (Travis, 2003) who have made a living for centuries by diving 30 feet under water and harvesting sea cucumbers and clams. Few could believe that Moken children could see clearly at that depth without goggles, something that most humans cannot manage because of the way sunlight is refracted under water, so not falling on the retina in the usual way. The Moken however, learn to control the size of their pupils and the shape of their lenses. This is not a genetic capacity, as an experiment was done with Swedish children, who were able to learn this if they were taught early enough. Here what were assumed to be hardwired circuits in the brain were changed through cultural influences.

It also is increasingly being shown that people in different cultures might have somewhat different cognitive architecture. In experiments Americans and Japanese people have been shown to perceive a slightly different reality (Masuda & Nisbett, 2001). Subjects in both cultures were shown animations of coloured fish swimming, and in each animation there was one 'focal' fish which was larger, more brightly coloured, and faster. Afterwards the Americans usually remembered the focal fish while the Japanese referred far more to the less prominent fish, and to background features such as rocks. Americans recognised the focal fish whether shown with its original background or not, whereas the Japanese only recognised it in its original context. Such experiments suggest that people reared in sociocentric ways perceive things more 'holistically' whereas Westerners might see things more analytically, with a more focused vision. Interestingly, children of Asian immigrants to America tend to have both capacities.

To survive in a Western post-industrial world one might need a sharp analytical focus. In other contexts it might not be such an advantage. The sea gypsies were one of the few groups who, like many animals, survived the Indonesian tsunami in 2004 despite living in the heart of where it hit. When the elephants left for high ground, and the cicadas fell silent, they began telling an ancient story of 'the wave that eats people' and retreated to either higher ground or very deep water, and all survived. One member of the tribe said of other fishermen who did not survive (Leung, 2005) 'They were collecting squid, they were not looking at anything. They saw nothing, they looked at nothing. They don't know how to look.' It seems that Moken sea gypsies were in some senses living in another world to those other fishermen.

Summary: culture's central place

This chapter has aimed to give a flavour of the complexity of the interface between culture and child development. It is not simply that we can talk about different societies having different cultural or psychological habits, but more radically the very psychology of another culture, its concepts, ideas, and presuppositions, can differ hugely. This can be of major significance for anyone living or working in multicultural environments, or who travel to societies where values are very different to their own.

The chapter has aimed to illustrate and even celebrate the extraordinary richness of cultural diversity and avoid the trap of assuming that any practices are right or best. It has particularly focused on the differences between sociocentric and egocentric cultural beliefs, and has tried to steer a path between universalism and relativism. Despite having a separate chapter, culture is central to understanding child development generally. The chapters about attachment, language development, play, gender identity, or childcare, for example, all would be poorer without taking a cultural slant on the findings. Culture is not so much a separate topic as another lens for examining the whole range of questions concerning children's psychological and emotional development.

Chapter 8

Biology and the brain

In the last 20 years there has been an explosion of research about psychobiological processes, and in particular the human brain. We now know a lot more about the brain regions involved in emotional processes, and how brains develop differently depending on early experiences. This chapter will give a basic overview of some of the more relevant and accessible elements of research. Neuroscientific ideas have already made an appearance in earlier chapters such as in discussions about hormones like oxytocin and cortisol, and mirror neurons, and will do later, for example in the descriptions of changes in the adolescent brain.

Neuroscience has confirmed Freud's view that much mental processing occurs in nonconscious ways. In a classic study by Libet (1985), subjects informed researchers when they had made a conscious decision to undertake an action. Scans showed that somewhere in their brains these subjects had unconsciously made the decision to act several seconds before they thought they were making the decision. Such findings challenge whether we consciously make decisions in the way we think we do (Soon, Brass, Heinze, & Haynes, 2008). Such research, as well as findings from areas such as hypnosis (Fromm & Shor, 2009), has shown that what drives us to act often occurs far out of consciousness.

Similarly the habits and patterns through which people relate to others are often set down as almost biological or physiological templates when very young, and we are rarely conscious of such patterns in ourselves. Our attachment templates are of this kind, as might be seen in a child whose upset was never responded to and so learnt (nonconsciously) never to reveal any upset. Such learning and body-based memories are often called procedural or implicit memories. These include both skills such as riding a bike or playing a violin, and also memories of how relationships go and the expectations people take into new social situations; which are the result of prior learning.

Much early emotional learning in the first year or so of life is of this procedural kind, occurring before parts of the brain that encode and retrieve more factual or explicit memories, such as the hippocampus, are fully 'online'. There is a small almond shaped part of the brain called the amygdala that humans also share with our reptilian ancestors (see Figure 8.1). The amygdala is already well developed at birth and is central to emotional learning, particularly in relation to fear responses. The fear of something, like loud sounds, can be 'written' onto the amygdala well before conscious memories are possible, and one might remain afraid of that same thing well into adulthood. This kind of learning can be very useful, and even ensure a human's survival, but such learning can also be hard to unlearn, even when it is no longer pertinent.

The development of **procedural memory** can be seen in action through brain scans (Schwartz & Begley, 2002). The brain activity of a man was monitored as he tried to work out a mystery sequence on a keyboard, and showed tremendous activity across various brain regions, echoing his huge conscious effort. Once he had mastered the task and it became second nature then his brain activity quietened with only his motor regions active. When he was then asked to again pay special attention to the task the scans again showed lots of activity. One might think of the huge effort infants make in imitating an adult gesture, or in the interactive sequencing games children learn in the playground; these require copious amounts of attention before they become more automatic and semi-conscious. Similarly procedural learning about relationships early in life takes great effort and once learnt is not based on conscious

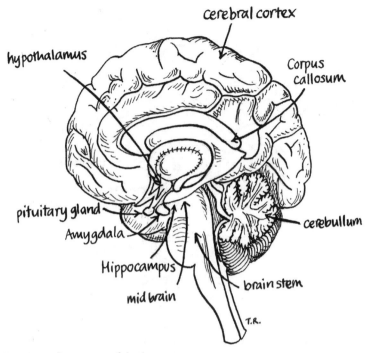

Figure 8.1 Some key areas of the brain

Figure 5.3 from p. 65 in Music, G. (2009b). Neuroscience and child psychotherapy. In M. Lanyado & A. Horne (Eds.), *The handbook of child and adolescent psychotherapy*. London: Routledge. Reproduced with permission of Taylor and Francis

understandings. Adults and children enter new situations guided by prior procedural learning and internal working models of relationships.

Our brains and evolutionary past

Our brains are by far the most complex of any animal on earth, and have extraordinary capacities. The fundamental units of the brain are neurons, long entities with a central nucleus (Figure 8.2). Neurons connect to other neurons, via synapses, which enable electrical and chemical signals to be sent to areas of the brain and nervous system. The brain is highly complicated, able to make incredibly complex calculations about psychological matters within fractions of a second. The average neuron connects *directly* to 10,000 other neurons, and the average brain has 100 billion neurons. We are born with nearly all the neurons we are going to have but in the period from the end of pregnancy to early childhood all kinds of complex connections between them are being formed. Neurons send messages to other neurons via synapses, and we have far more synapses than neurons, some 100 trillion in fact (Pinker, 2002). Each neuron has a cell body and tens of thousands of tiny branches (dendrites) that receive

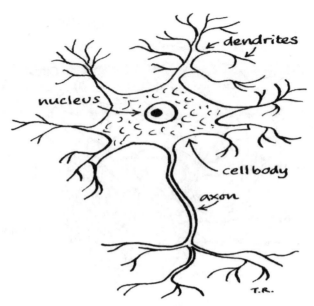

Figure 8.2 A neuron

Figure 5.1 from p. 53 in Music, G. (2009b). Neuroscience and child psychotherapy. In M. Lanyado & A. Horne (Eds.), *The handbook of child and adolescent psychotherapy*. London: Routledge. Reproduced with permission of Taylor and Francis

electrochemical messages. A piece of brain the size of a grain of sand contains 100,000 neurons; 2,000,000 axons; and a billion synapses (Siegel, 2007).

The development of the human brain has been uneven, and different parts have evolved at different stages of evolutionary history and serve different functions. Although slightly simplified, MacLean's (1990) concept of the triune brain is a useful starting point, suggesting that the human brain can be related to three main stages in our phylogentic history. He distinguished the reptilian brain, the limbic system, and the neocortex (see Figure 8.3). Many 'reptilian' brain functions have changed little in the last 250 million years. As well as controlling functions like heart rate, breathing, temperature, and balance, it also contains structures such as the brain stem, which manage vital survival instincts such as fight, flight, and freeze responses. It is also the brain region concerned with social dominance systems and 'pecking orders'. These brain systems are effective at learning fast, but can also be somewhat rigid, and once something is learnt it does not easily get unlearnt.

By about 150 million years ago the limbic system had developed in mammals. Its roles include making judgements, learning whether an experience is likely to be pleasurable or not, and forming emotional memories, and is sometimes seen as the seat of emotional life. Emotions such as fear, joy, pain, and pleasure would not exist without the limbic system.

Finally, the 'new kid on the block' is the neocortex, a mere two or three million years old, and its most complex form is seen in humans with our two cerebral

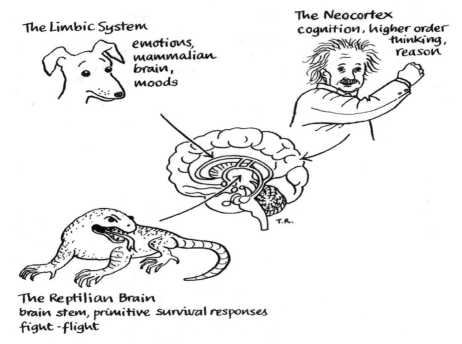

The Limbic System
emotions, mammalian brain, moods

The Neocortex
cognition, higher order thinking, reason

T.R.

The Reptilian Brain
brain stem, primitive survival responses
fight-flight

Figure 8.3 The triune brain (after MacLean, 1990)

Figure 5.2 from p. 54 in Music, G. (2009b). Neuroscience and child psychotherapy. In M. Lanyado & A. Horne (Eds.), *The handbook of child and adolescent psychotherapy*. London: Routledge. Reproduced with permission of Taylor and Francis

hemispheres, responsible for human thought, language, imagination, and consciousness. The three parts of the brain are not separate units by any means, and complex relationships and pathways have developed between them over the millennia.

The neuroscientist Daniel Siegel (2007) has argued that psychological health is marked by ever increasingly complex interdependence between brain areas, and that many who present with psychological or psychiatric issues show a less complex or interwoven structure, with fewer links between brain regions. An exercise I sometimes undertake when working with clients is to ask myself what brain region is active at a particular moment. For example basic instinctual responses such as fight, flight or hate, lust, and aggression emanate from more reptilian brain regions. If one is confronted by anger or hatred in someone who at a particular moment has a highly active brain stem and is in 'fight' mode, it is folly to make a joke or an intellectually complex comment that only their cerebral cortex could make sense of (Music, 2009b). When we are very frightened we tend to return to very basic modes of functioning, in which our more developed cognitive capacities are barely active.

Experience dependence

In recent years we have increasingly understood that the human brain is malleable or experience dependent, and that particular experiences give rise to specific brain pathways and structures. The brain can be thought of as like an extraordinarily complex muscle system that strengthens and grows, or withers, according to how much it is exercised. At birth the human brain has an overabundance of cells, but very few connections between them. In the postnatal period there is a process often called 'use it or lose it' or 'pruning', in which cells that are not used simply die off. Schwartz and Begley (2002, p. 117) quote a figure of 20 billion synapses pruned every day between childhood and early adolescence; they state 'like a cable TV subscription canceled because nobody's watching, synaptic connections that are not used weaken and vanish'. Once a connection forms it remains wired, and neurons that are unused, that do not form part of the pathways needed by experience, are 'pruned' and wither away, although new wiring can still form later in life. For example, each time a child is held and soothed by its mother, connections and links are being formed in its brain. Next time it experiences distress and its mother is nearby, it might equally expect to be soothed. Experience begins to be filtered through such ready formed pathways, just as water naturally flows down existing channels. Once an expectation is formed it remains, and the world is later experienced according to such preconceptions.

The phrase 'cells that fire together wire together' (and survive together) has been termed Hebb's law, after the neuroscientist Hebb (1949). This describes the process whereby experiences are filtered through specific neuronal pathways, so that we expect X to follow Y if they have previously gone together, and the cells involved in that process link together and strengthen. The brain is a powerful predictor of the future. If encountering a strange adult triggers fear, as might happen in children who have suffered trauma, then these same fear responses might also be triggered with other more benign adults, such as kindly teachers or adoptive parents. Early on the human brain is particularly malleable, something known as 'neuroplasticity' and vital emotional learning is taking place. The period from the last trimester of pregnancy to the second year of life is crucial, and at its peak in prenatal life the brain is producing 250,000 cells every minute. Thankfully there are other 'sensitive periods', particularly the first 5 years and during adolescence, and some plasticity remains throughout the lifespan.

Many have argued that the limbic system and the right hemisphere are central for emotional development in the early years (Schore, 2005). More sophisticated capacities arrive considerably later, such as **explicit memory** and more complex cognitive skills, and parts of the cortex are still developing in our early twenties. Parents might be described as psychobiological regulators of the developing infant brain, and development in infant brains takes place through experiences such as face-to-face interactions with an attuned caregiver. This is less of a mystical process than it might sound. When a mother is in tune with an infant and is regulating its feelings then both parties show remarkable similarities in heart rate and in their nervous system functioning. Similarly when infants are happily in the company of an adoring adult then this has a physiological effect, with the release of hormones that enhance optimistic feelings and in turn forge positive attachments. The opposite is also true, with infants of depressed mothers showing low dopamine levels at a month, mirroring the low dopamine of their mothers, for example. These days we are moving away from models of single brains towards an understanding of how one brain activates another.

Hormones and opiates

Experience affects not only the structure of the brain, but also the way the system of chemicals in the human body works. Chemicals, such as hormones (released from an endocrine gland into the bloodstream) and **neurotransmitters** (released by nerve terminals) send signals between neurons and other bodily systems, and some commonly known ones I have mentioned already include serotonin, dopamine, adrenaline, and oxytocin. We have seen how high levels of stress in pregnancy lead to the production of the stress hormone cortisol; which crosses the placenta and can affect the developing foetus. Experiences of neglect or trauma, even when not consciously remembered, can affect not only behaviours and attitudes but also hormonal systems. The **hypothalamus–pituitary–adrenal (HPA)** axis is a complex system that controls reactions to stress, and is linked to the release of adrenaline into the bloodstream, increasing heart rate, blood pressure, and cortisol levels; preparing the body for fight or flight. Cortisol is easily measured on saliva samples and quite an industry has developed doing this. Children's cortisol levels are higher when they are fearful or subjected to ongoing trauma or anxiety. Cortisol has a number of pernicious effects, and can destroy cells in the hippocampus, a brain region central to memory (Mc Auley, Kenny, Kirkwood, Wilkinson, Jones, & Miller, 2009). Ironically some victims of serious trauma such as many Holocaust survivors have extremely low rather than very high cortisol levels (Yehuda, 2004). Both high and low cortisol levels are often a sign of severe stress.

Good or loving experiences, however, are accompanied by different hormonal releases. As already described, oxytocin particularly promotes warm and affiliative feelings. Primates that 'pair bond', such as humans, have more oxytocin receptors than species that do not. Oxytocin levels increase when we are with someone we love, or when breastfeeding, having sex, or receiving a massage. An interesting experiment (Kosfeld, Heinrichs, Zak, Fischbacher, & Fehr, 2005) in Zurich showed how oxytocin increases trust. Subjects were given either oxytocin or a placebo, and asked to participate in a game in which they gave money over to a trustee, and depending how much they gave away they 'could' receive up to four times as much back. The group who were given oxytocin were more trusting, gave more away and received more back. A linked experiment by Zak and colleagues in California looked at generosity to unknown partners, and found that those with naturally higher oxytocin levels in their bloodstreams gave away more, and also received more in return (Zac, Matzner, & Kurzban, 2008).

Another experiment found that when shown pictures of threatening and scary faces, those given a placebo showed much higher activation of the amygdala, a brain area linked with stress and anger, and the group given oxytocin showed much lower activation, suggesting that oxytocin lowers social fear (Kirsch et al., 2005). Much research demonstrates the benign and positive effects of oxytocin, in bolstering the immune system, being a buffer against the impact of stress, as well as being implicated in feeling good. It is interesting that a recent study comparing Romanian orphans adopted about 3 years earlier with children brought up by birth mothers, found that the adopted children did not release oxytocin when cuddled by their mothers in the way that the birth children did (Fries, Ziegler, Kurian, Jacoris, & Pollak, 2005). This suggests that the capacity to give and receive affection, and its neuronal concomitants, might atrophy with neglect.

Many medical and recreational drugs mimic the chemical effects the body produces naturally when we feel good. Cocaine impacts on the dopamine system, and experiments have shown that stressed low-status monkeys self-administer more cocaine than dominant ones (Banks, Czoty, & Nader, 2007). Stress and anxiety increase desire for substances such as cocaine, something that occurs less when we feel good. Similarly, if we have high status and confidence then our serotonin levels are naturally high. Many antidepressants work with the serotonin system, and low levels of serotonin are seen in people who are more irritable, volatile, and unhappy. In an experiment a well-known antidepressant was given to a male monkey in a troop that at that point had no alpha male. The monkey taking fluoxetine (Prozac), with higher serotonin levels, then became the troop's alpha male (Raleigh, McGuire, Brammer, Pollack, & Yuwiler, 1991). Indeed, as Wilkinson and Pickett (2009) and others have shown, low status gives rise to lower serotonin, higher stress levels, worse immune systems, and also worse health outcomes.

Inevitably nature–nurture questions arise when such research is discussed. High cortisol levels are seen in strains of rats bred to be highly reactive, but these same rats have far lower cortisol levels than their peers when they are adopted by a calmer, less stressed rat mother (Francis, Diorio, Liu, & Meaney, 1999). Similarly rat pups removed from their mothers for brief periods showed high stress levels throughout their lives, while rat pups that were handled and licked showed lower cortisol levels and reacted less to stressful situations as they grew older (Ladd, Huot, Thrivikraman, Nemeroff, Meaney, & Plotsky, 2000).

The same appears to be true for primates and humans. Infant monkeys raised in stressful circumstances have elevated cortisol rates. Suomi (1997) undertook cross-fostering experiments with monkeys in which those bred to be highly stressed were fostered by calmer mothers, and as in rat experiments the cross-fostered monkeys became calmer, with lower cortisol rates. In humans the nearest equivalent is research undertaken with children adopted or fostered from stressful or depriving backgrounds. Mary Dozier and colleagues studied children fostered after traumatic starts, and as one might expect she found that the younger the children were fostered, the more likely they were to recover (Dozier, Stovall, Albus, & Bates, 2001). If fostered in the first 18 months then recovery was far better. Insecurely attached infants fostered by well-trained carers became secure and developed similar cortisol levels to those seen in nonfostered children.

One large study found that 5-year-old children with stressed mothers had high cortisol levels, but their cortisol levels were only high when the mothers had also been highly stressed when the children were infants (Essex, Klein, Cho, & Kalin, 2002). In other words, if a stressed pattern sets in early it is hard to shift and almost becomes an inbuilt biological programme. Change is possible though, and looking at samples of Romanian orphans, the findings mirrored those of Mary Dozier, in that those adopted earliest showed the lowest cortisol levels and most normal stress regulation systems (Gunnar, Morison, Chisholm, & Schuder, 2001). Environmental stressors and the lack of emotional regulation gives rise to stress reactions that are hard to turn off, and can have an effect throughout the lifespan.

Left and right hemispheres

The human brain is divided into a left and right cerebral hemisphere. There are many popular misconceptions that there is definite lateralisation of functions in which 'only' the left or right hemispheres 'do' certain things, as if there was a complete separation of tasks. However, there are some general differences that can be stated. The left frontal cortex generally is dominant for positive feelings, and people who are happier, more cheerful and hopeful have more activity there. Children and adults who are depressed show more activation in the right frontal cortex and have less left brain activity, and this has been shown even in very young infants (Davidson, 2008). Left frontal dominance is linked to approach as opposed to avoidance strategies, and people who are more positive are generally more outgoing, more likely to actively seek novel situations, and less likely than depressed people to be inhibited. Such left frontal brain functioning includes qualities such as autonomy, self-acceptance, and being purposeful. It is not simply about pleasure in the hedonic sense, but is more about openness and acceptance of experiences, including of negative ones. Recent research shows that meditation gives rise to a 'leftward' shift, as well as improving immune systems (Davidson et al., 2003). Writing down negative events as a way of processing them also activates the left hemisphere, something one would also expect to see in psychotherapy, and Siegel (2007) suggests that the crucial factor is being prepared to face all experiences, whether good, bad, frightening or exciting, rather than shrinking from them.

The better known, and more popular, difference between the left and right hemispheres is that the left hemisphere tends to lead on language, instrumentality, and logic whereas the right brain has particular strengths in intuitive, emotional processing, creativity, and more 'holistic' skills. These are different parts of the brain to those involved in positive and negative affect. As a rule of thumb, the right brain receives signals from and controls the left side of the body, and vice versa. Big strides in our understanding of the functions of the different hemispheres were made by Sperry (2001) who researched how the left and right brain are linked by a bundle of nerves, called the **corpus callosum**. When some of Sperry's patients' corpus callosum were removed for clinical reasons he discovered that the two hemispheres functioned independently. For example, when a pencil was shown to such a patient's right hand and eye (controlled by their left hemisphere) the patient could name the pencil but not describe what it was used for. In contrast when shown to the right eye and hand, the patient knew what one did with the pencil but could not name it. Schore (1994) and others have argued that it is the emotionally dominant right hemisphere that is most significant in earliest infancy, and that the left brain and the cortex, dominant for logic and cognition, play a lesser role in the early first years when many vital neuronal pathways and synaptic connections are forming.

Neuroscientists such as Siegel are convinced that mental health is characterised by increasing complexity, richer neuronal pathways and connections, including better links between the left and right sides of the brain, in the form of a better functioning corpus callosum. Indeed, following emotional trauma one is likely to have a thinner, less effective corpus callosum, and hence the more logical left brain is not working so well in tandem with the more emotionally dominant right hemisphere. Similarly, telling stories and forming narratives is primarily a function of the left side of the brain, but to develop autobiographical memories there is a need to link this with more processing of emotional experiences that takes place in the right brain. It is the links between the parts of the brain that are needed for emotional health. Some evidence suggests that certain treatments for trauma, such as eye movement desensitisation and reprocessing therapy, might facilitate various changes in the brain, including better communication between the hemispheres (e.g., Harper, Rasolkhani-Kalhorn, & Drozd, 2009).

There can be disjunctions between our nonconscious beliefs and the stories our left hemispheres tell ourselves and others. Pretending to oneself one is not jealous when a friend gives someone else their attention might be one example, or having racist feelings despite professing to not being racist might be another. People were asked to immerse their hands in freezing water for as long as they could, and some had been told that their life expectancy was greater the longer they could keep their hands in it while others were told the opposite (Quattrone & Tversky, 1984). People genuinely experienced more or less capacity to keep their hands in the freezing water depending on whether the result was likely to predict their longevity. In another experiment avowedly homophobic men who did not hold such views watched X rated films showing heterosexual, lesbian, and homosexual sex (Adams, Wright, & Lohr, 1996). Their sexual arousal was monitored, and it was the stridently homophobic group who showed by far the most arousal in response to the films of gay sex, but not other forms of sex. These examples show how much goes on beyond consciousness and part of the aim of much therapeutic work is to bring these two aspects of ourselves, our conscious and nonconscious worlds, more in line with each other.

Trauma and neglect: the amygdala, hippocampus, and HPA axis

The early years are vital. Just as the rat pup licked by its mother copes better with stress as it gets older, so a parent's good emotional and physical contact with its infant is an innoculatory factor in its growing up. To describe it somewhat simplistically, with loving care helpful and calming hormones are released, more receptors for these hormones develop, and a template for future emotional experiences is set up. When early experience is of trauma or neglect then different chemicals are released and high stress levels can become the infant's natural way of being. The amygdala is vital in such processes and is particularly involved in fear responses and how humans are primed to respond in microseconds to threat. Infants and children subjected to trauma might have an amygdala on constant hyperalert.

We are biologically predisposed to respond to potential danger via flight, fight, or freeze, and quick surges of adrenalin and the release of cortisol are essential and lifesaving when a predator such as a lion comes into view. Generally after such shocks the body quickly goes back to normal, with blood pressure and heart rates reducing as we relax. For example during the Strange Situation Test (Chapter 6, p. 61) securely attached children show stress and anxiety, but when their mother returns they quickly return to their baseline levels of arousal. Insecurely attached children take far longer to calm down after stressors. If one has been subjected to constant trauma it is possible to become either chronically hyperaroused, sensing danger everywhere and rarely calming down, or the opposite, developing a, closed down underaroused self-protective state that one sees in dissociation. Hyperaroused and multiply traumatised children can seem like soldiers still trying to fight a war that in fact ended long ago; on constant alert.

The psychiatrist and neuroscientist, Bruce Perry (Adams et al., 1996) has expanded our knowledge of the impact of trauma on brain development, and has described how many traumatised children can barely relax, are often constantly 'on the move', and are in a desperately anxious and hypervigilant state. Such heightened physiological responses are a sign of a highly activated **sympathetic nervous system**. There is a different response by the nervous system to stress and trauma, an activation of what is called the **parasympathetic nervous system**. In this the body closes down, rather like a creature playing dead in front of a predator. Blood pressure becomes low, as does heart rate. The parts of the brain which specialise in logical thought can often shut down when faced with trauma, while primitive survival mechanisms take over. This can give rise to the phenomenon of dissociation, in which people can seem to be cut-off from their own experiences. In dissociation, as well as in allied states such as derealisation or depersonalisation, people often just do not react emotionally, or indeed even bodily, to unpleasant or frightening emotional stimuli (Sierra, Senior, Phillips, & David, 2006). This might be part of the explanation for why many children from highly stressful or abusing backgrounds often do not achieve well academically. They have learnt to cope either by being hyperalert to danger, which impedes ordinary relaxed concentration, or they can go into a shut down dissociative mode in which the thinking part of the brain becomes inactive. Both are linked to the survival responses of fight, flight, and freezing. Following trauma aspects of more ordinary cognitive functioning are dampened down, there are weaker links between the left and right hemispheres and an overactive amygdala and it seems likely that cells in the hippocampus might die off as a result of exposure to trauma, with cortisol being directly implicated in this (Hageman, Andersen, & Jorgensen, 2001).

Severe neglect, different from trauma, can lead to atrophy in parts of the brain and developmental delay, as well as serious deficits in the ability to empathise, regulate emotions, manage intimacy and ordinary social interaction. Studies of extreme cases of deprivation such as neglected children adopted from Romanian orphanages (Chugani, Behen, Muzik, Juhász, Nagy, & Chugani, 2001), have shown the impact of such early deprivation on their actual brains. Scans revealed that parts of their brains were showing diminished activity, particularly the sites concerned with language development. But worse, brain areas that are primed for emotional understanding and expressiveness seemed in these seriously neglected orphans to be almost like a 'black hole', with shockingly little activity and life. Perry (2002) published research that demonstrated that the actual circumference of the brain of severely neglected children is often much smaller than the norm, although actual brain circumference will recover for those adopted sufficiently early. Experience affects the brain, particularly very bad experiences such as of severe trauma or neglect.

Summary: hope or hopeless?

We have learnt in this chapter that experiences, such as of trauma and neglect, affect neuronal pathways and hormonal systems. Early experiences can be fundamental to forming procedural knowledge and particularly the expectations of relationships that we take into our later experiences, expectations that often remain out of consciousness. We have looked at some of the key areas of the brain involved in emotional functioning and seen how emotional health appears to be characterised by more connections between brain areas, including between the left and right hemispheres. We have seen that established behavioural patterns can be hard to shift.

However, lest gloom overtakes the reader, we also know that new circuitry can grow and that change can take place throughout the lifespan. Change is genuinely possible, even if it is sometimes the result of slow and painstaking work. This can happen for example, through good parenting, such as is seen in studies of successful adoption or fostering. Also helpful can be therapeutic work, and indeed neuroscientist Joseph LeDoux (1998, p. 265) has argued that therapy is 'another way of creating synaptic potentiation in brain pathways that control the amygdala'. The amygdala's emotional memories are indelibly burned into its circuits, but we can regulate their expression. The way we do this is by getting the cortex to control the amygdala, as shown in Figure 8.4. The amygdala is the seat of primitive fear responses and reacts in nanoseconds to perceived danger. Experiences will often be filtered straight to the amygdala via the thalamus. However, there is a slightly longer route whereby experience is filtered via the thalamus to the cortex, the cognitive part of the brain. Thus the 'direct route' can be mediated by benign new experiences. For example, a loud noise

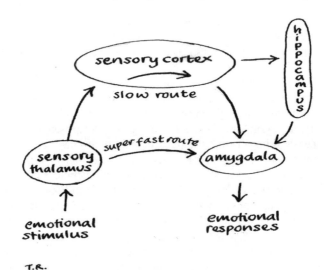

Figure 8.4 The fear response (after LeDoux, 1998)

Figure 5.4 from p. 69 in Music, G. (2009b). Neuroscience and child psychotherapy. In M. Lanyado & A. Horne (Eds.), *The handbook of child and adolescent psychotherapy*. London: Routledge. Reproduced with permission of Taylor and Francis

might cause a startle in a war veteran who then becomes aware that the noise was simply a carpenter hammering next door, not a bomb going off. He then relaxes. Therapeutic work can enhance such processes, building up the capacity to interpret experience in new and less frightening ways, and this is but one way in which change can take place. Other byproducts of therapeutic work are likely to include a better link between left and right brain, better thinking capacities, more ability to form coherent narratives about oneself and to regulate emotional experiences, an enhanced ability to tolerate difficult emotions without losing control, as well as the ability to form and manage attachments better. Indeed research studies have begun to show that therapeutic work does indeed change brain structures (Ressler & Mayberg, 2007).

One hopeful feature of the recent neuroscientific findings is that the brain remains plastic throughout life. A classic example of brain changes later in life is the case of the research findings on London black-cab (taxi) drivers. Scientists took a close look at their brains (Maguire et al., 2000) and found that they had something in common that was different to other males of similar ages. The hippocampus of black-cab drivers was significantly bigger at the back and smaller at the front, and the research plotted quite clearly how the changes in shape of the hippocampi were directly related to the number of years they had been driving. There is much similar research with equally exciting findings, such as stroke victims recovering functioning as new parts of the brain colonise functions previously undertaken by now dead brain regions (Begley, 2009). There are many other such tales of massive brain and life changes and the plasticity of the human brain is one of the exciting discoveries of our time (Doidge, 2008). New learning can give rise to new neuronal connections and new brain organisation throughout life. We might never erase old experiences and their related brain circuits, but we can build new experiences, new expectations, and brain pathways. There are of course some important 'windows of opportunity' when big developments take place and the brain is changing more rapidly. Particularly important are the first few years of life, and also adolescence, which as we will see in Chapter 16 is a time when the brain is developing hugely and real change is possible. To some degree learning, new experiences and their accompanying brain changes are possible until the end of our lives.

Developmental capacities and stages

Language, words, and symbols

For most of the history of psychology language has been considered in relation to the development of cognitive capacities, with words primarily seen as developing **scaffolding** for thinking. This sat comfortably with an ethos that saw emotion and affect as relatively poor cousins to cognition. In this chapter I will stress the social, emotional, and cultural aspects of language, how linguistic abilities are being laid down in the earliest months of life, and are linked to early emotional and gestural communication, as well as the understanding of other minds.

A relationship with language is even developing *in utero* and infants start to recognise sounds in their first months. By about 9 months infants generally begin to understand the meaning of some words, and just before a year first words often appear. Then between about 12 and 20 months vocabulary grows, and by the end of their second year many infants can use between 20 and 50 words, some in combination. Through the next year the rudiments of grammar are learnt, leading sometimes to the quaintly overzealous application of rules in statements like 'he fallded over' or 'she winned the race'. More complex capacities for stories and communication begin to take shape after 5 years of age. Such milestones are always only the roughest of guides and some children reach them earlier, others later, while some might never reach certain milestones.

The world is never the same after we acquire language. Words can determine how we see and understand the world, altering one's perspective, as Eva Hoffman (1990, p. 29) describes in her autobiographical account, *Lost in Translation*, where she writes 'Sometimes, when I find a new expression, I roll it on the tongue, as if shaping it in my mouth gave birth to a new shape in the world'. Language can open up new vistas, as poetry often does, and it is necessary for developing the autobiographical and narrative capacities that are central to forming a coherent sense of self. Yet language can be a loss as well as a gain, as Daniel Stern (2000, p. 176) shows. He describes a child perceiving a patch of yellow sunlight on a wall, 'experiencing the intensity, shape, brightness, pleasure', having what is a global sensory experience which can be disrupted forever when someone says something like 'look at the yellow sunlight'. Putting experiences into verbal boxes (e.g., yellow sunlight) inevitably reduces the complexity of experience. Stern says that language can 'fracture amodal global experience' (p. 176) so that one becomes distanced from it.

Some argue that people are 'prisoners' of their language, unable ever to think outside its confines. Other experts such as Stephen Pinker (2002) argue that thoughts and thinking occur independently of the ability to use language, and neuroscientists such as Antonio Damasio (1999) equally argue that thinking is occurring most of the time, irrespective of language. One must distinguish language and thought, and also language and communication, even though they are linked. Infants are biologically primed to communicate, and their early communications contain emotional understanding, intentionality, and expectations. This differs from a traditional view of communication as one person 'sending' a 'parcel' of information to another, with an understanding that the other can receive and understand this parcel. An infant's urgent vocalisation is a kind of proto-communication, which a mother might respond to in a way that makes it meaningful, communicating back this understanding so that the baby learns to make sense of their own feelings. In this way meanings are socially constructed through dialogic interaction.

Central to language is symbolism, Words are *arbitrary*, and alternative random sounds could just as easily be used to denote the same things. For example, while we use 'paper' to denote that thing that words are printed on, it would be equally possible for another symbol to do the same job. With the exception of onomatopoeic or iconic words, such as 'bang' or 'woof woof', in our use of linguistic symbols there is a distance between the word and that which it describes. This allows a psychological distance between the user of symbols and the thing being described. When we label something with a symbol this increases our capacity for self-reflection, as the symbol and that which is symbolised can be reflected upon and spoken about, increasing cognitive flexibility and control over thoughts (Jacques & Zelazo, 2005).

Central to emotional development is learning to label and monitor feelings and thoughts. The ability to use symbols in their full richness, such as in poetry, or to use words to understand thoughts or feelings, is something that some children never develop. Because symbols are arbitrary, without fixed meanings, and can mean something different depending on a speaker's state of mind and intentions, some people who struggle to grasp intentions and mental states are particularly challenged, such as some people with autism. Linked to the ability to use symbols is the capacity to understand other people's minds. What distinguishes human language from the rudimentary copycat words that parrots can use, or the alarm calls that monkeys make, is such psychological understanding. Language use is not just about signs, that one word 'stands for' a thing. It requires the ability to 'tune in' to another's mind, to make sense of their intentions. To begin to explore this, once again, I will begin with early infancy.

Parentese and infant-directed speech

The precursors of language can be seen in the early parent–infant relationship. Mary Bateson originally coined the term **motherese** to describe a way of communicating with babies seen in most cultures in the world (Bateson, 1971). Many now use the word parentese instead, to avoid the gender-biased assumption that only mothers do this, and academics use the label **infant-directed speech (IDS)**. Parentese has clear characteristics; we tend to speak to babies using a higher pitch, longer hyperarticulated vowels, shorter pauses, and more repetitions than in usual speech. Infants show an interest in the rhythm, prosody, and tempo of speech long before they understand the meaning of words. Not only mothers, but fathers, grandparents, and children as young as 4 years of age tend to automatically adopt this way of speaking with babies, even speaking to pets in the same manner (Fernald, 1985). In experiments with infants using language stripped of its grammatical meaning, parentese has been shown to be far superior to traditional adult-directed speech as a way of communicating intentions and expectations.

Infant-directed speech or parentese is common in nearly all cultures studied. Central to it is a musicality that facilitates the regulation of social and emotional relationships (Mithen, 2006). There is some variation between cultures, such as Japanese mothers using a slightly lower level of emotional expression, but these tend to be minor, as was found by Anne Fernald who has travelled the globe examining mother–infant speech patterns. In an interesting experiment, parentese that was expressing prohibitions was played to babies in four languages, and also in English using nonsense words. In addition loudness, which is generally the most significant difference between approval and prohibition, was filtered out, so infants were primarily responding to 'melody'. The infants consistently frowned when the speech expressed prohibition and smiled at the phrases expressing approval, showing how intentions in a speaker can be communicated simply via the musicality of speech (Fernald, 1993).

Infants can understand extremely subtle differences in sounds, and differentiate separate words from what is really a continuous 'sound-bath'. Saffran and Thiessen (2003) describe the sophistication of this task, which requires detecting statistical regularities in spoken sentences, and is how one differentiates specific words and part-words from a stream of sound. Spoken sentences do not have gaps between them like written words, making this feat all the more remarkable. In one experiment 8-month-olds were exposed to sound streams denuded of all prosody and melody, and a few nonsense words, such as like 'bo-ti-nim' were placed several times into the sound-stream. The infants somehow worked out which sounds had appeared regularly. They could similarly extract the patterning when listening to musical tones, again suggesting a link between linguistic and musical abilities.

Musicality is fundamental to early language use. Sandra Trehub and colleagues found that six-month-olds show greater physiological response to their mothers' singing than to their speech, as gauged by measuring their cortisol levels (Trehub, Unyk, & Trainor, 1993). Across cultures babies are soothed by lullabies, which generally have similar melodies, rhythms, and tempos. Interestingly Jayne Standley (2003) found that a female voice singing lullabies to premature infants increased their sucking abilities, thereby aiding weight gain, stabilising oxygen saturation levels, and improving general physical development. Singing helps improve infant mood, which has a knock-on effect on sleeping, eating, and learning, and is central to how infant emotional life is regulated.

The role of positive emotion in this is crucial. When infants are presented with both adult-directed speech and parentese, they generally prefer parentese, but when emotion is held constant, neither negative nor positive, infants show no preference. When adult speech forms express more positive emotion than infant-directed speech, then babies clearly prefer the positive adult speech forms (Singh, Morgan, & Best, 2002). The lilt and melody of parentese has a positive tone that naturally inspires interest. What is unique about parentese is its rich emotional expressiveness and positive affect quality (Trainor & Desjardins, 2002). Parentese is more emotionally expressive than ordinary adult speech, which tends to be more emotionally inhibited. Via parentese the precursors of early language learning are interwoven with learning about the world of emotion.

Culture and language

There are a few rare exceptions to the universality of motherese or parentese. One example is seen in the Kaluli, a tribe in New Guinea, who confer high status on skilled language users (Ochs & Schieffelin, 2009). They have no lilting parentese with its soft, high-pitched tones, and infants and children are not even addressed directly. Rather they are taught to speak clearly through adults modelling correct speech that infants are expected to follow. Infants learn by observing how adults or older children speak to each other, not through parentese nor the dyadic interactions we in the West might assume to be natural. The Kaluli expect children to fit into adult speech patterns and barely attempt to understand what a child might be thinking; believing that one can never know what is in another's mind.

Similarly the Gusii of Kenya believe that if you talk too much to your children then they end up self-centred (LeVine, 1994). Gusii children are immersed in adult conversation but are not talked to or taught to talk. The Western middle-class ideal of lots of dyadic mother–infant communication again does not pertain. As ever, we cannot assume universality for what we take for granted as natural.

The relationship between culture and language is more complex than such variations. One cannot understand culture without language or vice versa. Language provides basic tools for thinking, and as importantly, for ways of becoming culturally embodied. Birdwhistell (1970) showed that a bilingual Kutenai tribesperson consistently moved in a different way according to whether they were speaking Kutenai or English. They took on and literally embodied not just rules of speech, but also the feeling and cultural mores embedded in the language. Language can thus be viewed as 'performance' (Butler, 1999), and for those learning a second language it is often accompanied by new social roles (Burck, 2005).

As we have seen, infants are learning about language even before birth, and are able to recognise voices and words from their time in the womb (De Casper & Spence, 1986). Two-day-old babies have a preference for their native tongue, presumably because of exposure *in utero*, and humans are primed to be socialised into their own cultural mores (Moon, Cooper, & Fifer, 1993). Infants are born very sensitive to sounds, but their ability to distinguish between them diminishes greatly during the first year. Babbling has the same sounds across all cultures, but by the end of the first year infants become less capable of differentiating any sounds that are not used around them. For example, at around this time a Spanish baby would stop distinguishing so well between a 'b' and a 'v' sound. Patricia Kuhl and colleagues undertook research in Japan, watching when babies stopped noticing that the sounds in certain words were changed from what we know as 'l' to 'r' sounds (Kuhl, Stevens, Hayashi, Deguchi, Kiritani, & Iverson, 2006). When the babies successfully noticed a change she was relieved and smiled, only to look around and note that her Japanese colleagues had not noticed anything. The infants still had this skill but her adult colleagues were long past the stage when they could notice such subtle differences.

Interestingly, the Beng people have a religious explanation of such infant capacities. In their belief system, babies are born able to speak every language. It is believed that in *wrugbe* or the afterlife, where babies are believed to come from, all languages are spoken. Children are said to only slowly shed other linguistic understandings during the first years, understandings that had derived from wrugbe. If we translate wrugbe as evolutionary or cultural inheritance, theirs might seem a surprisingly accurate view, much more so than the idea of humans as a *tabula rasa* in relation to language. Language use becomes culturally distinct in the first year or so and is a way of distinguishing whether someone belongs in one's group or not, aiding processes of group cohesion.

Intersubjectivity and language learning

In the West developmental psychology has tended historically to focus more on individual than social development, but there is an increasing understanding of the social and emotional nature of language. The Russian psychologist Lev Vygotsky (1962) particularly emphasised the influence of social factors on individual development and stressed the links between social learning and language, describing how children internalise culture, thinking capacities, and ways of being from parental figures and other adults. In recent times social constructionist theory has particularly emphasised how the world is partly constructed through culturally specific linguistic understandings (Gergen, 2009).

It is often assumed that children learn words for objects through things being pointed out to them. Parents often ask questions like 'what colour is that?' or say things like 'that is a doggy'. Many other cultures do not have this form of 'teaching' language, and instead words are picked up from the ordinary flow of social interaction. Children particularly learn through making sense of the intentions of those around them. It is almost definitely no coincidence that mirror neurons are situated in Broca's region of the brain, which is also the seat of language use. These neurons allow us to read the intentions of others, something that is necessary to use language effectively. In one experiment with 2-year-olds, Michael Tomasello (2003) invented verbs for actions, and these verbs were then used (e.g., 'plinnock') when a particular act was performed. The infants were later able to associate this made-up word with the action, but only when they could read the intentionality that went alongside the use of the word. Such infants were entering a complex **intersubjective** universe requiring an understanding of adult's intentions, and building on skills like social referencing and joint attention. This is why some children on the autistic spectrum, lacking in understanding other minds, struggle with the subtle nuances of meaning. Simple statements such as 'that's hot' mean something completely different depending on whether the speaker is complaining about the temperature of a drink, or showing pleasure in the summer sun, describing an item that is fashionable, or subtly hinting that someone should turn up the air conditioning.

As the philosopher Ludwig Wittgenstein (1974) taught us, the meaning of a word derives from its use in the language games of social discourse, rather than simply referring to something external in the world. In another experiment by Tomasello (2003), an adult told a child that they were looking for a 'toma'. The adult then picked up various objects, which were unfamiliar to the children, and made gestures, such as disappointment or excitement, indicating whether they had found it, and sure enough these infants soon picked up the meaning of 'toma'. This is more than pointing at an object and naming it; they had to understand wishes and intentions to decipher the meaning. Such learning is quite a feat for young children faced with a new sound and several possible things to which it might refer. Children as young as 18 months work out the meaning of words through deciphering adult behavioural cues, such as by watching lines of vision and emotional expressions, thus joining a joint-attentional world.

The skills infants are learning in their first months, such as imitation, the to-and-fro of early proto-conversations, the subtle dances of dyadic interaction, are all building blocks for later language use. Beebe showed that the rhythms of adult–infant communication are similar to those in conversations between adults, in terms of timings, pauses, and how infants look at and away from conversational partners (Beebe et al., 1997). Preverbal interactions are providing a rhythmic understanding of how conversational dialogue works. There is a developmental line from very early interactions to joint attention at about a year. The discovery of mirror neurons has added weight to the link between language use and understanding other minds. Nonverbal gestures are central to spoken conversations. Moving in the same rhythm as someone's speech is often a sign that one wants to join in a conversation. Skills such as switching a conversation, or changing emphasis, are achieved through nonverbal means such as facial expression and hand movements, skills that are being learnt well before words.

It is no coincidence that words arrive more or less when children become aware that people have separate minds. Proto-declarative pointing, such as pointing excitedly at an object that you want someone else to appreciate, demonstrates a wish to share an experience, and so to build intersubjective bridges between people. Some children with autism cannot do this, only managing proto-imperative pointing, such as pointing because they want something passed to them. For them the motivation is not the intersubjective sharing of experiences but is more instrumental.

Children work out what another person understands and adjust their communications accordingly. In an experiment children of about 2 saw a toy being hidden. Some knew that their mothers had hidden this toy, while others knew that their mothers did not see the toy being hidden (Akhtar & Tomasello, 1998). Children were more likely to name both the toy and where it was hidden when they assumed their mothers did not know its whereabouts. In other words, they had worked out what was in their mother's mind and hence what they needed to communicate to ensure the object was successfully retrieved. Slightly younger preverbal children similarly used different kinds of gestures depending on whether or not they thought their mothers knew where the toy was. Such skills need some understanding of another's mind. When adults express incomprehension to 1-year-olds these children tend to try all manner of tactics, from repeating themselves to exaggerating gesticulations to substituting different gestures, requiring considerable intersubjective sophistication (Golinkoff, 1993).

Joint attention at 14 months predicts language development at 2 years, or in other words, the better a child is at understanding other minds and intentions, the better their language skills are likely to be (Mundy & Burnette, 2005). How well a child follows its mother's attention during interaction predicts word comprehension when language proper comes into play (Silvén, 2001). Writers such as Tomasello therefore believe that language is an inherently intersubjective process that 'human beings have collaboratively invented for establishing, regulating and maintaining intersubjective interactions with fellow human beings' (Akhtar & Tomasello, 1998, p. 334).

Language and brains

A common view is that language primarily occurs via the left hemisphere, the part of the brain which generally specialises in logical, linear, and rational thought. Babies when babbling open their mouths more on the right side, suggesting that even then their left brains are getting to work on the skills needed for language (Holowka & Petitto, 2002). Magnetic resonance imaging (MRI) scans show that the same regions of the left brain that adults use in speech are also very active in infants (Dehaene-Lambertz, 2000). However, to be a language user one must be able to use and bring together many facets of the personality, and link many separate brain functions and regions.

Two particular regions, Broca's and Wernicke's areas, are central to language use, both found in the left hemisphere. Damage to Broca's area in adults leads to an inability to produce words, even if sufferers can generally still understand them. If Wernicke's area is damaged sufferers can form words, but their understanding is limited. Such discoveries suggest a difference between thought and language, and that words can be used to capture thoughts. For example Solms and Kaplan-Solms describe a patient (2001, p. 104) suffering from the brain and language disorder Wernicke's aphasia, who said 'I know what I want to say but I can't find the words; they just aren't there. And then, before I can find the words, the thought is gone'. This is a graphic if painful example of how words and thoughts cannot be conflated.

Language use depends on procedural rather than **declarative memory**. For example, patients who have lost their memories and do not make meaningful sentences still use the same grammatical structures as other people (Ferreira, Bock, Wilson, & Cohen, 2008); these being based on nonconscious learnt templates. While vocalisation in most primates takes place in emotional brain regions, human language is controlled by the cortex yet remains closely linked to the brain's emotional centres. Both cognitive and emotional capacities are central to language use.

There are definite windows of opportunity for developing the ability to use language. If one learns a second language after one's first few years, then one uses a different part of the brain for that second language than for one's first language (Perani et al., 1998). Children with little exposure to speech in their first years rarely use language fully, and often have problems with complex grammatical forms, and many severely neglected children show an inability to use language normally. Reports of feral children suggest something similar (Newton, 2002).

A famous recent example was Genie, imprisoned by her father at 18 months and discovered at 13 years of age in the 1970s who, despite attempts to teach her language, managed only rudimentary speech with little syntax. It seems likely that brain areas for learning language atrophy with lack of use at the right time. Similarly many late-adopted children reared in depriving orphanages in Eastern Europe had deficits in linguistic capacity, and also in social capacities (Rutter et al., 2007). Social interaction and having someone attuned to one's experience, as well as exposure to language, are all necessary for verbal and communicative abilities to flourish.

The case of children with autism casts light on the link between language, social skills, and understanding other minds, as so often people with autism might not feel their way into another person's world of meaning and thus cannot participate fully in social discourse. Not surprisingly, recent research suggests that children with autism have deficiencies in their mirror neuron functioning (Oberman et al., 2005). To communicate verbally we need to understand something of the other's states of mind. This can be hampered by developmental disorders such as autism, but also when the cultural expectations of speaker and listener are alien. Charlotte Burck (2005) quotes a second language speaker who was asked by a teacher 'what is the magic word?', the teacher assuming that the pupil would understand this magic word to be 'please'. However, the pupil came from a culture that did not require such expressions so his lack of the use of 'please' was considered rude in Britain whereas in his own family doing things for others required no words signifying gratitude. Having such an understanding of others, and being able to work out something about their thoughts and feelings, is a prerequisite of successful language use.

Language and emotional processing

We have seen from the attachment research that parents who score 'secure-autonomous' in the Adult Attachment Interview are likely to have securely attached children (Chapter 6, p. 64). Such parents can use language to make sense of emotional experiences, creating coherent narratives. Using words to describe internal states such as emotions is an aspect of affect regulation. In one study, participants were asked to look at anxiety-provoking pictures that were sufficiently frightening to stimulate subcortical amygdala alarm responses in their brains (Schieffelin & Ochs, 1986). When subjects 're-appraised' the pictures, re-interpreting what they saw using language, this lessened their arousal levels and helped regulate their emotions. Labelling angry or frightening emotions reduces blood flow to the amygdala, the brain's fear centre, helping emotional regulation (Hariri, Bookheimer, & Mazziotta, 2000).

Reflective self-functioning and putting feelings into words helps an individual to manage difficult emotional states. Indeed, it has consistently been found that writing about difficult experiences aids both emotional and physical health, and in particular that it is the ability to shift from first person pronouns ('I') to third person ('he', 'she') or 'we' statements, that is linked with enhanced health outcomes (Campbell & Pennebaker, 2003). The ability to use words to process experiences, and in self-reflective ways, facilitates both affect regulation and also executive functioning (Winsler, Fernyhough, & Montero, 2009).

If we develop the psychological equipment to process difficult experiences, we no longer have to defend against them so much. Using words in a coherent narrative to reflect upon emotional states is linked with secure attachment. Meins and colleagues' research about mind-mindedness, a mother's use of words that describe their child's mental states, has shown that using more mind-minded interactions in early infancy predicts later theory of mind skills and verbal ability, as well as secure attachment (Meins, Fernyhough, Wainwright, Das Gupta, Fradley, & Tuckey, 2002). Such findings have consequences for practitioners. Children who show conduct problems often have low verbal skills (Loney, Frick, Ellis, & McCoy, 1997); and insecurely attached children tend to have parents who do not develop complex narratives about their emotional lives. Avoidantly attached children and their parents often have a limited capacity to use words to describe emotional experiences. Using language to put thoughts and feelings into words is a primary way in which what is often termed emotional intelliegence (Salovey & Grewal, 2005) or emotional literacy develops as well as being a central tool of therapeutic work.

Language ability and social advantage

Language skills, perhaps particularly in the West, confer considerable advantages on children and adults. Linguistic skills differ according to how much language is valued in a family, social group, or culture as a whole, and how much children are exposed to it. In an extremely fine-grained study Hart and Risley (1999) taped the speech of families and children throughout their first years. The families were grouped according to whether they were welfare (i.e. out of work), working-class, or professional families. The researchers aimed to count the words a child heard in every interaction with its parent or caregiver. The analysis revealed stark class differences. A professional's child had had 50 million words addressed to it by the age of 4, compared with the working-class child's 30 million words and the welfare child's meagre 12 million. In other words the welfare child heard less than a quarter of the number of words that a child of professionals heard. In an average hour the child of professionals had 2100 words addressed to them while the working-class families had 1200 and the welfare families just 600. Maybe even more worryingly, by 3 years old children of professionals had received about 800,000 encouragements and only some 80,000 discouragements. However, the children of welfare parents had only been encouraged 60,000 times thus far, but had received twice as many discouragements. This is indicative of how psychological outcomes are closely connected with factors such as poverty and social position.

These children generally turned out to be similar to their parents in terms of vocabulary and verbal interaction styles. A child's measures at 3 years old also predicted later school results. Of equal worry was how IQ corresponded with vocabulary, with the professional child having an average IQ of 117, and the working-class child one of only 79. By 3 or 4 years old children given more affirmative input were more affirmative to other children. The sample was followed until age 10 and the early findings held up right until that age. The sample size was admittedly relatively small, but nonetheless these results fit with other research. Exposure to a wide vocabulary, more encouragement, less discouragement, more ordinary interest in children's mental states, less stress, and more positive feeling, all are likely to stimulate verbal and other abilities. Lest one becomes too deterministic, these results were not just about words spoken to, or indeed 'at', children, but this and other research has consistently shown that what counts is how much parents respond verbally to a child's gestures, communication, or other initiation of communication (Tamis-LeMonda, Bornstein, & Baumwell, 2001). As ever, it is being involved in two-way interactions that counts most.

Hart and Risley's (1999) work is just one example of how a social dimension can inform an understanding of language. Others might include having a particular dialect or vocabulary, such as an English public-school accent or a working-class dialect, as yielding tremendous advantages or disadvantages. Words and speech forms have meanings that take on a particular flavour for individuals and as Bakhtin (1982, p. 293) writes, 'each word tastes of the context and contexts in which it has lived its socially charged life'.

Summary

Sophisticated language use is unique to humans. Other primates and animals produce sounds patterns, monkeys can warn of predators, birds sing in complex ways, but none match human language. Attempts at teaching chimps to speak have met with limited success; they have been taught up to 100 signs, and even to joke and lie, but they never really develop syntax or sentences (Savage-Rumbaugh & Lewin, 1994).

Considering humans diverged from Great Apes some 6,000,000 years ago, we gained language relatively recently, about 70,000 years ago; about when humans expanded into new territories, developed cultural capacities as seen in cave paintings, and became the only surviving hominid, after the extinction of the Neanderthal. Most evolutionary theories suggest that humans achieved their success at least partly through social solidarity and communicational skills. Robin Dunbar (1998) from an evolutionary perspective has argued that language helped ensure group unity when human group sizes increased such that ways of establishing group cohesion seen in other primates, like physical grooming, no longer worked. Evolutionary psychologists argue that language allowed social conventions and information to be stored in group consciousness, maybe via chants, songs, and stories. Humans could then pass on information across generations, such as about plant species, hunting skills, seasonal changes, as well as cultural and religious conventions.

In much Western thought, dominated by rationalism, the logical and cognitive content of words has been emphasised. Language was viewed as a way of communicating ideas from one person to another, ideas conceptualised as discrete entities passed from mind to mind rather on the model of a telegraph. This leaves out how speech is an emotional, bodily, and sensuous process, and a feelingful expressive act, the roots of which can be seen in earliest infancy. Communicating is about more than just words and humans were communicating with gesture long before formal languages arrived. One only has to witness the complex hand gesticulations of mobile phone users to be reminded of the link between speech and gesture. Imitation, mirror neurons, word use, gesticulation, and social understanding are all fundamentally interlinked.

We communicate in all kinds of ways for all kinds of reasons. Sometimes we want someone else to know how we feel, while sometimes we want to deceive the other; sometimes we say one thing in words (e.g., professing love) and our body communicates something quite different, what Gregory Bateson (1972) called a double-bind. When we listen to another person we listen to far more than simply their words.

Language can be used in a dead, stultifying way or in a lively, expressive way; it can open up previously unthought symbolic or imaginary realms, or close down thinking; it can be the medium for the most intimate of communication and yet can also be the way people distance themselves from others, and from their own emotional selves. Language, as the philosopher Charles Taylor (1989) states, is not monologial but dialogical, it is potentially a way of knowing the other, and of course oneself. Language development arrives as infants realise that minds can be joined and can share in attending to something, whether an object of fear, or a pleasurable moment. This is a skill that we cannot take for granted, and is a developmental achievement that some sadly never manage. As Michael Bakhtin (1982, pp. 293–294) wrote 'language only becomes ones own when the speaker populates it with his own intention, his own accent ... language is not a neutral medium that passes freely and easily into the private property of the speaker's intentions; it is populated – overpopulated – with the intentions of others'.

Memories: learning who we are and what to expect

In this chapter I look at memory, and the different ways in which people's past impacts on their present lives. In Chapter 8 I distinguished two forms of longer-term memory, procedural and explicit, and this is further explored in terms of how past experiences are taken with us into our present functioning through procedural memories. I also examine declarative memories, the ability to remember facts and events from the past, including the thorny issue of memories of traumatic experiences. I will look too at autobiographical memory, and how people develop a sense of themselves as having a history and continuity over time.

The brain as predictor of the future

To ensure survival any creature needs to predict what is likely to happen next. We need some continuity, and if we do not know that the sun will rise tomorrow, or if we cannot predict the mood of a tyrannical parent, we can feel anxious. Children who desperately watch for clues about their unpredictable parent's next move are undertaking an extreme form of such predicting. We try to imagine the future by making sense of the present, and do so by using past experiences. If my father usually smiles and hugs me when he sees me then I probably expect this in the future from him, and maybe from other adults too. The brain is predictive, not in the sense of predicting lottery numbers or football results, but rather in its attempts to predict forthcoming moments. Daniel Siegel (1999, p. 24) states that memory is 'the way past events affect future function', thus taking the concept of memory beyond just the recall of facts or events. Such predictions are happening outside of consciousness almost all the time, in fractions of seconds.

Ironically predicting what will happen can alter what actually happens. If I predict good weather and the sun shines, I have not altered the weather. However, if I expect someone to be uninterested in me then I might relate to them in such a way that in fact they do not show interest in me. Similarly, approaching people with an expectation that I will be responded to with openness and warmth is likely to lead to a more open response from others. We bring our past expectations into the present in the form of a 'template' of relationships, attachment patterns being typical of this, and generally if a strategy has worked then it tends to be stuck to.

This approach is mostly successful and 'economic', swiftly giving a sense of whether a situation, person or moment is safe. However, a risk is that we can make wrong surmises about people, such as in what psychologists call the 'fundamental attribution error'. This describes how we can too easily expect people to be consistent over time. Many experiments show how hard it is for humans to learn from new evidence. In a classic study subjects were asked to converse with a woman posing to be an undergraduate (Goethals & Reckman, 1973). With half of the subjects she was told to be friendly and warm, and with the other half she was cold and aloof. The students were asked to evaluate not her behaviour but her true personality. Unsurprisingly those who had witnessed the unfriendly version rated her personality as cold and rejecting, while those exposed to the friendlier incarnation 'knew' she was 'really' nice and kind. More interesting was that these same subjects were then told that she was just an actress playing a role. They were then asked again what they thought her *real* personality was like, and despite knowing she had been acting they more or less gave exactly the same answers. The new facts had not altered the power of their earlier view of her personality.

People generally ascribe stable characteristics to people after seeing only fleeting behaviours. If someone is shown a picture of a neutral face and told the person was a Nazi, they tend to see cruelty in their features, but if shown a science equation next to the same neutral face they might see a studious face. Depending on our mood we can also ascribe all manner of characteristics that say more about our state of mind than the person in the picture, a phenomenon that psychoanalysts call **projection**. Emotional learning from powerful early experiences has a particularly strong effect on how the brain constructs a particular version of reality, seeing what others do not see. If I am an adopted child who was abused and I am offered a helping hand by a teacher or parent, I might experience this as an aggressive gesture. This is why therapists can lay such store by conscious self-reflection as a means of challenging nonconscious predicting. If I am able to step back from my preconceptions and examine the evidence I might just see that my teacher/parent/therapist in fact was not being aggressive. Of course other, more superficial factors also alter how we see the world. If one asks people about their overall happiness levels in their life, they give higher ratings when the sun is shining than when it is raining (Schwarz & Clore, 1983). Indeed, candidates are even more likely to be admitted to medical school if their interviews take place on sunny days (Redelmeier & Baxter, 2009). Our perception of what we think of as 'reality' is hugely influenced by both such superficial influences, and particularly by past experiences.

Predictions change experiences, and for example pain increases when it is predicted. When we get a mild electric shock, we physically react, and particular brain regions fire up, something that can be measured with functional MRI scans. Amazingly, when people are then told to expect such a shock, then these same brain regions have begun to react even before any actual stimulus. Furthermore, after applying a cream that subjects are told removes the pain, but is in fact a placebo, these same brain regions for pain do not react (Wager et al., 2004). Interestingly, depressed people tend to feel physical pain more acutely (Wagner, Koschke, Leuf, Schlösser, & Bär, 2009), and presumably have developed more expectations of unpleasant experiences.

We need such procedural and automatic understandings to efficiently do things like ride a bicycle or play the violin. The centipede would fall over if expected to be aware of every step it took. Emotional learning, and our expectations about how relationships are likely to go, are forms of procedural memory that can have lasting psychological effects. Someone who has been badly criticised as a child might protect themselves by shirking the limelight and withdrawing from social situations, which in turn might harm their capacity to manage later social situations. Yet to change such a pattern requires conscious effort, which is often resisted, as somewhere nonconsciously and deep in our beings we have learnt to trust our automatic procedurally based judgements. We can learn to adjust our tennis serve, or driving style, and emotional re-learning is also possible but may be resisted more. It might seem like I am describing classic **conditioning**, but this is only part of the story. A child who is often subjected to verbal attacks might become conditioned to expect danger, and be likely to interpret a neutral cue as a sign of threat. Yet there is also a mental correlate to the distrust (e.g., 'she is just out to get me' or 'if I trust her I'll be let down again').

Conscious and mindful practices can help counter such expectations and enable people to realise when they are wrong.

Memories of events and facts

Through our memories we integrate our experiences into a coherent subjective sense of ourselves. Memory is how we make sense retrospectively of events. As Daniel Stern (2004) shows, experiences that can be thought of as mini-moments of sensation can become episodes or 'chunks' of experience that are organised by our minds and brains. For example, if we have an experience that resembles a previous one seeing a grandparent smiling and carrying a bag, we may begin to believe there is a pattern; perhaps like last time the person with a bag will give us sweets and kisses and make us feel good. Even in infants such expectancies develop after something happens only twice, and when similar events happen several times children develop what Stern termed representations of interactions generalized (RIGS). These RIGS arise from an ability to do abstract averaging from past events, working out what the likelihood is of something happening next.

Infants of depressed mothers have learnt to expect low mood in their mothers, and a few months later they also expect and show such flattened mood with attuned others (Field et al., 1988). As we have seen, in the 'still-face' experiment (Chapter 4, p. 34) babies are disconcerted because their preconceptions (predictions based on memories) are confounded when their mother does not respond as expected. The accumulation of memories gives rise to a sense of who we are, and what is possible and likely. The child who is struggling with a task will draw on their previous experiences, consciously or not. They might respond to being faced by a difficult puzzle by smashing it up, or asking for help, or saying the puzzle is wrong, or maybe determinedly trying to solve it and saying aloud 'I can if I try, I can if I try', as one child I saw in treatment did. These various approaches all draw procedurally on past experiences.

In early infancy most learning is of the implicit or procedural kind, and although things, faces, and other 'facts' might be remembered for a short while, they are rarely available for recall later on. It is true that 2-month-old babies can remember objects such as a mobile 24 hours later, and 5-month-olds remember faces after 2 weeks (Greco, Rovee-Collier, Hayne, Griesler, & Earley, 1986). Yet it is less common for adults to remember events that happened much before the age of 3 or 4, a fact often described by the term **infantile amnesia**. By 4 children can definitely remember some things that had happened previously. Some children between 3 and 5 were asked about a trip to Disney that occurred in the past 6 to 18 months, and seemed to have very accurate recall, as validated by adults, even if they would not remember this trip 20 years later (Hamond & Fivush, 1991). The older ones had better recall, and giving them prompts helped. The research on imitation similarly shows that 14-month-olds who witness motor sequences can reproduce these same sequences 24 hours later (Meltzoff, 1988). This is called deferred imitation and requires a kind of memory that is a 're-experiencing of past events' and linked to procedural memory and remembering 'how to' do something.

Psychologists still have many questions about exactly why infantile amnesia occurs, and why some memories do or do not make it across this 'divide'. Bauer (2006), one of the leading researchers, has argued that due to neurological immaturity our early memories are less likely to be consolidated, and that consequently there are more storage failures. She states that prior to about the age of 4 memories are lost faster than they are gained, but with developments in the frontal cortex after 4 years of age memories are formed faster than they are forgotten.

We can, however, underestimate the young child's capacity to remember events that are not encoded in language. They can often remember a lot from their previous few years, without having conscious verbal recall, but can express their memories nonverbally. Emotionally charged events are more likely to be remembered than others. Children who have a stressful medical procedure (e.g., having an injection) remember this better than those who have a less stressful one (von Baeyer, Marche, Rocha, & Salmon, 2004). Gaensbauer (2002) described children as young as 7 months seemingly retaining memories of traumatic events several years later. He described an infant who had a car accident at 9 months that had not been talked about, and yet he later re-enacted the accident scene with toy cars at nearly 2 years of age. Gaensbauer and others have reported accounts in which abuse experienced preverbally, including sexual abuse, was later represented in children's drawings or play with seemingly surprising accuracy, such as a child depicting an abusive act to a very specific part of her body that was then corroborated by video evidence found later. These are anecdotal stories and might not count as research evidence, but the combination of such reports and the research suggests the ability to retain memories of events from the first few years, at least nonverbally.

In these examples the memories were recalled through a medium other than language. Language was not available at the time of encoding the memory, and the memories had not been translated into a verbal format. There is higher likelihood of later recall of early trauma when the child is able to verbally narrate some of what happened at the time of the trauma (McNally, 2003). It is possible but not easy to 'infuse' a preverbal memory with language to transform a nonverbal memory into a verbal one and Bauer (2006, p. 321) has shown that when this occurs, perhaps when a parent talks about an event with a child, then that memory is more likely to survive and cross the barrier of infantile amnesia. Preverbal experiences are not recalled via linguistic cues, which makes evoking them more difficult, and this is why research about children's early memory can be flawed if researchers only provide verbal cues.

Our ability to remember is influenced by other factors such as how safe people feel. If one is too stressed one's capacity for recall is reduced, although one also needs a degree of stress to remember something. In one test distressed and crying babies did not remember a mobile they were presented with 3 weeks later, whereas the nondistressed ones did (Fagan & Singer, 1983). Similarly the hypervigilant child in school who is overalert to danger will have less ability to concentrate and take in information.

Stress also impacts on how the brain develops, and the hippocampus, a region especially involved with memory formation and retention, is smaller in traumatised war veterans as well as sufferers from major depression (Sapolsky, 1998). Neglect as well as trauma can affect developing memories. The memories of young children adopted from Romanian orphanages into more 'enriched' families were much worse when asked to undertake tasks such as deferred imitation (Bauer, Kroupina, Schwade, Dropik, & Wewerka, 1998).

Unlike chronic ongoing stress, however, a small amount of stress aids memory. If we walk down a street and nothing remarkable happens we are less likely to remember the walk than if a car drives fast and noisily the wrong way down the street. People remember unusual and emotionally charged moments, sometimes called **flashbulb memories**, such as what they were doing when President Kennedy or John Lennon died. This has been called a stress signature, after the biological process whereby a mark of a previous event leaves tell-tale signs on an organism. Too little stress is not likely to lead to memories being encoded, but too much stress can inhibit memory.

Autobiographical memory

When a child can put events into language then memories take on a new form. Before the age of about 2, as we have noted, the main areas of the brain involved in encoding explicit memory are not fully 'online', and most learning is of a procedural kind. In the next few years the explicit memory system gradually consolidates. By 2 years old infants can see that someone has an intention to do something (e.g., to reach up and grab an apple), even if the person does not act on that intention, and children start to develop stories about their own and other's desires and wishes. This is also around the age when infants realise that the mark they see on the face in the mirror is actually a mark on their own face. This is sometimes seen as the beginnings of a sense of self that includes autobiographical memory.

A fuller version of autobiographical memory is not really seen until about 4 or 5, when full-blown theory of mind capacities become evident. At around this age most children start to think of themselves as existing over time, and can relate stories and facts about themselves that suggest a more cohesive idea of self. They develop a sense of themselves as ongoing in their own and other people's eyes. This is when they can really recognise themselves when watching a video, so that if the child in a video (them) has a sticker on their head, and they are asked where the sticker is, it is at this age that they can point to their own head (Suddendorf, Simcock, & Nielsen, 2007). This is seen as a sign of a child's more sophisticated representational capacities, in which they can hold multiple versions of the world in their mind simultaneously. Now events are more likely to be remembered declaratively and encoded in memories that can be recalled.

Having an 'autobiographical self' depends on having organised memories of situations that characterise our life, such as who our parents are, our names, where we were born, what we like or dislike, and our usual reactions to situations. Damasio (1999, p. 172) characterises such a sense of identity as a kind of feeling, what he calls a 'felt core self', which uses both nonconscious experience and memories that can be recalled to form an ongoing idea of who we are in time, and in relation to others. This is called **episodic** memory.

The 'felt' aspect of such memory is central, as episodic memories are not simply stored but 'lived'. Language and the ability to use narratives to reflect on oneself are important in this and require a self-reflective capacity that is more likely if one has had mind-minded input. Parents of securely attached children tend to have more elaborated and sophisticated narrative styles, and their children develop these too. As Damasio says 'whether we like it or not, the human mind is constantly being split, like a house divided, between the part that stands for the known and the part that stands for the knower' (1999, p. 191). This autobiographical sense we have, this certainty about our own ongoing identity, depends, to use Damasio's metaphor, on a sense of self in which we are the storyteller of our own stories. We might add that we feel we exist insofar as we are in other people's minds, part of other people's stories. The importance of being in another's mind is obvious to those who know the effect on some unfortunate children of having never really been in anyone's minds, nor having a clear story told about themselves, such as many children in the care system.

Autobiographical memory is never an exact filmic reproduction of what happened in the past. Autobiographical, and indeed all memory, is hugely influenced by our current concerns and preoccupations, and by the context in which they arise. When we feel happy we can more easily remember pleasant childhood events. Context is central. Some scuba divers were asked to remember words while underwater. They were later tested both above and below the water and were more able later to recall the words underwater than on dry land (Godden & Baddeley, 1975). The specific autobiographical details we recall are influenced by our current contexts.

Autobiographical memories are expressed verbally, and so are dependent on linguistic and narrative skills, and so some children are advantaged in this area. Children who are quick to develop skills in autobiographical memory are also early to recognise themselves in the mirror, and have mothers who tend to elaborate more in complex narratives and conversations about past events (Welch-Ross, 1997). This tends to occur earlier in Western, more egocentric, cultures. Korean and Chinese children, for example, are far less likely to have as many specific personal memories as American children; they make fewer references to themselves, and describe more generic and less specific events (Han, Leichtman, & Wang, 1998). As we saw in Chapter 7 on culture, some societies have far less emphasis on the self, let alone on the ability to develop stories about oneself. Nonetheless, whatever the cultural influences, children exposed to a more elaborative style in which events are reported and described, will tend to internalise that narrative style and way of remembering and describe personal events within autobiographical memory. In the West at least these are generally the children who become securely attached.

Trauma, memories, and forgetting

One of the big controversies within the world of psychology concerns traumatic memories, how reliable or accurate they are, and whether traumatic memories from the past can be repressed and only remembered later. Memories are not like exact photos or videos of the past stored in a hard drive in one's brain, and they can be notoriously unreliable. The brain only stores traces of information later used to 'make' memories. As Bateman and Fonagy (2004, p. 105) describe 'A complex neural network, involving many different parts of the brain, acts to encode, store and retrieve the information, which can be used to "create memories" '.

In one study over 70 boys were asked questions like 'how often did your father hit you when young?', or 'how concerned were you with particular issues'. Some 30 years later many of these boys were re-interviewed about their memories of what they believed when younger. Their memories, which they would have sworn by, were mostly completely wrong. For example, some remembered themselves as outgoing but in fact at 14 had described themselves as shy, and their ability to guess how they had described themselves 30 years earlier was no more accurate than chance (Offer, Kaiz, Howard, & Bennett, 2000).

Experiments consistently show the unreliability of memories. In a classic experiment people were shown a film of a blue car stopping at a traffic light on a clear day with no traffic (Loftus & Palmer, 1974). Some were asked questions such as whether there were many clouds or if there was another car and what colour it was, and something about their 'memories' changed as a result of the questions. The group that was not asked anything still had the same memory, but the questioned group had different 'memories', such as of other cars or clouds. This process, that psychologists call **priming** is seen more powerfully in a similar example when people watched a film of a car accident. If asked 'how fast was the car going when it *smashed* into the other one', then the 'memories' become entirely different from the responses seen when the word *hit* was substituted for *smashed*. When the subjects heard smashed they assumed the car was going faster, and later they often claimed to have witnessed things not in the film, such as windscreens breaking. Research has shown the ease with which it is possible to foster such false memories. False autobiographical memories can be implanted with the right 'priming' because memories are so vulnerable to suggestion.

This question of the reliability of memory gets more controversial when the memory is of something traumatic like sexual abuse in childhood. Not only are memories vulnerable to suggestion, but also the memories we recall at a particular moment are coloured by the context one is in and the influences on us at the time. Although it is possible for therapists to suggest events to patients, as in so called false-memory syndrome (Loftus, 1997), evidence also suggests that forgetting traumatic events certainly occurs. Brenneis (2000) analysed a number of cases in the therapeutic literature. Some could not be substantiated but for others the evidence compellingly suggested that the stories of remembering abuse were true.

In one example a woman had always remembered being sexually abused as a child but had no memory of any abuse in adulthood. Someone mentioned to her that child victims sometimes also become abused as adults. Driving home afterwards she was reported to have remembered being raped by a stranger at 22 years old, some 13 years before. She investigated this, and later brought charges against the assailant who was convicted after the facts were confirmed in court (Geraerts, Schooler, Merckelbach, Jelicic, Hauer, & Ambadar, 2007). Yet she had not remembered these events for many years. Brenneis reports several similar cases, and also analysed others where the evidence was less certain. In the cases where memories seem to have returned there were similarities. The memories were cued by linked information, and once prompted, memories unwound straight away and did not need any deciphering. They were accompanied by powerful emotional reactions, such as the person recalling the memory starting to shake and in none of these cases were the memories suggested by therapeutic work.

Forgetting traumatic memories is not uncommon. For example, research (Epstein & Bottoms, 2002) on 1400 women found that in interpersonal trauma, particularly sexual abuse, forgetting was seen in as many as 20 per cent of cases. It was less likely in noninterpersonal traumas such as car accidents. However, the mechanism of forgetting was not necessarily that of Freudian repression, and in many cases the forgetting reported was partial, and was explained as an active avoidance, and sometimes as a re-labelling.

Procedural memories are different to memories of trauma as they generally are 'content-less'. The expectation of danger in a child subjected to violence is engrained in brain circuits, and might cause them to flinch at the slightest noise, but is not necessarily accompanied by conscious memories. There is, however, another form of memory that is neither quite a normal declarative memory nor a procedural memory. The flashbacks of post-traumatic stress victims seem to be also embedded somewhere in the amygdala, and have content, but are not explicit memories in the sense we usually mean. One theory is that such traumatic flashback memories are not contextualised in terms of time and place by the hippocampus, so that they lack a 'signature' of context. Sufferers of these intrusive and overwhelming memories seem not to be open to the influence of suggestion in the way that is seen in cases of false-memory. Their memories rarely become part of a narrative with verbal processing. The flashback type of memory is not so amenable to distortion or influence. It certainly feels to the sufferer that they are reliving the original events.

Children who have experienced horrors such as violence or torture often cannot stop images of violence intruding. An example was reported by McNally (2003, p. 105) in which children who had survived the brutal Pol Pot regime were constantly disturbed by images of killing. There is uncertainty about whether the contents of the memories are replicas of what originally happened, but they seem to be reliving something of the emotional experiences of the events, often in a way that includes other senses such as smell and taste. It seems it is the emotional experience of the trauma that is remembered, rather than any photographic re-representation, and the details are not necessarily accurate. In secondary trauma, for example, people whose loved ones had been murdered can experience nightmares and flashbacks of the murder, even though they were not there (McNally, 2003, p. 116).

There remains much controversy about traumatic memory, and whether such memories can be repressed, or be dissociated from. What certainly happens in traumatic experiences is that we narrow our focus, and afterwards cannot remember wider details of an event. For example, some people were shown some neutral pictures, while others had a rather shocking image of a murder victim slipped into their sequence of pictures (Kramer, Buckhout, & Eugenio, 1990). Those who saw the gruesome picture were not so able to remember the pictures that came afterwards. When we witness something terrifying such as violence we focus on the most salient details (who had the knife and how near it was) and are less aware of peripheral details (whether it was raining outside). This can make witnesses in court seem unreliable, as they are less likely to have as much detailed information in their minds. Show people a violent or nonviolent version of the same event, and then ask questions about the details, and the group who see the nonviolent version have a much more accurate recall of the peripheral details (Loftus & Burns, 1982).

After trauma there is impairment in the ability to recall autobiographical details. This has been shown, for example, with some Vietnam veterans who had what is called an 'overgeneral' personal memory, and struggled to remember specific events in the way we usually can (McNally, Brett, Litz, Prassas, Shin, & Weathers, 1994). In response to cue-words, like 'kindness' or 'panic', they could not find memories or narratives that fitted the words. Children who are traumatised also find it harder to put feelings into words or to organise their memories. It is possible the lack of the kind of parenting that gives rise to narrative capacities in children intersects with the impact of trauma, leading to even less likelihood of forming and processing memories. The narratives of trauma victims can often be filled with thoughts that seem unfinished, and language that is vague, unclear, and repetitive, and that have more narrative fragmentation (Foa, Molnar, & Cashman, 1995).

The nature of what and how we remember is extremely bound up with our capacities for reflecting on our own and others' states of minds, for mentalisation and narrative coherence. A goal of much therapeutic work with trauma is to ensure that traumatic memories are not re-evoked too powerfully, so that as well as building up areas of thought and memory which concern more well-functioning parts of the personality, we might also integrate traumatic experiences so that they can be reflected upon, modulated, and processed. This is something seen in some parents who were traumatised in childhood and yet who still score 'secure-autonomous' on the Adult Attachment Interview (AAI). It is not seen so much in the AAIs of more 'unresolved' adults who were traumatised. A telling difference between these two types of adults traumatised in childhood is that one type (the secure-autonomous) has developed self-reflective capacities, and an ability to integrate experiences in the form of a coherent narrative within autobiographical memory.

Summary

Memory concerns the relationship between past, present, and future. As Susan Hart (2008) points out we use our memories to make sense of new experiences. The meaning we give to a present experience is partly determined by our past experiences and these in turn also have an effect on which of our present experiences we select and store in our memories. The human brain is especially efficient at predicting the future on the basis of what has happened in the past. Experiences are engrained in implicit memories, becoming patterns of relating that we take into new relationships. This is happening before children gain the ability to encode, maintain, and retrieve explicit memories. We can learn new ways of relating but we do not necessarily unlearn what we already know. Confounding our expectations and learning new possibilities about ourselves is possible, but can be an emotionally challenging undertaking, one seen for example when an abused adopted child tries to learn new ways with a new parent or therapist.

Memory is notoriously unreliable, greatly influenced by our current experiences and preoccupations and some supposed memories are simply the result of suggestion. Other traumatic memories can be intrusive, frightening, and overwhelming, and are not linked to narratives or reflective functioning. We remember more in certain moods, such as when mildly stressed, as in flashbulb memories, but not when there is little stress or too much stress. For some anxious children who have suffered trauma, their states of mind mean that forming new explicit memories may not come easily. Similarly, if we have been thought about, and our lives spoken about a lot by carers with sophisticated narrative capacities, then we will probably develop complex autobiographical memories in which indepth stories about ourselves are in place. Such children feel 'held in mind' by others, and are similarly likely to hold themselves and others in mind. Others are less lucky, such as children who have not had adults around them who tell stories about their history, including many children in the care system. Our memories have conscious and nonconscious aspects, and the kind of memories and expectations we develop depends a lot on the kind of mind-minded input we have received. Procedural memories, when laid down, are hard to shift, but nonetheless we need not always be a slave to them. New learning can take place, particularly with the development of a more self-reflective capacity, in which develops what Siegel (2007, p. 309) called a 'witnessing self', something that is more likely to develop if our own emotional and psychological selves have in turn been witnessed by another reflective mind.

Chapter 11

Play: fun, symbolising, practising, and mucking about

Play is an important childhood activity, one that is necessary for many other capacities to take root, and yet one that can only develop if certain other developments have already occurred. Children who are lost in play often evoke a sense of awe in adults. Play is generally seen as having intrinsic value; we do not do it to achieve anything else, although there are often rewarding byproducts. We can get lost in play, be taken over by it, and it is no coincidence that the psychoanalyst Winnicott (1971) contrasted play with reality, and argued that the capacity to play, to symbolise, and creativity in general are fundamentally linked. As Fonagy and Target show (1996), even very young children can distinguish the worlds they create in play from reality. Harsh realities can sometimes come crashing in to destroy fragile moments of play. Think of the little girl who puts on her mother's shoes and hat and is pretending to be a teacher until her father comes in and harshly asks what she thinks she is doing.

What makes something play rather than not play, or even work? There is no single overarching definition of play. It comes in all manner of shapes and sizes. It can be solitary or social, imaginary, or rough and tumble, more or less rule bound, verbal or nonverbal, object based, pretend, and more. Play is often characterised by its flexibility, such as putting things in new combinations, changing roles, or making objects represent other things. Play also is generally characterised by positive affect, as seen in Tom Sawyer's classic ruse when ordered to whitewash a fence by his aunt Polly (Twain, 1986). Begrudging the duty, he managed to trick his friends into believing he was going to paint the fence for fun, whereupon they all fought to do the task that a moment before had been drudgery and work, but suddenly became play. Mark Twain writes 'work is whatever a body is obliged to do, and play consists of whatever a body is not obliged to do' (p. 14). Various experiments back this up, such as one in which participants were paid to problem solve a task, while others were not paid for the same task, and the remunerated ones gave up earlier than the others (Deci & Ryan, 2000). Similarly, a group of nursery children were given felt tip pens. Some were rewarded for using them with stars and ribbons whereas others were given no reward. Yet next time felt tips were left casually around the classroom it was the unrewarded children who wanted to play with them (Lepper, Greene, & Nisbett, 1973). Just wanting to do something is itself motivating.

Play produces benefits in its own right for the player, spurring other developments, yet it is generally undertaken simply for its intrinsic rewards. Panksepp and colleagues have shown how in rats with a neurological propensity for hyperactivity, enhanced opportunity for play decreases hyperactive behaviours and lead to more self-regulation (Panksepp, Burgdorf, Turner, & Gordon, 2003). They argue that the same applies to children, and interestingly much therapeutic work with children is undertaken through the medium of play.

Yet not all children or animals are able to play. Children are less playful when under strain, when less confident, or when anxious. In research by Harlow, Dodsworth, & Harlow (1965) on monkeys reared in isolation they were found to be unable to play, either when alone or with other monkeys, whereas those reared by mothers in group settings were delightfully playful with each other. Children reared in orphanages without emotional nurturing or stimulation have similarly been found to be less playful. A study from Harvard showed that men whose mothers had been affectionless and cold were less likely to play games with friends, play sports, or even take holidays, later in their lives aged 45 to 65 years old (Vaillant, 2002). The predictive factor was how loved they felt as children. Feeling secure and at ease allows the possibility of play, and play in itself can facilitate development.

Play in infancy

One of the quotes about play that I like best is that play is 'training for the unexpected' (Spinka, Newberry, & Bekoff, 2001, p. 141). Play almost by definition cannot be rigid and planned; it is generally spontaneous and has elements of uncertainty and surprise. Classic infant games such as 'peekaboo' are typical of play that has both a structure and an element of surprise. Often both parties know what is coming next but do not know exactly when. In such games skills are being learnt, such as taking turns and understanding and predicting another's thoughts and actions.

Infants are active partners in interactions, through using imitation and proto-conversations for example, and by the third and fourth months of age more sophisticated communications can occur, such as pleasurable responses to nursery rhymes accompanied by rhythmic use of their bodies. These games tend to be marked by clear patterns within which spontaneity occurs. Often a playing pair becomes entrained to each other's rhythms, pitching their gestures in time to the other. This helps to build a sense of agency, social confidence as well as flexibility.

By 5 months infants can engage in humorous exchanges with peers using active imitation of postures, as well as gestures and grimaces. By then games between mothers and babies can last longer, with a structure, sequence, and a crescendo. Songs have a complex pulse, prosody, and melody, and infants enjoy timing their own gestural and vocal responses to salient moments, such as clapping hands at a special instant, leading to mutual enjoyment and what is usually called playfulness. Positive affect is central here, and the lack of musicality in a depressed mother's voice can lead to an infant not joining in, but instead to act in rather a flat way. By 3 months humour and teasing can come to the fore, and shared pleasure is more openly dialogical, as beautifully described by Vasuveddi Reddy (1991), who experimentally illustrated the kind of teasing and mucking about which happens later in the first year. By the end of the first year, as skills such as proto-declarative pointing develop, games can increase in complexity, with more likelihood of two partners playing together with a third object. By then ways of interacting and being together are remembered and repeated, and routines can develop.

Such play depends on experiences of subtle mutual attunement and understanding, and requires a complex combination of flexibility and predictability in an atmosphere of mutually positive affect. Exuberance, enjoyment, and pleasure are emotional states that perhaps are not given enough credence in developmental accounts. Infants between 7 and 12 months have been studied in playful episodes, in both dyadic and triadic interactions, and here pleasure and joy increase and neutral and negative emotions all but disappear (Kugiumutzakis, Kokkinaki, Makrodimitraki, & Vitalaki, 2004). From the end of the first year there are exciting developmental leaps, especially with increased mobility, dexterity, and speech, and one sees the beginnings of role play, fantasy, and imaginary games. As Daniel Stern writes 'playing can only occur in a setting where there is a feeling of ease, of security, of not having to be vigilant, being free of pressing other needs' (Stern, 2001, p. 145). He was commenting on experiments undertaken by infancy researchers Beebe and Jaffe, who studied in fine-grained detail interactions between mothers and their 4-month-old infants. At this age they can barely grasp or move, but are particularly adapted to face-to-face learning, and their interactions are less 'playful' when they are not at ease, such as when a stranger is present. Play is richer and fuller when a child feels safe and positive.

Play in other species

Playing has a biological and neurological base and Panksepp (2007) argues that there is a discrete play system, just as there are systems for fear, sex, aggression, or attachment. Human children across all cultures play, so one might assume that playing has been positively selected for evolutionary reasons. Play seems biologically linked with a period of high arousal and almost boundless energy seen in many mammals in mid-infancy. Play can stimulate aspects of brain organisation, developing what Schore (1994) describes as an exploratory-assertive motivational system. Playing can 'solidify social habits' as well as developing physical and cognitive capacities, the social circuits of the brain and executive functioning (Panksepp et al., 2003).

Play of various kinds is seen in many animals. Think of kittens and their skittish moves, puppies chasing balls or tiger cubs play-fighting. Such play has similar characteristics to human play. Dogs will signal they are playing by lowering themselves onto their forelegs, and chimps have their own 'play face' that signals to other chimps that an action is play and not serious (Bekoff & DiMotta, 2008). Play in young animals tends to be hugely energetic, without obvious 'point', and there is some uncertainty about why animals, including humans, play. A common theory is that play enhances skills and abilities needed for roles taken on later. The speedy dashes of the young deer might be play now, but later on running fast from predators might be lifesaving. Experiments with rats suggest that animals deprived of opportunities to play are disadvantaged. Rats reared in isolation without opportunities to play-fight were more immobile and harshly attacked when introduced to strangers.

Animals do many things strikingly like pretend play in humans. An orangutan, who could sign, was seen to pretend an invisible cat was present by signing 'cat', and acting fearful, while a dolphin was reported to observe a human smoking through an underwater window, and then obtained a mouthful of milk from her mother and squirted the milk underwater in simulation of smoke (Mitchell, 2001). More common in animals is mock-fighting and energetic rough and tumble. Play is seen in species that live in complex social groups, such as chimps and dolphins, who have imitative skills and a degree of social sophistication. Here the young often play using exaggerated social gestures, trying out behaviours, sounds, movements, and ways of being that will be performed seriously later, such as in fighting or hunting.

Rough and tumble

Anthony Pellegrini (2007) defines rough and tumble play as characterised by positive affect, a 'play face', high energy, exaggerated movements, and soft, open handed hits or kicks'. Such physical play arises in infancy in most mammals, and begins to tail off with sexual maturation. It can aid muscular skills, build strength, stamina and stimulate brain development.

Rough and tumble is a very specific form of play, which superficially looks like fighting but is different in definite ways. Generally there are not real threats at the start of it, and afterwards the partners renew friendly relations. In childhood it generally facilitates closeness, and Pellegrini's research confirms that affiliative bonds increase following rough and tumble. Aggression and rough and tumble are not particularly related in primary school boys but in adolescence, Pellegrini argues, rough and tumble tends to be much more to do with dominance and gaining status in a pecking order. Pellegrini even found that partner choice is linked to dominance status in adolescence and that there are direct correlations between boys' fighting ability at 12 years old and their later status, which in turn relates to successes such as dating popularity.

The gender differences noted in the West are true across most cultures studied, with boys indulging in much more physical play, and the same is seen in monkeys and great apes. Indeed exposure of foetuses, male or female, to **androgens** such as **testosterone** predisposes children to indulge in more rough and tumble play later on (Hines & Collaer, 1993). Versions of such rough and tumble are seen not only in most cultures studied, but indeed in many mammalian species.

Different kinds of play, different kinds of learning

Children play differently in different societies. In most pre-industrial societies children spent much of their lives in cross-age groups, learning from the older ones. In most cultures play involves pretending and imagination. Children often work out the scripts of everyday life by role playing adults, whether Mayan boys in a Mexican town play being bar owners at a fiesta, European children pretending to be teacher and pupil, or !Kung children of the Kalahari playing at pounding, digging, and cooking.

Adult beliefs about the role of symbolic play similarly differs across cultures. Americans tend to see play as a way to aid learning whereas Korean mothers are more likely to see play as amusement. Japanese infants are likely to be encouraged in play that has a sociocentric emphasis, with more 'other directed' attention, such as 'feed the dolly', whereas US mothers might be more likely to stress play that promotes individual autonomy or assertiveness ('yes, you can do that if you try'). In Taiwanese middle-class families influenced by Confucian values the roles children were expected to take in play involved 'proper conduct' and addressing elders appropriately (Göncü & Gaskins, 2007). In a study of a poor rural Turkish community, where children had to contribute to the workforce at an early age, play was less highly valued, and adults did not join in, but rather left children to get on with it (Göncü & Gaskins, 2007). The same is true of many other cultures, such as Yucatan Maya children, where play is actively curtailed to encourage more 'productive' activity. Many cultures do not value symbolic play highly.

Many of these examples describe reality-based pretend play, particularly trying out real-life roles and scripts. There can also be more abstract fantasy play, seen more often in Western cultures that encourage abstract learning in which ideas are used in a decontextualised way, allowing more 'playing around' with concepts that are less bound by actual roles and realities than in some other societies (Harris, 2007). Maths questions such as 'take three pink horses and add four red cows' would be met with incomprehension in cultures where such abstract thinking was not part of their cultural repertoire.

Many theorists of play have struggled with the paradox that play is indulged in for its own sake, but must have some purpose, otherwise why would most children and animals indulge in it. One theory that goes back several hundred years is that in play one is practising skills and abilities needed in adult life. Smith (2004), for example, argues that playing at fighting, cooking, or hunting teaches essential skills but is less dangerous than actually doing them. The pretend pounding of grain develops all the necessary skills to actually do it. In the societies studied, play pounding peaked at about 6 years old, and tailed off around 8 or 9, when the children were expected to contribute more by actually pounding real grain (Bock, 2002). Although we cannot know for sure exactly what functions play serves, we know that children and mammals who are deprived of it are at a disadvantage.

Yet over and above developing practical skills needed later in life, whether pounding yam or using computers, such play can help develop a wide range of other capacities. Much Western educational thinking has seen debates about the relative merits of 'free' play, in which children follow their own interests, as opposed to structured activity in schools and nurseries. Much of the thinking behind spontaneous, free play is the recognition that children learn better when they are self-motivated. For example in an experiment reported by a pupil of Vygotsky, children who were told to stand still managed only about 2 minutes, but when asked to play at being soldiers on guard they lasted nearer 12 minutes (Bronson & Merryman, 2009).

There can though be a slightly false dichotomy between free play and structured teaching, as educational researchers such as Kathy Sylva have long found (Sylva, 1984). She discovered that children learn more, and indeed do better educationally, not when tasks are too structured, nor when play is totally free, but rather when play is organised via scaffolding (Bruner, 1966) to help children move to the next level of challenge. Such ideas have been used to good effect in recent programmes in America such as the tools of the mind approach (Barnett et al., 2008). This harnesses many of Vygotsky's ideas (1962) such as **zones of proximal development**, whereby children are facilitated to build on and use current knowledge and skills to reach a next level, using a child's intrinsic motivation to learn, generally via play. For example, in playing hospitals, teachers facilitate children's range of roles that they take on (e.g., doctor, nurse, porter), encourage children to plan the tasks, and help them use a variety of props (e.g., any doll can be a doctor). Such play-based learning can keep children busily active for long periods, building a range of capacities, not least the ability to plan, concentrate, self-regulate, as well as engage in complex interpersonal interactions. Such research links to the thinking of Panksepp (2007) and others on how play, and indeed play therapy as well, may increase the capacity for self-regulation and executive functioning. The children in programmes such as tools of the mind also gain considerable educational as well as emotional advantages as they progress in school.

Play as a window into the psyche

The way children play reveals a lot about their preoccupations and state of mind. Much research has linked the meaning of children's play to what is happening in their minds and everyday lives. Child psychotherapists since Melanie Klein, Margaret Lowenfeld and Anna Freud have used children's play therapeutically, seeing play as the childhood equivalent to the adult's free associations. Freud was possibly the first to analyse the meaning of a child's play, in his case of his grandson, who he witnessed playing with a cotton reel in his cot, throwing away the cotton, and reeling it back with a pleased 'da' (there). Freud (1920/1973) understood this to be the boy's way of managing his mother's absences, inventing a scenario of disappearance and return that *he* was in charge of, despite not being in charge of his mother's actual absences and returns.

Children use play to express their preoccupations symbolically. A child's play provides a vital window onto their psychological state. Commonly, children who have had a tough day at school might return home and act being the strict teacher with a younger sibling. We would worry about a child whose play is constantly full of themes of death and destruction, or whose play manifested constant violence, or inappropriate sexualised contact between children and adults.

There are now standardised ways of understanding children's play that back up therapists' clinical theories. Perhaps best known is the story stem technique, taken forward in Britain by attachment researchers such as Hodges, Steele, Hillman, Henderson, & Kaniuk (2003) of the Anna Freud Centre in London. Here scenarios from everyday life are presented to children, using dolls and props. Children are shown the start of a story (hence called a story stem) and are then asked to finish these stories using the toys and their imaginations. A condensed example of one such stem is that a child is at school and has made a picture that their teacher praises and they then take home. The interviewer uses dolls to enact the child coming home and asks the child to 'show me what happens next'. Depending on their background and history, the children respond in a surprisingly rich variety of directions in their stories. Some describe children who come home and show their parents the picture and it is praised and everyone is delighted. However, in other children's stories the parents ignore the picture, violence might ensue, the picture can be forgotten or end up in the bin. The way the story is told, its content and how the various characters are portrayed, as well as the narrative structure, are all analysed, rated and coded. This has provided clear empirical evidence for the meaningfulness of children's fantasy play and its related-ness to their life situations and experience. This is something that child psychotherapists have long known. In particular, a child's expectations of how adults might treat them are often graphically illustrated in play. Children who have been abused or traumatised and are about to be adopted often narrate stories full of violence and neglect. Interestingly, within 3 months of being adopted many children have begun to develop more hopeful versions of the adult world, with some caring and concerned characters creeping into their narratives. Old versions do not disappear altogether but new ones develop alongside them.

Children will naturally enact their worries and preoccupations, as well as their hopes and wishes, through play. After 9/11 many American children were reported to enact scenes of trauma and disaster. Clark (2003) found that asthmatic children often played doctors and nurses, and much amusement was had when in a game a big bad wolf is to blow a house down but does not have enough 'puff'. Of course, some children can get stuck in play, often after trauma, and in these cases we might well not be witnessing symbolic play so much as a traumatic re-enactment akin to the flash-backs common in trauma sufferers (Osofsky, 2007). It takes care and experience to decipher the difference.

Children play for a variety of reasons. A child who has been bullied might come home feeling horrible and play a game of bullying their younger sibling, thereby projecting (Klein, 1975) an unwanted feeling into another. When people have had a blow to their self-esteem they tend, experiments have found, to be nastier to others, more prejudiced and take more pleasure in demeaning others, in an attempt it seems to bolster their own self-worth (Fein & Spencer, 1997). One severely disabled child in a therapy session tied up her therapist's legs with sellotape, unwittingly giving the therapist some idea of what it feels like not being able to move one's limbs. Sometimes this is less symbolic and more 'getting rid of' feelings into another, and play can teeter between being symbolic and re-enacting scenes in which experiences are 'discharged', so communicating something like 'see how you like it and learn how bad it feels'. Experiences can thus be 'got rid of', but also shared, and relief gained by someone else knowing what an experience is like.

Of course, positive experiences are similarly passed on, and a much loved child is likely to care fondly for her doll or younger sister. In more hopeful situations the roles a child takes on are not so stuck, and infinite permutations and reversals are possible. Such children are prepared to take on the role of a helpless baby as well as a devoted parent, while other less fortunate children are not so flexible. What has been learnt from the research, as well as parents and generations of therapists, is that in symbolic and fantasy play important experiences, feelings, worries, and hopes can be expressed, enacted, and processed. Some believe that the experience of play alone is therapeutic when done in the presence of a sympathetic adult.

Play, pretending, symbolism, and growing minds

Those of us who have experienced a sense of hushed awe on hearing little children enact a complex fantasy story behind closed doors can be aware of witnessing some-thing magical and rather delicate, a rich bubble of a world that might suddenly burst with the self-conscious knowledge that a less than sympathetic person is listening. The 3-year-old whose mother is away and enacts a complex game about journeys and reunions is able to objectify their personal and interpersonal experience, express it in a form that is both make-believe and true, and thus playing around with such experi-ences and processing them. Part of the richness of play is that it can accommodate ambiguous meanings, unresolved questions, and is rich with multiple interpretations. The player can 'try on' ways of being, identifying with one party then another, being both the doctor and the patient, giving an injection that might be done kindly, sadistically, or with a mixture of both, thus developing skills in empathising or mentalising.

The possibilities in such play are almost infinite. Such pretend play is unique to humans, even if the rare great ape has occasionally demonstrated behaviour somewhat akin to pretend play. Apes have been described playing games in which they are definitely attempting to trick other apes into thinking something, such as that the ball they are playing with has disappeared (Mitchell, 2001). This though is different from a sustained narrative with characters. To pretend one needs not only a pretender and a reality, but also a mental representation that is projected onto this reality, and this excludes just about all nonhuman behaviour. This implies an ability to distinguish between a pretend reality and actual reality, to function in a meta-representational way, and to be able to symbolise. Acting in such an 'as-if' and genuinely imaginative way is more sophisticated than the trickery of deception that some animals manage.

I have described how play can be imitative of adult activities, being not only practice but also a way of learning to understand from the inside how adults think, act, feel, and understand the world. For example, children when playing at hunting, fighting, or preparing feasts are not simply indulging in blind mimicry or trying to really be, say, a warrior. True, children at times get so into role that they do believe they have actually become what they are playing. But if a toddler pretends that a rag is a baby and then pretends to cuddle it, they and others present know that one cannot really comfort rags, and the pretend aspect of the behaviour is somehow signalled. A child similarly knows that the parent is not just stupidly confusing a rag with a baby. Toddlers of 18 months of age when they observe pretend play respond with pretend play, but when they observe a mistake, they tend to correct it. If a child watches an adult genuinely trying to write with a pen lid still on, or pretending for fun to write with the same pen lid on, they know the difference (Rakoczy, Tomasello, & Striano, 2004). Pretence involves a different way of being. One smiles more in pretence, and the smiles are longer, more than the 4 seconds that seems to mean that the smile is a signal not just an expression of pleasure. When mothers pretend to eat they look much more at their play partner than when they really are snacking, and they also talk far more in pretend play, with more repetitive speech, and more variation in pitch. Pretending adults also tend to move more quickly, perhaps not surprisingly as in pretend play it is possible to have a major battle, sleep, become a parent and age several years, all in a matter of minutes.

For a child to be able to play symbolically he or she needs to have reached certain developmental milestones. To move from being the teacher to the taught, the doctor to the patient, the attacker to defender, requires an ability to place oneself imaginatively in another role, and hence have the capacity to 'feel' one's way into another's state of mind. In play one can enter a liminal world, where reality is suspended, where one is on the threshold of a range of potential experience. This is a skill that can be taken for granted until one comes across children lacking or limited in this capacity.

Participating in symbolic play with a sophisticated play partner, such as a parent or older sibling, enhances the ability to symbolise. Cross-culturally, mothers who value symbolic play have children who play more symbolically. One way this happens is via 'scaffolding', whereby a slightly more sophisticated play partner raises the level of the less sophisticated partner. Returning to a theme described often in this book, the ability to play is linked to social and interpersonal skills. Attunement and accurate emotional signalling during the first year of life predicts symbolic play abilities in later years (Feldman, 2003), once again demonstrating the social and intersubjective foundations of play as well as so many important human abilities.

The ability to decontextualise is central to pretend play, especially with objects that stand for something else. Object-supported imaginary play, such as pretending to drink with a cup, can start at about 9 months, and develops more in the next year and a half, but is more likely to be used in earnest after 3 years of age. Children tend not to use substitute objects for imaginary ones when actual ones are present until that age. By 4 years old children know that if they are to pretend to be something, say a tiger, they must convey an intention to simulate or pretend, which again suggests that the capacity to pretend depends on theory of mind abilities. Also central is the ability to set aside one's identity and take on another role; which again requires some ability to understand mental states in oneself and others, to appreciate different perspectives and have some fellow feeling.

Role shifting takes place in complex ways from 2 years onwards. Nadel and Muir (2005) worked with 13 2-year-old triads and found that there was symmetry in terms of how much time each toddler spent either imitating or being imitated, showing temporal coordination and synchrony and a natural readiness to move in and out of roles. Not surprisingly children on the autistic spectrum find it considerably more difficult to imitate and switch roles, and lack the skills necessary to invite the other to imitate them. Even when actively taught to imitate they did not switch roles and alternate between being the imitator or imitated. To manage pretend play one needs to have acquired some theory of mind abilities, but such play also enhances these skills.

Children who play symbolically can stand outside reality, providing a 'meta' perspective, something also seen in what the attachment theorists have called reflective-self functioning. The securely attached adult or child, as we have seen, has a coherent narrative about their experiences and feelings, and is able to tell a consistent story about themselves using such meta-cognitive capacities. There is a link between storytelling and pretend play. Nicolopoulou (1997) has helpfully shown that there are two separate lines of development that come together as children get older. In one line the early phases of pretend play emphasise increasing attention to understanding character representation, moving towards more understanding of what someone is like, starting to understand different perspectives on people. The second line is more about early storytelling and is less about character but more about plot, and developing themes of how one event follows after another (e.g., 'she did that and then he went bang and then they cried'). These different skills generally come together in the early school years, to generate an ability to play out pretend fantasy play which has both plot sequence and character, using the parallel and complementary skills of play and storytelling.

Summary

Play, particularly symbolic play, is for many people one of the most treasured human gifts, which marks out humans as distinctively human. I have described how play is undertaken seemingly for its own sake but also how it leads to many other benefits. It is generally accompanied by positive affect and is something one gets immersed in. Play is also indulged in by animals, particularly play-fighting and rough and tumble. Much of such play appears to also be building skills for later life and it is clear that animals deprived of play show severe developmental deficits. Play is differently valued in different cultures. In the West complex symbolic play is often associated with children who are able to understand other minds, process experience via imaginary play, and understanding such play provides a window into the preoccupations and psychic life of children. Through such play a child's preoccupations and deepest feelings can be expressed and understood.

The psychoanalyst Winnicott argued that what he called the 'transitional space' of imaginary play is the basis for all cultural activity, and he stated that 'Cultural experience begins with creative living first manifested as play' (1971, p. 100). A symbol is partly an arbitrary or conventional sign, one thing representing another, but it is potentially much more than that. Using symbols, for example in pretend play, means 'bracketing' here-and-now experience in order to participate in another reality. A symbol represents or evokes another world, and is separate from that which it symbolises. The use of symbolism, which seems to occur in all cultures, is a skill and an achievement. Some children's developmental trajectories are such that symbolic and imaginary play is beyond them, as seen particularly in many children with autistic-spectrum disorders as well as some neglected or maltreated children (Cicchetti & Lynch, 1995). Yet play also ultimately is not play if it is not fun, so despite the differences across cultures, what seems to be universal is not only that children indulge in play, including pretend play, but that it is mainly undertaken with feelings of pleasure and wonder. Maybe playing touches us so deeply because it is something that many in busy post-industrial society have so little time for; that ability to be in the moment and engrossed in an activity and in one's own being.

Boys, girls, and gender

This chapter examines gender differences and the extent to which they are the result of society or biology, nurture or nature. Some argue that different physiologies, brain structures, and hormonal systems lead to different behaviours in males and females. In contrast others deconstruct gender stereotypes and believe that gender difference derives from cultural influences, such as parenting styles, role models, and the way society and its meaning systems are organised. Judith Butler (1997, p. 49) developed the idea of gender as performativity, whereby people are said to 'do' gender. She wrote: 'The doctor who receives the child and pronounces – "It's a girl" – begins that long string of interpellations by which the girl is transitively girled'. How different that sentiment is from statements like this from the book *Brain Sex* (Moir & Jessel, 1992, p. 38): 'If brain structure and hormones are different in men and women, it should not surprise us that men and women behave in different ways.' This can be a dangerous fray to enter, with powerful pressures to espouse particular views.

In recent decades people began to talk of the gender rather than the sex of a child, to challenge the idea of gender as biologically given, and suggest a cultural influence on these matters. Research about gender reveals a mixture of clear facts and more fuzzy ideas. We know that most violent criminals, physics professors, and political leaders are men and that most childrearing is done by women, but these facts ask as many questions as they answer. A complication is that if we look for similarities between genders then we find them, but we can also seek out and find differences, and these are more likely to make published headlines.

There is also a danger of generalising with insufficient evidence. For example, on average males have slightly superior spatial ability, but one can too quickly link this to stereotypes about men reading maps better, attributed to spear-throwing hunter–gatherer pasts. In fact, there is on average a gender difference, but it is mainly in a small subcategory of spatial abilities, the ability to do mental rotations, and so is possibly less important than is sometimes trumpeted (Linn & Petersen, 1986).

Stephen Pinker suggests that we think of differences in terms of a bell-shaped curve (Pinker, 2002). While in the middle there are fewer differences between the genders, these are larger at the extremes. Boys suffer more from dyslexia, learning difficulties, and ADHD than girls, but also most of the highest scorers for maths are boys. Males make up the majority of university professors but also of pupils who fail in school, and of the prison population, so from one perspective males are both the higher- and lower-achieving gender.

Yet culture also has a strong sway, and this chapter will try to tease out these respective influences. It is also possible to be, or be seen to be, either more or less masculine or feminine, irrespective of biological gender, and many males are considered feminine and women masculine. Baron-Cohen (2003) for example argued that irrespective of biological gender, one can have a more male or female brain.

Biological differences and rare conditions

There clearly are some biological differences that, on average, differentiate males and females. Women produce ova and men produce sperm. Men cannot do many things a woman can, like give birth, breastfeed, or menstruate. The male body produces more androgens, such as testosterone, while female bodies produce more oestrogens. Men are more hairy on average, taller on average, and the genders have different body shapes, with women generally having bigger hips and men wider shoulders. Males generally have bigger brains, whereas female generally have more complex neuronal connections in their brains. Generally males have a more lateralised brain, in which language takes place more in the left hemisphere, and visiospatial tasks in the right, whereas more females use both hemispheres in language. A stroke in the left hemisphere usually has a more profound effect on men's language than women's, but women's language is affected worse by strokes affecting their right hemispheres, which men use less for language (Kansaku & Kitazawa, 2001).

Biologically at conception genetic information from the mother and father combine. One of our 23 pairs of chromosomes, which are packages of genetic material, are the sex chromosomes. If the pair consists of two X chromosomes then we become female, and if we have both an X and a Y chromosome we become male, although there are rare variants leading to less clear-cut differentiations. Mothers pass their X chromosomes to all their offspring whereas fathers pass their Y to their sons and their X to their daughters. Interestingly both genders start their *in-utero* existence with the same sexual organs but at about 6 weeks male gonads differentiate into testes. These produce androgens (male hormones) such as testosterone, which are released into the bloodstream, a chemical cocktail that hugely affects gender development. When sufficient testosterone is released then a penis and scrotum form, recognisably so by the third month. In the absence of such testosterone release then these very same structures become the clitoris and labia. Such facts have led some to argue that femininity is the 'default' human position and masculinity needs to be 'formed'. The hormonal bath also impacts directly on the brain and nervous system, which then develop in line with biological gender. At puberty further penile growth occurs, stimulated by testosterone and its related hormone, dihydrotestosterone, while girls' breasts are stimulated to grow by oestrogen.

If the levels of hormones released are different from usual, then less typical results ensue, challenging our preconceptions about what we mean by gender. Boys without working androgen receptors, whose testosterone cannot get to work in the usual way, can look female, have small penises, and perform much like females on visual-spatial, verbal, and other personality tests (Hines, Ahmed, & Hughes, 2003). Reductase-deficient males, whose hormones act unusually, develop female genitalia. Their brains have been masculinised but they are generally reared as girls, although many with this condition opt to change from female to male after puberty (Lippa, 2005, p. 125). In a study of over 25 boys born without a penis and 're-assigned' as girls, all showed typical male attitudes such as rough and tumble play, and half later independently declared themselves to be boys (Reiner & Gearhart, 2004). Male hormones had a more powerful effect than simply not having a penis.

Girls with one genetic disorder (congenital adrenal hyperplasia or CAH) have androgen levels similar to boys and ambiguous genitalia, sometimes a clitoris so enlarged that they are misidentified as male at birth. This leads to a propensity for increased aggressive tendencies, disliking stereotypical female play, and also for some a greater likelihood of being either lesbian or bisexual (Dittmann, Kappes, & Kappes, 1992). Androgen-exposed female rats and monkeys also indulge in rough and tumble play and sexual mounting while males whose androgen release is artificially stopped display female sexual behaviours.

Other rare genetic disorders challenge our ability to conceptualise male and female as obviously distinct. For example, infants with another disorder called complete androgen insensitivity syndrome (CAIS), have both an X and Y chromosome but can be identified and reared as girls, and they have internal genetic organs that cannot be said to be either female or male. Turner's syndrome can equally leave someone's gender unclear.

Girls tend to make more eye contact than boys, and there seems to be a biological basis to this (Knickmeyer, Baron-Cohen, Raggatt, & Taylor, 2005). Testosterone levels in foetuses were measured via amniocentesis and irrespective of gender, the higher the testosterone levels the less the eye contact. Indeed in Turner's syndrome, in which the second chromosome can be either an X or a Y, those with two X's (nearest to female) tend to be more sociable than those with an X and a Y. A typical result was found by Simon Baron-Cohen (2003) with 1-day-old babies who were presented with a choice between a mobile and a face. The experimenters were unaware of the gender of the babies, and the mobile was designed with the same colours as the face, even having the face's features inscribed on it in scrambled form. Interestingly the newborn boys looked longer at the mobile than the girls who looked longer at the face. The biological nature of these preferences has been reinforced by experiments with vervet monkeys who were given a range of toys (Alexander & Hines, 2002). The males played for longer with the trucks and the females longer with the dolls, presumably biological factors playing a part here. It is important though to be clear that these are small and average differences, so even if there are biological propensities, many girls, for example, make poor eye contact and play with cars and vice versa for boys.

A weaker sex? Gender and the impact of early experiences

Much research has shown that males gain unfair advantage in many situations. Much inequality remains, such as males being paid more for doing the same jobs. In Western playgrounds boys tend to dominate physical space (Karsten, 2003), and on average are reported to demand more attention in classrooms. Most leadership positions are held by men, males on average earn more, and of course it is only relatively recently that females were even allowed to vote in Europe.

Yet other research shows that in other ways boys are vulnerable (Kraemer, 2000). Most accounts suggest that about 140 males are conceived for every 100 females, and on average for every 105 male babies born there are 100 females, so many more males do not even make it to birth. Higher male mortality rates means that by late adulthood there are equal numbers of men and women and by old age women far outnumber men. Male foetuses are far more likely to succumb to congenital abnormalities, premature and stillbirth and cerebral palsy. Interestingly in times of serious economic and social difficulty even less male foetuses survive (Catalano, Bruckner, Anderson, & Gould, 2005). Boys born prematurely do less well than girls, are more prone to childhood illness, and are more likely to die from these. Girls are born developmentally ahead, some say about 4 to 6 weeks even at birth, and if anything their maturity increases through childhood. Boys are more likely to suffer from disorders such as autism, Tourette syndrome, or reading delay. Throughout the lifespan men are more prone to disease and early death. One explanation is that males must make do with the genetic material on their single X chromosome, whereas for females if a gene on one chromosome is defective, the parallel gene of the other chromosome might become dominant instead (Jones, 2002).

From birth onwards girls respond better to social stimulation, seem better equipped on average to regulate their emotions, and are less badly affected by disruptions in parenting. Mothers tend to work harder to imitate and respond to their sons than their daughters, and researchers have suggested that boys need more input in order to feel emotionally regulated (Trevarthen, Kokkinaki, & Fiamenghi, 1999). Following postnatal depression Lynne Murray and colleagues found that boys fare worse, having less capacity for object constancy at 18 months and showing more behavioural problems at school age (Murray, Kempton, Woolgar, & Hooper, 1993). Lou Sander (2007) looked at newborns separated from their parents and placed with new carers. After a few days the girls had all entrained to their new carers' day–night rhythms but the boys took several days longer to adjust, suggesting they were more vulnerable following disruptions of care. Many accounts suggest that boys on average are more susceptible to poor care, as well as being more irritable and emotionally labile.

Tronick (2007) found that depressed mothers consistently showed angrier emotional expressions to their sons than to their daughters. By 6 months the boys were gesturing more anxiously, and were three times more likely than female babies to resort to self-comforting strategies such as sucking their thumbs. It seems that boys generally are more demanding of their interactive partners. A recent study in France showed that mothers with a propensity for depression were more likely to actually become depressed if they had male babies (de Tychey et al., 2008), who were presumably more demanding than female ones.

One study casts light on how weakness can look like strength in boys. Six-year-old children were exposed to the taped sound of an infant crying. The girls were sympathetic, whereas the boys were more likely to turn away, or try to turn the sound off. Interestingly though, when their heart rate was measured, the boys were more anxious than the girls, their turning away due to being less able to tolerate the distress (Adam, Keller, & West, 1995). This might be a typical example of male fragility masquerading as toughness. A similar relative fragility has been observed in rhesus monkeys, suggesting a biological basis for this in primates. Boys are more active than girls from earliest infancy onwards (Campbell & Eaton, 1999). Higher activity might be biological but might possibly also be linked to having less ability to self-regulate. Increased muscular activity, such as moving about a lot, is something that ill at ease babies often resort to, what some psychoanalytic researchers describe as a **second-skin defence** in which infants hold themselves together by physical movement (Bick, 1968).

Boys seem to be more affected by poor-quality childcare, especially if the poor care is both at home and at nursery (Hungerford, Brownwell, & Campbell, 2000), and they also are more vulnerable to the effects of mothers being away at work, showing more **externalising** behaviours, defiance, and poor self-regulation. They also do worse following marital disharmony and divorce (Wallerstein, Lewis, & Blakeslee, 2000). Of course, as children get older it is harder to know if one gender is worse affected, as they respond differently, with girls tending to internalise; which is less noticeable than the acting out and aggression of boys.

Later on too males react more strongly to stress and trauma. In male adolescents trauma leads to more adverse brain development than in girls. De Bellis (2003) has accumulated so much evidence of this that he even suggests that just being male is a neurobiological risk marker for stress-related vulnerability. Another researcher looked at adults in their 70s and found that almost 40 per cent of the physical and mental illness of the men could be accounted for by early childhood experiences, but barely any at all for the women (Patterson, Smith, Smith, Yager, & Grant, 1992). Males occupy the odd position of seeming to be both stronger and weaker. They have more power, are more violent (including to women), perpetrate more abuse, and dominate in all kind of ways but are also more vulnerable in other ways.

Different cultures, different genders

Biology might be important but it is not the whole story. Looking at other societies can challenge biologically led notions of gender difference. In arguing against the idea that men and women live on the different linguistic planets of Venus and Mars, Deborah Cameron (2007) describes The Gapun women of Papua New Guinea. They have an aggressive form of verbal exchange called *kros* whereby they vent their rage against those who have annoyed them, particularly their husbands. Here the target cannot answer back, and *kros* is a woman's perogative. She describes one irate woman whose husband received a feisty attack, which in typical fashion lasted at least 45 minutes. A flavour of this is seen in the following extract (p. 33):

> You're a f****** rubbish man. You hear? Your f****** prick is full of maggots. Stone balls! F****** black prick! F****** grandfather prick! You have built me a good house that I just fall down in! You f****** mother's ****!

In this culture women's language is assertive, direct, and aggressive, while men pride themselves on indirect and careful speech, confounding Western stereotypes. Cameron also described the Malagasy people of Madagascar where women are more assertive and quicker to anger. In this culture, unlike stereotypical Western gender role divisions, people believe that women are naturally the assertive, aggressive, competitive, and less verbally subtle gender.

Some cultural practices even challenge the idea of a binary division of genders. The Xanith, found in Omani, an Arab Sultanate, act like a third gender (Wikan, 1991). These biological males sell themselves in passive homosexual relationships, become domestic servants, have male names, dress as females, and practise female rites such as purdah. They are allowed to speak intimately to women in ways that men cannot, and they never sit or eat with men. They are highly perfumed, speak in high-pitched voices, and while women wear their hair long and men short, theirs is medium length. They occupy a cultural space that, albeit being an oppressed and even abused one, seems rather like a third gender.

Another well-known example is the Native American Berdache, reported in over 150 tribes. The Berdache were often called *Two-Spirits*, a male and female spirit in the same body, and have sexual relationships with either gender. The Berdache was a respected and honoured role. They might take on male activities such as fighting or joining men in sweat lodges, or traditional female actions such as cooking (Jacobs, Thomas, & Lang, 1997). If nothing else, such examples challenge us to look at our preconceptions about gender.

David Gilmore's (1990) account of masculinity across cultures, *Manhood in the Making*, describes many societies where masculinity is hard-won through rituals, exhibitions of strengths, physical prowess, and 'macho' acts. Such cultures are extremely common, but at the same time there are plenty of exceptions. Typical of such a 'heroic image of achieved manhood' are the Truk fishermen of the South Pacific who undertake dangerous 'manly' actions in order to prove themselves, like treacherous deep-sea fishing. Males who do not are teased and denigrated. Many cultures have similar rites. Masai warriors were taken from their mothers and sub-jected to bloody circumcision rites, and if a boy cried out they were shamed for life. For the Sambia too, mentioned earlier, masculinity must be 'made', by taking boys away from their mothers and inculcating them into male ways (Herdt, 1994). In such cultures masculinity must be earned, and there is always a risk of sliding back into the feminine world. One might think too of the boarding-school system devised for males of the British upper classes where boys as young as 5 years old were brought up in a regimented harsh regime by strangers and where toughness and physical prowess was highly valued.

There are exceptions that show that such extreme versions of masculinity are by no means universal. Horrocks (1994) quotes a social organisation in Tahiti where women have high status and there is no pressure to prove one's manhood. Their economy fosters cooperation over competition, and material striving is frowned upon. Here men do not have to take the role of providers and have no ideals of 'proper' manhood.

Another culture that challenges gender stereotypes is the Semai of Malaysia, a people who survived through fleeing rather than fighting (Dentan, 1968). They believe that to resist the advances of another is tantamount to being aggressive, and that one should accede to another's requests. They say that they do not get angry, and believe that one should run away when threatened. Here children are not disciplined and they have an interesting concept of *bood*, which roughly means to not feel like doing something. If a child says 'I *bood*' then that is the end of the story, as putting any pressure on another is not deemed appropriate. There are no competitive, or violent games, or pressure to act 'manly'. This is an unusually gentle people where there is no violent crime.

Gender cannot be conflated with biology and alternative potential destinies exist, an idea which of course helped fuel the growth of feminist ideas in recent decades. For many living in multicultural communities questions about appropriate gender roles can stir up other issues, such as conflicts between generations and crises of identity. This is, perhaps, particularly the case for young people influenced by both their parents' cultural beliefs and those of the local culture, as is seen for example in British–Asian young women (Dwyer, 2000). Seeing gender as partly something that is 'done' (Butler, 1999) can give rise to exciting possibilities, although sometimes also to confusion and disagreements as well.

Venus and Mars: language and different planets

Girls in the West seem to develop higher verbal competence than boys, but it is not clear if this is to do with biology or nurture. Clarke-Stewart (1973) observed American infants and found that girls' language skills were better, but also that mothers and daughters spent more time together, and had more mutual eye contact and engagement. On this basis one could make an argument for either nature or nurture making the difference.

In many popular psychology texts one reads that men withdraw when under pressure while women want to talk. Women are said to be more verbal in contrast to men being more physical, men supposedly being better at reading maps but worse at reading people. Much of the actual research suggests that the differences are smaller than are often made out and are not statistically significant (Hyde, 2005).

As Cameron (2007) points out, language use differs according to social context. Western females tend to use more 'hedges', words expressing a tentative meaning, such as 'perhaps', or 'you know'. Yet such conventions can change, depending on who is speaking to whom, and what power relations exist between them. In Japan a more restricted linguistic range has traditionally been available for female use, with women not using deprecatory pronouns, and this results in their speech sounding more polite. The same is not true of 'laddettes', tough talking, aggressive females in Britain. In many cultures females use higher status linguistic variants, and males use more non-standard slang and swear words (Coates, 1993). Different ways of speaking are available to those in different social positions, including different genders. Girls might use more 'hedges' like *'isn't it'*, but are perfectly capable of more direct, less tentative conversational modes, if the context allows it.

Much learning is from same-sex peers, and research shows that in playgrounds girls tend to use more talk while boys more often engage in activity. Gender appropriate linguistic styles can thus be learnt so that one performs according to one's gender. In the West, for example, girls are given the message that to be loud and dominating is unfeminine, and teachers often have this expectation as much as children, unwittingly being more tolerant of boys' boisterous assertiveness in classrooms than girls' and teachers giving much more of their attention to boys, presumably unconsciously (Einarrson & Granstrom, 2002). These are difficult patterns to change. One head of science who managed to work hard and achieve a balance between the attention he gave to boys and girls said that 'he had *felt* as if 90 per cent of his attention had been devoted to the girls' (Whyte, 1986, p. 196). This is, perhaps, a chastening example of how gender is at least partly something that is 'done', as Judith Butler (1997) stated, and so also can sometimes be 'undone'.

Preferred cultures, different gender preferences, and beliefs

In many cultures boys are preferred by parents, but not always. While the usual birth ratio is 105 boys to 100 girls, in China with its one-child policy, the ratio for second born children is 125 to 100, and thousands of girl babies disappear. Here, the lack of girls is most acute in rural areas where male labour is at a premium. Hrdy (1999) has researched the link between infanticide and gender and found that in much of India parents pray for a male child, and in one Indian clinic of 8000 abortions, 7997 of them were female foetuses.

In more patriarchal societies where males control resources and females leave their community to marry, having a male child is advantageous. The attempt to control the ratio of boys to girls is more than just about ideology, and has much to do with which gender brings the most rewards. Other species indulge in gender preferences in certain circumstances. For example alligators can determine the gender of their offspring by ensuring its eggs will hatch at a particular temperature. Triver's (2002) evolutionary theory seems to most successfully explain gender preference in humans, stating that if one gender brings more rewards then it is more highly invested in. The Mukogodo people of Kenya are lower ranking than neighbouring Massai, and acquire bride-wealth by becoming second and third wives to Massai men. They preferentially invest in their daughters and ignore their sons (Cronk, 1993). It is rarer for daughters to be preferred but there are other examples, such as Hungarian gypsies, or the Tonga of Zaire where wealth is inherited through matrilineal lines, and the custom is two cries for a girl and one for a boy. Interestingly more Tonga boys die younger than girls, and infanticide and early death, possibly from neglect, is higher for the least preferred gender in many cultures studied.

The balance of gender desirability is not static. In some monkey species, where rank is inherited via mothers, in tougher conditions more daughters are produced (or less sons are killed or die young), but as conditions alter so does the sex ratio bias. In Europe and America there are generally less strong gender preferences, with research studies (e.g. Andersson, Hank, Ronsen, & Vikat, 2006) suggesting that most families prefer a child of each gender, and preferences for the third child being more variable across countries than many of the extreme examples I have quoted. Indeed, in some societies preferences are changing towards girls, and gender bias often is a calculated response to specific conditions.

Different genders, different psychological presentations

In the West certain kinds of mental disorders, known as internalising ones, are more common in girls; these include depression, anxiety, and eating disorders. More children with externalising disorders, such as ADHD or conduct disorders, are boys, and adolescent males are more likely to commit suicide, while girls are more likely to self-harm.

This difference in mental health outcomes makes sense in relation to what we have learnt so far. Girls seem better able to self-regulate, and are more verbally skilled. Males tend to be more active from as early as *in utero* (Campbell & Eaton, 1999), and in most studies boys move from activity to activity much more frequently than girls. Rough and tumble play is similarly seen more in boys than girls, and more in male primates than females. Cross-culturally boys and girls from about age 4 tend to play in same-sex groups where cultural and biological patterns are likely to be reinforced. Infants will make assumptions about gender simply by observing body movements (Kujawski & Bower, 1993), and young males prefer watching males and females watching females. The play of boys and girls tends on average to be different, with boys' play being much more active and their calorific intake higher (Pellegrini, 2007).

In the West girls' play is generally more verbal, less physically active, more symbolic, and is more likely to have a nurturing component such as looking after pretend babies. The wish to play with those of the same sex seems to be as much to do with the gendered style of play as actual gender, as boys seem to prefer girls with masculine play styles over boys with a feminine style (Alexander & Hines, 1994).

Males generally take more risks, especially young men (Byrnes, Miller, & Schafer, 1999), which of course does not mean that all men are risk takers and women are not. Young males die more often from activities like motor racing, bungee jumping, mountain climbing, and violent incidents. Even in pre-school the genders show different levels of aggression, and boys show more violent themes in their fantasies (Ostrov & Keating, 2004). In most species males are more violent. An exception from the animal world is the hyena, and female hyenas are more aggressive, and also interestingly have higher testosterone levels than males.

Evolutionary theorists have argued that risk taking evolved in males as a result of sexual competition. In humans and other primates some males can monopolise several females, and then not all males have an equal chance to procreate. Females can theoretically produce far fewer children in a life time than males. Studies of human deoxyribonucleic acid (DNA) show that in human history some men have been very successful at producing offspring while many more men than women have entirely failed to become parents. As Lippa argues (2005, p. 92), it is due to such competition that some young men are literally 'dying' to attract young women through risk taking.

However, evolutionary theories also postulate the idea that there are different niches to be occupied. A commonly given example is of the bluegill sunfish, where there is a dominant male with distinctive colouring, but also many other males who maintain female colouration and sneakily mate with females (Magurran & Garcia, 2000). Something similar is seen in primates such as male orangutans, where there is generally one huge, brawny, and hairy male with a harem, and other males often remain in a 'Peter Pan' adolescent body for decades, while occasionally indulging in underhand copulation (Utami, Goossens, Bruford, de Ruiter, & van Hooff, 2002). However, when the alpha male dies or disappears one of these Peter Pan males will transform into an alpha male, its body becoming as large, hirsute, and powerful as its predecessor. There are diverse ways of being male.

Testosterone again, and other hormones

Most violent criminals are male, most murders are male-on-male and generally males are more violent than females, although there are exceptions. High levels of testosterone are associated with increased aggression. Prisoners with higher levels of testosterone commit more violent crimes, Vietnam veterans with high testosterone had more behavioural difficulties as children, and college fraternities with lower than average testosterone levels were more polite and less rowdy (Dabbs & Dabbs, 2000). Yet high testosterone also leads to less success in jobs, less likelihood of successful marriages, less politeness, and even less smiling in company. In women high testosterone levels is also associated with more dominance, aggression, and competitiveness.

Men with low testosterone show lower than average visual-spatial skills but when given increased doses of testosterone such abilities improve, again illustrating the role of hormones. Foetuses exposed to high levels of testosterone in the second trimester of pregnancy become more masculine when they grow up, and those with lower testosterone levels tend to have more flexible gender identifications, becoming more feminine when their mothers encourage them to be so (Udry, 2000). Those with high testosterone interestingly were less influenced by their mothers, which raises a fascinating question about whether high testosterone levels might make children less amenable to parental influence.

Other hormones also show up gender differences. Males with low serotonin tend to be more reactive and violent, and social deprivation or abuse leads to lower serotonin levels (Cirulli, Francia, Berry, Aloe, Alleva, & Suomi, 2009). Low serotonin in females is linked to increased anxiety and depression rather than violence.

Much research points very firmly to the impact of hormones on gender development, but it is worth making a caveat. Our hormones are not god given or set in stone, and levels can change in response to social stimuli. For example male sportsmen have considerably higher testosterone levels when playing in front of their home crowd, or when playing against bitter rivals (Neave & Wolfson, 2003), and after the American election results in 2008 McCain supporters and not Obama supporters had lowered testosterone levels (Stanton, Beehner, Saini, Kuhn, & LaBar, 2009). Levels of hormones can change when the context changes. Males in Texas respond with more aggression than males from the North of America to exactly the same stimuli, such as a deliberately but unsuspectingly administered insult in an experiment (Nisbett & Cohen, 1996). Here it is the more *machismo* culture that is central, and probably leads to higher testosterone levels. Aggression and testosterone might be linked, but the direction of the influence of nature and nurture are not always clear.

Social learning

Most children can identify their gender by about 3 years old. At this age they still might assume that another child's gender is not fixed, and that the child who puts on a dress after wearing trousers changes from boy to girl. Between 4 and 6 children often still ascribe gender according to superficial characteristics, such as hairstyle or clothes. By 6 or 7 this is more stable, and by this age in most known cultures children separate into gendered groups for play.

It is easy to ascribe biological explanations to behaviours that have their basis in social roles. Women have been found to do worse on intelligence tests, and describe themselves in more feminine ways, when meeting a man who states a preference for traditional women (Zanna & Pack, 1975). Women can eat less and put on softer voices when talking to a man they find attractive, while girls can become less competitive when boys are present (Salomone, 2003), and often do worse at 'male' subjects in mix-gendered schools, all illustrating the role of social context in gender roles. This allows rigid gender roles to be viewed more sceptically. Typical is how well women adapted to occupations during both world wars that were previously seen as men only occupations in Britain.

Children identify with gender appropriate play. For example a task of threading a wire through a small space was described to children as either needlework or electronics. Performance improved when the task was seen as appropriate to the child's gender identity (Davies, 1989). In classic studies babies were dressed in the clothes typical of the other gender, and labelled with a name of the opposite sex to see how adults reacted. Such studies reveal real, if small, differences (Stern & Karraker, 1989). For example those thought to be boys were often played with more roughly, using bigger bodily movements and children were subtly encouraged to choose gender typical toys. Fathers especially are prone to pushing boys towards being traditionally masculine in appearance and discouraging signs of feminine play (Lamb, 2004). In Western cultures deviating from gender norms can be a risk factor for depression in boys, as well as for bullying.

Few would disagree that learning from others, whether siblings, peers, parents, teachers, or the media has an impact. If children have an older sibling of the same gender then generally they behave in a more gender typical way than if they lacked such a same-sex older sibling. Similarly only children behave in more gender typical ways than children with older siblings of the opposite gender (Rust, Golombok, Hines, Johnston, Golding, & ALSPAC Study Team, 2000). We are influenced by those close to us and by the culture one lives in. In a Canadian town that had not had television due to transmission problems, the children deprived of television had weaker gender stereotypes than children in neighbouring towns. This changed when television eventually reached this part of the Rocky Mountains (Kimball, 1986). As much later research has found (Bryant, 2008) cultural learning, whether from the media or siblings, definitely makes a difference, but once again it is uncertain just how much.

Summary: nature and nurture and fuzzy genders

While I have highlighted some clear biological gender differences, it is important to reiterate that differences between genders are partly a question of emphasis, and statistically remain relatively small. Most differences are average ones and more importantly, men can vary in their masculinity and women in their femininity.

With the women's movement in the West some even challenged the very concepts of male and female. Masculinity and femininity were seen as traits that were not necessarily opposite, but rather that one could be either low or high on both. For example one might be both independent and dominant, but also compassionate and empathic. Some psychologists argued for a new ideal of **androgyny** as the most psychologically healthy profile (Bem, 1974).

Uncertainty and debate remain about the relative roles of biology and culture in gender differentiation. Possibly environmental influence diminishes slightly with age, given peer pressure for gender appropriate behaviour, and how some parents police gendered behaviour, particularly fathers with their boys. The research by Udry (2000) adds another dimension in suggesting that those with lower testosterone levels, might be more amenable to the influence of socialisation. It may also be true that active boys are attracted to play with other boys, but this then leads to the development of same-sex play groups in which initiation into gender appropriate roles and subcultures occurs, so that biology is reinforced by culture. Chicken and egg are hard to untangle.

Men die younger than women, masculine men die younger than feminine men, and masculine women younger than feminine women (Lippa, 2005). This could be biology, for example the effect of testosterone. Alternatively, it could be the impact of lifestyle, such as being more aggressive, taking more risks, or working harder. Overall it does seem that emotional development is different for males and females in most cultures, but is differently different across cultures and such differences are only ever going to be average ones, with plenty of exceptions. Ultimately we are more alike than different, but we are nonetheless still different, and whether we stress the similarities or differences is partly a personal choice.

Part IV

Not just mothers

Nonmaternal care and childcare

In this chapter I examine nonmaternal childcare as seen in Western and other societies, including more formal organised childcare such as nurseries. Humans are what is often called a cooperative breeding species, in which childcare has historically been shared by adults in the community. Yet this happens in different ways in different cultures, accompanied by very different beliefs about the right way to care for children. Bowlby (1969) received harsh criticism when his theories about attachment were interpreted as arguing that mothers should stay at home with their children, while working mothers can still be publicly maligned and politicians try to win votes by arguing for the importance of what they call the traditional nuclear family.

Non-parents have always looked after children. It is likely that evolution selected infants who developed ways of attracting adults, such as with big eyes or symmetrical features, optimising their chances of survival by enhancing the motivation of others to look after them. Humans, but certainly not all primates, have an evolutionary history of breeding cooperatively, or in other words there have always been people other than mothers who have shared in the task of childcare. Although paying for childcare is a recent phenomenon, mothers leaving children at nurseries or with childminders is part of a long tradition of nonmaternal care. Humans produce some of the costliest infants, in terms of the required investment of time and energy, and by the time the next child comes along, it is extremely unlikely that the previous one will be anywhere near independent. A human infant requires more physical and emotional resources than a mother alone can provide, and the social nature of human childrearing allows humans to keep more offspring alive and to reduce the intervals between the birth of children.

The best predictor of infant survival, Hrdy (1999) and other researchers argue, is maternal commitment, and this in turn is strongly influenced by a mother's perception of the degree of social support and alternative care that is available to her. Such nonmaternal care is sometimes termed alloparenting by biologists and primatologists, 'allo' having its roots in the Greek for 'other'. This is likely to include close relatives, such as grandparents, fathers, aunts, and siblings, and in most species kin are the main contributors. Grandmothers seem to traditionally have played a central role. In a study of the Hadza, a hunter–gatherer group in Tanzania, in times of food shortages children were more likely to survive when they had grandmothers alive and on hand (Hawkes, O'Connell, & Blurton Jones, 1997). Hazda mothers could leave their infants while they went to forage and return in time for the next breastfeed. Higher rates of survival of children, and shorter spaces between births, have been found in many societies where grand-maternal support is strong. German, Finnish, and Canadian children were also found to be more likely to thrive with grandmothers present, although the same was not true for the presence of grandfathers (Sear & Mace, 2007).

A large role in human alloparenting is often played by adolescent girls, who in many pre-industrial societies undertake a very high proportion of childcare, freeing mothers to care for infants and undertake tough physical work (Hewlett & Lamb, 2005). Societies vary in the amount of nonmaternal care used, although all seem to indulge in this to an extent. For example in Efe society (Tronick, Morelli, & Winn, 1987) babies are likely to be transferred between about eight people in an average hour. Efe infants still have a primary attachment to their mothers, but this is a society where, when asked 'who cares for the children?' the answer is 'we all do'.

As described earlier humans are a species that sometimes abandons newborn infants, and in many cooperative breeding species, like humans, maternal commitment to their newborns depends on a mother's assessment of their social support systems. The historical literature detailing the history of abandonment of infants, such as in European foundling homes, and the frequency of human infanticide in history, is a challenge to the assumption that maternal instinct is universal (Hrdy, 1999). This again might explain why infants seek out faces and gaze from the first moments of life, to elicit the positive responses that aid survival. As they get older, human infants become adept at working out who might be able to provide care and support by using the kind of mind-reading skills detailed in earlier chapters. Humans, compared with other apes, might be equally competitive and violent, but more likely to be altruistic and cooperative (Tomasello, 2009), presumably something which has aided survival. Infant's propensity to 'babble' occurs primarily in species who cooperatively breed. For example pygmy marmosets babble at just the age that alloparents come on the scene, presumably because such vocalisation helps to maintain contact with important adults.

Long childhoods are the other clue to the human evolutionary propensity for cooperative care. Cooperative breeding species with whom humans otherwise have little in common tend to have longer childhoods, such as wolves and many species of birds. The logic is that one does not have to skimp on a job like childrearing when there is help around. Humans seem to have evolved to nurture infants in a community context, in which social support is central for infant survival and growth.

Adoption is common in some societies

An extreme form of nonparental care is adoption. Historically in Europe a high proportion of adoptions were of babies who for various reasons were 'given up' at birth. In some Western countries adoption has increasingly been used as a solution to finding homes for children who have had to be removed from their birth parents following neglect or abuse. Such children often come with extremely complicated histories, and can prove to be a huge challenge to care for (Kenrick, Lindsey, & Tollemache, 2006).

In fact adoption has been much more common across the world than people may realise, and the view that children 'should' be raised by their birth parents is by no means universal. In many cultures, for example, clans or descent groups 'own' children, who are circulated within lineages. As the anthropologist Fiona Bowie (2004) has found, adoption and fostering are not always seen in a negative light. In the Wogeo society of Papa New Guinea in some villages as many as half the children are adopted (Anderson, 2004), while in the Eastern Cameroon about 30 per cent of children between 4 and 10 were not living with their biological parents. Sometimes the motivation is to better a child's opportunities, and in Brazil it is common for poor families to send their children to live with better off foster parents (Fonseca, 2004). In these cultures one can have more than one mother, and new ones do not cancel out the biological mother's importance. Such practices do not always mean transferring all rights over children to a new carer, something that can cause conflict and confusion in cases of overseas adoption.

We tend to use words like 'real' and 'natural' to describe biological parents, and cross-cultural comparisons can be helpful in challenging assumptions about the sanctity of the blood ties. For example, the Baatombu in Northern Benin simply do not have terms for biological parents, and the term which translates as 'giving birth' is used by both adoptive and birth parents (Alber, 2003). In parts of the Cameroons women discriminate between children by whether they are part of a lineage, not on the basis of whether they are biological children, and grandmothers are actively competitive in building matrilineages. Thus in many societies children are not simply seen as 'belonging' to a biological parent. In some West African cultures babies were regarded as belonging to the wider kin group, and in some traditional Japanese households a child was viewed as belonging to the house (Hendry, 1986). As Fiona Bowie (2004) makes clear, it is never easy for a mother to give up a child for adoption, nor for children to suffer such changes, but the anthropological evidence suggests that where this is culturally sanctioned and seen as normal, then the effect is not as obviously damaging as some disruptions to care seen in Western societies.

Purchased nonmaternal childcare: nurseries

In contemporary societies completely new forms of nonparental care have developed in the form of organised purchased childcare. In Britain there are now 1.6 million mothers of under 5-year-olds who work full time, and 75 per cent of these mothers had their own mothers at home in their own infancy, so this is a relatively new phenomenon (Leach, 2009). Increasing numbers of young children are placed in various forms of childcare while parents go out to work. There has been debate as to whether such childcare helps or harms children, yet the issues are complex. In the case of nurseries, one cannot any longer simply ask whether nurseries *per se* are good or bad for children, or whether children would be better off staying at home with their mothers. There are so many other factors to consider, such as that some nurseries seem on most criteria better than others, and similarly for some, the move to nursery might give access to more stimuli and emotional care than that received at home. I use words like 'good' or 'poor' to describe quality of childcare, aware that 'quality' is partly a question of judgement and is an elusive thing to measure. I follow the definitions of studies that suggest that good ratios, well-trained staff, continuity of staff, and especially those who invest time and energy and who are emotionally responsive, all contribute to better outcomes, whether behavioural, emotional or academic. Penelope Leach quotes a useful definition from the National Institute of Child Health and Human Development (NICHD) Early Childcare Research Network by Scarr that 'quality child care is warm, supportive interactions with adults in a safe, healthy and stimulating environment, where early education and trusting relationships combine to support individual children's physical, emotional, social and intellectual development' (Scarr, 1999, p. 375).

Early attachment research stressed that prolonged separations from attachment figures can be harmful. Bowlby had seen the effects on children of wartime separations from parents, and his colleagues such as James and Joyce Robertson had studied in detail the moment-by-moment impact on children of being separated from parents. Perhaps the most famous and indeed heart-rending of the Roberstons' studies is the film made of an 18-month-old boy, John, whose caring parents were having another baby, and placed him for a week or so in a residential unit (Robertson, 1971). The film graphically shows a normal and happy little boy trying hard to find the internal resources to cope with an overwhelming new situation, unsuccessfully competing for the matron's attention, then becoming upset and tearful, protesting hard for a few days, and in time becoming hopeless, listless, given-up, and depressed. The nursery setting was not cruel or abusive, but simply could not give him the attention he needed or expected.

Although such research was used by some to argue that children should be at home with their mothers, in fact the main lesson from such research was that a child needs to be able to depend on a known and reliable attachment figure. A child can have several attachment figures, even if one person, often the mother, is the primary one. Such understanding in principle could have a big impact on childcare practice if taken seriously, but as yet there is surprisingly little research which has used these ideas to examine nursery practice in detail.

There is no doubt that going to a nursery is a stressful experience for children. A recent study showed that toddlers starting nursery after being at home since birth experience high levels of stress, with cortisol levels after starting nursery between 75 per cent and 100 per cent higher than when they were at home (Ahnert, Gunnar, Lamb, & Barthel, 2004). Secure attachment does not buffer this effect much, and insecure children had higher stress levels than secure ones in nursery while their parents were present, but not once the parents had left them. Stress levels lowered slightly in time but they were still showing 'chronic mild stress' 5 months later, irrespective of security of attachment. These children showed little outward sign of stress or anxiety, which is possibly why nursery staff often reassure parents that their children are 'just fine'.

To make sense of the impact of childcare we need to take several factors into account, such as the nature of the childcare provision itself, factors in a child, such as temperament, and the quality of family life. No factor alone tells the whole story. The risks are far higher if a child is born into a chaotic family, say with a psychiatrically ill mother, and then attends poor-quality childcare. In other words, having unresponsive caregiving both at home and in a nursery makes things considerably worse. On the other hand, high-quality childcare, whether nurseries, childminders, nannies, or grandmothers, can buffer the effects of a riskier home situation, leading to better than expected outcomes, and helping children develop social and coping skills that they might not otherwise have gained (Ramey, Campbell, Burchinal, Skinner, Gardner, & Ramey, 2000). However, children from loving and encouraging families can lose out through attending poor-quality childcare. A child's temperament also has an effect, not only on how they cope with daycare, but even whether they are placed in it. A British study of over 1200 families suggested that children with more fussy temperaments were left in daycare for longer than other children (Sylva, Stein, Leach, Barnes, & Malmberg, 2007).

Most research shows that family factors, such as a stable home and sensitive parenting, are far more likely to predict later outcomes than the quality of childcare. Nursery care generally has less of a negative effect than many people have assumed, but has an effect nonetheless. For example, securely attached children who had been in childcare longer were more hostile in structured interactions with their mothers at

42 months, and were rated by teachers as more aggressive (Egeland & Hiester, 1995). The differences might be small but are still significant. Children who start low-quality nursery care earlier are more likely to be rated as distractible and less task oriented at pre-school than children who enter nurseries later (Hungerford & Cox, 2006). Lamb (1996) found that children in daycare were more likely to have an avoidant attachment than those being looked after at home, even if statistically the difference between the two groups was not huge. Belsky et al. (2007b) in particular has amassed much research suggesting that longer hours in childcare have a persistent effect, which is not massive, but is real and measurable, such as more externalising problems. What clearly does make a difference, as previously suggested, is the 'dual risk' of low parental sensitivity coupled with low-quality daycare or longer periods in daycare, often leading to externalising behaviours and poor peer relations.

With such vast numbers in daycare of one form or another, an understanding of these matters is crucial. The biggest ever study of childcare was an American one (National Institute of Child Health and Human Development (NICDH), 2004) that found that 50 per cent of infants under a year were in daycare for over 30 hours a week, and 74 per cent for at least 10 hours. This again is not an issue for moral judgement. The amount of time a child spends in childcare is generally related to how much a family relies on a parent's income, particularly a mother's, with many mothers not having the luxury of choosing to stay at home. Political support for parents to care for children can make a big difference. A study across 20 Western countries led to the startling finding that just by increasing paid maternity leave by 10 weeks infant mortality decreased by over 4 per cent, and presumably might decrease more if more leave were granted (Tanaka, 2005).

Going out to work can also of course have different effects on mothers. Employed mothers who are less satisfied with their work roles, and who have less support at home, in fact tend to be more controlling of their children, who in turn tend to become more defiant. Yet many employed mothers who get satisfaction from their work are reported to be both happier and more responsive parents (Grzywacz & Bass, 2003). Mothers who go out to work often compensate for the time they are away by spending more time interacting with their child, such as in story times or doing household activities together, so that in many cases the total amount of time spent together adds up to the same as that spent by stay-at-home mothers (Bryant & Zick, 1996).

Most studies show that quality of childcare does make a real difference. For example children between 2 and 4 years old have been shown to have less behavioural problems the higher the quality of daycare provided, and for children from more deprived backgrounds, more time in daycare benefitted them (Votruba-Drzal, Coley, & Chase-Landsdale, 2004), and provided social, emotional, and cognitive boosts.

Workers in group childcare rarely become substitute mothers. Analysis of over 2000 cases found that, more often than not, in nurseries attachments were of an avoidant or ambivalent rather than a secure kind (Ahnert, Pinquart, & Lamb, 2006). Most of the children studied had secure relationships with their mothers and their response to their daycare staff is a testament to their capacity to develop different kinds of attachment styles with different carers. Even though some sensitive and well-trained nursery workers can potentially be more sensitive than many parents, even the most sensitive staff member inevitably becomes less sensitive when activity is geared to the needs of the group as a whole, rather than to specific children. It might be for this reason that secure attachments are more common when childcare is provided in home-based settings, such as by nannies and childminders. Childcare providers in daycare settings are often unable to modulate infant distress, and consequently are less often sought out for comfort. Lamb (1996) suggests that children realise that such carers are primarily interested in providing a learning environment and minimising misbehaviour in the interests of group harmony.

Some years ago Trudy Marshall, while working for a London local authority, did a study of childcare that brought many of these, sometimes upsetting, issues to life. She found that most staff were young, little trained and had a fear of getting close to the children or of 'spoiling' them. A typical comment made by one staff member was 'if they cry and it is just because they want to be cuddled, then I would try not to do it' (1982, p. 28). Dependence was feared and discouraged, and as Marshall wrote 'there appeared to be an underlying belief that to nurse a child was to spoil him, particularly if he was crying' (1982, p. 24). In these nurseries a child was never held for more than a few seconds, except when he or she had just arrived in the morning. Similarly, no child received ongoing sustained attention from an adult, as staff would drift from child to child quickly, concentrating on the group as a whole (Marshall, 1982). Anxious and withdrawn children received even less attention than crying ones, and when children cried, physical reasons were generally sought, such as the child being 'dirty' or 'cold' rather than emotional reasons, such as being sad, homesick, scared, or unhappy.

More recently Peter Elfer (2006) has undertaken detailed observational research in nurseries, in order to bring the child's perspective more centrally into view. He has described the contrasting experiences of children in nurseries where emotional under-standing and attachment is or is not central to the practice and philosophy of the institution. He found that in many nurseries staff actively defend themselves against being aware of the emotional and attachment needs of very young children in their care, and for example may actively discourage a child from becoming dependent on them. The children in turn learn to adapt to the expectations of the staff, and secure attachment relationships often will not be formed in such environments. Nursery life is often characterised by a lack of mind-mindedness; which may be as much a func-tion of working in such an institutional setting as the psychological capacities of the workers. Although Marshall's and Elfer's studies are relatively small they illustrate some of the difficulties that toddlers have to manage when their childcare environ-ment is less than ideal. Yet for many parents, a daycare setting, often full time, is the setting of choice, preferred over childminders and nannies. Nursery care has generally as yet not taken on-board the lessons from attachment theory, particularly the benefits of developing an attachment relationship with a known and trusted worker who can buffer anxiety levels in very young children (Bowlby, 2007).

As Rutter has argued, there is a danger of exporting the findings from poor residential care to daycare settings, and the overwhelming evidence that children can be extremely adversely affected by living in residential settings simply is not the case for daycare, where the effects are far smaller (Rutter & O'Connor, 1999). It is true that long days in nursery from an early age lead to a less secure attachment with mothers, and that being placed in daycare full time, before the age of 1, especially where there is instability and a lack of continuity of care, are real risk factors (NICDH, 2004). Overall though, the research shows that the effects are real, but not huge.

Nurseries, nannies, grannies, and childminders

One of the biggest decisions parents often have to make is what kind of daycare to use. Various factors come into the equation, not least cost. In a recent large British sample mothers were asked, soon after having their first child, what kind of childcare they would choose in an ideal world (Leach et al., 2006). Nearly half stated that their ideal was to stay at home with their children, far ahead of the next choices, grandparents or nurseries, both of which scored about 10 per cent, with nannies and childminders coming in at about 6 per cent and fathers rock bottom at 0.5 per cent. In fact over half of the mothers in this, the largest ever British study of childcare, did not end up with the childcare that they had anticipated.

This study looked at the quality of the different forms of childcare, comparing nurseries, childminders, nannies, and grandparents. Having attuned and empathic carers made a big difference (Leach, Barnes, Malmberg, Sylva, & Stein, 2008) and particularly important factors are the stability and availability of caregivers, the ratio of adults to child, the experience and training of staff, and how stimulating the environment was. Interestingly, Leach's study suggested that parents might not always be the best judge of how good childcare is, particularly of nursery care, and might sometimes make judgements on the basis of factors such as how well they get on with the carers rather than what actually goes on while the child is in that care.

The most central finding from this study was that at 10 months, on just about all counts, nursery care came out worse than care from one main carer in a home. Nursery care was consistently associated with less positive interactions and less emotional responsiveness from adults. In comparison, the results for nannies, childminders, and grandparents were fairly similar, and much better than nurseries, with grandmothers coming out slightly lower than the others for the amount of positive interaction, but not significantly so. Health and safety and quality of equipment were better in nurseries, but not the quality of interactions. Maybe more worrying for parents was that there seemed to be very little relationship between the cost of childcare and its quality.

Childcare in nursery is often provided by young staff with few qualifications, and an interesting finding was that older staff tended to be less punitive and have more positive interactions with the children. Overall the research findings were perhaps not surprising. Nurseries did provide good stimulus for cognitive development as children got a little older, and certainly provided better physical environments and more facilities. However, the emotional environment of group care generally was considerably less supportive. Maybe slightly surprisingly, grandparental care on average showed slightly more punitive behaviour than the other forms of home-based care, and the grandparental homes were also slightly less safe. Yet overall the study found that home-based forms of care offered the best forms of attention. As ratios got better in nurseries, then there were also some improvements on all these scales. Such findings, I think, fit well with others in this book. Children benefit from consistent, positive, warm, and ongoing relationships with stable figures who provide security, safety, and stimulation and who are interested in their minds and emotions. Children feel safer, as attachment theory attests, when they can be confident of gaining a response from a carer who helps them manage anxiety and worry. As well as needing safety and security, children thrive in environments where they feel confident, are cared for, at ease, and where they are stimulated.

Summary

Nonmaternal care has been a central part of rearing children in almost all known societies. In the money economies of the West this increasingly takes the form of purchased childcare. A question that policy-makers, students of child development, and maybe most of all, parents, find themselves asking is what effect does placing a very young child in such forms of childcare have on how the child later develops. The biggest ever study of these effects in America (Belsky et al., 2007b) found that child-care until 4½ years, defined as being nonparental care for over 10 hours a week, had different effects on different aspects of development. Higher-quality care, as already mentioned, can improve readiness for school, and help with cognitive and linguistic skills. Yet social and emotional skills do not improve, and the more time a child spends in such childcare, the more likelihood there is of behavioural problems by school age. Perhaps educational gains are sometimes made at the expense of some emotional difficulties. Many of these effects still exert an influence later on in their school careers, such as in academic performance and peer relations.

Maybe the most important finding is that the quality of relationship a child has with its parents is a far better predictor of children's academic performance and social functioning than the quality of childcare. Nonetheless better childcare, of any form predicts better vocabulary and other academic advantages at 12 years old. Conversely, the more time a child spends in childcare, the more behavioural problems they show in the ensuing years, and although such problems do not predict serious psycho-pathology, these children consistently show up as not doing as well (NICDH, 2004). It seems that it is particularly in an institutional daycare environment such as a nursery that such issues are exacerbated As Belsky points out, irrespective of family factors, 'in the case of non-relative care, it is centre (i.e. institutional) care that has unique and enduring impact of a seemingly adverse kind' (Belsky et al., 2007b, p. 697).

Humans fit into the class of animals designated as cooperative breeders, and have always needed more than just mothers to bring up children. Humans seem biologically primed to respond to children other than their own, this often being accompanied by the release of hormones that help develop bonds between adults and children. Similarly babies are born primed to interact with and attract other human adults, and they might develop some of their capacities for understanding other minds in order to enhance nonmaternal care. As in many other species, other females, such as adolescent girls, and grandmothers, are often prominent in communal child-care, although there seems to be no biological reason why males could not undertake such roles more (Lamb, 2004). The degree and kind of nonmaternal care varies hugely across societies, but in all societies studied, primary attachments tend to remain with the mother, even though other attachments can form with other members of the community.

The forms of parenting mostly seen in the West, with nuclear families and a sometimes isolated stay-at-home mother, are relatively unusual in human history. I have not mentioned fathers in this chapter, as they feature in one of their own, but they too of course often play a significant role. Human infants are born immature, and require a huge investment, and without nonmaternal support a child's survival might be compromised. Bearing in mind this human history of cooperative parenting, in this chapter I have looked at how in contemporary Western societies, with wage economies and a decrease in both community support and extended families, alternative forms of childcare have developed. Recent research studies have aided our understanding of what can be helpful, and not so helpful, in how childcare is provided. Such information can aid policy-makers at both a macro- and micro-level, help parents and others think about their preferred ways of providing care for children, and influence how childcare is organised on the ground in a child's best interests. The understandings gleaned from the research back up other findings in this book, about the importance of consistent attachment figures and attuned sensitive attention to children's psychological and emotional states in order to enable children to thrive.

Chapter 14

Siblings, peers, group life, and middle childhood

This chapter examines how children's development is influenced not just by parents but also other children; peers as well as siblings. I look particularly at middle childhood, a period that I am defining as roughly 6 to 12 years old, although some people define the age range slightly differently. I discuss both how children are influenced by peers, how children are born primed to be part of group life, but also how their home situations and their temperaments influence how they interact with other children. In Western societies the nuclear family plays a more central role than in many cultures, and young children are often home based in their early years, reducing the influence of people outside the family. Thus, much developmental research focuses on mother–infant interactions, and has had less to say about siblings or peers. In many cultures children are part of a larger social group from much earlier on and are regularly interacting with, and influenced by, others across the age range.

By school age children are beginning to find a place for themselves in groups, separate from their parents, and fitting in is easier for some children than others. Whether or not a child is popular can be a central preoccupation, not being invited to birthday parties can be a painful experience, and children who are bullied or shunned are a cause for concern. Some are introverted and seen as loners; others seem to be always involved in fights, while luckier ones develop sophisticated social skills and become popular. Part of the job of this chapter is to think about why children tend to move along such trajectories.

We know that a child's attachment status is likely to impact on what kind of relationships they develop in nursery and even later in school. A child's capacity to empathise and understand other minds will similarly affect their ability to get on with others. Yet some, such as Judy Rich Harris (2009), have argued that the influence of parents has been overestimated and that peers have more influence on children than parents. Such views are not universally accepted but have challenged a more commonly held view that the primary direction of influence is from parent to child.

Many factors affect children's capacity for social interaction, and much social development takes place in middle childhood, when the inbuilt propensity for social and group life generally comes more to the fore. By this age children normally spend increasing time with peers; cognitive and social skills are developing fast, children become more reflexive, more capable of abstract thought, develop better memories, and can hold onto several different ideas at once.

Children can by now compare themselves with others, and can work out where they fit into a peer group. They might understand that they are better at maths than some but worse at football than others, or liked by some but not by others. They can become more emotionally self-aware, describing feeling states with increasing subtlety. They can become more able to manage conflicting emotions towards the same person or event, maybe liking certain aspects of someone but not others. They also begin to understand that others, too, can have mixed emotions (Hemenover & Schimmack, 2007). Such developing interpersonal skills means that children, if all goes well, are more able to understand others through predicting their actions and making sense of their states of mind. They gain abilities such as pretending or deception, and learn how to behave in order to gain group acceptance. The group is increasingly important, and in terms of role models to emulate, peers become a central reference point. Not all children are equally successful at this, and children with few social skills and an inability to understand other minds are particularly vulnerable, such as children who have suffered serious maltreatment and neglect who often struggle to form stable friendships.

Siblings

Relationships with other children often begin in the home, with their siblings. Having an older sibling generally enhances capacities such as theory of mind and executive functioning (McAlister & Peterson, 2007), especially if the siblings are close in age. In many hunter–gatherer communities infants were kept with their mothers until the next child was born, and then spent more time with peers, siblings, and other adults, and socialisation occurred in such groups. For example, one study showed that Polynesian children, once they could walk, were 'released' into the care of 3 or 4-year-old siblings (Martini, 1994), with mothers and other adults nearby. The children valued this so much that when the older siblings occasionally left them with their mothers, they would cry with disappointment.

Judy Dunn (2004) has particularly stressed the important role in emotional development played by siblings, arguing strongly against focusing too much on parent–child relationships. For example, children who engage in pretend play and role enactments with siblings in their early years display more sophisticated social under-standing later. Children living in families learn from interactions, even interactions in which they play no active part but simply observe. Of course, because children benefit socially from having siblings does not mean that sibling relationships are not often fraught and full of rivalry and aggression. Indeed, it is sometimes seen as the most common form of conflict in families (Kramer & Radey, 1997), and the bane of many parents' lives. Despite this, social advantages can accrue from interactions with siblings.

Dunn's (2004) research found that as children get older the relative influence of other children increases, and in her sample talk with other children about feelings and mental states quadrupled between 33 and 47 months, whereas such talk with mothers almost halved. Children talk differently with other children to how they talk with parents, developing skills in engaging with those they are on an equal footing with. These are important skills. In Dunn's studies children who interacted best with other children had spent more time interacting with siblings. Such children played more cooperatively in pairs and used more statements that referred to the thoughts and feelings of others. Such capacities may have roots in mother–infant relationships, but are honed with siblings and peers. Dunn found that children who had more emotional understanding at 3 continued to be ahead in these capacities at 6 years old, leading to less interpersonal conflict and more cooperation.

Power of the group

Humans are profoundly social creatures who have evolved to survive in group contexts, and are influenced by others from their first months. Babies are like baro-meters of emotional atmospheres, and a 4-month-old is likely to smile when the atmosphere is jolly, and become fretful if things become tense. An infant's capacities for communication and imitation are by no means reserved simply for mothers and the capacity for social interaction does not just depend on attachment relationships (Nash, 1995). Peers do not have to look after each other but they still mutually interact and this begins much earlier than previously thought. Researchers such as Cathy Urwin (2001) have described how young babies are surprisingly equipped for interchanges with other babies. Ben Bradley and Jane Selby (Selby & Bradley, 2003, p. 213) looked at what happens when babies of about 8 months were placed together in groups of three, without an adult present, and here is a typical sequence captured on video:

> towards the end of a long session (15 minutes), we recorded a cat's chorus of interwoven vocalizations from three babies, lasting more than a minute and a half. One baby, close to crying, gave voice to a querulous intermittent wail and a second copied quite precisely the vocal contours of the wail made by the first. The first baby, seemingly contained by the second baby's mirroring of him, then repeated and modulated his initial utterance.

Later:

> Ann began to make frequent staccato vocalizations, predominantly whilst looking at Joe ... Ann's vocalization rate increased markedly after Joe vocalized back to her once (from 2 sounds in 20 seconds prior to his vocalization to 10 in 10 seconds after; throughout all this Mona was mute). After watching Ann make this flurry of vocalizations, Joe then turned to Mona to make a huge initiation, as if bringing her in to the conversation. He reoriented his body towards her, lent towards her, waved both his arms up and down, all accompanied by an 8-second-long wide-open smile and raised eyebrows.
>
> This attracted Mona's attention, who had also been watching Ann vocalize. In contrast, as Ann saw Mona and Joe make mutual gaze, her legs, which had been stretched out towards the other two, drop down and she looks down at herself, seemingly deflated. Joe looks briefly back at her, still smiling and they make mutual gaze. But then he turns back to Mona, still smiling. After this, 30 seconds pass before Ann and Joe make mutual gaze again. Five seconds after Joe's big initiation to Mona, Ann turns and scowls at Mona, an expression she never made to Joe.

There can be little doubt that these are complex social interactions, including mutual regulation, rivalry, assertively demanding attention and playfulness, illustrating how infants can manage multiple relationships, not just dyadic ones, and are able to participate in group life. In these brief excerpts one sees an acute awareness of the pressures of belonging, of being 'in' or 'out', even in young babies, and as they get older humans tend to invest a lot in group identities and seem to have a natural tendency to divide the world into 'them and us'.

Moving to older children, most research has shown how children want to belong to groups. In one experiment boys were shown pictures comprising only of dots and asked to estimate how many dots the pictures contained. They were then told randomly, with no grounding in reality, that they had over- or underestimated, and were either 'overestimators' or 'underestimators'. They were then asked to interact with other boys who were described to them as either over- or underestimators. Surprisingly they tended to favour and be more generous to others in their own, in fact spurious, group of over/underestimators (Tajfel & Turner, 1979).

Belonging and being part of a group is important. Beebe reported LaFrance's work examining postural matching that found that those who shared similar postures had more mutual rapport (LaFrance, 1979). Some college students unwittingly mimicked the posture of their teacher. When the teacher placed his right hand under his chin, the students mirrored this by placing their left hand under their chin. Those who reported having good rapport with their teacher were the ones who unconsciously mirrored his posture, suggesting that feeling good is partly a function of being in synchronous harmony with those around them.

Birdwhistell undertook similar analysis in various cultures and found that not only language but postures and ways of moving are culturally distinctive. He found that speakers of French tend to bulge their lips forward, and tilt their heads while undertaking specific hand gestures (Birdwhistell, 1970). Similarly a bilingual Kutenai tribesperson consistently moved in a different way according to whether they were speaking Kutenai or English. Children pick up such cues and learn to act in culturally expected ways, not just according to the norms of their parents.

Humans have a tendency to split into 'in-groups' and 'out-groups' and be extremely influenced by social pressures. Children are learning at a young age about what is necessary to be 'in', such as with which nuances to speak, what games to play, or what to wear. Infants as early as 1-year-old recognise their culture's language. Intergroup 'bias' and believing in the coherence of one's own group increases self-esteem (Hewstone, Rubin, & Willis, 2002), so it might be good for us to feel that we belong. Prejudice about ethnicity, class, or nationality are perhaps extreme examples of this predisposition. In a classic experiment a teacher divided her class into brown- and blue-eyed pupils and announced that the brown-eyed pupils were better in various ways (Peters, 1987). The children with the low-status eye colour showed a marked deterioration in many ways, and also previously well-functioning friendships between blue- and brown-eyed children were suddenly not working well. We might speculate that this need for group belonging has sensible evolutionary roots; unknown males straying into the territory of strangers are at risk in many species, including humans.

Yet this human propensity can have shocking implications, as seen in the well-known Stanford prison experiments. In this, adults were arbitrarily asked to play the role of either prisoners or guards. In a very short time the two groups, who in reality again had little to differentiate themselves from each other, had taken on their respective roles, and the prisoners became distrustful of, and angry with, the guards who in turn became surprisingly vindictive and cruel (Zimbardo, Maslach, & Haney, 2000). Their overidentification with these roles led to hatred and mutual enmity, a prisoners' revolt and guard violence ensued, and the experiment, which was due to last 14 days, was abandoned after a mere 6. The participants identified very profoundly with the group they belonged to, and were unable to see the point of view of those in the other group who had become 'alien'.

Other experiments similarly illustrate the power of role expectations and ask profound questions about human nature. In a famous experiment by Stanley Milgram (1974) subjects were asked to participate in what they believed to be a method of helping students learn by giving them mild electric shocks when they got an answer wrong. It was then 'slipped' into the conversation that the putative student had a heart condition. What is alarming and hard to believe about this experiment was that around 65 per cent of the subjects, despite questioning the experimenters, were prepared under pressure from a white-coated male in authority, to administer what they believed were potentially fatal levels of electric shock in order to conform to the experimenter's wishes. When the subject showed reluctance the experimenter used verbal prods such as 'the experiment requires that you continue', and subjects were allowed to stop if their reluctance remained after 4 such verbal prods. This experiment, which would be unlikely to get past ethics committees today, has been replicated on numerous occasions and consistently showed that over 60 per cent of subjects were prepared to administer potentially fatal doses. This confounded all predictions, and is a stark example of the power of social pressure.

Children are similarly influenced by peer pressure, answering questions in a certain way in class because everyone else does it that way, or joining in the scapegoating of a child that others are ganging up on, as classic experiments have shown (Bond & Smith, 1996). The felt wish to be 'in' and belong starts early. Working out who is a stranger or who is safe is something that babies as young as 6 months do. A different part of our brains lights up when we look at a familiar face as opposed to a stranger, although interestingly this does not happen with autistic children (Dawson, Carver, Meltzoff, Panagiotides, McPartland, & Webb, 2002).

Group biases can be less than savoury. In a typical experiment in America white subjects were shown both black and white faces for 30 milliseconds, too short a time for the conscious mind to register. When shown black faces, scans revealed that there was heightened amygdala response, suggesting a nonconscious fear reaction. When the pictures were then shown for long enough to register consciously what they were seeing, the scans showed activation in brain areas involved with conflict resolution (Cunningham, Johnson, Raye, Gatenby, Gore, & Banaji, 2004), suggesting that the subjects now were grappling with their own racism. Our biases are nonconscious and implicit, generally develop early in childhood (Baron & Banaji, 2006), and play a powerful role in terms of how we defines ourselves.

Learning to fit in has profound social consequences for children. Whether we are accepted or rejected by one's peer group in childhood and adolescence predicts aspects of social adjustment right into adulthood (Bagwell, Newcomb, & Bukowski, 1998). Children adjust their natural temperaments to gain peer acceptance. Children are born with particular temperaments, such as of shyness or extroversion, and such temperamental predispositions remain fairly constant until about 6 years old. At this age children begin to adjust their tendencies, and for example timid boys become less shy and more outgoing, presumably because timid boys might suffer socially (Kerr, 2001). Middle childhood is an age when such social adaptation develops apace, and when influences outside the family become more important.

Peers: are they most important?

Judy Rich Harris' (2009) argument, that parents have little influence on their children, may not hold up fully under the weight of evidence, but her theories demand that we rethink the relative balance of influences. Important environmental influences include the impact of other children and adults, as well as the communities children live in. Seeing a child's environment as synonymous with their mother is a notion that puts tremendous pressure, and blame on mothers, and ignores other central influences. The prototypical example that Harris describes is how children use language. Parents who are immigrants and speak little of the local language have children who soon pick up local expressions and dialects, not speaking in the often stilted way that first-generation immigrants are likely to. They learn how to speak like their peers, not like their parents.

Harris argues that what a child learns in one context, such as with parents, is not necessarily useable in other contexts. What is undoubtedly true in her argument is that children learn that different environments have different rules. What works at home does not necessarily work in school. She gives many persuasive examples such as that Polynesian children are raised to be subservient and modest with adults, but pushy and assertive with peers; having different rules for different contexts.

Parents understandably like to believe that their attitudes have the biggest influence on a child's views, but Harris warns against this. Children tend to have similar attitudes about their studies to their peer group, and not only because children from similar backgrounds choose each other, or because parents facilitate certain kinds of friendships. In one study of children who switched peer groups, they then also changed their attitudes to study to fit in with their new peer groups, and this affected their academic performance (Kindermann, 1993). As Harris points out, neither their IQs nor their parents had changed, only their peers. Harris admits that parents can make a difference by influencing a child's peer group, such as by ensuring they live in certain neighbourhoods or go to certain clubs. Children want to be like the children they associate with, and adopt their attitudes, dress code, and behavioural styles. The logic of this argument leads to the theory that children, particularly by the time they reach middle childhood, are aiming to be like peers rather than parents.

Children learn to speak the dialect of their peers, rather than their parents, as well as taking on their social nuances, and these are often important survival strategies enabling a child to fit in. Similarly, children quickly learn how to use the technology that their parents did not even have when young, and they learn from each other, whether this is computers or mobile phones. Harris described how a young macaque monkey on a Japanese island chanced upon a way to separate out grains of wheat from grains of sand by throwing the grains into water and seeing what floated. Soon all the other young monkeys were doing this, but not the older ones (2009, p. 202). It makes evolutionary sense that the young must learn from each other, not just from their parents, if they are to 'stay ahead of the game'.

Thus much social learning in middle childhood is from peers, which is why parents so often worry about bad influences on their children. There is increasing evidence that effective interventions for youth at risk of criminal behaviour work best when they address the peer group (Henggeler, Schoemwald, Borduin, Rowland, & Cunningham, 2009). When boys are moved away from such peer groups then crime and behavioural difficulties diminish (Youngblade & Curry, 2006). The neighbourhood they live in, and the young people they associate with, are very influential. Young African–Americans living in inner-city areas have a higher than average tendency to get involved in youth crime. Yet children whose background seemed almost the same, in terms of race, socioeconomic status, and family constellations, were less likely to be aggressive when living in more middle-class areas; adapting their behaviour in part, to neighbourhood norms (Wikström, 2000).

In some research on gender and sociocultural influences, Hopi Indian and African–American girls were playing dodgeball competitively. Then some boys came on the scene and joined in and the girls became less competitive, standing around or joking more (Weisfeld, Weisfeld, & Callaghan, 1982). These girls changed their behaviours according to cultural sanctions about gender roles and it has also been found that girls can perform on average better in subjects such as maths and science in single-sex schools, where it is not seen as unfeminine to succeed in them (Steele, 1997).

The effect of peer group experiences can last right into adulthood. For example, maybe surprisingly taller men generally tend to have higher status, hold more leadership positions, and are even more successful in job interviews than their shorter counterparts. Yet it is not their height as adults that has this effect. Some children were small in childhood but later in adulthood caught up with those peers who had matured earlier. Nonetheless, they never caught up in terms of status. Adult status and confidence was linked more to relative status in adolescence, which in turn was linked to height in adolescence. Males who were smaller than others in adolescence when their peer group status was being worked out, kept their lower status despite catching up with their adult peers in height (Hall, 2006).

Thus early group learning can last, and timing of influences is all important. Some Japanese children were transplanted to California (Minoura, 1992). Their parents ensured that the culture in the family home retained its traditional Japanese style, as they were intending to return and wanted their children to manage the transition back. Yet if the children stayed too long, they became completely assimilated to the local culture and struggled to re-adjust on their return. If children had not returned by the age of about 12 or 13 they struggled much more, whereas the younger ones remained more malleable and could still adjust more easily. This makes sense in part because the period of middle childhood is such an important time for social learning from peers and the wider culture more than just from parents.

Peers, parents, and attachment

Despite the arguments of Harris and others, the role of earlier relationships should not be underestimated. How children relate to their peers is influenced by previous relationships. Dunn and others described how infants and toddlers in ordinary nonabusing homes show concern and empathy for other children in distress. Main and George (1985) studied toddlers from less advantaged backgrounds, some of whom had been abused and others who had not. Although their sample was small, they found that not a single abused toddler showed concern or sympathy for another child in distress, whereas over half the nonabused sample did. Nearly all of the abused toddlers responded with aggression or anger to children crying. Typically, they described one toddler as making a 'ferocious, threatening face at another toddler in distress with whom she had had no recorded previous interactions' (p. 409). They linked the ability to show concern for others to having had relatively nurturing experiences at home. These young toddlers seemed to already be part of an intergenerational cycle, whereby such experiences are passed on to others. These children were aggressive to caregivers in the daycentre, and avoidant of adults and peers who made friendly approaches. Children with a disorganised attachment categorisation, who have been subjected to frightening and inconsistent parenting, are very likely to show all kinds of difficulties with peers when they reach school age (Lyons-Ruth, Yellin, Melnick, & Atwood, 2003). Disorganised attachment predicts both violent and controlling behaviour in school-age children and is the best predictor of hostile relationships in pre-school. Children who are hostile at a young age with peers often come from backgrounds of severe psychosocial deprivation, again illustrating the influence of home life.

The converse is also true and securely attached children tend to be more socially competent and popular with peers in pre-school (Dunn, 2004). By school age securely attached children are better liked than their insecurely attached peers who in turn are perceived as more aggressive. Children with ambivalent attachments are more prone in general to being victimised and having social difficulties. Attachment theorists (Sroufe, 2005) argue that social skills learnt at home through attuned reciprocal social interactions translate into better capacities for peer relationships. Children develop representations of themselves in relationship to others that become templates for future relationships. This suggests that Harris might not be right that learning from one context is not taken into new situations. Children who are rejected at home have been found to attribute hostile or malevolent intentions to peers, whether known or relative strangers; their prior expectations being transferred onto new relationships.

A big question is whether such early effects last into later childhood or adulthood or 'wash out'. The longitudinal attachment studies by Sroufe in Minnesota and the Grossmans in Germany suggested that young children with secure attachments to either parent were more likely to develop high-quality friendships as they got older (Grossmann et al., 2005), and that secure attachment predicts later social competence, and participation in reciprocal friendships (Sroufe, 2005).

Mothers who are demanding, or show aggressive behaviours, often have children who struggle to get on with other children. Such children often interact with peers in ways that are similar to how their mothers interact with other adults, presumably learning directly from their parents (Putallaz & Sheppard, 1992). Coercive parent–child relationships are associated with children who are more aggressive towards peers, and maybe not surprisingly, when parents are more controlling or intrusive then their children have more friendship difficulties (Dodge, Bates, & Pettit, 1990). On the other hand, maternal overprotectiveness increases the likelihood of being victimised at school, especially for boys (Finnegan, Hodges, & Perry, 1998).

Children who are socially competent tend to have mothers who display more positive emotions, and respond thoughtfully to feelings. Considerable matching has been found between a child's interactions with both parents and peers, showing similar proportions of taking turns, and forms of expression (Black & Logan, 1995). Where parents were more responsive to children, the children were more responsive to their peers, and similarly where parents were closer to their children then these children were more prosocial and empathic towards peers and had better friendships.

It is clear that what happens at home has a big impact on how children function in other relationships. Not surprisingly the more stressors a child experiences in the home the worse their peer relationships (Bolger, Patterson, Thompson, & Kupersmidt,

1995). Harris (2009) still makes an important point in that children who pick out and interact with unpopular children with few social skills then cannot model themselves on more competent peers, and worrying behaviours can be reinforced by peer groups. Yet early relationships in their own right influence how children relate to peers.

Emotionally abused and maltreated children often struggle to form good relationships, sometimes being shunned or attacked by other children. The research has also been done the other way around, and found that boys who were aggressive in school tended to have backgrounds that included abuse and violence (Schwartz, Dodge, Pettit, & Bates, 1997).

It is easy to see why this might happen. Popular children seem more able to be accepting of interactions initiated by others, and respond in an appropriately contingent way. When they receive an initiation that is unwelcome they will often offer an alternative possibility rather than just being rejecting. These tend to be the same children who are able to play well in a social and imaginative way. Popular children are by no means all sweetness and light, and most studies show that they know how to be aggressive, assertive and at times quite nasty, alongside the ability to be socially attuned and prosocial (e.g., Cillessen & Rose, 2005). On the other hand unpopular children tend to be more unremittingly controlling, bossy and contrary (Hay, Payne, & Chadwick, 2004). Children do learn from each other, but who they interact and learn with, and how they do this, is also very much related to their family relationships.

Temperament

Some research has suggested that a child's temperament accounts for much of the difference in how children get on with other children. Children who are more positive, and have a milder temperament, do get on better with peers. Children who are more emotionally labile and struggle to regulate emotions have worse peer relationships, although this can be moderated by parenting style and cultural influences (Russell, Hart, Robinson, & Folsen, 2003). So a child's temperament might influence how they respond to others, and also how they are responded to by parents or peers. Children with aggressive temperaments will elicit different reactions to children who have easygoing temperaments, and these will in turn evoke different reactions to shy and anxious children. Genes and environment interact in multifaceted ways. Some very recent research is suggesting that popularity and where one positions oneself in social networks has some definite genetic components (Fowler, Dawes, & Christakis, 2009). Yet it is never simply a case of either genes or environment. A toddler may have temperamentally worse capacities for emotional regulation, but when combined with insensitive parenting then some, especially boys, become more aggressive (Rubin, Burgess, Dwyer, & Hastings, 2003). Similarly children will often find a niche for themselves in a family or peer group that suits their temperament, yet the roles that they take on might then be socially reinforced by interactions with others around them, so that nurture reinforces temperament.

Children who are distractible, low in mood, and easily aroused tend to be less popular than the norm (Walker, Berthelsen, & Irving, 2001). Very active children engage less in interpersonal or pretend play than other children and research with American schoolchildren has shown that high activity can lead to popularity in boys but not in girls, who often favour less active peers (Gleason, Gower, Hohmann, & Gleason, 2005). High levels of emotional expression and poor emotional regulation has an adverse affect on peer relationships and there seems little doubt both that temperament has an impact on a child's capacity for peer relations, but also that this is moderated by factors such as parental input. Children with different temperaments elicit different kinds of parenting, and while inconsistent discipline might increase negative emotionality in children, children's irritability can evoke inconsistent parenting in its own right (Lengua & Kovacs, 2005).

Intervention studies show that social influences and not just genetic destiny has an effect (Ladd, 2005, p. 338). Interventions that aim to increase children's social competencies and inhibit acting out behaviours result in improved peer relationships, and more acceptance by other children. The same changes are not seen in the untreated, control groups, suggesting that social competencies are at least partly learnt and not just due to temperament. Such studies suggest that real change is possible, that some forms of help can lessen the likelihood of children becoming victims, can end cycles of bullying and give hope that, despite a child's temperamental endowment, they are not condemned to a particular model of interacting with others.

Summary

This chapter has focused on the importance of children's relationships with other children and looked at the natural human propensity to be influenced by the group that they identify with. The research shows that peer relationships are very important for children's development, particularly during middle childhood, when many social skills are being developed. As Harris stressed, family influences are not everything, and for example there is no reason to think that two siblings brought up in the same family should turn out the same. As well as genes and temperament playing a role, children find their own particular niche in a family. There is less incentive to be the family joker, for example, if another child already has that role. A child's temperament might cause a parent to act differently rather than just the other way around. Harris turns the traditional idea on its head, suggesting that rather than good parenting producing good children, good children also produce good parenting. What researchers like Dunn and Harris are showing is that parents can neither take all the blame nor all the credit. Relationships with siblings and peers, as well as temperament, should not be underestimated as central influences in how peer relationships develop.

There remains though a relationship between early attachment and peer relationships. There are significant links between early attachment and both middle-school peer relationships, and adolescent social competencies (Sroufe, 2005). The role of parents is shown to be increasingly important when parenting input at later stages in childhood, as well as early attachment is taken into account. Children who are socially incompetent are more likely to expect rejection, to act in ways that flout social norms, are less likely to see the world from another's point of view, and are also less likely to have fun with other children. As Ladd states 'a picture emerges of socially incompetent children as having thought patterns that motivated, justified and perpetuated behaviour that undermined the formation and maintenance of positive peer relationships' (2005, p. 331). In other words, some children expect and elicit a bad reaction from other children. The social competencies that develop in middle childhood have residues that can last right into adulthood. Ladd suggests that in the average Western classroom there will be two or three children with no friends, a similar number with at least one enemy, between three and seven being rejected by classmates, and between three and five actually being victimised. For this reason interventions that facilitate a child's ability to appropriately interact with peers can be vital.

The research about the impact of parenting challenges the views of others, such as Judy Rich Harris, who have argued that parents are not that important, and children are mainly influenced by other children or by genes. Harris' thesis helps to shift the focus away from mother–child interactions and take seriously how children learn from each other as well as parents, and that humans have a propensity to be influenced by groups and those who surround them. It makes complete sense that children will learn from peers and siblings, and others apart from their parents. The ability of new generations to adapt and change would be hindered if children gained all their understanding only from earlier generations. Children's development cannot be understood without taking into account parental, peer, and a range of sociocultural influences.

Chapter 15

The place of fathers

Like other subjects, questions about the role of fathers can stir up controversy. Most readers will have a view about what a father should or should not do. Some people argue that children should be brought up in heterosexual marriages, others that fathers should do much more for their children, while still others think fathers are becomingly increasingly irrelevant. The role of fathers has undergone shifts in the West alongside demographic changes such as more babies being born outside marriage (Stevenson & Wolfers, 2007), higher divorce rates, and more children living in 'blended' families, as well as more women working, full or part time. This has all impacted on paternal roles. A recent study by the Equal Opportunities Commission in Britain looked at nearly 20,000 children born at the turn of the twenty-first century (Dex & Ward, 2007). It suggested that in Britain the old idea of stay-at-home mothers and working fathers was true in less than 30 per cent of families. The most common pattern in Britain (35 per cent) now is of a full-time working father and a mother working part time, whilst in 11 per cent of cases both parents work full time. In the West generally fathers have become more involved with their children in recent decades, although the bulk of childcare still falls to mothers (Lamb, 2004).

This chapter looks primarily at father's involvement with, and effect on, their children. As Lamb suggests, fathering can constitute a variety of tasks in contemporary societies, such as moral overseer, breadwinner, gender role model, and father as nurturant/participant parent. Societies have been organised in a huge variety of ways, and fathers have played a vast array of roles and there is no 'natural' paternal role in any idyllic past to use as an ideal. Thus, although many of us might ask what makes a good father, to answer this presupposes a theory of what a father is, or is supposed to do, that is distinctive.

What a father is and does varies enormously from society to society and epoch to epoch. Anthropological studies suggest that as nomadic existences shifted into settled pastoral life, and then into moneyed wage-earning economies, fathers became more absent from the day-to-day care of children. Yet even in Western Europe men's participation in childcare differs widely. Swedish men, with the longest paternity leave, are the most involved with their children, considerably more so than British fathers, for example, who in turn contribute more than fathers from other European countries (Smith & Williams, 2007).

The greatest known involvement of fathers is seen in the Aka forager communities in Central Africa. Here a father is holding or within arm's reach of an infant for about half of a 24-hour period, is near the baby 88 per cent of their waking time and holding an infant for about a quarter of the time (Hewlett, 1991). An Aka father is expected to be physically affectionate to his child, and very supportive of the mother, and Aka males can slip into more traditionally female roles with no loss of status.

The opposite extreme is families with little male presence. In America the proportion of female-headed households quadrupled between 1960 and 1990 (McLaughlin, Gardner, & Lichter, 1999). The highest rates of female-headed families are seen in African countries, with Botswana topping the bill with nearly half headed by women (Flouri, 2005), and interestingly in Botswana, with their strong matrilineages, it is often the mother's brother who becomes the important male in a child's life. Ways of conceptualising masculinity and femininity, or fathers and mothers, that are accepted currency in one culture do not necessarily have universal significance.

Given the cultural and historical variations, it is not possible to say what a father's role is or should be but it is possible to look at the effects of different kinds of fathering, and of the presence or absence of fathers. Much psychological thinking, such as in psychoanalysis, has emphasised the role of the father in helping to separate symbiotically bonded mother–infant pairs, and also in providing support or 'holding' for the mother so that she can in turn emotionally support the baby. It is clear that a father's emotional support to a mother can enhance a child's care, even when the father is less directly involved in that care (McHale & Fivaz-Depeursinge, 1999), although support for mothers does not only come from fathers. The importance of fathers in supporting mothers is less relevant for those living in different constellations, such as when there are lesbian parents, or in matrilineages where biological fathers live away from children and maternal relatives play the supporting role. Research on Western populations shows that father involvement is often associated with some good outcomes (Flouri, 2005), but like much research cited in this book, research about fathers is increasingly complex and multidimensional, which means there are no easy answers, or even easy questions, about whether having a father present is a good thing or not for a child.

Biological priming

A widely held view is that looking after children is 'naturally' done by mothers, and it is worth asking whether there is any truth in this idea. After all, in nearly all known societies mothers do the bulk of the childcare. Hrdy notes (1999, p. 109) that females are more primed in most species to respond to infants, both in terms of neurocircuitry and hormonal predispositions, whereas males in most species remain more aloof from infants. Yet males, even in the least nurturing species, like patriarchal hamadryas baboons or languors, can be induced to care for infants, and there is an unanswered question about why male parenting does not happen more. Hrdy suggests that biological differences are nowhere near as great as the childcare gender divide that has occurred in humans. Rather she thinks that slight biological predispositions, due maybe to factors like hormonal systems or the ability to breastfeed, might turn into ongoing expectations and social rules through parents taking the line of least resistance, much like water tends to run down the same rivulets, thereby increasing the likelihood of water taking this route in the future.

In fact most evidence suggests that fathers are biologically no less sensitive potentially to infant signals than mothers. Given the right circumstances they interact and imitate in much the same way as mothers (Lamb, 2004), are equally able to identify their children by touch as mothers when blindfolded and not able to use smell (Bader & Phillips, 1999), and have been shown to be as sensitive as mothers in feeding, allowing appropriate pauses and recovery time. Comparing how securely attached children related to their mothers and fathers, it appears that there is not a very clear difference (Day, Lewis, O'Brien, & Lamb, 2005). This kind of research does not show that fathers do anything unique. In research in Western samples fathers relate to their children with more physical stimulation and by being more playful, but there is no evidence that this is a biological given, and for example the Aka fathers mentioned above, who spend more time with their children, indulge in less of this kind of active play than Western fathers.

Cultural ideals contribute fundamentally to paternal practices. The Kipsigis of East Africa do not feed, dress or carry infants for about 4 years and believe that infants can be damaged by their masculine gaze (Hewlett & Lamb, 2005). It is likely that it is attitudes, female as well as male, that play a role in the lack of paternal input into families in the West. In the British childcare study led by Penelope Leach mentioned in Chapter 13, 1200 mothers were asked soon after their first child's birth what their ideal childcare arrangement would be, if money and other factors were not an issue. Fathers were right at the bottom of the list, the preferred choice of only 1 in 200 mothers, scoring 8 times less than the next worst choice, childminders (Barnes, Leach, Sylva, Stein, & Malmberg, 2006). In reality by 18 months nearly 8 per cent of the children were being looked after primarily by their fathers. This might be an example of the quite mixed feelings members of either gender might have about the other gender taking on roles that are less traditional.

Males in many species may tend to be less nurturing of infants, but retain a predisposition to become nurturing if given the right triggers. Many men who seem reluctant to become parents can become adoring fathers the moment a child is born. This has a biological root. In human and other primate males prolactin levels rise when males care for offspring (Ziegler, 2000). Prolactin elicits protective feelings, and cohabiting males have higher prolactin levels during their partner's pregnancies. Once so primed, males are likely to respond in a more nurturing way with subsequent infants. Men living with pregnant wives, as well as having higher prolactin levels, also have considerably lower testosterone levels after birth, suggesting a biological tendency to become more protective and less sexually active (Storey et al., 2000).

One obvious disincentive for male participation in childcare is that until the recent advent of genetic testing fathers could never be 100 per cent certain of paternity. Hrdy (1999) shows that paternal care across species increases the more certainty there is about paternity. For example, male dunnocks (sparrow-like birds) provide food to infants more or less in proportion to how frequently they copulated with the mother, and male baboons similarly tend to help children of polyandrous females more if they think paternity is theirs. Males are biologically capable of having many more children than females who tend on average to invest more in each one. Analysis of the human genome shows that in evolutionary history males are more likely to have had multiple partners than females, and a higher proportion of men than women have had children with more than one partner, but also a higher proportion of men than woman have not been successful at having any children at all (Hammer, Mendez, Cox, Woerner, & Wall, 2008).

From the studies we have, we can say that infants generally fare better with paternal support. Hrdy and others have even shown that in many societies having children with more than one male is a way of eliciting useful extra help. Particularly in an environment where male life expectancy is low, this increases the chances of children being provided for and protected. This is even enshrined in the belief systems of some societies. The Canela, a matrilineal Brazilian tribe, not only sanction women having intercourse with more than one man but are seen as selfish if they do not do so (Crocker & Crocker, 1994). This society has a belief in what is called 'partible paternity', or in other words a child can have several fathers. In some variants it is even believed that more than one man's sperm is needed for a foetus to grow properly. Partible paternity confers advantages on children in many societies. For the Bari people of Venezuela those who had a primary and secondary father, have survival rates in late adolescence that are considerably higher than those with only one father (Beckerman et al., 1998). Pregnant Bari women accept sexual advances from higher-status males, such as successful fishermen, giving themselves and their children a better chance of flourishing. We might speculate that such practices are less necessary in Western monogamous cultures where males live longer.

Children with a father and a mother

From studies of American and European samples we have learnt a lot about the effect of a father's presence in children's lives. A major British study followed all children born on one day in 1958 (Flouri, 2005), and asked how much fathers were involved with their children at 7, 11, and 16 years old. The study asked straightforward questions such as how often did a father take a child on an outing, or read to them. It found that fathers were more involved with their children when mothers were also highly involved and when the quality of the parents' relationship was better. Social factors also strongly influenced behaviours, and there was less father involvement, and more behavioural problems, where families were of low socioeconomic status.

Analysis of the research by Flouri and others suggests that father involvement is protective. The children of fathers who were not living with them were more likely to have ADHD and conduct problems. The presence of a father is also linked to a child's sense of happiness, and to less likelihood of antisocial behaviour. Many of these effects are lasting, and for example Flouri shows that early father involvement predicts educational attainment in adult life for both genders. Where the couple relationship is stronger, fathers tend to be more committed to their children (Waller & Swisher, 2006). Indeed, one research study showed that children benefit more from parents working on their couple relationship in counselling than from receiving direct parenting skills trainings (Cowan & Cowan, 2003). Having a better parental relationship seems to pay dividends for a child's later development.

Having more father involvement is not necessarily a good thing though, as different fathers have different effects. Fathers as well as mothers have a propensity for postnatal depression (Ramchandani, Stein, Evans, O'Connor, & ALSPAC Study Team, 2005), which is seen in as many as 10 per cent of new fathers, although this differs from country to country (Madsen & Juhl, 2007). The children of depressed fathers show emotional and behavioural difficulties such as hyperactivity at $3\frac{1}{2}$ years of age; affecting boys more than girls. This is just one example of how we have to be careful about suggesting that fathers in general are either a good or bad thing, without looking more closely at what kind of fathers. Depression diminishes a father's ability to be empathic and attuned with their child, and to manage a harmonious relationship with the other parent.

One interesting study looked at the effect of having a father who indulged in antisocial behaviour (Jaffee, Moffitt, Caspi, & Taylor, 2003). Fathers with antisocial tendencies were less likely to be highly involved with their infants, to be living at home with them, or to have married the mother. Striking a blow against the idea that two-parent families are always best, when antisocial fathers were living at home then the children were much more likely to show behavioural difficulties than if such fathers were absent. Some but not all fathers foster children's development. Fathers who are aggressive and violent to their partners are also often not good for children (Sternberg, 1997).

Generally when fathers are nurturing, playful and encouraging, advantages are conferred. Children starting school with such fathers on average have higher IQs, better vocabulary and cognitive skills, and more readiness to manage the demands of a school environment. This can pay dividends right up until adolescence, where such children gain higher grades and achieve better overall. Cognitive and emotional developments are finely interlinked. Children achieve better academically when they feel good about themselves, and nurturing active parenting, including fathering, helps to achieve this. Children from a loving home who feel attuned to, encouraged, and understood tend to be more confident and have fewer mental health or behavioural problems (Yeung, Duncan, & Hill, 2000). Children whose fathers are highly involved are less likely to suffer from depression or anxiety, to get involved in drugs or delinquent behaviour, are more likely to have high self-esteem, and do much better on most scores (Dubowitz et al., 2001).

Such better outcomes occur when the fathers actively choose to be more involved. Just spending time with a child need not necessarily confer the same advantages. This is particularly the case when fathers are involved by default rather than choice, such as when they become unemployed and the mothers become the main breadwinner, and in such cases children do not tend to do so well (O'Brien, Commission, & Britain, 2005). Similarly, father involvement increases when mothers encourage this, and mothers have been found to often be gatekeepers of paternal involvement (Schoppe-Sullivan, Brown, Cannon, Mangelsdorf, & Sokolowski, 2008). When both parties actively value the closeness in the parental relationship and coparenting, then all seem to reap rewards, but if there is resentment, such as unwilling childcare by fathers, or unwilling labour by mothers, then this is likely to create a less harmonious family atmosphere.

Children seem to benefit most from authoritative parenting (e.g., Simons & Conger, 2007), which includes dimensions of being caring and accepting, showing appropriate discipline, and fostering autonomy. Although in many families such tasks can be divided according to gender stereotypes, with fathers dispensing the discipline and playfulness, the research does not suggest that this is in any way inevitable, or that fathers necessarily do anything unique that mothers or other adults cannot do. What it does suggest, as stated throughout this book, is that good relationships, empathy, nurturing, and playfulness, among other things, breed happier children who feel more confident, secure, and held in mind.

Children with no biological father present: single mothers, lesbian parents, and step-fathers

One way of working out how important biological fathers are is to see what happens when they are not around, such as with children brought up by single mothers, lesbian couples, or step-fathers. Most data suggests that children do worse when they are brought up by lone parents. They often achieve less educationally, and are more likely to have behavioural and emotional difficulties. On the face of it sole parenthood looks like a major disadvantage. One American study found that 3-year-olds of single parents were more likely than children in two-parent relationships to have lower social and cognitive skills, more behavioural issues, worse relationships with adults, and a greater likelihood of insecure attachment (Clarke-Stewart & Dunn, 2006).

There is plenty of similar research that can be used by those opposed to single-parenthood. However, extreme caution is necessary in interpreting these findings. Economic and social factors make a huge difference, and are likely to exercise more influence on child outcomes than whether a father is present. Single parents often come from lower socioeconomic groups, have many social disadvantages, and are more likely to be socially excluded. For example, children from single-parent households have lower attendance at college *except* when family income was taken into account as a factor (Huang, Garfinkel, & Waldfogel, 2000). Research suggests that it might well be poverty and lack of support, rather than single-parenthood, which has the main effect on the poor outcomes for such children.

In such studies, when factors such as income and social disadvantage are screened out, the differences between the children of single parents and two-parent families tend to almost disappear (Spencer, 2005). Financial difficulties are often compounded by the stresses of bringing up a child with little or no other adult support, something which, even without the economic disadvantages, is likely to lead to less ability to parent with both authority and sensitivity. This can often be further affected by mental health issues such as depression, which are more prevalent in single mothers, and this again can be affected by economic circumstances. Overall the research suggests that it is income and social position rather than single-parenthood, which we should most worry about as risk factors for children. A 15-year-old, single mother living in a deprived inner-city community is likely to fare far worse than a middle-class, wealthy single-parent living in an affluent area with social support.

Longitudinal research comparing children brought up in female-headed households (i.e. lesbian or single parents) with children brought up in heterosexual couples has found that as they enter adulthood the children of female-headed households were functioning emotionally as well if not better than their counterparts on all scores (Golombok & Badger, 2010). The clear finding was that neither sexual orientation, nor the absence of a father, had negative consequences for the children's development at 20 years of age for either boys or girls. Children of lesbian and heterosexual couples show more similarities than differences. A large-scale research study (Patterson & Wainright, 2007) has found that there was no effect on overall emotional adjustment, school outcomes, substance use, family and peer relations from living in a lesbian-headed household. The differences in adolescent functioning were not as a result of family type (i.e. lesbian, heterosexual couples, or single parents) but rather were related to overall emotional functioning in the families. In general it would appear that growing up in a female-headed household is not a risk factor.

However, children living with a step-father and their mother, compared with those living with a biological father, on average have worse outcomes, including lower academic achievements, more criminal behaviour, substance misuse, and teenage pregnancy (Hofferth & Anderson, 2003). This might partly be explained by the likelihood of children in 'reconstituted' families having already often lived in less harmonious circumstances, and suffering dislocations. But also step-parents have been consistently shown in the research to be on average less warm and nurturing, and less likely to become attached to their step-children (Pryor & Rodgers, 2001). A strong hypothesis is that parents invest more in genetic children. More extreme and worrying, bodies of research have shown that child abuse, violence and even child murder is more common when living with a step-father (Daly & Wilson, 1999). Yet of course many children do extremely well in step-families (Ganong & Coleman, 2003), especially when the new relationship is close and stable, and where there is more cohesion and family bonding. Thus reporting such research must avoid the danger of type-casting step-fathers.

Studies suggest that not having a biological father present can be a disadvantage in some, but by no means in all cases. Children of lesbian couples seem to do as well as children in heterosexual couples. Children brought up by single mothers do seem on average to be handicapped, but economic and social pressures are as much the cause of this as the lack of a father. Children brought up in 'blended' families with step-fathers are more likely to do worse, but once again this depends very much on the particular step-father and the state of the adult relationship.

Practical lessons from research on fathers

Given that so little can be said about what a father 'naturally' is or should be, it might seem hard to use the evidence available to think about what practices might seem preferable, at least in Western cultural contexts. In so-called 'high-risk' groups parenting interventions are increasingly used in which specific paternal roles are encouraged that could be construed as supporting gender stereotypes, such as 'father as disciplinarian'. Much therapeutic literature, such as in some psychoanalytic thinking, defines the paternal role as one which provides an outside perspective or 'third position', a view which fits well with the widespread conception of the father as 'outside' the mother–child relationship, representing the external world (Music, 2004). Fathers in much of both the research and parenting literature are often encouraged to act in such traditional roles, as provider, as a bridge into the wider world, encouraging autonomy, and also providing discipline. Research does not show that fathers are any better at these tasks than mothers, but it certainly seems that when such ideas are put into practice as interventions to help families then the outcomes are often good.

It is also clear that many parenting interventions are more effective when fathers participate (Bakermans-Kranenburg, van IJzendoorn, & Juffer, 2003). One consistent finding that is maybe not surprising is that a positive relationship between fathers and mothers helps children, and interventions which help the couple relationship also help the children (Cowan, Cowan, Pruett, Pruett, & Wong, 2009). Thoughtfulness and respect in a couple can be modelled and passed on to the next generation, just as violence, hatred, and disrespect can also be transmitted. Fathers who are negative, critical, who withdraw or attack too quickly, have been shown to have a negative effect on family life (Almeida, Wethington, & McDonald, 2001).

Consistent with the themes of this book, children do better in relationships with others such as peers when they have had good relationships at home, and fathers can be important in this respect. When fathers spend time with children in a playful and enjoyable way this can build bonds and enhance good feelings, and indeed also make fathers more sensitive to a child's needs. Furthermore fathers who are able to remain calm under pressure, manage children's upset and remain supportive and nurturing, are likely to have children who are more popular in school, with boys being less aggressive and girls getting on better with peers (Parke et al., 2002). Children whose fathers are not very involved with them have a greater likelihood of problems such as poor educational performance, delinquency in adolescent boys, and teenage pregnancy in girls (Flouri, 2005). In other societies the disadvantages can be more extreme, and as Hrdy (1999) points out, in hunter–gatherer societies children without fathers are more likely to die.

It was once thought that infant–mother attachment was all important, but increasingly it has become clear that a child's attachment to their father can be central too, sometimes having almost as much effect on the child's attachment status as the mother's. Children who have secure attachments with their fathers, for example, tend to show more empathy with other children in primary school (Biller, 1993). A secure attachment with a father can offset an insecure one with a mother and vice versa, and of course best of all is having a secure attachment to both. The characteristics of fathers who have securely attached children are seemingly very similar to those of mothers of securely attached children. They tend to be more agreeable and outgoing, and to have more stable and better functioning marriages and more satisfaction at work (Belsky, 1996). In other words, maybe not surprisingly, men who manage the challenges of their relationships and working life with more ease, tend to have more securely attached children.

Ultimately what counts is a father being there for their children in the context of harmonious relationships. A father's influence does not just magically rub off, but depends on actual interaction with his children, and whatever the father's character traits, they are unlikely to influence a child if he rarely sees them. Fathers in two-parent families, who are present in their children's lives, add more benefits the more they put in. One early study showed that when both parents visited their child's school, as opposed to only the mother, the children's reading and maths scores were up to 7 months ahead (Lambert & Hart, 1976). When neither parent visited their children were on average 13 months behind, although of course there might be other explanations for this as well. When fathers have more warm contact with their children then their children do better, even if 'doing better' can have different meanings in different times and cultures. I mentioned previously (Chapter 1, p. 5) the research from the 1950s that suggested that involved fathers tended to have sons who were more 'masculine', in American studies at least. At the time it was thought that this was a father's central influence. Contemporary studies suggest that involved fathers lead to happier and more fulfilled sons, but sons who are often more sensitive than their more masculine forerunners from the 1950s and 1960s (Lamb, 2004). Children want to be like the people they admire, whatever the current cultural ideal, whether the admired fathers are warm and involved or more distant and 'macho'.

Some children are brought up only by their fathers and research with these relatively small samples is showing that they tend to do very well (Pruett, 2000), and one might surmise that given the cultural expectations, these fathers were likely to be particularly committed. They had stable gender identifications, good friendships with children of the opposite gender, and were active and curious. Such parenting practices challenge gender stereotypes, and are becoming increasingly common in Europe and America.

Summary

What it means to be a father varies hugely over historical periods and across different kinds of social organisation, from the most involved fathers, such as Aka foragers, to matrilineal cultures where biological fathers play very little part in parenting. In recent decades in the West there have been major demographic changes that have influenced the roles of men, and so also of fathers. Fathering in the West has over time undergone changes, from the strict patriarch to the distant wage-earner to more involved dads. Fathers, it seems, these days in the West are more involved with their children than they were in the past (Lamb, 2004), although despite the hopes of a gender or sexual revolution, in fact mothers continue to do the bulk of parenting and other work in the home (Craig, 2006). How much change there really has been, and how much such change is really wanted by both parties, is uncertain.

Most research has looked at the effects of a father's presence or absence, and generally shows that the presence of a father benefits children. There are of course exceptions, such as antisocial fathers. Lamb (2004) argues, having perused thousands of studies, that it is less clear whether there is anything a father can provide that mothers cannot, and vice versa, even if there are clear tendencies for fathers and mothers to do different things.

Certain behaviours are more typical in fathers than mothers in Western research samples. Fathers tend, for example, to use humour more or to indulge in more rough-and-tumble play which provides measurable benefits. In such studies fathers are more likely to treat their sons and daughters differently to mothers, being more likely to encourage their sons' autonomy and individuality, being more disciplinary and directive with boys, and more reactive to any signs of atypical gender behaviours.

We live in a society where a stable parental relationship and the presence of more than one caring adult in the home can confer advantages on children. It might suit the way Western society is currently organised, around the nuclear family as a unit of consumption, for children to be brought up in such groupings, but there is nothing 'god-given' or natural about such arrangements, and in other societies this is not the case. The research clearly suggests that being parented without a father need not be a disadvantage to children. There are too many different ideas about what a father should be to argue that one way is any better than another. Monogamy might be highly valued in the West, whereas ideas about partible paternity might suit other societies, and in some cultures females actively prefer to be in a polygamous relationship with a high-status man, over being in a monogamous relationship with a man with no access to resources.

I have tried to steer clear of the complex moral issues that inevitably arise in relation to fathers, marriage, and relationships. Following the changes in Western cultural attitudes in recent years, many women have argued that men should do much more. Other surveys paint a different picture and suggest that while many men want to spend more time with their children, and many women would like to work more, it is also true that some women do not want fathers any more involved than they are, and that some women value the breadwinning functions of fathers above all else (Gutek & Gilliland, 2008). Maybe the main message again echoes that seen elsewhere in this book. Children benefit from good, loving, thoughtful relationships with their caregivers, ones that offer both nurturing and clear boundaries and a relatively harmonious and stimulating environment. Fathers can play a crucial role in this, and in most societies do this in a different way to mothers. However, fathers are not essential to this happening, and in some circumstances their presence can hinder rather than help children, such as when they exert a more malign influence. However, the research evidence overwhelmingly suggests that on average the presence of an active, nurturing father is likely to be beneficial to many aspects of a child's development.

Moving towards adulthood

Children are moving even further away from their parents as they move into adolescence, a time of huge and exciting developments. In this chapter I outline some of the main developmental challenges of this period and look at the extent of continuity with earlier experiences. Adolescence is sometimes seen as a transitional time, a stepping-stone between childhood and adulthood, a view which perhaps underestimates how important it is in its own right. It begins with a series of neuroendocrine changes towards the end of the first decade. From the first signs such as breast buds in girls and larger testes in boys, there is a cascade of development lasting well over a decade. Something akin to adolescence is seen in most primates and mammals. For example rodents and primates also engage in more peer-directed social interaction during the equivalent period (Sisk & Zehr, 2005), as well as increased risk taking and novelty seeking, and there is increased mortality in most species, including humans, during adolescence (Steinberg, 2007). Human adolescence is marked by major hormonal and brain changes, startling physical transformations, particularly into distinctive male and female bodies, new capacities for abstract thinking, the development of a conscious and autonomous identity, all of which set the stage for adult life by putting clear developmental capacities in place.

During adolescence one tends to see an abandonment of many attachment and dependency needs, although these may continue to exert more influence than most adolescents admit. Real changes take place that adults, in particular parents, are often slow to recognise, such as huge strides in cognitive, emotional, and social abilities, a push for developing independence, and the locus of identifications moving further away from family, towards peers.

It is often described as a period of emotional upheaval, G. Stanley Hall (1904, p. 306) as early as 1904 calling it a time of 'storm and stress'. However, it is parents who sometimes find adolescence more stressful than teenagers, and adolescents themselves can be less disconcerted by family disputes and arguments; which they see as simply part of life and learning (Holmes, Bond, & Byrne, 2008). Research has questioned Hall's idea that adolescence is always a painful and difficult time, but during adolescence the effects of childhood experiences can certainly come home to roost, with early stress, trauma, or family difficulties often leading to turbulent teenage years.

Some such as Margaret Mead (1943) have argued that adolescence is a more culturally specific than a universal phenomenon, and in some cultures adolescence is not generally a time of turmoil. A study of over 170 societies (Schlegel & Barry, 1991) showed that most cultures had a clearly defined period between childhood and adulthood, often with accompanying rites and rituals. For example the tribal Okiek of Kenya (Kratz, 1990) between 14 and 16 undergo various rituals including circumcision. They live secluded from adults of the opposite sex for up to 24 weeks, are painted with white clay and charcoal to appear wild, and esoteric knowledge is imparted to them by elders. Many societies have such processes through which youth become integrated into traditional roles and values. One of the best-known examples is the Native American Vision Quest, whereby boys of about 14 undergo a process that includes ritual purification and a sweat lodge (Foster & Little, 1987). Assisted by a medicine man, the adolescent partakes in prayers and chanting and then will be brought to an isolated place where he stays alone, and fasts, for about 4 days. Once there he awaits a vision, which will illustrate his future path in society.

Adolescence is both a social and biological phenomenon, is turned on by a rush of hormonal and other changes, but its form is also much influenced by cultural factors. The Nso of the Cameroons are considered adult by virtue of marriage and parenthood as young as 14 years old, whereas for them a 24-year-old childless person would be considered immature. Different rites, rituals, and expectations mark transitions into adulthood across the world. Even the timing of menarche varies across cultures, from 12 years old on average in middle-class city-dwelling Venezuelan girls to 18 for girls living in the Burundi Highlands of New Guinea. In Western Europe the average age for the onset of menarche dropped over the last century. Such changes are probably influenced by changes in diet and affluence, and some think that age of menarche has now stabilised in the West (Viner, 2002).

Adolescence is often divided into early (11–14) middle (14–17) and late (17+) phases, and many textbooks state that there are different developmental tasks at each age. For example, in early adolescence the primary task is often seen as developing autonomy from parents, leading to struggles over separations and reunions. In middle adolescence young people are said to be struggling with mastery and competence, and late adolescents to be working out issues of intimacy and closeness. While these can be useful working models reflecting common developmental processes, the 'tasks' of adolescence are conceptualised differently across cultures, social classes, and historical periods. For the same reasons it is hard to talk about 'adolescent states of mind' in a universal rather than culturally specific way.

A recent change in the West is that, while the timing of adolescence has shifted slightly earlier, the age when adulthood is 'taken on' has got later. People get married on average later in the West and adolescents are becoming part of the workforce later than previously, and more go into higher education. Thus a young person's biological readiness to both reproduce and become part of the adult world is increasingly out of kilter with what society expects. Arnett (2004) describes this as a new life stage he calls 'emerging adulthood', when many young people do not regard themselves as adults, but as only on the threshold of adult commitments.

There is no definite time that adolescence starts or stops. Puberty can be earlier or later and this has different causes and effects. It is usually earlier in girls, but it is possible that different patterns are seen in homosexual youth, with earlier puberty in gay male adolescents (Savin-Williams & Ream, 2006). Girls who reach puberty earlier often show many more signs of psychological distress, have more mental health problems, and generally are more at risk (Ge, Conger, & Elder, 1996b). Early puberty may be partly due to genetic factors, or exposure to chemicals, but also research shows the importance of psychobiological factors and that better interactions between family members, paternal presence, and good father–daughter interactions all lead to later puberty (Ellis & Essex, 2007). High stress levels early on in infancy are also linked to early pubertal development in girls, as is being adopted from abroad. Evolutionary theorists explain this in terms of a psychobiological push to reproduce earlier and more often when there is more stress and an expectation of a less safe world and a shorter lifespan. Of course purely physiological factors such as a very poor diet can lead to later puberty as well, and in one interesting Polish study both factors were observed and it was found that poverty led to later puberty, but this was sometimes counterbalanced by stress and father absence, which led to girls reaching menarche earlier (Hulanicka, 1999).

The adolescent brain

Adolescence is marked by massive brain development and hormonal upheaval. Not so long ago people believed that the brain was almost totally formed by the time children started school but in recent decades we have discovered that much brain development and reorganisation occurs in adolescence. These changes almost rival those of early childhood (Giedd et al., 1999). There is a major process of pruning, the loss of grey matter and an increase in **myelination**, the white wrapping around neurons leading to brain signals travelling about 100 times faster. The adolescent brain becomes more efficient, but also less adaptable, and new knowledge is not soaked up as effortlessly as in earlier childhood. Adolescents do not, for example, learn languages as easily as 5-year-olds. Pruning enables specialisation and honing of specific skills, in preparation for the adult life tasks they might be preparing to take on. Every society has different skills to prepare for, from hunting with spears, to pounding yam, to working on computers, to living in forests or arctic snow. Adolescence sees leaps in cognitive skills, working memory, and the ability to manage competing information, all aided by pruning and myelination.

The frontal lobes, central for what is often called executive functioning, are one of the last areas to develop fully, often not until the early 20s, even though there is a growth spurt in early teenagehood (Blakemore & Choudhury, 2006), while the limbic system, where risk and emotionally driven behaviour is rooted, is definitely 'online'. Not surprisingly impulsivity and pleasure seeking is often more intense than in other life stages. The parts of the brain to do with risk taking and rewards are generally much more active in adolescence, and for example light up when scanned, whereas the parts which are involved with more 'top-down' control and executive functioning are at a level more like a child (Hare, Tottenham, Galvan, Voss, Glover, & Casey, 2008).

The brain areas involved in social understanding are reorganising in adolescence. Teenagers need to negotiate complex relationships, which is essential if they are to find a place in peer groups. In some experiments adolescents, who had been given a pseudonym and were anonymous but who believed other unknown adolescents were witnessing them, had to answer questions about themselves. At those moments the parts of the brain involved with managing danger and distress lit up (Bronson & Merryman, 2009). How adolescents are thought about can be crucial to how they feel about themselves.

Adolescents often interpret social cues differently (Yurgelun-Todd & Killgore, 2006). When adults see strong facial signals such as fear, scans show that their prefrontal cortex normally fires. With adolescents it is generally the amygdala, that more primitive region to do with fight or flight responses. This maybe makes sense of why some teenagers over-react and erupt so quickly. They respond with amygdala-led and other subcortical reactivity rather than the as yet underdeveloped prefrontal cortex, which only in time will regulate emotionally reactive brain regions (Sowell, Trauner, Gamst, & Jernigan, 2002). One thesis is that the time lag between the onset of emotional reactivity and later prefrontal regulatory capacities has become more marked as puberty has shifted earlier, meaning that an earlier maturing body develops even further ahead of the immature adolescent brain.

In fearful and anxious adolescents the amygdala can become even more over-reactive and dysregulated (Thomas et al., 2001), and adolescents anyway show greater activity and vulnerability in their amygdala than adults. Anxious adolescents find screening out vicarious stimuli harder than less anxious young people. In one test some young people were given the task of labelling objects according to their colours. These objects had words written on them, and when the words were emotionally stimulating, like 'death', then adolescents at risk of anxiety disorders were especially likely to lose focus. Similarly when adolescents were asked to watch for a nonemotional cue in a picture which also contained anxiety-inducing images, then anxious adolescents did far worse than the nonanxious ones. Their attention was caught by angry faces, which to them signalled interpersonal threat, and they were less able to concentrate (Monk et al., 2006). Anxious and maltreated teenagers spot danger incredibly fast, seeing an angry face in the crowd much quicker than others (Pine et al., 2005). Those subjected to inconsistent care or trauma are likely to be more hypervigilant and less able to concentrate. Teenagers with still-maturing brain structures are driven more by immediate emotional stimulus and are generally more easily distracted than adults.

Yet impulsiveness and risk taking, often bemoaned by parents, open up important developmental possibilities. Adolescents need to move away from parental control and take risks. In many species one sees increased interactions with peers, risk taking and more fighting with parents. Increased novelty seeking and risk taking might be developmentally appropriate as adolescents need to try out who they are, and experiment to prepare to leave the safety of parents and make their own way.

The teenage brain is fast reconfiguring but also vulnerable, easily damaged, and the effects of adolescent experiences such as alcohol or drug use can be lasting (Crews, He, & Hodge, 2007). Teenagers who drink more than average, perhaps only two alcoholic drinks a day for 2 years, consistently recall less on memory tests. The effect of such alcohol use is seen on the hippocampus, which has a particular role in memory formation and retention, and is smaller in teenagers who drink. Adolescent rats, with similar hippocampi to humans, are also more affected by alcohol than adults, being less able to find their way through mazes. Teenage alcohol use also affects the frontal cortex and cerebellum as well as the hippocampus. Other drugs, and nicotine, can have an effect. The changing teenage brain is vulnerable and when teenagers smoke then more nicotine receptors develop, and remain in place. Other recreational drugs such as marijuana impact on memory loss, psychomotor speed, attention, verbal memory, and planning ability (Medina, Schweinsburg, Cohen-Zion, Nagel, & Tapert, 2007), while exposure in adolescence to drugs such as cocaine increases the likelihood of later addiction in adulthood, and cannabis use hugely increases the risk of adolescents developing psychotic symptoms later (Moore et al., 2007).

The human reward system, strongly implicated in seeking new and exciting activities, is linked with the dopamine system. This, in many adolescents, can seem as if it is in overdrive, as they experiment and seek thrills. Nearly all addictive drugs (cocaine, heroin, nicotine, alcohol, marijuana) increase dopamine levels, and dopamine levels anyway are typically altered in adolescence (Volkow & Li, 2004). Dopamine stimulates novelty seeking, which pushes forward development, aiding the learning gained from experimentation. If one blocks dopamine receptors in rats, they no longer experiment with new food, and tend to get stuck in old patterns (Bevins, 2001). Interestingly, adolescent rats are similarly more likely than their adult counterparts to take risks and to imbibe stimulants presented to them, such as alcohol. In some ways contemporary adolescents cannot win, as parents can worry if teenagers show fierce independence, but also if they are unadventurous and rarely leave the home.

Dopamine-stimulated novelty seeking is adaptive and aids learning. When rats venture into unknown territories their dopamine levels shoot up (Rebec, Christensen, Guerra, & Bardo, 1997) and the same is seen in humans. Teenagers take risks, but some more than others. Some teenagers were divided into groups according to how they answered questions like 'I want to parachute from a plane' or 'I don't like new things'. The group who were clearly risk takers were 10 times more likely to take drugs in adolescence (Cain, Saucier, & Bardo, 2005).

Several studies suggest that adolescents require pleasure seeking and dopamine 'hits' to counter low mood, suggesting that adolescence is typically a more unhappy time, possibly for biological reasons (Garber, Keiley, & Martin, 2002). Average self-reports of feeling positive drop in adolescence and such mood falls occur frequently enough for this to be thought of as a biological predisposition of adolescence (Weinstein, Mormelstein, Hankin, Hedeker, & Flay, 2007).

Hormonal and chemical changes in adolescence can lead to increased aggression. A group of adolescents whose physical/sexual development was late were given hormonal treatment, testosterone for the boys and oestrogen for the girls (Finkelstein et al., 1997). For 3 months they were given the hormones and for other periods they received a placebo. For the period that they took the hormones all the adolescents became more aggressive. The hormone treatment also coincided in boys with more masturbation, nocturnal emissions and 'touching' girls; and in girls more kissing boys and sexual fantasies. Similar hormones are increasingly released in most adolescent bodies anyway, with their attendant levels of mood changes.

Yet there is an important interrelationship between biological and psychosocial experiences. Boys with high testosterone and poor family relationships are more likely to take risks, lie, steal, drink, or miss school. Similarly high testosterone girls show more risk taking when parent–teenage relations are poor (Booth, Johnson, Granger, Crouter, & McHale, 2003). Adolescent boys with low serotonin levels often become aggressive, while adolescent girls with low serotonin levels are more likely to be depressed. However, when family relationships are good then serotonin levels tend to be nearer the norm.

A final biological change that worries adults, but might well be natural, is the adolescent propensity to sleep longer and on a different time clock. It seems that adolescents need more sleep, and suffer badly when they do not have it. Their body clocks might be shifting the timing of their melatonin release, meaning that they 'naturally' sleep and wake up to 2 hours later than adults (Hagenauer, Perryman, Lee, & Carskadon, 2009), something that also seems to happen in other mammals. This is a possible biological explanation for parent's perception that adolescents are 'being lazy'. Indeed when American States experimented with starting school later for adolescents then not only did school performance improve but even the frequency of car accidents involving teenagers reduced (Danner & Phillips, 2008).

Overall physiologically and neurologically adolescence is a period of huge shifts. Mood swings and personality changes are often seen as 'down to hormones', but now we know that accompanying the physiological changes and rush of powerful hormones there is major brain reorganisation making adolescence a time of huge potential, but also of massive vulnerability.

Becoming less attached

Adolescence is a period when young people tend to identify increasingly with their peer group and become less dependent on families. Adolescents (human and animal) are more adventurous and risk taking, and have higher levels of conflict with parents (Steinberg, 2007). Yet dependency and independence can be seen as two sides of the same coin. Winnicott (1958) once described the very young child's capacity to be alone as deriving from a safe experience of being alone with their mother and something very similar can be seen in adolescence. Becoming autonomous is not necessarily established at the expense of attachment relationships, but rather the earlier attachment relationships can act as a solid platform from which independence grows. The ways in which adolescents approach new relationships, including romantic and sexual ones, are strongly influenced by earlier experiences of closeness and intimacy in families and relational templates. With good parental support adolescents are generally more secure, in attachment terms, but also manage peer-group negotiations, and their studies with more confidence. Despite being more autonomous, at times of crisis many still turn to their parents as a 'secure base', albeit less frequently and only for certain issues (Allen & Hauser, 1996).

Because adolescents seem to have become 'detached', parents can struggle to believe that they continue to play an important role, but most studies show the importance of parental input. Having a problematic relationship with parents increases the likelihood of depression and problems with peers, and good adolescent peer relations tend to go with better relationships with parents (Lieberman, Doyle, & Markiewicz, 1999). Adolescents who are better adjusted score highly on measures of attachment to both parents and peers, and those who score as secure have much less likelihood of depression, suicidality, anxiety disorders, antisocial behaviour, as well as substance misuse (Cooper, Shaver, & Collins, 1998).

I discussed earlier (Chapter 14) Judy Rich Harris' (2009) controversial view that parents have less influence on children than peers. It is complicated to tease out their relative influence. While good relationships at home aid an adolescent's transition into independence, peer groups also assert their own separate influences. Some adolescents move in circles that are supportive, and through which they develop new confidence in their ideas, beliefs, and abilities, and in which experimentation feels safe. Others are not so lucky. Adolescents from backgrounds of maltreatment are more likely to be attracted to peer groups involved with delinquency and drug use. But also adolescents can 'fall into' a peer group more by chance, taking on their ideals and values, irrespective of parental ideals, and a peer group's aspirations can be more influential than parents. Parents who try to get their children into good schools intuitively know the importance of peer group influence.

Adolescents are especially influenced by peers as they try to establish a new identity away from their families. Such identities can be fragile and fluid, and in the contemporary West it is not unusual for young people to change hair and clothing styles regularly, as they identify with new groups, each with their own norms, cultural styles, music, and ideas. The in-group and out-group phenomenon described in Chapter 14 is often seen even more strongly in adolescence. An experimental example of this was seen in the famous 'Robbers Cave' experiment. Here 24 young adolescent boys, indistinguishable in terms of class and background, were randomly split into two groups, and unbeknownst to each they set up camp near each other. Unlike the anarchy of Lord of the Flies, these groups became organised but extremely separate, each devising their own names, and developing their own identity and sense of 'groupness'. These ordinary, well-adjusted young people showed enormous competiveness, aggression, and prejudice against the other group. They demanded competitions, made their own flags and chants, and refused to eat with the other group's members. These children split into separate groups on very flimsy and insubstantial grounds, the real differences between them being almost nonexistent (Sherif, Harvey, White, Hood, & Sherif, 1961). One might think of the many groupings adolescents form, with their very clear uniforms. Some research even suggests that young people drawn to more extreme looking groups, such as Goths and Punks, are often shyer than average and trying to overcome this and find a sense of identity (Beši & Kerr, 2009).

Humans are group creatures, and adolescents are particularly influenced by other young people. Parents and peers both exert influences, but often in different ways (Meeus, Oosterwegel, & Vollerbergh, 2002). Peer groups often have more influence on social aspirations, and a surprisingly powerful influence on adolescents' sense of identity, while parents often retain a degree of influence on academic and career matters. One study tested Harris' (2009) hypothesis by looking closely at the relative influence of parents and peers, and a detailed look at 14 personality variables showed that adolescents were more influenced by peers on many variables (Bester, 2007). Interestingly there was also a gender difference, with boys less influenced by their parents than girls.

The primacy of the direction of influence is somewhat chicken-and-egg. When parents are threatened by their child's peer group, and there is conflict, then adolescents withdraw even more from their parents and their peer group becomes more important. Most research does not back up Harris' stronger claims, as it shows that parents retain an influence, in both direct and more subtle ways, but they maybe have less influence than they either think they have or than they would like. As adolescents develop, families must find ways of adapting, and families with more flexible modes of relating minimise the degree of conflict that can ensue (Allen, Moore, Kuperminc, & Bell, 1998).

Although peers begin to take on many of the attachment functions that were previously played by parents, the styles in which these are negotiated are linked to previous learning. If one has received a dismissive style of parenting one is more likely to treat both peers and romantic partners in a similar way. Similarly if one has had a secure relationship then adolescence tends to be marked by more autonomy and flexible peers relationships, and more open communicative styles with both parents and peers (Laursen & Collins, 2004). Early attachment styles at the very least predispose young people to meet later relationship challenges in particular ways.

Sex and romance

No discussion of adolescence is complete without mentioning sex and love. With the explosion of hormonal and bodily changes and increased sexual maturity one often sees a massive surge in powerful emotions. Pubertal changes include males releasing

pheromones that affect courtship. For example the steroid andostadienone that is present on men's skin produces physiological relaxation in women who are given it intra-nasally (Grosser, Monti-Bloch, Jennings-White, & Berliner, 2000), and other male odours can enhance ovulation (Stern & McClintock, 1998). Similarly men have been shown to be more attracted to women who are ovulating (Grammer, Fink, & Neave, 2005), so much so that careful studies have even shown that lap dancers earn more money when they are ovulating (Miller, Tybur, & Jordan, 2007). Lesbian and gay people in turn respond to pheromones differently but equally strongly (Berglund, Lindström, & Savic, 2006). Such sex drives are developing powerfully in adolescents who find themselves in the throes of hormonally driven urges and desires.

Competition and rivalry marks the adolescent move into sexual experimentation. Socially and sexually successful boys tend to be attractive, athletic, and also early maturers (Weisfeld & Woodward, 2004). Early maturity in girls can be a mixed blessing. Depression is linked to boys having fewer sexual partners, and girls having more. Just having a lesbian or gay orientation in itself hugely increases the chances of mental health problems (Fergusson, Horwood, Ridder, & Beautrais, 2005), maybe largely as a result of the social stigma that is feared or encountered.

In the West the age of first sexual encounters has been lowering (Rosenthal, Von Ranson, Cotton, Biro, Mills, & Succop, 2001), while average age of first sexual intercourse varies from country to country (Mackay, 2000). For example for females, the average age is 15 in the Czech Republic, 16 in the USA and 20 in Egypt and Italy. Most adolescents in an American sample reported having had a romantic relationship in the previous 18 months (Carver, Joyner, & Udry, 2003) and young people can spend a lot of time thinking about real or potential romantic relationships. While the ways adolescents relate to romantic/sexual partners has links with earlier relationship styles and attachment patterns, there are also differences. Adolescent sexual relationships are more reciprocal, both parties potentially having a similar need of the other, unlike parent–child relationships, and in later adolescence sexual partners can become attachment figures, used for emotional solace and comfort (Hazan & Zeifman, 1994).

The quality of caregiving in the first 42 months of life significantly predicts the 'quality' of romantic relationships in early adulthood (Sroufe, 2005), and whether an individual is in a romantic relationship between 23 and 26 is partly predicted by teacher rating of peer competence in middle childhood. Adolescents who experience a 'secure' model of parenting, as adjudged by their Adult Attachment Interviews (Chapter 6, p. 64), generally have a greater capacity for intimacy in romantic relationships (Mayseless & Scharf, 2007). Young people with an insecure preoccupied attachment style are more likely to struggle and suffer in relationships, often developing mental health problems such as depression (Davila, Steinberg, Kachadourian, Cobb, & Fincham, 2004). Having nurturing and involved parents seems to lead to more warmth and less hostility in romances. On the other hand, rigid parenting styles, marked by more conflict, lead to more relationship difficulties for adolescents, and aggression at home leads to more antagonism in young couples (Andrews, Foster, Capaldi, & Hops, 2000).

Popular adolescents, who get on well with peers are also more successful in romantic relationships (Connolly & Johnson, 1996). Young people who worry about losing their friends tend to be the ones who also worry that their relationships will fail (Diamond & Lucas, 2004), whereas those with good peers relationships tend to have easier romantic relationships. There are exceptions to these patterns, but findings definitely show an interrelationship between attachment experiences and how adolescents relate to peers and romantic partners (Furman & Simon, 2004). Once again we find that good experiences tend to breed good experiences and vice versa.

Risks, problems, and resilience

Adolescence is often an unstable time for those from difficult backgrounds, who are at increased risk of emotional disorders. Most adult mental health problems, such as antisocial behaviour and substance misuse, as well as sometimes psychosis, are first seen in adolescence. Relationship break-ups is the most likely precipitating cause of adolescent depression, suicide attempts, and indeed of successful suicides (Joyner & Udry, 2000). The epidemiological evidence suggests that as many as 1 in 5 adolescents have a mental health disorder in Britain (Collishaw, Maughan, Goodman, & Pickles, 2004). Without effective treatment children with ADHD diagnoses before adolescence often end up displaying symptoms such as antisocial behaviour, academic failure, criminal behaviour, and substance misuse after they reach puberty (Babinski, Hartsough, & Lambert, 1999). In girls one sees more internalising disorders such as depression, anxiety, or eating disorders, and these often are precursors of adult mental health issues. In boys one is more likely to see externalising disorders such as conduct disorders, as well as ADHD, autism, Tourette Syndrome, and antisocial or criminal activity. These are typical gender differences but there are historical and cultural variants, such as the increase in violent behaviour in girls in the USA and Britain (Ness, 2004). Mental health problems in adolescents in Britain and America have been getting worse in recent years and this is an age associated with psychological risks as well as gains.

A good predictor of adaptation in adolescence is the **social capital** accrued in early childhood, such as the gains from a caring home, good social and academic skills, a close peer group, better schools, and safer neighbourhoods, all of which stand young adolescents in good stead for the next stage of life (Fitzpatrick, Piko, Wright, & LaGory, 2005). Bad neighbourhoods and poverty increase the likelihood of mental health and social problems (Hull, Kilbourne, Reece, & Husaini, 2008). Neighbourhoods vary hugely. One study in New Orleans reported that 25 per cent of 9 to 12-year-olds had witnessed a shooting and 20 per cent had seen a stabbing (Osofsky, 1999). Neglect and maltreatment are associated with later problems such as depression, anxiety disorders, antisocial behaviour, drug use, and poor academic performance (Masten, 2006). Harsh, punitive parenting and delinquent peer groups consistently come out as major risk factors.

A degree of subtlety is always necessary when interpreting such findings. What might be a good strategy for parenting adolescents in one environment might not be so helpful in another. Mothers in violent crime ridden neighbourhoods who are more disciplinarian have children who do better academically. However, in low-risk environments such stricter parenting strategies can lead to less successful academic outcomes (Gonzales, Cauce, Friedman, & Mason, 1996). By the same token democratic parenting that facilitates autonomy might be an excellent strategy in an affluent middle-class suburb but is less helpful in an inner-city ghetto rife with violence and crime.

Research consistently shows that the riskier the setting, and the worse the poverty, then the less resilience factors one finds. Highly competent children, as assessed at 4 years old, living in high-risk environments do much worse than less competent children who happen to live in lower-risk ones. Adolescents who had high intelligence and good mental health as children still fared worse than young people with lower intelligence and worse mental health who lived in better neighbourhoods (Sameroff, Gutman, & Peck, 2003). Psychological help and good families can only help so far, as in the face of serious environmental adversity then individual protective factors are of less consequence.

Much longitudinal research attests to continuity from childhood to early adulthood. Disorganised attachment at a year is perhaps the best predictor we have of serious psychopathology in adolescence (Cassidy & Mohr, 2001). When there is serious early trauma then the long-term effects are clear. When the situation is less serious a more complex analysis of potential influences is needed. Sroufe (2005) found for example that there was a definite but not very large statistical correlation between care in infancy and global adjustment at 18 years old. This correlation became a little more predictive when they added in attachment at 18 months. This increased still further when other factors were put into the equation such as peer competence in elementary school. When you add in still later factors such as levels of stress and social support in middle adolescence, then the predictability of such early experiences on later outcomes increases dramatically. As Sroufe says, 'adaptation at the edge of adulthood builds on a cumulative history beginning in early life' (p. 202).

Such findings have led researchers to suggest the idea of a cascade of effects (Masten et al., 2005). A presenting symptom or behaviour shown at one age spills over into and influences another phase and domain of functioning. For example one piece of research looked at how the development of violent behaviour occurs across the lifespan, again suggesting a cascade of effects (Dodge, Greenberg, & Malone, 2008). Many children who would later become violent were born into poor, unsafe neighbourhoods, and also had difficult temperaments as infants. This meant that they were harder to care for, which meant more likelihood of parenting difficulties. This in turn affected their ability to manage peer relationships and learning in school and nursery. They often then showed behavioural disturbances and conduct problems earlier in school, which could give rise to negative reactions from teachers, and their academic achievements became more limited. As they got older they began to drift into more delinquent peer groups. Each symptom, such as conduct issues early in school, can be seen both as predictive of later violence, but also as a potential moment for intervention. Help at the right moment, such as supporting parents when their children were young, might move a child from one potential trajectory to another. Our previous experiences affect how we approach new ones, but each new experience also presents new opportunities.

Summary: adolescence and emerging adulthood

It is hard to generalise too much about adolescence as it takes such diverse forms in different cultures and periods, and can be experienced so differently, depending on factors like social class, gender and sexual orientation, cultural values, and capacity to manage interpersonal or academic challenges. Many nonWestern cultures have had very clearly ritualised ways of managing the move into young adulthood. In contemporary Western cultures there are not obvious equivalent rites of passage seen in other cultures, such as the Vision Quest of Native Americans. One might cite school exams and leaving ceremonies, or the experience some young people have of a gap year. What is different is that the transition into adult roles is later, slower, and more piecemeal in contemporary Western cultures, with less adult involvement than in other societies, and less clearly defined expectations and end-points.

Arnett (2004) has described a new phase of 'emerging adulthood' in the West. As the age of marriage, having children, or entering the workforce has grown later, young people have spent longer in activities such as studying or travelling. There is an extended period that has been described as 'drifting', with less likelihood of 'settling down', whether into a career or long-term relationship. Arnett acknowledges that this is a phenomenon that concerns affluent young people more than more deprived populations, but he shows that demographically there have been clear changes in this direction. This is an age where identities and possibilities are tried out, and can be a transitional time in which one feels neither adolescent nor adult. It seems that social and workforce changes have forged a new relationship with an adolescent brain that often does not finish maturing until about 25 years of age.

Late adolescence and the transition into adulthood affords new developmental opportunities, and during this period, maybe surprisingly, a new resilience can emerge even for those who have really struggled up until this point providing a second chance for developmental change (Masten, 2006). Ideas about the immutability of early influences are giving way to newer ideas of cascades of developmental influences with various moments of potential change.

Adolescence has some features that are common across cultures, while others show divergent paths. Physiological and hormonal changes are the norm, with a considerable amount of change in the brain. One sees the increased importance of peer relationships, and parental influence begins to wane. There are increases in experimentation, including sexual experimentation, and more risk taking, as adolescents prepare to move away from their families and begin an independent existence. In many cultures, particularly in the West, this period can be one of fluidity of identity, as adolescents 'try on' different roles and ways of being. In some young people new hair styles, fashions, and personality styles seem to be tried on regularly, as identity is experimented with. Group life, gangs, cliques, and crowds can become more important. There are huge cognitive and intellectual developments, which allow the possibility of much more complex and profound thinking about oneself in relation to others, and about life in general.

Adolescence is a period of both vulnerability and possibility, sometimes a time of emotional turmoil, change, and upheaval. The ways adolescents approach tasks, such as peer group interaction or academic work, are influenced by earlier experiences within their families. Yet new influences emerge that can open the possibility of new trajectories. Mental health worries can become much more prominent during adolescence, which is generally the time where issues such as depression, anxiety disorders, psychosis, eating difficulties, as well as antisocial behaviours and violence, can all rear their head. The adolescent brain is reorganising and re-forming and is vulnerable, both to the impact of substances such as alcohol or cannabis, as well as to levels of stress and anxiety, and a cocktail of hormonal, psychological, and bodily challenges. Yet this is also a period of exciting developmental possibilities. For many it is the most intense and memorable period of their lives. Adolescence can no longer be considered simply a transitional time, but rather one that is central for psychological, emotional, and social growth, possibly the making of the adult life to come.

Part V

Consequences of early experiences

Trauma, neglect, and their effects

In this chapter I discuss the effects of childhood abuse, neglect, and trauma. In Chapter 6 I looked at some of the defensive processes infants resort to when under strain and now I build on this by describing how abuse and neglect impact on children's lives and minds. I make a distinction between neglect and abuse because they describe different kinds of experiences that have different effects, even though in the definitions of social workers neglect is a form of abuse. I define neglect as the absence of experiences that a child is primed to receive, such as consistent care or the presence of a safe attachment figure. Neglected children tend to learn to rely on their own limited emotional resources rather than other people, and they can struggle to make an impact on others or share good experiences with them. In contrast, children whose experiences are primarily of abuse live in a world that is likely to seem a much more terrifying place, with considerable uncertainty and fear about what might happen to them next.

A trauma is an experience that our normal defences cannot protect us against and so is overwhelming, and both abuse and neglect can have this effect. Some children are unfortunate enough to suffer both neglect and abuse and I think the word trauma can be applied to both. The original medical meaning of trauma is literally a piercing of the skin, and we might think of psychological trauma as piercing a psychic skin or membrane. Some forms of abuse and neglect are likely to leave any child scarred, such as living in a Nazi concentration camp. Other events may be traumatic for one person but not for another; for example some people develop serious symptoms of **post-traumatic stress disorder (PTSD)** after an event that others quickly recover from.

Neglect

Neglect is hard to define and not always easy to spot. Social workers act more easily on seeing bruises or broken bones, or parental drug use or violence, than neglect. It is not always clear when behaviour is neglectful, particularly as neglect is the absence of something rather than its presence and to some extent is always a question of judgement. It is also a question of timing; infants need holding, touching, and soothing in a way that adolescents do not, and what is neglectful at one age is not at another. We know though that the lack of basic nurturing can lead to serious psychological, emotional, and physical delay, and even death, as the pioneering studies of institutional life by Renee Spitz (1945) in the 1940s showed. Spitz filmed infants in institutional settings who displayed excruciating behaviours to witness, staring into space, rocking, turning from side to side, and lying still for long periods with glazed expressions. They had given up hope of human contact and had withdrawn into a self-contained world, becoming very hard to reach.

Spitz's abandoned orphans are an example of what happens when the minimum basic expected input does not arrive. Human infants who have no or very little social input do not develop language and other skills normally. They have not received experience expectant input, and this is different to experience independent factors that need little external input to come on-stream, such as hair growing or eyes forming *in utero*. Experience dependent capacities are different again, and describe how we develop different interactional patterns depending on the kind of relationships experienced.

Probably the most extreme forms of neglect studied have been those seen in institutional settings. In Romania in the 1980s about 65,000 infants were placed in orphanages, mostly in the first month of life. These tragic children became a spectacle that shocked the world. They also became a source of important scientific information, as their development could be compared with children with more usual upbringings. These infants could spend up to 20 hours a day in their cribs unattended. Many showed serious cognitive retardation, much of which persisted in later years. Others indulged in stereotypical or self-stimulatory behaviours.

Bruce Perry and colleagues found that children who had experienced such global forms of neglect had a considerably smaller head circumference than average (Perry, Pollard, Blakley, Baker, & Vigilante, 1995). Their head size grew nearer the norm if they were adopted in the first year to 18 months, but the later the adoption the less the catch-up, much less so after the age of 6. The lack of certain experiences 'on time' means that some capacities might not develop properly. Severely neglectful early environments can lead to medical problems, impairment in cognitive and language abilities, social and communication skills and also in emotional regulation. Behavioural and attachment difficulties often follow neglect, which at its worst can lead to symptoms similar to autistic ones, such as stereotypical rocking and self-soothing (MacLean, 2003). Early neglect has been shown to lead to considerable deficits in IQ, compared with control groups, as well as having a range of severe effects on brain development, hormonal functioning, and general emotional development (De Bellis, 2005).

In other species something similar is found. When rats are separated from their mothers their growth becomes seriously impaired. It is the lack of touch more than anything that inhibits the work of growth hormones (Kuhn & Schanberg, 1998). Stimulating premature infants with massage has been shown to increase growth compared with children left in incubators (Dieter, Field, Hernandez-Reif, Emory, & Redzepi, 2003). Harlow and colleagues' early studies with rhesus monkeys showed that those reared without maternal care and in relative isolation were fearful, easily startled, did not interact or play with other monkeys when introduced to them later on, and overall showed chronic difficulties. They indulged in much of the behaviour seen in human orphanages, such as rocking, blank staring, walking around in circles, and self-mutilation (Harlow, Dodsworth, & Harlow, 1965).

Generally the more severe the deprivation, then the worse are the effects. A group of British children adopted from Romania have been examined over a long period by Michael Rutter and colleagues (O'Connor, Bredenkamp, & Rutter, 1999). Many at 6 years old showed serious attachment issues, such as indiscriminate sociability, but those with the worst symptoms had spent twice as long in institutional care. In an important study Bucharest orphans were split into two samples and then compared. One group received standard institutional care in which 20 caregivers worked on a shift basis with about 30 children. Alongside this was a pilot project in which the group size was reduced to 10, with 4 carers to look after them (Smyke, Dumitrescu, & Zeanah, 2002). The pilot group did much better, were more able to accept help, and a battery of tests showed that in many respects they did not differ from children who were never institutionalised. The institutionalised children with the worse ratio of carers and poorer input showed higher levels of reactive attachment disorder, and were more withdrawn, unresponsive, and disinhibited.

An early, now classic, account of the comparative effect of good and neglectful care was reported in *The Lancet* in 1951 (Widdowson, 1951), and concerned children in two linked orphanages in Germany. In this experiment the children lived on rations, and after 6 months food supplements were introduced to the children in only one orphanage and the effects were observed. During the first 6 months, when the food was identical, children in one orphanage grew more than those in the other, and in this orphanage there was a kindly matron who cared for her children; who enjoyed their company, played and laughed with them and comforted them. The matron in the other orphanage was a harsh disciplinarian who bestowed little emotional warmth and care, forbade the children to be picked up, and seemed not to like them. Here the children grew at a slower pace and generally did less well, all except a small group of her favourites who thrived. Interestingly food supplements were introduced to the first orphanage, but at the same time the 'kindly' matron was replaced by the harsh disciplinary one, who had also taken all her favourites with her. Surprisingly, despite the food supplements, the growth rates in this orphanage fell, except in the favourites who continued to thrive, yet the children in the orphanage without the food supplements began to grow. It seems that a harsh and punitive matron had a detrimental effect on the children's growth rates, and her presence over-rode the potentially beneficial effects of the food supplements. This is a graphic example of something that other research has borne out, that sensitive and nurturing care (and indeed in this case even the good care the disciplinarian matron bestowed on her favourites), led to considerably better outcomes. Such cases are now technically known as 'non-organic failure to thrive' (Block & Krebs, 2005).

Neglect impacts on brain development and the developing nervous system. Many children adopted from Romanian orphanages showed much less brain activity in the prefrontal cortex and the temporal lobes. These children had cognitive and emotional impairments, difficulties in concentrating, and in regulating bodily and emotional states as well as neurological deficits (Eluvathingal et al., 2006). Other research showed that children adopted from orphanages produce lower levels of hormones that promote loving feelings, like vasopressin and oxytocin (Fries et al., 2005). Such neglect remains a serious issue. Unicef estimated that there are 1.5 million children living in institutions in central and eastern Europe (Browne, Hamilton-Giachritsis, Johnson, & Ostergren, 2006).

Less extreme forms of neglect are often seen by professionals such as social workers and described by Howe (2005, p. 113) as 'chronic parental failure to meet some developmental need, either physical or psychological . . . neglectful parents tend to avoid, disengage and de-activate their caregiving under emotionally taxing conditions'. Not surprisingly rates of neglect are considerably higher when unemployment and social deprivation are present (Barnett, Miller-Perrin, & Perrin, 2005). Such children are often very passive, and listless. This might be expected because, as Howe graphically stated, 'the psychological traffic between minds has all but stopped' (p. 137) and these children can seem lost in an empty world of their own. Their carers can be unresponsive too, unaware of any signals being sent out, and there can be a defeated look to these children. The attachment researcher Patricia Crittenden (1993) has studied emotionally neglectful parents and found that neglect can take various forms, from parents not perceiving infant signals, to perceiving them but assuming no response is needed, to simply being unable to find a response.

Neglected children, particularly those who have been in institutional care, can be passive and show little desire to interact with peers or caregivers. Some disinhibited ones go off with total strangers, maybe sitting on laps indiscriminately, without any sense of fear or danger. Such contact is generally very superficial. The official psychiatric diagnostic manuals describe both an inhibited and disinhibited form of reactive attachment disorder, and children from extremely deprived institutional care often fall into the disinhibited category. These children do not have an idea of adults who can provide comfort at times of anxiety. In the Strange Situation Test (Chaper 6, p. 61) for example, they generally perform in peculiar and rather unclassifiable ways. Orphans adopted in the study from Bucharest did not form normal attachment relationships with subsequent carers (Zeanah & Smyke, 2005).

These studies echoed earlier research showing that the effects of institutional care persisted into late adolescence, when the young people were less able to form friendships and lasting relationships, even when adopted into emotionally supportive families (Tizard & Hodges, 1978). Neglected children generally interact less with other children and show less aggression but more passivity under stress. Despite their poor prognosis they often do not come to the attention of professionals as often as overtly maltreated children. They draw less attention to themselves, and can easily 'fade' into the background, becoming further neglected by professionals and other adults. This is unfortunate for them as the prognosis after neglect is often far worse than after active maltreatment. On a more hopeful note, many of those adopted early on from the most deprived orphanages made a good recovery, especially the younger ones (Rutter, 1998), even if often retaining some signs of disturbed attachment patterns.

Neglected children have not had an experience of a parent sensitive to their bodily and emotional states, who psychologically holds and imitates them, and is attuned to their gestures. They do not learn to experience that wide-eyed delight so often seen between infants and their carers. Nor do they have anyone to help them with anxious or frightening moments. Their signals are not read by others, and they can stop communicating, becoming out of touch with their own emotional states. Neglected children often do not believe that they can have an impact on others. Tragically the experiences that normally help build emotional confidence and resilience are lacking in severely neglected children who so often live in a flat and desultory world.

Maltreatment, trauma, and abuse

The experience and effect of abuse and maltreatment is profound in different ways. It often leads to high stress levels, a difficulty in focusing and concentrating, problems regulating emotions and in executive functioning, a hyperalertness that can make it difficult to relax, and many interpersonal difficulties. Young children who are victims of abuse, with no safe adult to rely on, often resort to desperate measures to survive. Some identify with the abusive parent or carer, and become violent, while others survive through dissociation, an extreme form of psychic numbing often seen in trauma victims.

Traumatised people who are later exposed to frightening images show extreme arousal in primitive brain regions such as the amygdala, a deactivation of the brain regions for thinking, and little capacity to inhibit strong emotion or translate feelings into words (Rauch et al., 1996). Adults who are sexually abused as children show different brain responses when exposed to traumatic stories than control groups

(Bremner, 2006). The more 'primitive' parts of the brain can become the default pathways for responding to stimuli. If the trauma or abuse starts early then a child's repertoire to deal with such affronts is more limited. Children and adults who have been subjected to trauma and abuse are generally not able to use their emotions and bodily reactions for effective guidance about what is or is not safe. Their bodies can become geared to acting fast to avoid danger, this being a useful survival reaction in times of danger but one that when overly relied on does not help in ordinary social interactions.

The sympathetic nervous system prepares our bodies for action, generally fight or flight, and in the face of threat our heart rate goes up, as does our blood pressure, adrenaline is pumped around our systems and stress hormones are released. While this is happening there is a deactivation of other systems, such as for digesting food, and our immune systems. The need for immediate survival over-rides other bodily functions. In some trauma victims one sees the activation of the parasympathetic nervous system, seen in the freeze response, as when animals 'play dead'. Heart rate can go right down, systems slow down, and the thinking parts of the mind shut off in dissociative responses.

It is possible for both of these seemingly so different emergency responses to occur in the same person at the same time. Post-traumatic stress disorder (PTSD) sufferers seem to tragically suffer this, showing both hyperarousal and lower heart rate (Sahar, Shalev, & Porges, 2001). Trauma victims often have inhibited capacities for executive functioning, and struggle to plan for the future, to manage strong emotions or be aware of the consequences of their actions.

Therapeutic practices that specifically aim to develop the brain functions associated with the cerebral cortex, such as being more self-aware, also change the brain, and so give hope that traumatised people's lives can improve. Sarah Lazar and colleagues for example found that **mindfulness** meditation, which can lead to more awareness of psychological, emotional, and physical sensations, can actually result in a thicker cortex developing (Lazar et al., 2005). Change is possible, and even if trauma affects the very structure of our brains, these same brains can later be more healthily structured by subsequent better experiences.

Many trauma victims suffer from PTSD and its symptoms, such as flashbacks and intrusive thoughts. The most damaging form of trauma is interpersonal trauma, which is far more likely than other traumas, such as car accidents, to give rise to post-traumatic symptoms (Van der Kolk, 1989). Maybe the worst form of interpersonal trauma is that inflicted by a child's carers. When a carer turns abuser, then the world feels unsafe and unpredictable. Serious abuse often leads to fear, helplessness, shame, rage, betrayal, and resignation. Not surprisingly many children who have been maltreated are seen as 'problems' in schools and elsewhere, and are oppositional and aggressive. Such children are easily overaroused and can seem particularly ill-suited to the structured and ordered learning environment of the classroom or chaotic playgrounds. Stimuli such as the loud voice of a teacher, the stare of a peer, or the humiliation of not understanding something, can quickly trigger disturbed behaviour. The traumatised child will easily become hyperaroused, seeing threat where there is none, leading to an escalation of challenging behaviour.

Early stress and trauma causes changes in brain circuitry and hormonal systems and these can become patterns, or as Perry and colleagues writes, 'states can become traits' (Perry, Pollard, Blakley, Baker, & Vigilante, 1995, p. 271). Trauma thus can impair a child's ability to manage everyday life, in particular impacting on the ability to benefit from relationships with others, whether adults or peers. Children who have been deprived often tragically reject the help that they so badly need, a phenomenon the child psychotherapist Gianna Henry described as double-deprivation (Henry, 2004). Maltreated children struggle with peer relationships, are more aggressive than other children, and also show less empathy to other children in distress. One might hypothesise that such children are not able to be in touch with their own distress and upset, and so are unlikely to have sympathy for other upset children.

Long-term effects

There is increasing evidence that early trauma and neglect have an impact that lasts through the lifespan. Adults traumatised as children have more psychological and physical problems than others, are more likely to use drugs and alcohol, to end up in prison or the psychiatric system, are less likely to manage stable relationships, to do well educationally, or to hold down stable employment. Children who have been abused or neglected in childhood are far more vulnerable to serious mental health disorders as adults such as borderline personality disorder and major depression (Zanarini, 1997). For example, a large-scale, longitudinal study (Shea et al., 2004) in the USA has shown that a very high proportion of people suffering from personality disorder experienced serious sexual trauma as children. Another study followed over 600 children from New York for about 20 years and found that children with proven experiences of childhood abuse or neglect were more than four times as likely, as adults, to develop a personality disorder (Judd & McGlashan, 2003). Another group of boys were studied whose childhood abuse was proven in court. By the time they reached 30 years old they had a 75 per cent higher than average likelihood of adult depression (Widom, 2007). Serious trauma and maltreatment also hugely increases the likelihood of young people suffering educationally and socially and becoming involved in substance misuse and crime (Gilbert, Widom, Browne, Fergusson, Webb, & Janson, 2009).

Maybe the best known form of childhood trauma is sexual abuse, which has many long-lasting consequences, including the likelihood of higher numbers of sexual partners, more chance of contracting sexually transmitted diseases, and of teenage pregnancy, as well as other enduring psychological scars. For example, victims of sexual abuse have been found to be much more at risk of suicidality, mental health problems and also being in harmful relationships (Dube et al., 2005).

One of the biggest studies is an American one called the ACE (Adverse Childhood Experiences) (Dube, Felitti, Dong, Giles, & Anda, 2003). This focused not just on single traumas but on the effects of combinations of bad experiences. Not surprisingly factors such as having a mentally ill parent, being physically neglected, subject to violence or exposure to drug-using adults, tend to occur in clusters. The higher the numbers of adverse experiences, then the worse were the later physical and psychological outcomes. One of the researchers, Felliti (2002), stated that a male child with an ACE score of 6 has a 4600 per cent increase in likelihood of later becoming an intravenous drug user when compared with a male child with an ACE score of 0. This study of over 18,000 people showed how childhood adversity reduces life expectancy, even increasing the likelihood of early death from physical causes, such as heart disease and cancer, as well as from violence or suicide.

Disorganised attachment

It can be difficult enough to contemplate a child being maltreated and abused by an adult, but even worse if the adult is the person who the child relies on for solace and care. The group of children Mary Main was to define as disorganised in attachment terms suffer this. They do not develop a coherent strategy to deal with being with their unpredictable caregivers and show many odd and unusual behaviours. In the Strange Situation Test (Chapter 6, p. 61) they might move towards their mother but then veer off, or become dazed, as if uncertain whether they want to approach. Their movements are often incoherent, with many mistimed and awkward actions, often falling over or becoming disoriented. Other responses include freezing, or huddling on the floor. For example, Main and Solomon (1986) wrote 'One infant hunched her upper body and shoulders at hearing her mother's call, then broke into extravagant laugh-like screeches with an excited forward movement. Her braying laughter became a cry and distress-face without a new intake of breath as the infant hunched forward. Then suddenly she became silent, blank and dazed' (p. 119).

Children who have suffered trauma can be quite chaotic but they can also become controlling and rigid. Professionals who work with children who have been fostered or adopted and with their carers, are often surprised at how difficult such children find changes in routine, or transitions, and how much they need to control interactions. Events that most children would look forward to, such as holidays or trips, can be disconcerting for such children who often urgently feel the need to be in charge of every moment.

Such children have had very unpredictable and complicated early lives, and have developed a controlling strategy as a desperate attempt to predict a volatile world (Solomon, George, & De Jong, 1995). Yet when one looks below the surface at what is going on in these children's thoughts and fantasies, their worlds are frightening, chaotic, and unpredictable. In their stories and play the research shows that disorganised children tend to enact scenes in which both children and carers are untrustworthy, dangerous, and likely to cause damage. The self in such play tends to be depicted as powerful and dangerous, or as very helpless and desperate. Beneath a controlling and rigid presentation the minds of these children can be filled with dangerous and frightening thoughts, disasters, and tragedies, and a belief that the world is unsafe and unpredictable (Hodges, Steele, Hillman, Henderson, & Kaniuk, 2003).

Many children traumatised by their parents show oversensitivity to their parents' signals. It can be vital for them to work out things like whether a violent father is angry, tired, drunk, or in a rare good mood. One very common way of coping that is different to fight and flight is what is called the 'tend and befriend' response (Taylor, Klein, Lewis, Gruenewald, Gurung, & Updegraff, 2000). This is resorted to when it might be safer to reverse traditional parent–child roles. Such children stay safe by becoming acutely aware of the state of mind of their parents, trying to ensure that

208

parents stay in a better mood, and they tend to be extremely sensitive to any change of emotional temperature. Such children have sometimes been termed 'parentified', an common response to a frightening family situation (Chase, 1999).

Adult Attachment Interviews (Chapter 6, p. 64) show that parents who have children with disorganised attachments have narratives that are 'unresolved'. They describe themselves and their childhoods in inconsistent and incoherent ways, and many show 'frightened or frightening' behaviour towards their children. They often cannot integrate and process painful and fearful affects. Not surprisingly many such parents describe having childhoods in which they themselves suffered a great deal of trauma. Such parents can unwittingly induce high levels of fear in their own children, by being both inconsistent and unpredictable.

Disorganised (D) attachment generally comes with a secondary classification of disorganised insecure or disorganised secure (Lyons-Ruth et al., 2003). Children with a D-secure label are more likely to show withdrawing behaviours than D-insecure children who are more likely to be aggressive and hostile. Both are acutely aware of their caregivers and struggle to stay safe in the presence of adults who do not inspire trust. As previously stated, children classified as disorganised are not necessarily suffering from the psychiatric diagnosis of attachment disorder, although a disorganised classification tends to predict later psychopathology. These children find it hard to find a strategy that consistently keeps them safe. They can resort to hypervigilance and controlling behaviours, and at other times give up and have no strategy at all. A child's need for a safe attachment figure can be in conflict with the pull to move away from a cruel or abusive carer. The tragedy is that the figure upon whom they should be relying on for succour, comfort, and support is the very person who is putting them in danger.

Summary

Research shows that trauma and neglect both have very real and often long-lasting effects on a person's emotional, psychological, and social development, and indeed on their very brain development, immune systems and on their physical well-being. I have in this chapter distinguished between neglect and abuse. Children who are overtly traumatised but whose experiences remains unacknowledged by anyone else, do not develop the ability to manage such affects in themselves or others. When their primary experience is of neglect, rather than abuse, then a child can develop little hope that they will be helped by adults or have enjoyable interpersonal experiences, and such children can end up quite cut-off. Unlike abused children, they do not need to be vigilant of others, and their preoccupation is less with danger and more with trying to self-regulate in the absence of external help. The outcome of neglect can be even more damaging than that of abuse, with many basic building blocks of the personality not forming, particularly cognitively and socially (Music, 2009a).

The play of maltreated children reveals a belief that the world is dangerous, frightening, and unpredictable, in which adults are not protective figures, and things rarely work out for the best. Abused as well as neglected children tend to resort to very controlling strategies to manage interactions. They have not learnt the playfulness and give-and-take of reciprocal play or the belief that interactive ruptures can be mutually repaired. They develop less confidence that human interaction can be rewarding or that people can understand each other's thoughts and feelings. The child who is secure, who feels loved and thought about, is likely to approach the world feeling confident, with more capacities for emotional regulation and mind-mindedness. The maltreated child has little of this. They are likely to have a highly aroused stress system, be vigilant, untrusting and out of touch with their emotions. Intruded upon and abused children often work hard to read other minds, but from a fearful place, to avoid danger, rather than with genuine interest, empathy, or sympathy for another person. Children who are abused have terrible things done to them, but maybe even worse, they can make little sense of what they are forced to endure and experience and they struggle to develop the cognitive and narrative tools to understand these experiences.

Those parents abused as children who somehow manage to break the cycle of abuse are those who develop a capacity to form narratives and stories that make sense of their lives (Roisman et al., 2002). Such reflective functioning or mentalisation seems to be a major resilience factor, something that therapists hope will develop through their work. Generally trauma and abuse is likely to take place in families where there are lower levels of reflective functioning, and abused children in turn tend to show less self-reflective capacities. Trying to tolerate and survive trauma is difficult enough, given their accompanying impact on brain development, stress, and immune systems. On top of this, in the face of trauma many psychological capacities simply do not develop. Sadly the capacity for affect regulation, reflective functioning, and inter-personal relationships is often beyond children who suffer so terribly when young.

Resilience and good feelings

In recent years there has been increasing use of concepts such as resilience and well-being and a more widely held view that our understanding of how positive feelings and happiness develops has been neglected in a field that has focused more on mental ill health. In contrast to the focus in the last chapter on trauma and neglect, this chapter examines the impact of positive experiences on emotional health, and on what gives rise to the ability to manage emotional challenges. Underlying this chapter is an idea that is not intuitively obvious, which is that 'being happy' is not the same as 'not being unhappy', and similarly the absence of happiness is different from the presence of unhappiness. Our biological systems process negative and positive emotions differently, using different brain circuitry and hormonal systems. Humans have evolved two separate emotion systems, one which takes care of our survival needs by responding to danger and threat, and another which is more concerned with enjoyment, pleasure, and positive experience (Zautra, 2003). The number of positive emotions someone experiences does not predict the number of negative emotions they have. Very confident and outgoing people experience more positive feelings, but not necessarily less negative ones (Bradburn & Noll, 1969).

It seems likely that in evolutionary history humans thrived so successfully partly by anticipating danger, an ability linked to our fear response and the negative emotion system. If we do not predict danger we are in trouble, and worrying can sometimes be helpful in a pre-emptive way (Tamir, 2005), although it is also possible to anticipate too much danger, as seen in some depressed people who always expect the worst. Humans might be more prone to the effects of negative than positive emotions. One study suggested that in marriages where there are equal numbers of positive and negative exchanges, both partners tend to be unhappy, and a marriage requires about six times more positive than negative interactions for it to be considered satisfying (Gottman, 1994). Our taste buds detect sweetness if we place just one part of sugar into 200 parts of a food sample, but we are far better at spotting bitterness, which we perceive in only 1 part per 2,000,000 (Harris & Ross, 1987). Maybe humans are more adept at spotting danger than experiencing pleasure. Some people are more likely than others to note the bitter tastes in life, while optimists taste sweetness unnoticed by pessimists.

The systems for seeing a cup as half full or empty, for having positive and negative emotions, are different. The dopamine system for example is central to goal-directed behaviour and positive emotion, involved in desire and seeking and reaching out. We saw in earlier chapters that both depressed mothers and their infants have low dopamine levels. Positive and negative emotions also tend to be processed in different brain areas, with people experiencing more negative emotions generally having high right prefrontal brain activation, and those showing more optimistic and positive emotion having a higher left brain activation (Demaree, Everhart, Youngstrom, & Harrison, 2005). Either one of these separate systems might be dominant in a particular moment.

The negative emotion system is often called the defensive system, and is concerned with avoiding danger, and its activation leads to more pessimism, more worry, and its motivation will be to seek safety and security. The positive affect system is sometimes called the appetitive system and leads to interest, pleasure, hope, is linked with moving towards and not away (e.g., in extroversion), and aims to increase good feelings, not just avoid negative ones. These systems involve very different hormonal and neuronal activity. Some people rely more on their appetitive system and others on a more defensive one, depending on whether they gravitate more towards caution, fight–flight and inhibition as opposed to aiming to actively fulfil interests and desires. Ideally humans build two sets of capacities, to manage both difficult situations and positive experiences. Children who are traumatised and have had little positive experience might need help to process their difficult experiences, otherwise these might remain to haunt them, but they also need help to enjoy the good things in life, to build up hope and the ability to have pleasure. Yet the two systems can work separately, and as Zautra has pointed out (2003, p. 105), people can be high on one or the other, or high on both or low on both.

Positive emotions and health

The distinction between positive and negative affect is not purely academic but has vital consequences, not least for life expectancy and health. For example, the more negative emotion we experience, the lower our immune responses are likely to be. In experiments exposing people to the influenza virus, more negative people with more activity in their right prefrontal cortex had less anti-influenza antibodies and were more likely to succumb to the virus (Davidson, 2000). Richard Davidson, with the Dalai Lama, trained people in mindfulness meditation. This both increased activity in the left prefrontal cortex, and heightened immune systems (Lutz, Dunne, & Davidson, 2007). Such personality differences linked to brain asymmetry is seen even in very young children. Toddlers were observed in play sessions and classified into two groups, inhibited or uninhibited, depending on how exploratory, talkative or outgoing they were, or how near to their attachment figures they stayed. The inhibited children, while at rest, had greater right-sided brain activation while the more outgoing ones had greater left-sided brain activity.

A fascinating retrospective study suggested the large health benefits of having a positive outlook. Over 300 nuns in Milwaukee (Danner, Snowdon, & Friesen, 2001) all wrote diaries when they entered the Order in the 1930s, and these were recently examined in detail by researchers, for example in terms of how many positive and negative words were used. Although their lives once in the convent barely differed in terms of routine, diet, climate, physical amenities, or activities, their relative longevity differed, and in direct proportion to how happy they were six decades earlier. One nun for example wrote 'The past year has been a very happy one. Now I look forward with eager joy to receiving the Holy Habit of Our Lady . . .' (p. 806), and we might note words like 'happy', 'eager', 'look forward' and 'joy', which did not appear in more negative diaries. Of the less positive nuns, two-thirds had died before reaching 85 years old, whereas 90 per cent of the happy ones were still going strong. It was having more positive feelings that predicted longevity, not the amount of negative ones. The nun quoted above was still alive at 98 years old, and on average the happier ones lived about 9 years longer than the more pessimistic ones. This study, using several scales and tested for inter-rater reliability, found a statistically significant link between positive emotion and a decrease in mortality rates.

The positive and negative emotion systems are complementary, and mental health requires both the ability to manage distress and to feel positive. In recent years a 'positive psychology' movement led by writers such as Martin Seligman (2002) has offered a counterpoint to the preoccupation with psychological and mental pain. A major finding from such research is that, given the same psychological stressor, those less badly affected find a way to believe that some good has come out of their experiences, taking positive learning from it. Both groups have similar levels of anxiety, depression, and unrest, but it is levels of positive feeling that differentiates them. Research shows that those who are more resilient have a more hopeful, 'meaning-giving' outlook, even if they have no less distress than those who fared worse (Zautra 2003, p. 81).

Positive emotions can be protective. A typical study was one of over 300 heart patients that showed that what most predicted recovery was self-esteem and optimism, and those scoring high on these were over three times more likely to survive (Helgeson & Fritz, 1999). The presence of negative emotions did not predict relapse but the presence of positive emotions prevented relapse. When exposing people to the influenza virus, those people who showed more positive mental states had a reduced likelihood of contracting the virus, irrespective of the amount of negative emotion (Cohen, Alper, Doyle, Treanor, & Turner, 2006). More positive feelings also equate with higher levels of natural killer cell activity, and those with a degree of psychological distress gain the biggest immune system boost via their positive affect states (Valdimarsdottir & Bovbjerg, 1997). Indeed we are even more likely to recover better from a cold if our doctor shows more empathy (Rakel, Hoeft, Barrett, Chewning, Craig, & Niu, 2009).

Resilience is the ability to remain positive in the face of adversity, which is not the same as not having distress or denying it. Why some are more resilient than others, has become a major research issue. Some people recover better than others from trauma and bad experiences. Early resilience research looked mainly at factors within individuals, such as the capacity for self-regulation or levels of autonomic reactivity. Researchers soon realised the need to look wider, at factors in people's life circumstances that led some to even thrive following adverse circumstances. Recent research adds data from genetic studies, and from experimental interventions which examine whether boosting protective factors, such as providing good nurseries, increases resilience. A contemporary understanding of resilience takes a more ecological approach, linking factors in an individual, the family, and wider social influences and the relationships between these (Bronfenbrenner, 2004).

Particularly central to such resilience is being part of social groups, which requires being sociable and outgoing. Participating actively in social networks, and having a sense of group identity, has been shown to enhance health outcomes and reduce the risk of an array of potential difficulties from memory loss to halving the risk of suffering another stroke for previous stroke victims (Jetten, Haslam, Haslam, & Branscombe, 2009). Such research suggests that belonging to social groups predicts health outcomes better than diet or exercise. Of course, one might need a degree of resilience and good functioning to manage to participate in social groups, and as ever, explanatory factors themselves often need explaining.

Stress and negative emotions can be damaging in themselves and so there is a kind of 'double whammy,' in that positive affect raises immunity, but stress and anxiety lowers it. In a typical study two groups of university students were given slight wounds by their experimenters. Those given wounds in the holidays healed faster and better than those whose wounds were inflicted in stressful exam periods, who took on average 40 per cent longer to heal (Glaser, Kiecolt-Glaser, Marucha, MacCallum, Laskowski, & Malarkey, 1999). Similarly, patients experiencing more marital hostility heal less well after major medical procedures (Kiecolt-Glaser et al., 2005). Increased stress can lower immune systems, reducing the effectiveness of healing mechanisms. Children subjected to trauma, abuse, and neglect often have chronically high stress levels, and this affects their physical as well as emotional health. Data shows that children from troubled and disrupted backgrounds, such as those in public care, suffer worse health outcomes (Williams, Jackson, Maddocks, Cheung, Love, & Hutchings, 2001). Policy-makers often try to improve the health of children in public care through improving access to good medical care rather than taking seriously the impact of having insufficient good experiences, and too many negative ones.

A major effect of neglect is the absence of positive experiences. Neglected children are more likely to show a lack of interest in life, and little positive emotion. Spitz's (1945) early studies of barren institutional care regimes showed this, and even rats lacking maternal care show less interest in pleasurable experiences, such as the taste of sugar. Meaney and colleagues studied rats in bleak and deprived environments and not surprisingly on most measures they did badly (Francis et al., 1999). They then enriched the animals' environments by stroking and handling them. The handled mother and pups in turn licked and groomed their own pups, and this had a knock-on effect, the pups became more interested in suckling, and eating more. As they got older the groomed pups had lower stress responses and better immune systems. Maybe most strikingly, the pups that had been licked and stroked grew up to become the rat mothers who licked and groomed their own infants. As in humans, Meaney suggests that there were two separate mechanisms involved here. There was the mechanism for fear, which for example is more active when there is maternal separation, but also a set of neural circuits of social engagement that links with feelings of well-being and a heightened immune system. The rats who did well not only received less bad care, they also received more good care.

Similar processes are seen in humans, such as in the research that showed that, when cuddled, adopted but previously deprived Romanian orphans did not release oxytocin, the 'love' hormone, in the same way as children brought up in their birth families (Fries, Ziegler, Kurian, Jacoris, & Pollack, 2005). Another study tracked down in middle age those who 35 years earlier had participated in a study in which they had rated their parents' care (Russek & Schwartz, 1997). Those who had rated their parents as uncaring 35 years before had five times higher rates of illness in middle age, as assessed via careful medical examinations. What was striking was that better health arose not from the absence of uncaring parents, but from the perceived presence of at least one caring parent. Good experiences it seems can inoculate against ill health.

Optimism is natural in children

It is helpful for children to have a slightly overconfident view of themselves, and this aids later competence, as Bjorklund (2007) has demonstrated. In tests adults,

7-year-olds and nursery children were shown a series of 10 pictures and asked how many they expected to remember in the right order. The adults and older children generally guessed they would remember about 5 to 7, and tended to be right, whereas the little ones massively overestimated (Yussen & Levy, 1975). This is fairly typical. Children when young tend to think they can climb higher mountains, balance more balls, score more goals and generally perform excellently, and they are adept at ignoring evidence that contradicts this. For example, in the early years at school most children think they are one of the cleverest in the class (Stipek & Gralinski, 1996). Children of various ages were asked to rate how well they understood the mechanics of complicated devices such as toasters, and the kindergarten children gave themselves the highest ratings of all (Mills & Keil, 2005). Unlike older children, their confident levels of self-belief barely lowered after they heard an adult's 'proper' explanation, and again unlike older children, a quarter even increased their ratings after hearing the actual explanations.

Bjorklund describes this as a form of 'protective optimism' as not just a defensive denial of unwelcome realities. Young children when told stories about people with positive and negative personality traits are likely to believe that the negative traits will change to more positive ones in time, and that things will work out for the best. They do not generally have the opposite belief, that positive traits turn negative (Lockhart, Chang, & Story, 2002). Bjorklund explains such optimism in terms of its usefulness for children who need to try out new things with confidence and persist at tasks that feel too difficult. Of course, within every group there are children who are more or less optimistic or pessimistic, partly because of experiences, such as whether or not they have come from families which displayed much negativity.

Many if not most adults are also prone to such self-deceptive beliefs, such as being adamant that they are better than average drivers (Horswill, Waylen, & Tofield, 2004), or less prejudiced than their peers, something called the self-serving attribution bias by psychologists. Such tendencies are even more marked in little children, and seem to have a protective function. In another 'picture remembering' study, the children who overestimated their skills in a first round, who we might have assumed had an almost delusional level of self-belief, in fact tried out more strategies second time around and improved the most. Their overoptimism encouraged them to keep trying (Taylor & Armor, 1996).

One might contrast such optimism with the children of depressed parents who tend to be more passive, or children who have been traumatised, whose sense of confidence is so badly affected. Obviously there are dangers in overestimating one's ability but optimism does give rise to a sense of self-belief and self-efficacy. Children who have less confidence can easily give up and become less effective. Optimism is a trait which, when seen in children, often continues into adulthood. Furthermore, if a child's scores on optimism and pessimism are the same as those of an average adult this can be a sign of depression, as depressed children and ordinary adults generally come out about the same on such scales (Seligman & Nathan, 1998). Optimism is a quality children begin life with more of, at least when things are going well, and reality slowly creeps in to revise expectations, but hopefully not too much or too soon. Optimism, even laced with a degree of self-deception, can give rise to resilience, and although Freud's view that reality must eventually be faced has some truth, too much reality too early might not be in a child's best interests.

Control, stress, and predictability

Consistently being in the presence of unpredictable events leads people to feel stressed and anxious. Experiments have demonstrated the stress induced by what is called learned helplessness (Peterson, Maier, & Seligman, 1993). When subjects are given tasks to perform, but are intermittently interrupted by very loud noises, they do better when the noise comes at predictable intervals, even if the noise is louder when it was predictable. Similarly, subjects are less stressed and perform better when they are told that they can press a button that will reduce the noise, even if they did not use the button. Knowing what is going to happen, or feeling one has some control over it, reduces stress. Babies who are responded to, whose parents are fairly consistent, and who feel they can influence their interactive partners, feel more confident and less stressed than babies whose parents are unpredictable and abusive, or are neglectful and unresponsive. Give any animal a major stressor (the classic test was cruelly giving electric shocks to dogs), and those with some control do not become hopeless and helpless, whereas those without control become despairing, withdrawn, and fearful, showing symptoms rather like human clinical depression.

We see an exaggerated and more deeply engrained version of learned helplessness in children brought up in abusive or neglectful situations. Once an animal or human child has learnt that there is nothing they can do to change their situation, then they no longer look for or see opportunities that are actually there. Children who have disorganised attachment patterns, for whom the world is unpredictable, have little sense of control except that gained by vigilantly watching the adults or becoming overly 'controlling'. Most research on resilience suggests better outcomes when people feel more positive, can take an active stance, believe that they can influence events and feel confident that the world is predictable, none of which is true of children who suffer extreme neglect, unpredictable trauma, or both.

Stress, resilience, biology, and the brain

Humans and other primates who experience early stressors, such as abuse or separation, are vulnerable later on (Haglund, Nestadt, Cooper, Southwick, & Charney, 2007). They are likely to grow up with abnormally high physiological signs of such stress, such as higher cortisol levels and altered brain organisation. Resilient individuals tend to look forward to good things and maintain an appetite for life. To deal successfully with stress we need a well-functioning reward system, in which dopamine is centrally implicated, and trauma and stress adversely affect reward systems (Bogdan & Pizzagalli, 2006). Research with animals, and clinical accounts with humans, have shown that highly stressful experiences diminish enjoyment and make people and animals averse to social contact, although some are less affected by trauma than others and are more resilient.

Interestingly individuals who use humour tend to be more resilient, as seen both in war veterans (Hendin & Haas, 2004) and at risk children (Werner & Smith, 1992). Humour seems to neutralise anxiety-provoking situations by somehow reappraising and looking at them from another perspective, and of course humour is very much a social, interpersonal act. Indeed laughter in itself has been show to increase immunity-boosting hormones. Breastfeeding mothers shown a Charlie Chaplin film had higher levels of immunity-enhancing hormones in their breast milk than mothers who watched the weather report, thus helping their babies resist allergies (Kimata, 2007). Similarly exposure to humour actively increases the amount of pain someone can tolerate, such as how long subjects could keep their hand in freezing water (Zweyer, Velker, & Ruch, 2004). Humour has many health benefits, from lowering cortisol levels, to heightening immune systems, as well as improving cardiorespiratory functioning (Bennett & Lengacher, 2009).

An active coping style is also helpful. This links with the advantages of being more extroverted and not being an 'ostrich', as being able to face one's fears rather than shirk situations fosters resilience. These three factors, facing one's fears, using humour, and an active coping style, are marked by an ability to 'move towards' experiences, to meet the world 'head-on' rather than shrink from it. This is seen in individuals who have more left hemisphere dominance and are outgoing, reaching out to new experiences, whereas more depressed and introverted individuals show less resilience under stress.

The flipside of positive mental states is seen in **neuroticism**, a cluster of personality traits that includes a tendency to feel anxiety and worry, to be pessimistic, introverted, have a propensity for depression, and to struggle with regulating emotions (Eysenck, 1988). Such people show less resilience, and are more affected by trauma. Interestingly people who are securely attached seem to show more extrovert characteristics (Carver, 1997), and there are links between insecure attachment and neuroticism, and as one might expect a more secure child is likely to be happier, more at ease and confident, and more outgoing.

If one examines the brain activity of extroverts and introverts when showing them both positive images, such as happy couples or children playing, and also some negative sadder or worrying images, the result is fascinating. Subjects high in neuroticism barely respond to the positive images, their brain activity being more or less unchanged, but their brains are very active in response to the negative images. The converse is true for extroverts, who have little brain activity when shown negative images but lots when shown more positive ones (Canli, Zhao, Desmond, Kang, Gross, & Gabrieli, 2001). We perceive and react to a version of the world that we expect and understand.

There are clear biological correlates to these mental states. For example higher levels of the hormone DHEA (dehydroepiandrosterone) is seen in soldiers who perform best under stress, or veterans who recover best from post-traumatic stress (Yehuda, 2004). Similarly low testosterone, which is also linked with depression, is often seen in PTSD, whereas testosterone gets a boost when one is confident. Chicken and egg questions abound here, as it is not clear what causes what. Serotonin is known to be linked to mood, and well-known antidepressants such as Prozac (fluoxetine) target the system involving it. When the serotonin receptors in the brains of mice are 'knocked out' they become more anxious and fearful, so we know that these brain receptors have a role in protecting against stress (Parks, Robinson, Sibille, Shenk, & Toth, 1998). It seems likely that early anxiety and stress down regulate the receptors in the brain for serotonin, basically stopping people experiencing happiness and also reducing resilience. Depressed patients generally have less dense serotonin receptors, as do those with panic disorders. However, one can also have a genetic predisposition to be more or less receptive to serotonin. Children with one kind of serotonin transporter gene, the short *5HT*, are more likely than others to be badly affected by neglect or trauma in childhood, exhibiting more behavioural problems as they get older (Beitchman et al., 2003). Thus experience alters genetic potentials, including for resilience.

Longitudinal studies and protective factors

Living in an enriched environment with plenty of stimulating, positive input seems to actually 'grow' the brain. Rats reared in isolation have thinner cortical regions and less neuronal connections than their counterparts reared in stimulating settings (Curtis & Nelson, 2003). Infants brought up in deprived environments similarly often have smaller head circumference and less complex neuronal pathways (Perry, Pollard, Blakley, Baker, & Vigilante, 1995).

Many intervention studies have attempted to improve children's outcomes by 'enrichment' programmes and early intervention, perhaps the most famous being Headstart in the USA. Most of the studies showed large gains in IQ in the early years in targeted children, but often these gains did not last into adolescence. One exception was the Abecedarian Project in Carolina, which has been going for over 30 years. Here high-risk infants were given interventions in subjects such as language, reading, and maths, with a number of hopeful results. The intervention group were more likely to get through higher education, had higher IQ scores right into adulthood, began having children later and generally the effects lasted longer than in other programmes. The children who gained the most were the ones who started off most at risk, with less good quality input at home (Campbell et al., 2008). We have to be careful in comparing this kind of intervention to enrichment programmes for rats, especially as the human brain continues to mature for at least the first two decades, which is not true of rats. Similarly the enriched rats have their entire environment designed to enhance their potential, but in human intervention programmes children remain in the same homes and neighbourhoods. Furthermore, most of the intervention programmes are targeting specific gains such as IQ, rather than more generalised ones. Nonetheless it does seem that enriching an infant's environment can have a big impact on their future.

Many thorny questions remain unanswered by the resilience research due to the complexity of factors. Behavioural problems in early childhood show considerable continuity into early adulthood but why this is the case is less clear (Masten & Powell, 2003). Antisocial behaviour affects academic performance, and peer relations, for example, yet this cannot in itself be taken as the primary cause, as other factors such as early trauma, lack of good attachment, living in poverty, or genetic factors, need to be taken into account.

Fortunately amidst this complexity some consensus is emerging about which factors are most crucial, through seeing which children come through adversity relatively unscathed. Following divorce, for example, a raft of protective factors is helpful for children (Hetherington & Elmore, 2003). The factors within individuals include having an easy temperament, a good internal locus of control, above average intelligence, higher self-esteem and a sense of humour, and basically the more of these the better. These traits are more likely to develop within a supportive family environment and when there are high levels of conflict in the family things are worse. It has been shown that supporting parents to be both warm and authoritative lessens the risk of mental health problems in children of divorced parents or those suffering the loss of a parent (Sandler, Wolchik, Davis, Haine, & Ayers, 2003). In other words, good loving support and clear boundaries breed resilience.

When interventions are put in place for depressed mothers, such as home visiting and maternal support, then insecure attachment reduces, again illustrating the role of protective factors (Lyons-Ruth, Connell, Grunebaum, & Botein, 1990). Without such help children are more likely to have cognitive, emotional, or behavioural difficulties. The factors that make a difference are closely linked to the kinds of parenting capacities that have been emphasised throughout this book. While depressed mothers tend to show more negative behaviours to their children, and disengage more from them (Lovejoy, Graczyk, O'Hare, & Neuman, 2000), better outcomes are more likely when there is a 'non-ill' father present and contact with other helpful adults. Some good experiences can counter the negative ones and boost resilience.

Studies of children of alcoholics also showed the importance of affectionate and nurturing relationships in early childhood, and particularly of there also being a nonalcoholic parent in the picture (Zucker, Wong, Puttler, & Fitzgerald, 2003). The experience of good relationships is the major protective factor, and in this study all the children had similar negative inputs (i.e., alcoholic parents) but the different amounts of positive experiences made a difference.

Examining the impact of maternal drug abuse throws up surprising findings that raise issues of cause and effect (Luthar, D'Avanzo, & Hites, 2003). The children of drug-using mothers often have serious problems including an increased likelihood of at least one lifetime psychiatric disorder. But the primary causative factor might well not be the drug use, and is more likely to be other factors, such as parental depression, or highly stressed family situations. In one study of at risk children in low-income families, when the drug use was isolated and analysed, it seemed less important than other factors. What seemed particularly significant was the severity of a drug-using mother's mental health problems, and with greater severity one sees less attuned parenting, and more likelihood of hostile interactions. Psychopathology was highest in children whose mothers had high levels of affective and anxiety disorders but without the drug use. It seems that the drugs might not be the main problem, and indeed maybe drugs can even be used to alleviate symptoms through self-medication.

Yet taking account of Bronfenbrenner's (2004) ecological model of influences at various levels, from the individual, family, community, and society as a whole, it is important to bear in mind both the effect of wider social factors and the possibilities for interventions at various levels. For example in one fortuitous natural experiment (Costello, Compton, Keeler, & Angold, 2003) a casino was placed on a Native American reservation and financial benefits came to the community. As a result some families were lifted out of poverty, and this reduced symptoms such as conduct disorders in the children. No such improvement was seen in the local white population who did not benefit financially from the casino. In fact, the mediating factors seemed to be that with decreased poverty the parents engaged more with their children and supervised them more. The families and their histories remained the same and this is a classic example of how a community-wide intervention can affect behavioural and psychiatric symptoms and enhance resilience factors.

What all these studies show, whether of children of divorce, of mentally ill, drug-using or alcoholic parents, is that some children are more resilient and less badly affected than others, while some environments are more likely to breed resilient individuals. The factors that seem to be protective are similar across many studies, and are a mixture of individual attributes, such as genetic inheritance and quality of care, and more distal factors, such as poverty (Kennedy, Burger, Ormel, Huisman, Verhulst, & Oldehinkel, 2009). When living in poverty or a stressful environment it is harder to be a loving, attuned, reflective parent (Kiernan & Huerta, 2008). Broad macro studies seem to back-up the more fine-grained micro research in much of this book that demonstrates the importance of good interactions between caregivers and children.

Ambivalence and emotional complexity

While stress is bad for people, equally a stress-free life is also not what is needed. Children who have come through mild stressors, such as moving home, or a parent becoming ill, are better equipped to deal with stressors later in life (Maddi, 2005) than those who had a stress-free early childhood. A typical example is of adolescent boys who had experienced early difficulties such as ill or divorcing parents, who had less reactive heart rates and blood pressure when performing challenging tasks than boys who had had a relatively easier early life (Boyce & Chesterman, 1990). Too much and/or too overwhelming early stress does not help later on, but interestingly nor does too little, and some exposure to manageable early difficulty builds resilience. This same stress inoculation model can be seen in most primates. Monkeys separated from their mothers for 1 hour every week exhibited acute distress, desperate calling out and high cortisol levels, but they coped better later in life with novel situations than those who had not ever been separated, showing less anxiety on all measurements (Parker, Rainwater, Buckmaster, Schatzberg, Lindley, & Lyons, 2007).

Thus some stress is helpful, and resilience does not come from having an easy life with no challenges. Learning to face difficulties, and to process and modulate one's emotions helps, and experiencing manageable stressors inoculates against later stressors (Lyons, Parker, Katz, & Schatzberg, 2009). This can be through behavioural exposure, or in other words habituating or getting used to difficulties. It can also occur through active conscious emotional processing. For example, some people were shown an upsetting film that featured an automobile accident. They recovered more quickly, and ruminated on it less later, if they were skilful at identifying and processing their own emotions (Mayer, DiPaolo, & Salovey, 1990). What we see in those able to face such adverse experiences is that they do not deny them, or retreat from them, but are able to process and make sense of them. The ability to sustain complex and mixed feelings, to have both positive and negative affect, is central. People who describe themselves in mixed ways tend to be more resilient (Niedenthal & Showers, 1991). Those who paint a rather 'Pollyannaish' too nice vision, who refuse to let any good feelings in with the bad ones or vice versa, turn out to be less resilient to stress. For example parents who score 'submissive' on the Adult Attachment Interview (Chapter 6, p. 64) tend to describe their own childhood experiences positively, irrespective of the reality, having no room in their minds for the negative and also distancing themselves from their children's difficult emotional experiences.

In one experiment, bereaved men and women described their relationships with their recently dead spouses. Those who recovered best were those who told stories about their spouses that contained both negative and positive emotions (Bauer & Bonanno, 2001). A child needs positive experiences, but also the capacity to face and manage negative ones without being overwhelmed; one might say to be positive about negative emotions. This capacity to see two sides of the coin, to manage mixed ambivalent feelings, is at the heart of much psychotherapeutic theory. One kind of feeling, whether positive or negative, cannot simply override another. In one study infants were deliberately mildly distressed with overwhelming lighting and sounds (Harman, Rothbart, & Posner, 1997). Next came an attempt to distract them with interesting noises and colourful shapes, and the infants stopped crying and were indeed distracted by these enticements. However, once the novelty was over the distress returned. It had not been transformed into another emotion but had lain there dormant. The distress was 'kept safe' so to speak, re-emerging when the distraction was over, and still needed managing in its own right. Just managing either positive or negative feelings alone is not enough, and children (and adults) are advantaged if they can manage both sets of feelings.

Summary

This chapter has shown how resilience and protective factors can develop in children, shielding them when difficult experiences arise. The resilience research discussed here asks what leads some children to come through such adverse circumstances better than others. Positive experiences predict positive outcomes. Resilience was once explained mostly in terms of factors internal to the child, but with the advantage of children's developmental histories, researchers have shown that the quality of care has a decisive impact. Sensitive early caregiving is innoculatory and leads to feeling better which in turn leads to better health, higher academic achievement, a more outgoing and confident personality and other positive traits (Werner & Smith, 1992).

When children suffer serious child maltreatment however, very few come through unscathed. In one study not one of the 44 children identified as maltreated were functioning competently in early schooling (Farber & Egeland, 1987). Another found that only 13 per cent of maltreated children were doing reasonably well in elementary school but even these did not sustain their adaptive behaviours into adolescence (Herrenkohl, Egolf, & Herrenkohl, 1997). Maltreated children are far more likely to be classified as low functioning on every measure and resilience always is relative to the severity of the bad experiences that children are exposed to.

Both proximal effects, such as the quality of family life, and distal factors such as inequality, poverty, and hardship, are important and interact with each other. Maltreatment occurs considerably more in poverty (Freisthler, Merritt, & LaScala, 2006). Maybe relative affluence and freedom from economic hardship is the most significant factor in fostering good outcomes. Families at the bottom of society's pecking order are more likely to be younger, single-parent families, have low educational attainment and bad work prospects, all of which increase the likelihood of poor parental mental health, and harsher as well as more neglectful parenting (Appleyard, Egeland, van Dulmen, & Sroufe, 2005). Parents in poverty are less likely to respond to infant cues, have less stable caregiving patterns and are more likely to convey a vision of the world as harsh, unstable, and frightening (Owens & Shaw, 2003). The more risk factors the worse the outcomes, yet the more resilience factors the better the outcomes, and resilience factors like good care inoculate against risk factors (Felitti et al., 1998).

In examining resilience Michael Rutter (2000), has rightly cautioned that one can easily underestimate genetic determinants something that is examined in more detail in the next chapter. Overall it is the loading in terms of risk factors whether genetic, familial, or social that makes the difference, and any one single risk factor taken in isolation has only a modest effect.

To return to where this chapter started, the psychobiological systems for processing negative and positive experiences are different. In emotional health children develop a capacity to manage both good and bad experiences. Good experiences are good for us, and having them can protect us when bad ones come along. Facing and managing bad experiences can also be good for us and foster resilience. This chapter has roamed across a wide terrain, taking into account more 'distal' social influences such as poverty and the wider environment, as well as personal factors such as neurological, biological, and genetic influences, and particularly emotional development in the family context. Individual attributes can be overrated and are less powerful than one might think. Children at social risk who also have high personal resources in fact tend to do worse than economically advantaged children with less personal resilience factors (Sameroff, 1998). For example very bright children from low socioeconomic backgrounds might start off well at school, but are nearly always overtaken in achievements by more advantaged children who had lower intelligence (Feinstein, Hearn, Renton, Abrahams, & MacLeod, 2007). A disadvantaged environment trumps good personal attributes nearly every time. On the plus side it is possible to make a difference on many levels of the system, whether by working with families, schools, individuals, communities, or society as a whole. Resilience is bred from hope and positive action, and there are grounds to have plenty of this.

Genes, nature, and nurture

This book has looked at a wide range of influences on how people turn out the way they do. I have particularly focused on the impact that different kinds of early experiences have on the forming personality. Although there has been mention of genes and inherited temperament, in this chapter they receive attention in their own right. There have been huge advances in understanding in recent years, opening many exciting new vistas, particularly since the advent of the human genome project.

However, there has been suspicion of genetic research in some circles, partly because such research has sometimes in the past been used for questionable purposes with insufficient evidence. An example that Michael Rutter gives is how genetic explanations were often given for the fact that people of Caribbean descent in the UK have a far higher than average likelihood of developing schizophrenia. Although genes can have a role in the development of schizophrenia, in this case genes are less likely to provide a proper explanation because rates of the illness are far lower for ethnically similar populations in the Caribbean (Fung, Bhugra, & Jones, 2006). One has to assume that distal factors such as inequality, racism, or socioeconomic status have a bigger effect. More worrying uses of genetic research include Eysenck's controversial work on race and IQ (Eysenck, 1971), or the questionable claims by Cyril Burt on the inheritance of IQ, which seems likely to have used falsified data (Ward, 1998). Even more worrying has been the use of simplistic genetic ideas in eugenics, which led to practices such as mass sterilisation of some 20,000 unwilling Americans with learning disabilities in the 1930s, or the unthinkable genocide in Hitler's Germany.

Yet despite this, important and surprising discoveries have been made in recent years that have forced people to take note of the importance of genetic influences. Rarely does a week go by when one does not see a newspaper article declaiming some newly discovered gene that is said to cause this or that kind of illness, such as a form of cancer, or a particular psychological symptom. Many such reports should not be taken too seriously. Genes do not generally work in isolation or cause such major effects on their own. More commonly, one sees genetic inheritance giving rise to an increased probability of certain conditions ensuing and there is nearly always some interplay between genes and environment. To take one example, a study of adolescent smoking patterns showed that when there is low parental monitoring of behaviour, a genetic predisposition is likely to lead to smoking, but when parental monitoring is high, then smoking is less likely (Dick, Viken, Purcell, Kaprio, Pulkkinen, & Rose, 2007). Here the parental environment snuffed out the genetic potential.

Genes are more important than many had realised and genetic research has been turning up some surprising results. For example, the idea that some men are good 'marriage stock' might provoke scepticism in some quarters. However, a new Swedish study seems extraordinarily to have isolated a genetic variation or **allele** (allele 334) in men that affects the likelihood of successful relationships (Walum et al., 2008). Men with this allele were nearly twice as likely to be unmarried. Having this allele even predicted what a wife said about how satisfied she was with her marriage. This is all the more surprising as in Sweden there is no financial or tax incentive to marry, and all the men in the sample had either been married or cohabiting for at least 10 years. Yet despite this, having this particular allele was more likely statistically to lead to cohabitation than marriage.

This is the same gene that is involved with vasopressin production, which rather like oxytocin is a hormone involved with producing loving feelings. It had previously been studied in mammals such as voles. There are two species of prairie vole, a monogamous and a nonmonogamous kind, and the main difference between the two seems to be a genetic variation that is very similar to that seen in men. Monogamous voles have a version that leads to the release of more vasopressin, as seemingly do the married Swedish men.

The idea that early experiences have crucial long-term effects holds less water if it can be shown that people are more influenced by their biological inheritance than by their experiences. This is the heart of the nature versus nurture question. What most of the research concludes, though, is that neither nature nor nurture is in charge. People are definitely all born with particular genetic predispositions, and, for example, some adolescent girls have more of a predisposition for depression, but this will only be realised if life events are particularly difficult (Kendler & Greenspan, 2006). Similarly, some people are more predisposed than others to have asthma. Genes matter but experiences can turn genes on and off, and chronically stressful family situations may inhibit the expression of genes which otherwise protect against asthma (Miller & Chen, 2006). Genetic predispositions for behaviours, disorders, or personality types generally do not become a reality without the trigger of particular experiences. While much research using genetics remains at an early stage, it seems clear that nature and nurture work in tandem and neither provides all the answers.

Many studies, such as the Swedish one mentioned above, have used both twin and adoption studies to try to work out whether nature or nurture is more influential, in the hope of discovering whether it is the genetic inheritance (of the adopted twins) or the environmental influence (of the adoptive family) that is primary. Studies of twins adopted apart are not likely to ever be seen again, as it is no longer deemed right to separate twins. Identical twins are of course genetically identical, and so if different life experiences or 'nonshared environments' give rise to different personality traits, we can learn more about the relative importance of genes or environment. Often, though, the research has not yielded definitive answers. For example, children in Finland who had been adopted were tested for their genetic liability to develop schizophrenia. At the same time the family dynamics of the adoptive families were studied carefully. When there was both a genetic liability and a dysfunctional family then schizophrenic symptoms were likely to develop, but the lack of either the genetic potential, or the presence of a well-functioning family, protected against this (Wynne, Tienari, Sorri, Lahti, Moring, & Wahlberg, 2006).

This is a good example of how life experiences can either afford protection against genetic potentials, or predispose people to fulfil such potentials. I have previously mentioned the role of serotonin in 'happy' feelings. Much research has been done on serotonin transporter genes. There are two versions of this *5HT* gene. Subjects, who have a 'short' version are more likely to have behavioural problems, high anxiety, and depression. However, good experience buffers the impact. In one study over 10,000 subjects were followed for 23 years (Caspi et al., 2003). While there was seemingly no difference between those with the short or long version in terms of the number of stressful life events experienced, those with this short allele were more likely to show symptoms such as depression in adulthood or behavioural problems as children, following adverse early experiences. Others with the long allele who suffered similarly bad experiences did not suffer the same seriousness of symptoms. Interestingly, people with this short version also react more to frightening images, with brain scans showing more right amygdala activation in response to them (Hariri, Drabant, & Weinberger, 2006). This *5HT* gene is one of several known to affect the serotonin system. Another is a gene called *TPH2* that has a different impact and seems to affect the likelihood of a range of disorders from ADHD, to panic disorders, bipolar disorder and even suicidality (Shamir & Sakowski, n.d.). Once again it is the combination of genetic potential and experiences that counts.

Similarly if children are traumatised or severely neglected, and also have a particular gene which produces low levels of an enzyme, monoamine oxidase A (MAOA), in the brain, then they have been shown to be as much as nine times more likely to engage in violent or antisocial behaviour than people with the same gene who were not mistreated (Alia-Klein et al., 2008). Treating children badly can affect them hugely, but all children are not necessarily similarly affected by the same mistreatment. In one study of over 1000 children, 85 per cent of the males with both the lower levels of MAOA and suffering severe maltreatment later became antisocial (Foley et al., 2004).

Equally pertinently, having the long rather than short version of a gene called *DRD4* increases the likelihood that children will be novelty seeking and suffer from ADHD (Faraone, Doyle, Mick, & Biederman, 2001). Having the same gene also increases the likelihood of a child having a disorganised attachment, which is of course seen in children who have had traumatic, frightening, and very inconsistent parenting. If one has the riskier long allele and receives insensitive rather than sensitive parenting then one is several times more likely to show such externalising behaviours, and much more likely to show signs of disorganised attachment (Bakermans-Kranenburg, van IJzendoorn, Mesman, Alink, & Juffer, 2008). Yet if the same children receive sensitive and attuned parenting these effects are not seen. Yet again we see that experiences and genes, nature and nurture, interact to produce their effects.

DRD4 is involved with dopamine production and the brain's reward centres, but there are other genes that affect this system as well. For example, one of two genetic variations of the *D2DR* gene gives rise to increased activation of people's reward circuits (Cohen, Young, Baek, Kessler, & Ranganath, 2005). In time we would expect to discover many more genes that give rise to varying amounts of susceptibility to environmental inputs.

Such findings may eventually affect what treatments get offered. For example higher doses of medication are needed to modify ADHD symptoms in children with this long version of the *DRD4* gene (Hamarman, Fossella, Ulger, Brimacombe, & Dermody, 2004). The effectiveness of parenting interventions also seems to depend on which version of this same gene one has. With one group of children who showed more acting-out and ADHD-type behaviours, a parenting intervention was designed which successfully reduced the children's stress and cortisol levels. Yet this parenting programme was more successful with the children who had the long *DRD4* seven-repeat allele, but was less successful for children with the shorter allele (Bakermans-Kranenburg et al., 2008).

Yet we might ask why nature, or evolution, would decree that any child should be born with a version of a gene that gives rise to such a poor prognosis as ADHD. It seems though that such a temperament might well be selected for evolutionary reasons as it proves advantageous in some environments. Examination of large samples of people involved in major migrations reveals that a higher proportion than average had the same 'novelty seeking' genetic variant that leads to ADHD in children

(Chen, Burton, Greenberger, & Dmitrieva, 1999). One can speculate that for these people such novelty seeking might have aided those whose survival depended on finding new territories. To add yet another twist, about one seventh of a Kenyan tribe, the Ariaal, had this long version of the *DRD4* gene. The Ariaal live either a nomadic life, moving from place to place, or a more settled pastoral life. Of those with the novelty-seeking allele, those living a nomadic life, wondering across territories with sheep and goats, were well nourished and healthy, whereas those with this same allele living a settled pastoral life were less well nourished (Eisenberg, Campbell, Gray, & Sorenson, 2008). It seems that having the 'ADHD-inducing' variant might well be a better option when living a less settled kind of life, and that different genetic variation might aid survival or success in different environments.

Thus what we are seeing is that some children are born with more genetic susceptibility than others to certain disorders, but also certain kinds of parenting, such as closely monitoring a child's behaviour, can hugely reduce the potential expression of genes that otherwise often give rise to symptoms such as conduct disorder (Dick et al., 2009). As Belsky (2005) has argued, one way of thinking about such research is that some children are more susceptible to 'rearing influence' or the effects of parental input than others. If one has a short version of the *5HT* then one is more influenced and affected by bad parenting, for example. He argues that this makes evolutionary sense because parents increase the chances of more children surviving and thriving if some of their children are influenced by their current environment, while others are more likely to flourish if the environment changes. What seems to be the case is that nurture, or some kinds of nurturing, has more effect on some children than others.

Genes affect behaviours in self and others

Genes can also have a definite effect on parenting styles. For example having the previously mentioned short allele of the *5HT* gene can give rise to less sensitive parenting, although this too is mitigated by factors such as social support or marital harmony (Bakermans-Kranenburg & van IJzendoorn, 2008). Studies of Swedish twins separated at birth have also demonstrated that a high proportion of the difference in both maternal warmth and marital harmony can also be explained by genetic factors (Neiderhiser & Lichtenstein, 2008).

One of course has to be somewhat careful about what conclusions one should draw from twin and sibling studies. A common assumption is that children in the same family have the same environment and are therefore subject to the same influences, and so if children turn out differently this must be due to their different natures. In fact this is not the case, and indeed ultrasound studies by researchers such as Piontelli (1992) of twins in the womb show just what different experiences twins can have from each other even *in utero*. Other studies have found that the behaviour and outcomes for same-sex adolescents in the same family differs according to how they are treated by their parents, and each child is treated quite differently (Reiss et al., 1996). Indeed if one child is treated harshly, this can have a protective effect on the other, a phenomenon Reiss calls a 'sibling barricade'. Similarly Caspi and colleagues (2004) found in a study of 600 identical twin pairs, who obviously shared 100 per cent of their genes, that the degree of positive or negative emotional expression from a mother to each twin predicted later antisocial behaviour.

On the other hand it is also true that different children evoke different reactions from parents, peers, and other adults. Parents react more similarly to identical twins than nonidentical twins, for example, and some children are more likely to evoke hostile responses and to be antisocial than others (Reiss, Neiderhiser, Hetherington, & Plomin, 2000). Thus their genes evoke an environmental response. Nonetheless, the interplay between the two remains and if parents are more consistently calm and less emotionally labile then this seemingly 'blunts' the genetic influence of such provocative children, leading to a calmer family life (Feinberg, Button, Neiderhiser, Reiss, & Hetherington, 2007).

Some researchers have argued that by as early as 5 months as much as 30 per cent of the variation in a mother's hostile behaviour can be attributed to an infant's temperament (Forget-Dubois, Boivin, Dionne, Pierce, Tremblay, & Pérusse, 2007). Another adoption study found that adopted children whose biological parents had shown more antisocial tendencies, or drug and alcohol use, were more likely to have adoptive parents who were harsh and inconsistent, a finding that is explained by these children inheriting temperaments likely to elicit more angry reactions in those around them (Ge et al., 1996a). Other studies have similarly shown that children born to antisocial mothers are also more likely to experience negative parenting from adoptive parents (O'Connor, Deater-Deckard, Fulker, Rutter, & Plomin, 1998), the children's disruptive behaviour and temperaments seemingly giving rise to more harsh parenting. Again caution needs to be exercised. In high-risk environments, such as where the adopted parents showed overt psychological problems, such effects are more likely to be seen than in low-risk ones (Riggins-Caspers, Cadoret, Knutson, & Langbehn, 2003).

A huge study of identical twins showed that marital conflict not in a man's marriage but in that of his identical twin brother's marriage, predicted antisocial behaviour in his child, irrespective of levels of conflict in his own marriage (Harden et al., 2007). In other words the shared genes of twins predict genetically driven behaviour not only in their own, but also their twin's children (these cousins being effectively half-siblings), suggesting a relationship between marital conflict and antisocial behaviour which has genetic roots.

Even more extraordinarily, the husbands of a large sample of both identical and nonidentical female married twins were asked questions about how satisfied they were with their marriage. The statements made by the husbands of these identical twins about their wives were more similar to each other than the statements made by husbands of nonidentical twins about their wives. This suggests that genetic influence affects not just a wife's marital behaviour, but also her husband's views on it, and even the response of the wife's twin sister's husband (Spotts et al., 2004).

Finally it is worth stressing that gene–environment interaction needs to be understood at a macro-societal level as well as at the level of family interactions. For example, in a massive Finnish study of about 10,000 twins (Rose & Kaprio, 2008), the use of alcohol and tobacco in adolescents was found to have a clear heritable element. However, this was modulated not only by different kinds of parenting and sibling interactions, but different schools and neighbourhoods also affected this, as also did differences between urban and rural environments. Thus again various levels of interaction and analysis are needed.

Genes are not everything

As well as the various kinds of genetic studies other, nongenetic, findings can cast light on what is genetic. For example, most of the evidence suggests that IQ is heritable to an extent but is also hugely affected by environmental factors. A typical example was seen in a large French study that found that the IQs of deprived children who were later adopted increased markedly after adoption, but also their IQs increased more when they were adopted into more advantaged homes (Duyme & Capron, 1992), thus demonstrating the important role of different environments on intelligence, irrespective of genetic inheritance.

Similarly the Romanian orphan studies showed clearly that these children showed common traits, such as quasi-autistic symptoms, cognitive impairments, disinhibited attachment and problems with attention and emotional regulation, all in much higher proportions than found in the normal adoptive population. Many of these effects were still present years later despite new environmental influences (Rutter et al., 2007).

In other areas genetic inheritance has not been shown to have particularly wide-reaching effects. One study looked at both genetic and environmental factors in the transmission of depression from mother to child, comparing a large adopted and nonadopted sample (Tully, Iacono, & McGue, 2008). The study showed how both genetic and nongenetic children were much more likely to suffer depression in adolescence when the mother (not the father) was depressed. As this was the case whether the child was adopted or not, it could only be the environment (i.e., a depressed mother, whether a birth or adoptive mother) which was the main factor.

Attachment patterns are similarly more influenced by the different treatment children get from their parents, particularly differences in parental sensitivity and mind-mindedness (Fearon et al., 2006). Genetics it seems has little effect on the very real connection between maternal sensitivity and a child's attachment classification. One study of twins found that genetic factors did not predict a child's attachment security at all. In this study maternal sensitivity was measured, and mothers were found to be differently sensitive with each twin, which in turn was a predictor of each twin's attachment security (Bokhorst, Bakermans-Kranenburg, Fearon, van IJzendoorn, Fonagy, & Schuengel, 2003). Even with twins there is a large nonshared environment. Indeed some twin studies, as David Reiss and colleagues (2000) has pointed out, show that having a strong attachment to one twin can suppress this possibility occurring with the other twin. Children in the same family do not necessarily share the same emotional environment, and while they might share some influences they also have some very different experiences. Measures are needed that are subtle enough to pick up the ways children are treated both differently and similarly within a family.

Summary

Much genetic research is currently being undertaken, and in many respects it is rather early to draw too many conclusions as there is so much we do not yet know. An example of the complexity of factors is seen in intergenerational influences, such as the transmission of abuse. We know that environmental inputs are crucial. For example, sensitive or insensitive mothering has been shown to have an impact on how a rat's offspring look after their own young (Cameron, Champagne, Parent, Fish, Ozaki-Kuroda, & Meaney, 2005). Rats licked lovingly as infants later become parents who do the same with their own pups. While genes make some difference and rat mothers of strains bred for generations to produce jumpy, insensitive rats, normally become less nurturing parents, however their pups still become calm and not at all jumpy when cross-fostered with rat mothers bred to be caring and calm. Yet, to complicate the gene–environment interaction question still further, what has also come to light in the last few years is that good or poor care might have an effect on a molecular, genetic level, a view which smacks of ideas that had been discredited since Lamarck. It is possible, according to some initial research, that in rats the memories of competent care leave their mark not only in brain centres of the offspring, but possibly as well the very genes are affected in a way that affects the next generation (Champagne & Curley, 2009). What this research suggests, but as yet has not proven, is that nurture not only turns on or off the expression of specific genetic potentials but can even alter the very form of genes that the succeeding generation might inherit. This is just one story that is yet to unfold in the debate about genes and nature/nurture.

It would make sense that the infant, or even the foetus, picks up clues about the likely world they will find themselves in, and not only adapts to it but also predicts (nonconsciously) that later environments might be similar. It also makes sense that a degree of heritability might develop over time. For example, some populations seem to have developed less diabetes than others, as the gene pool might well alter following consistent experiences in a population (Diamond, 2003). Yet most animals, including humans, retain a degree of plasticity in case these early predictions are wrong. The cross-fostering studies particularly are an example of this (Champagne & Meaney, 2007).

Genetic research has recently progressed hugely and is now better at avoiding simplistic understandings. We do know now that genes are important. We also know that the effect of the environment and experiences are important. Furthermore, we know that certain experiences seem to trump the impact of genetic factors. We also know that some people are more influenced by particular environmental stressors than others, in part because of the genes they inherit. Maybe the main overall conclusion we can draw thus far is that both genes and environment are important, and that genetic potentials can be turned on or off by environmental inputs. Almost definitely the most interesting research is yet to arrive, which will help flesh out in more detail the relative influence of genes and environment in specific instances.

Chapter 20

Conclusions: earlier experience and its longer-term consequences

This book has aimed to describe something fundamental about how the human infant, with all its unrealised potentials and possible futures, develops into a particular kind of person. Research findings have been at the heart of this endeavour, and they have cast an increasingly bright light on the subject in recent years. Any life lived means not having lived other potential lives, and it is the coincidence of being born into a particular family, in a particular culture, historical period, and social group, with the experience of unique life events, in combination with genetic inheritance, that provide the ingredients that form a person.

One of the main questions people ask when hearing about the range of influences on young children is how much continuity is inevitable from early life, and how much change is possible as time goes on. These are vital questions if we are to make a difference to people whose early experiences have not been good. We have seen that children are affected by earlier experiences, but also that they can build new experiences alongside past learning, develop new expectations, and new internal working models of relationships. This final chapter goes back over some of these issues and questions. I have described development in terms of an ecological perspective (Bronfenbrenner, 2004), which takes account of individual, family, neighbourhood, and societal factors, and the ways these all influence each other, allowing us to think of there being a 'cascade' of effects throughout life, as discussed in Chapter 16 on adolescence (Masten, 2006). Such perspectives suggest that there are a variety of levels of influence and potential points of intervention over a life course.

Attachment and the effects of early experiences

Attachment theory has been a constant presence throughout this book, so in this last chapter I look again at the long-term effect early attachments have. Attachment status at a year as measured in the Strange Situation Test (Chapter 6, p. 61) is on its own not a very good predictor of later developmental outcomes, even though there are interesting continuities. We have learnt that the main influence on what kind of attachments children form is the experiences they have had with their primary carers. While genes and temperament exert an influence on children, and for example some are born more or less reactive to stress (Frigerio, Ceppi, Rusconi, Giorda, Raggi, & Fearon, 2009), attachment status is more a function of the kind of parenting children receive rather than their temperament (Fearon et al., 2006).

A typical example of early continuity is children maltreated in infancy who in pre-school attack vulnerable children and are less able to show empathy to others in distress. Children who have been treated empathically at home respond to distress in others with care and concern (Sroufe, 2005). Here early nonconscious relationship patterns are being carried forward. The maltreated children are not maltreated in their next context, by their nursery staff, but they end up somehow being less liked and more shunned than other children. Researchers have found some continuity of such attitudes all the way into adolescence (Carlson, Sroufe, & Egeland, 2004). The premise behind the idea that early attachment has an ongoing impact is that one develops, in response to experiences, internal mental models of relationships that are then used in later relationships. Maltreated children will often ascribe aggressive intentions to actions that other children perceive more benignly. Such nonconscious internal models, based on procedural memories, can be challenged by new kinds of experiences, or be affirmed by continuity of experiences, and internal models always reflect a combination of current and earlier experiences.

Although the evidence overwhelmingly suggests that maternal sensitivity predicts attachment security, we still know less than we might about what the mechanisms are by which parents pass on attachment security, a lack of knowledge often termed the transmission gap (Van Zeijl et al., 2006). While leading child development researchers seem to concur that maternal sensitivity plays an important role (Steele, Steele, & Fonagy, 1996), a single, exact, and reliable measure for such sensitivity has not been agreed. It seems that maternal mind-mindedness, as defined by Meins et al. (2001), is as good a candidate as the research has found for being such a predictor.

A child who is securely attached at a year is unlikely to remain in such a healthy emotional state if external factors change. Belsky and Fearon (2002) looked at what happens when a secure environment becomes less secure and vice versa. Looking at factors like school readiness, linguistic capacities, and social skills children who were insecure at 15 months but then later received very sensitive parenting in fact outperformed the children who at a year were secure but whose parenting experience then deteriorated. Factors such as stress in the home and worsening social circumstances can lead to lessening parental sensitivity and so to worse trajectories.

As described also in the chapter on resilience, some children surprisingly come through adverse experiences and do very well, even if there usually is a cost to this. Werner and Smith (1992) found for example that adults who had overcome huge adversity in childhood, and seemed to be performing as well as their peers in adulthood, nonetheless suffered from more psychosomatic problems. Something similar has been found in rhesus monkeys who suffered early separations, and who in later life seemed fine, only to revert to previous odd behavioural patterns when placed in stressful situations (Suomi, Novak, & Well, 1996). The past can leave its mark, what the psychoanalyst Michael Balint (1968) described as a fault-line in the personality. Children with histories of positive care and competence are far less likely to show problem behaviours when placed in stressful situations than those who have had worse starts to life.

A child is constantly adapting to its current circumstances, using nonconscious relationship templates that have already formed. If a child loses a benevolent breadwinning father or gains a violent one, then their context changes and they adapt to it. What early attachment security seems to offer is a kind of buffer against such socioemotional blows. In other words a secure child at 15 months might have a head start on an insecure one, but they are maybe more likely to remain secure and confident 2, or 4, or 10 years later also because they have remained in a home where sensitive thoughtful parenting was present. To state the obvious, the best position of all to be in is to have good early experiences followed by good later experiences, allied of course with the right temperament.

Early attachment patterns can last, and even be transmitted across generations. Miriam and Howard Steele followed up first-time mothers who had been given Adult Attachment Interviews in pregnancy (Chapter 6, p. 64). The children of mothers who scored secure-autonomous in pregnancy were, at age 11, better able to manage complex emotions, to understand others' feelings, and on a range of other scores, to be more competent (Steele & Steele, 2005). We have seen how parents with a diagnosable mental health issue, such as maternal depression (Martins & Gaffan, 2000) or border-line personality disorder (Levy, Meehan, Weber, Reynoso, & Clarkin, 2005) are less likely to have securely attached children. Insecurely attached children are at more risk in many ways as they grow up, such as being more likely to have behavioural problems or interpersonal difficulties. Secure children tend to have better social skills, peer relationships, and cognitive abilities, as well as more empathy (Prior & Glaser, 2006).

The massive longitudinal studies of attachment by the Grossmans in Germany (Grossmann, Grossmann, & Waters, 2005) and Sroufe (2005) in Minnesota have found clear evidence of the very long-term effects of early experience. For example in Sroufe's Minnesota sample secure children, by age 10, were less dependent on adults than both avoidant and ambivalent/resistant children in a summer camp setting. These studies also found a link between attachment quality at 12 to 18 months and adolescent social functioning (Sroufe, 2005). Interestingly children who changed from secure to insecure functioning were found to have suffered more life stress than those who did not change. Sroufe's Minnesota study found that all in all the more factors that are measured and put into the equation, and the more moments in a person's life that data is examined, then the more sense one could make of how people end up as they do. There is definitely some continuity between early childhood and later life in relation to attachment, but this is mediated by a huge raft of other factors, and later influences, that can change a trajectory in one direction or another.

Childhood trauma and lack of good experiences

When these early experiences are of extreme abuse or neglect then even sceptics agree that early experiences have a longer-term effect. We have seen how stress and trauma has a marked effect on the hormonal system, on cortisol levels, as well as on brain pathways. In Chapter 17 I described research which showed the devastating effects of serious maltreatment on later outcomes, such as how borderline personality disorder is closely related to serious childhood maltreatment. Early abuse and serious childhood attachment problems affect a range of capacities such as executive function and the ability to form relationships (Minzenberg, Poole, & Vinogradov, 2006). Such children have not only had bad experiences, but many traumatised young people generally have never been lucky enough to receive the 'inoculation' of good care from adults possessing the kind of reflective functioning one sees in secure attachment (Bateman & Fonagy, 2004).

With extremes of abuse or neglect the longer-term outcomes are far less hopeful than with mildly adverse circumstances, and children do not have as much potential for change. We saw how in the widely studied cohort of orphans adopted from Romania, the longer they were in the orphanages the worse they did, and all showed some impairment in social and/or cognitive functioning. They were often adopted into extremely supportive homes, and although many did extremely well, there still was a limit to the amount of change that was possible (Rutter et al., 2007).

Generally children who have the worst experiences suffer the most in the longer term. Particularly worrying are those not living with their families, who often suffered abuse and neglect, and who the state have taken into the care system. As many as

50 per cent of them have mental health difficulties, and their overall prognosis educationally and psychologically is not good. Over a quarter of the prison population were formerly 'Looked After'. Bad things tend to come together. If a young person experiences more than 5 adverse factors in their families – these might be substance abuse, domestic violence, unemployment, disability, mental health problems or poor housing, for example – then they are as much as 36 times more likely to be excluded from school, and considerably more likely to be in trouble with the police or to be taken into the care system (Richardson & Lelliott, 2003). The American ACE study showed similar results (Dube et al., 2003). Bad experiences give rise to bad outcomes, and generally the more bad experiences the worse the outcomes.

What change is possible?

Yet change is possible, and interventions can really affect children's futures. A graphic example of both the effect of early experiences, and how later experiences can alter trajectories, is seen when children have been traumatised or abused and the radical intervention of adoption is used. Research using story-stem procedures (Hodges et al., 2003) shows that children subjected to trauma often have minds full of disastrous scenarios, and have little faith that adults can be trusted or that life could include order, routine, or safe boundaries. Their stories at the point of adoption are often full of blood, death, and violence, of adults acting like immature children, and people living in an unsafe world. Once adopted into safe homes changes are seen as early as 3 months later. These children develop new narratives with less disastrous scenarios, and their stories begin to show more order and narrative structure, and to describe a world where children can rely on adults to look after them. Yet their old stories remain, and they still often rely on their old view of the world, even though new versions are growing alongside the old. At different points children will rely on different under-standings of reality; and at times of stress the old models will often come to the fore again. In this study the children who did best were adopted by parents who scored secure-autonomous on the Adult Attachment Interview (Chapter 6, p. 64), or in other words, who had good capacities for processing emotions, for reflective self-functioning or mentalising, which has been another theme threaded throughout this book.

Equally hopeful are the changes seen in children's attachment status after they are fostered early in their lives. Mary Dozier and colleagues have done extensive research with fostered children who often come from very traumatising and abusive backgrounds (Dozier, Stovall, Albus, & Bates, 2001). Their striking findings are that infants fostered in their first year of life tend to reorganise their ways of relating to fit the relationship patterns experienced with their new carers. When placed with carers classified as secure-autonomous these fostered infants who had been subject to abuse nonetheless formed secure attachments. As was seen in the story-stem research with adopted children, being placed with carers who were sensitive to their psychological states gave clear advantages. Not only did the more fortunately placed children's representational worlds become more benign and hopeful, but the placements were less likely to break down or have serious difficulty.

Being adopted or fostered into a safe home after an abusive early experience is a more dramatic intervention than most children experience. We know that there are a range of influences and factors that might tip a child from one potential trajectory onto another. Such life changes might include, for example, a mother becoming depressed, a financial crisis, a supportive step-father arriving, or a child entering a very good or bad school, or a very different neighbourhood. Other important inputs include what professionals do, such as teachers, social workers, or therapists, or major community or social interventions. Many readers of this book will be undertaking activities with children and families that most definitely change a child or family's trajectory.

In terms of children's mental health, there is increasing evidence that early interventions can have an effect right into adulthood. Longer-term gains from treatment include a lesser risk of use of psychoactive drugs in children treated for ADHD, less risk of mortality for those treated for anorexia nervosa, and improved outcomes for those with autistic-spectrum disorders where language disorders are addressed early (c.f. Hazell, 2007).

In the world of child mental health recent years have seen increased evidence about how interventions can make a difference. I will not go into too much detail here about which methods work with which problems, as this has been reported in depth by experts such as Kazdin and Weisz (2009) and Roth and Fonagy (2005). For example we know that serious conduct disorders and oppositional behaviour can be treated successfully with forms of parent training, adolescent depression can be effectively treated with interpersonal psychotherapy, and that cognitive–behavioural therapy (CBT) can be effective for anxiety disorders and obsessive-compulsive symptoms.

Such findings give considerable hope, although a degree of caution should be used when arguing that one form of treatment is necessarily more effective than another. Other factors inevitably intervene and skew results. There are many forms of therapy used that have not as yet got an evidence base. It seems that some kinds of therapies, such as CBT, might be particularly amenable to accepted research formats such as **randomised controlled trials (RCTs)** and CBT practitioners have been good at gaining research funding. Other treatments, such as psychoanalytic and systemic approaches, have not yet been as well researched via RCTs, but still have a growing evidence base (Trowell et al., 2007; Kennedy, 2004). Not having an evidence base gleaned from a RCT does not mean that a treatment does not work.

Furthermore, there have been considerable difficulties in translating good treatment outcomes in experimental clinical trials to similarly good outcomes in the ordinary clinical settings that most clients attend. This might partly be because the zeal and belief of the originators of research trials cannot so easily be transferred to such everyday settings, and consistent belief in a treatment definitely affects outcome (Beutler, 2009). Also, most research trials compare treatments for children who present with a single disorder (such as anxiety or depression), while practitioners in the field rarely meet children with a single treatable disorder. Indeed many children referred for help have a range of issues, what is called comorbidity, such that they might even be unlikely to be accepted onto a research trial.

Maybe more importantly, there is also increasing evidence that factors other than the form of treatment make a difference. Evidence shows that often the quality of what is called the therapeutic alliance between a client and a therapist has a greater effect than the form of treatment offered (Green, 2006). In other words, children or young people suffering from the same disorder but being offered different forms of treatment are more likely to get better if the therapeutic alliance between therapist and client is good, irrespective of the treatment modality. Furthermore, it has been shown that outcomes are not particularly affected by whether clients like the therapist, but are measurably linked to the degree of skill of the therapist (Scott, 2008). In fact it seems that there are some common factors that make a good therapist (Lambert, 2005), which include being able to make a good alliance, being consistent, having hopes and expectations of improvement, as well as the effectiveness of the therapist (Messer & Wampold, 2002). Relationship factors such as the kind of therapist and the kind of patient often have a bigger effect on the form of treatment offered (Beutler, 2009). Even so, a good therapist nonetheless needs to use an effective treatment and neither the one nor the other alone is enough (Sexton, Ridley, & Kleiner, 2004).

This should all make sense in terms of the main themes of this book. The psychological attitude and skills of parents, and how they interact with their children, make a big difference, just as do the attitudes and capacities of professionals such as therapists, teachers, or social workers. Research in this book has emphasised how central maternal sensitivity, and in particular mind-mindedness and mentalisation, are in ensuring secure attachment in children. Several therapies have tried to target just this area, often with success, and children's attachments improve when parents get help in being sensitive to their child (Bakermans-Kranenburg et al., 2003). This can be especially crucial with mothers whose infants are at risk, either because of their socioeconomic position or because of infant temperament. In one study 78 per cent of the control group who did not receive help had children classified as insecure after a year, as opposed to only 38 per cent of the group who received help. When mothers are helped to become more responsive and thoughtful, and to read their children's emotional signals, then a real difference can be made to these children's attachment patterns (Cooper, Hoffman, & Marvin, 2003).

Similarly Lynne Murray's, as well as other clinicians' interventions, with postnatal depression have shown success. Without such help children become more passive, with less sense of agency, are more likely by age 8 to be showing conduct disorders, and by 15 daughters of depressed mothers in Murray's sample were showing above average frequencies of depression (Murray, Halligan, Adams, Patterson, & Goodyer, 2006).

There is also now an impressive array of research concerning the impact of various kinds of parenting interventions such as Webster-Stratton (Webster-Stratton, Reid, & Hammond, 2004) or Triple P (Prinz, Sanders, Shapiro, Whitaker, & Lutzker, 2009). Such findings can counter a gloomy pessimism that sometimes descends when thinking about the effects of bad early experiences. Even in the most serious cases, such as children and young people at risk of incarceration (Woolfenden, Williams, & Peat, 2001), there is clear evidence that interventions can make a real difference, including effective help based on the principles of attachment theory (Juffer, Bakermans-Kranenburg, & van IJzendoorn, 2008).

As stated, interventions can take place at different levels and have different effects depending on a multitude of factors such as where one intervenes (e.g., child, family, school system), its timing, individual factors in a child, the skill of the therapist, the quality of the intervention, and many others. For example the child of a depressed mother might get better as a result of a support group or parenting programme, or psychotherapy for the mother, the whole family or the child, or a community intervention. Not only can psychotherapy help a mother's depression, but more importantly, children of the mothers who are treated for depression improve more than children of nontreated mothers (Pilowsky et al., 2008), and so ameliorating a mother's depression aids their children, even when the children themselves are not treated directly. Children's lives can also be changed dramatically via changes in contextual factors such as poverty or socioeconomic status, and social care programmes. The main point is that there are many interventions, and many levels of intervention, that can alter worrying trajectories and can give us hope that change is possible.

Conclusions

We have learnt a huge amount about child development research in recent years. Although I have tried to avoid personal judgements and views in this book, it is hard to deny that too many children suffer through having less than optimal emotional experiences. Maybe these matters are more worrying in Britain, where, consistently on just about all scores the experience of childhood is worse than in other European countries. Typical is teenage pregnancy, which is over five times higher than in Holland, for example (Stone & Ingham, 2002). In total 1 in 10 British children has a diagnosable mental health disorder (Green, McGinnity, Meltzer, Ford, & Goodman, 2005), and many others have more minor difficulties. This matters because such serious issues, when untreated, do not just go away. A typical example is that 40 per cent of the children with conduct disorder at aged 8 were convicted of criminal activity in adolescence, and when looked at in reverse, 90 per cent of adolescents convicted of crimes had conduct disorders as children. Early problems are equally predictive of other worrying later outcomes, such as teenage pregnancy, drug use, or poor educational attainment for example (Romeo, Knapp, & Scott, 2006).

It would be naïve to think that these figures can be understood solely from a psychological perspective. Evidence from numerous sources has been mounting that mental health outcomes differ widely across the Western world, and indeed across the whole world, and in great measure these differences reflect the way societies are organised. A consistent theme is that the wider the income gaps in a society, the worse the mental health for those at both the top and bottom of the ladder. Epidemiological studies of large international samples (Marmot, 2005; Wilkinson & Pickett, 2009) have found that the more unequal and individualistic cultures are then on average people's levels of trust in others is lower, health outcomes are worse, mental health is also worse, and the overall prognosis deteriorates. It seems that the higher the inequality levels in a society then the lower the general levels of trust (Uslaner, 2008), and the weaker community life (Putnam, 2000). Social support systems do not work so well in such cultures, and for that reason communities can become more violent, families are less likely to stay together, and outcomes across the board can worsen. Many have argued that an increasingly consumerist culture is fuelling these changes (James, 2008).

Often research about family life is used as a rallying call by politicians and others who support ideas such as that marriage is good and family life is central. The facts they use are often right, but nonetheless the arguments do not necessarily hold water. For example, in Britain about one-third of 16-year-olds do not live with their biological father, and the same is true of a half of American youth (Bumpass & Lu, 2000), and it is true that children whose parents are not living together on average have 50 per cent more problems (Pryor & Rodgers, 2001). While a better family life is extremely important to children's mental health, the national and international epidemiological evidence suggests that the cause largely lies with larger, wider factors. Tackling psychological problems directly is important and helpful, but so is tackling social problems and both are needed. An important study looked at maternal depression and economic deprivation, and their combined and separate effects on children's outcomes (Kiernan & Huerta, 2008). It found that when both were present then children's cognitive and emotional development suffered, but it was not just either poverty or parenting that had the effect. While poverty had a big impact, parenting factors in their own right also made a big difference to the children's lives. Again, one can intervene at several levels in the system.

One of the exciting things about the current crop of research is that we can make links between individual children's experiences and more macro whole population findings. On a micro-level we know a lot about how children experience the world. We have seen the kinds of defences children build in response to stressful and painful situations, such as turning in on themselves and self-soothing in the absence of adult care. We can now understand how unsafe some children's worlds can feel, via research with their story-stems as well as directly from therapeutic work. We know for example from fMRI scans how fear affects the brain, giving rise to a more active amygdala, and how stressed children have higher baseline cortisol levels. We similarly have learnt a lot about how different family atmospheres and parenting styles affect children, as well as the effects of different kinds of neighbourhoods, different cultural beliefs, and the various ways societies and their economies are organised.

We are also better at interpreting our findings. As Rutter (2005) pointed out, it has been all too easy to confuse factors that indicate risk, such as what used to be termed 'broken homes', and the factors that really cause the risk, which might be more to do with the discord and violence in the home than the mere fact of parents splitting up. We have learnt to take into account both immediate effects, such as parental depression which can affect children, and also what are called more distal causes, such as poverty and inequality, which make parenting that much harder, and increase the likelihood of such parental mental illness. This can also help to take the 'blame' out of the research, particularly the blame of mothers. Parents affect their children, but often for reasons well beyond their control, such as violent neighbourhoods or abusive partners. Similarly direction of influences between parents and children are also by no means only one way, and children affect parents too (Rutter, 2005). The relationship between immediate and more distal effects still needs to be understood much more. There is also still a lot we do not know about the relationship between genes and environment, a field of study that is still in its infancy.

Interestingly the best predictor of childhood resilience in Werner and Smith's (1992) classic study was how 'loveable' a child was at 2 years old. This striking statement is typical of those that need a great deal of unpacking. The lovability may be something to do with a temperament a child was born with, or alternatively how much a child has been loved and enjoyed until then, or how mind-minded the parents were, which in turn will be influenced by more distal factors. This finding does though take us back to the fact that this research is about individual experiences and children's experiences and feelings, such as of being loved.

No human being can be reduced to the sum of the influences on them, even if such a comprehensive analysis was feasible. While this book has aimed to understand general principles, and wider external factors, ultimately it is trying to describe lives that are lived, and people who think, feel, and experience the world. Each child and adult is on a developmental trajectory, and understanding this trajectory inevitably means understanding the behaviours, but also the biological, psychological, and emotional states of a person, and how a whole being interacts with and responds to their environment. On an individual level this means being aware of each person as an active agent. The individual enters any new moment constrained by their current external situation and also by their history and prior expectations, their own set of emotional and biological capacities. Yet the next moment is always open to possibility, and although people have patterns in place, such patterns can be either confirmed or challenged by new experiences and new opportunities.

The last few decades have been an extraordinarily exciting time for understanding how children develop. The next few decades promise to be equally revolutionary and we can but await new findings with baited breath. What we can be sure of for now, and what the research has clearly shown, is that while the influences of temperament and genes are important and becoming better understood, the kind of parenting one receives and the kind of influences one has as a child can have a big effect, even if some children are more influenceable than others. This research can be a springboard for arguing that the kind of society we produce, and the kind of support and help we put in place for children and families, will make a big difference to future generations.

Glossary

Adult Attachment Interview (AAI)   A semi-structured interview that asks adults about emotional experiences and assesses their capacity for reflective self-functioning and assesses if they can develop a coherent narrative about their lives.

Affect   A person's emotional state, which they can sometimes recognise subjectively, and sometimes is linked to specific thoughts.

Allele   A form or variant of a gene.

Alloparent   An animal that behaves parentally towards a child that is not its offspring.

Ambivalent attachment   A form of attachment associated with more clingy behaviours, generally linked to more inconsistent parenting styles.

Amygdala   Small almond shaped area of the brain that links to many other brain regions, particularly involved with the fear response and other emotional reactions.

Androgen   Male sex hormones.

Androgyny   A state of ambiguous, mixed, or uncertain gender.

Attachment disorder   *see also* **reactive attachment disorder**.

Attention-deficit hyperactivity disorder (ADHD)   A diagnostic category describing impulsivity, an inability to regulate behaviour, to concentrate or attend to tasks.

Attunement   Being in tune with another's emotional state.

Avoidant attachment   An attachment style in which a child seems to be little bothered if their caregiver is nearby or not, linked with more 'dismissive' parenting styles.

Borderline personality disorder   A psychiatric diagnosis describing people with unstable relationship patterns, lack of a well-defined sense of self, and regular or constant changes in mood.

Conditioning In conditioning one learns to associate one stimulus (e.g., a bell ringing) with another (e.g., salivating because food is coming).

Containment A term from Bion describing emotional experiences, such as in an infant, are processed and made understandable by a mother or therapist.

Contingency The expectation that one event or act is likely to cause or give rise to another predictable one.

Corpus callosum A bundle of nerve cells that link the left and right cerebral hemispheres.

Cortisol The best know stress hormone; produced by the adrenal gland.

Declarative memory Sometimes known as explicit memory, a form of long-term memory of facts, such as dates.

Defence A way of protecting the self from the effects of experiences that otherwise might produce huge anxiety or feel unbearable.

Disorganised attachment An attachment style in children who have had frightening experiences with their primary carers and either have given up on developing a coherent strategy to respond, or who become hypervigilant.

Dissociation A split in the mind so that some aspects of experience are 'cut-off' from; often seen in trauma.

Dopamine A neurotransmitter that is particularly involved in the reward system and positive affect.

Duchenne smile A smile of genuine happiness that uses both eye and mouth muscles.

Egocentric A cultural belief that individualism and autonomy should be highly valued. Also refers to Piaget's (1976) theory of a very early stage of thinking when children cannot see another's perspective.

Episodic memory Stored personal experiences, often tied to specific people or places.

Executive functioning This describes a range of capacities such as being able to analyse situations, plan activities, and maintain focus to get a task done.

Experience dependent Developments and changes, such as in the brain, that depend on having particular experiences.

Experience expectant Experiences that a human might be born expecting, such as some care from an adult or being spoken to.

Explicit memory Memories of facts, such as dates (*see also* **declarative memory**).

Externalising Behaviours such as dramatic acting out, behaviour problems, violence and conduct issues, seen more in boys than girls as a result of adverse experiences, and contrasted with internalising disorders.

Flashbulb memories A memory that is stored after an emotionally arousing event (e.g., what one was doing when hearing of a famous person's death).

Habituation How a new, exciting, or worrying stimulus is got used to.

Hypothalamus–pituitary–adrenal (HPA) axis Regulates the body's stress system via the hypothalamus, pituitary, and adrenal glands.

Infant-directed speech A way of talking most adults across the world adopt with babies, often called **motherese** or parentese.

Infantile amnesia Denoting that humans retain no or few declarative memories from the period of infancy.

Internalising   A response to adverse circumstances via presentations that are turned inwards, such as in depression, self-harm, or eating disorders. Seen more in girls than boys, and generally contrasted with externalising disorders.

Internal working model   A mental model, based on previous experiences, which allows someone to predict what is likely to happen in relationships.

Intersubjectivity   The sharing of subjective states between two or more people.

Joint attention   Sharing one's experience of an event or object with another person through gestures or pointing.

Marking   An exaggerated demonstration of attunement with another's state of mind or feelings.

Mentalisation   The ability to reflect on one's own and another's experience.

Mindfulness   An ability to be aware of one's mental processes, often cultivated via meditative exercises.

Mind-mindedness   A mother's capacity to be in touch with her infant's psychological and mental states, and to refer to these.

Mirroring   Reflecting back to someone their mental or emotional state.

Motherese   A way of talking most adults across the world adopt with babies, often called parentese or infant-directed speech (IDS).

Myelination   A white insulating sheath around nerve cells that allows much faster communication.

Neuron   A basic cell in the brain that sends messages to other neurons via axons and dendritic connections.

Neuroticism   A tendency to experience negative emotional states, such as anger, guilt, anxiety, or depression.

Neurotransmitter   A chemical that transmits messages between nerve cells.

Oxytocin   A hormone centrally involved in good feelings between people, seen particularly in pair-bonding species.

Parasympathetic nervous system   Involved in slowing down heart rate and reducing blood pressure, particularly in response to trauma.

Peer review   Journal articles that are accepted for publication after being anonymously reviewed by professionals in the field.

Pheromones   A scent chemical used for communication, with a role in attracting those of the opposite sex.

Post-traumatic stress disorder (PTSD)   Psychiatric diagnosis for people who, following traumatic experiences, suffer a range of symptoms such as nightmares, flashbacks, high anxiety, and other emotional distress.

Priming   A disposition to act in a certain way due to prior exposure to specific stimuli.

Procedural memory   The most basic form of memory, learning 'how to' do something like riding a bike.

Projection   Seeing in another person what really belongs to oneself (e.g., attributing anger to one's partner when one is really angry oneself).

Prolactin   A hormone that stimulates milk production after birth, and its release is also associated with an increase in protective feelings for children.

Proto-conversations   The earliest, preverbal, forms of communication between an infant and its carer.

Proto-declarative pointing Pointing that aims to draw someone's attention to an object, particularly to share interest in it.

Proto-imperative pointing Pointing at something because one wants it.

Qualitative research Research based on non-numerical data, often relying on interpreting the ideas or thoughts of those being researched.

Quantitative research Research based on statistical or numerical forms, often presented through graphs and using maths.

Randomised control trials (RCTs) A clinical trial in which one or more treatments are tested for effectiveness against a control group or placebo.

Reactive attachment disorder (RAD) A psychiatric classification denoting the effects of severe early neglect leading to a compromised capacity to form attachment bonds with caregivers.

Reflective self-functioning The capacity to reflect on one's own thoughts and feelings.

Resilience The ability to be little affected by adverse circumstances, or to come through them relatively unscathed.

Scaffolding Bruner's (1966) idea of facilitating learning by building carefully on earlier learning, and revisiting previous learning to consolidate.

Secondary intersubjectivity A stage, at about 9 months, when an infant can share perception of another object, as seen in **social referencing, joint attention** and **proto-declarative pointing**.

Second-skin defence A psychoanalytic term denoting an infant defending against anxiety by 'holding themselves together', such as via muscular movement or clutching an object.

Serotonin A neurotransmitter particularly involved in positive feelings.

Social capital A metaphor taken from economics denoting how someone accrues social capacities and advantages that aid functioning in a range of contexts.

Social referencing The use of non-verbal cues to check another person's approval or not.

Sociocentric A culture that values having strong prosocial values and putting the needs of one's social group before the individual.

Strange Situation Test An attachment procedure testing the reaction of an infant of about a year to separations from a caregiver.

Stress A physiological and psychological response to changing circumstances, one often associated with anxiety and the release of the stress hormone, cortisol.

Symbolism Representing something by means of a symbol.

Sympathetic nervous system Responsible for arousal responses to danger, as seen in increased heart rate, blood pressure, and shallow breathing.

Temperament A disposition to react in a certain way, at least partly inherited.

Testosterone A hormone, seen more in men, that is linked to sexual desire and also levels of aggression, as well as regulating other bodily functions.

Theory of mind The ability to understand and make inferences about someone else's mind, mental state and feelings, normally fully developed by about 4 years of age.

Vasopressin A hormone that has a variety of functions, but has a role in loving feelings, and levels increase following sex.

Wet nurse   A woman paid to breastfeed another mother's child.

Zone of proximal development   A concept of Vygotsky (1962) describing how a child able to manage one level of learning alone can be facilitated to the next level.

References

Adam, K.S., Keller, A.E.S., & West, M. (1995). Attachment organization and vulnerability to loss, separation, and abuse in disturbed adolescents. In S. Goldberg, R. Muir, & J. Kerr (Eds.), *Attachment theory: Social, developmental, and clinical perspectives* (pp. 309–341). London: Routledge.

Adams, H.E., Wright, L.W., & Lohr, B.A. (1996). Is homophobia associated with homosexual arousal? *Journal of Abnormal Psychology, 105(3)*, 440–445.

Ahnert, L., Gunnar M.R., Lamb, M.E., & Barthel, M. (2004). Transition to child care: Associations with infant–mother attachment, infant negative emotion, and cortisol elevations. *Child Development, 75(3)*, 639–650.

Ahnert, L., Pinquart, M., & Lamb, M.E. (2006). Security of children's relationships with nonparental care providers: A meta-analysis. *Child Development, 77(3)*, 664–679.

Ainsworth, M.D.S. (1978). *Patterns of attachment: A psychological study of the strange situation*. Hillsdale, NJ: Lawrence Erlbaum Associates, Inc.

Ainsworth, M.D., & Bell, S.M. (1977). Infant crying and maternal responsiveness: A rejoinder to Gewirtz and Boyd. *Child Development, 48(4)*, 1208–1216.

Akhtar, N., & Tomasello, M. (1998). Intersubjectivity in early language learning and use. In S. Braten (Ed.), *Intersubjective communication and emotion in early ontogeny* (pp. 316–335). New York: Cambridge University Press.

Alber, E. (2003). Denying biological parenthood: Fosterage in Northern Benin. *Ethnos, 68(4)*, 487–506.

Alexander, G.M., & Hines, M. (1994). Gender labels and play styles: Their relative contribution to children's selection of playmates. *Child Development, 65(3)*, 869–879.

Alexander, G.M., & Hines, M. (2002). Sex differences in response to children's toys in nonhuman primates (Cercopithecus aethiops sabaeus). *Evolution and Human Behavior, 23(6)*, 467–479.

Alia-Klein, N., Goldstein, R.Z., Kriplani, A., Logan, J., Tomasi, D., Williams, B., Telang, F., Shumay, E., Biegon, A., Craig, I.W., Henn, F., Wang, G.J., Volkow, N.D., & Fowler, J.S. (2008). Brain monoamine oxidase a activity predicts trait aggression. *Journal of Neuroscience, 28(19)*, 5099–5104.

REFERENCES

Allen, J.P., & Hauser, S.T. (1996). Autonomy and relatedness in adolescent-family interactions as predictors of young adults' states of mind regarding attachment. *Development and Psychopathology, 8*, 793–810.

Allen, J.P., Moore, C., Kuperminc, G., & Bell, K. (1998). Attachment and adolescent psychosocial functioning. *Child Development, 69(5)*, 1406–1419.

Almeida, D.M., Wethington, E., & McDonald, D.A. (2001). Daily variation in paternal engagement and negative mood: Implications for emotionally supportive and conflictual interactions. *Journal of Marriage and the Family, 63(2)*, 417–429.

Alvarez, A. (1992). *Live company*. London: Routledge.

Anderson, A. (2004). Adoption and belonging in Wogeo, Papua New Guinea. In F. Bowie (Ed.), *Cross-cultural approaches to adoption* (pp. 111–126). London: Routledge.

Andersson, G., Hank, K., Ronsen, M., & Vikat, A. (2006). Gendering family composition: Sex preferences for children and childbearing behavior in the Nordic countries. *Demography, 43(2)*, 255–267.

Andrews, J.A., Foster, S.L., Capaldi, D., & Hops, H. (2000). Adolescent and family predictors of physical aggression, communication, and satisfaction in young adult couples: A prospective analysis. *Journal of Consulting and Clinical Psychology, 68(2)*, 195–208.

Appleyard, K., Egeland, B., van Dulmen, M.H., & Sroufe, L.A. (2005). When more is not better: The role of cumulative risk in child behavior outcomes. *Journal of Child Psychology and Psychiatry, 46(3)*, 235–245.

Argyle, M. (1988). *Bodily communication*. London: Routledge.

Arnett, J.J. (2004). *Emerging adulthood: The winding road from the late teens through the twenties*. New York: Oxford University Press.

Astington, J., & Gopnik, A. (1991). Theoretical explanations of children's understanding of the mind. *British Journal of Developmental Psychology, 9*, 7–31.

Ayers, S., Eagle, A., & Waring, H. (2006). The effects of childbirth-related post-traumatic stress disorder on women and their relationships: A qualitative study. *Psychology, Health & Medicine, 11(4)*, 389.

Babinski, L.M., Hartsough, C.S., & Lambert, N.M. (1999). Childhood conduct problems, hyperactivity-impulsivity, and inattention as predictors of adult criminal activity. *Journal of Child Psychology and Psychiatry and Allied Disciplines, 40(3)*, 347–355.

Bader, A.P., & Phillips, R.D. (1999). Fathers' proficiency at recognizing their newborns by tactile cues. *Infant Behavior and Development, 22(3)*, 405–409.

Bagwell, C.L., Newcomb, A.F., & Bukowski, W.M. (1998). Preadolescent friendship and peer rejection as predictors of adult adjustment. *Child Development, 69(1)*, 140–153.

Bakermans-Kranenburg, M.J., & van IJzendoorn, M.H. (2008). Oxytocin receptor (OXTR) and serotonin transporter (5-HTT) genes associated with observed parenting. *Social Cognitive and Affective Neuroscience, 3(2)*, 128–134.

Bakermans-Kranenburg, M.J., van IJzendoorn, M.H. & Juffer, F. (2003). Less is more: meta-analyses of sensitivity and attachment interventions in early childhood. *Psychological Bulletin, 129(2)*, 195–215.

Bakermans-Kranenburg, M.J., van IJzendoorn, M.H., Mesman, J., Alink, L.R., & Juffer, F. (2008). Effects of an attachment-based intervention on daily cortisol moderated by dopamine receptor D4: A randomized control trial on 1- to 3-year-olds screened for externalizing behavior. *Development and Psychopathology, 20(3)*, 805–820.

Bakhtin, M.M. (1982). *The dialogic imagination*. Texas: University of Texas.

Balint, M. (1968). *The basic fault: Therapeutic aspects of regression*. London: Tavistock.

Banks, M.L., Czoty, P.W., & Nader, M.A. (2007). The influence of reinforcing effects of cocaine on cocaine-induced increases in extinguished responding in cynomolgus monkeys. *Psychopharmacology, 192(4)*, 449–456.

Barker, D.J.P., Forsén, T., Uutela, A., Osmond, C., & Eriksson, J.G. (2001). Size at birth and resilience to effects of poor living conditions in adult life: longitudinal study. *British Medical Journal, 323(7324)*, 1261–1262.

Barker, G., Nascimento, M., Segundo, M., & Pulerwitz, J. (2004). How do we know if men have changed? Promoting and measuring attitude change with young men. Lessons from Program H in Latin America. In S. Ruxton (Ed.), *Gender equality and men: Learning from practice* (pp. 147–161). Oxford: Oxfam.

Barnes, J., Leach, P., Sylva, K., Stein, A., & Malmberg, L. (2006). Infant care in England: Mothers' aspirations, experiences, satisfaction and caregiver relationships. *Early Child Development and Care, 176(5)*, 553–573.

Barnett, O.W., Miller-Perrin, C.L., & Perrin, R.D. (2005). *Family violence across the lifespan: An introduction*. Newbury Park, CA: Sage.

Barnett, W., Jung, K., Yarosz, D.J., Thomas, J., Hornbeck, A., Stechuk, R., & Burns, S. (2008). Educational effects of the Tools of the Mind curriculum: A randomized trial. *Early Childhood Research Quarterly, 23(3)*, 299–313.

Baron, A.S., & Banaji, M.R. (2006). Evidence of race evaluations from ages 6 and 10 and adulthood. *Psychological Science, 17(1)*, 53–58.

Baron-Cohen, S. (2003). *The essential difference: The truth about the male and female brain*. New York: Perseus Books Group.

Barr, R.G., Hopkins, B., & Green, J.A. (2000). *Crying as a sign, a symptom and a signal: Clinical, emotional and developmental aspects of infant and toddler crying*. London: Mac Keith Press.

Bartels, A., & Zeki, S. (2004). The neural correlates of maternal and romantic love. *Neuroimage, 21(3)*, 1155–1166.

Bateman, A., & Fonagy, P. (2004). *Psychotherapy for borderline personality disorder: Mentalization-based treatment*. New York: Oxford University Press.

Bateson, G. (1972). *Steps to an ecology of mind*. Northvale, NJ: Jason Aronson.

Bateson, M.C. (1971). The interpersonal context of infant vocalization. *Quarterly Progress Report of the Research Laboratory of Electronics, 100*, 170–176.

Bauer, J.J., & Bonanno, G.A. (2001). I can, I do, I am: The narrative differentiation of self-efficacy and other self-evaluations while adapting to bereavement. *Journal of Research in Personality, 35(4)*, 424–448.

Bauer, P.J. (2006). *Remembering the times of our lives: Memory in infancy and beyond*. Hillsdale, NJ: Lawrence Erlbaum Associates, Inc.

Bauer, P.J., Kroupina, M.G., Schwade, J.A., Dropik, P.L., & Wewerka, S.S. (1998). If memory serves, will language? Later verbal accessibility of early memories. *Development and Psychopathology, 10(4)*, 655–679.

Beckerman, S., Lizarralde, R., Ballew, C., Schroeder, S., Fingelton, C., Garrison, A., & Smith, H. (1998). The Barí partible paternity project, phase one. *Current Anthropology, 39(1)*, 164–167.

Beebe, B., & Lachmann, F.M. (2002). *Infant research and adult treatment: Co-constructing interactions*. New York: Analytic Press.

Beebe, B., Lachmann, F.M., & Jaffe, J. (1997). Mother–infant interaction structures and presymbolic self-and object representations. *Psychoanalytic Dialogues, 7(2)*, 133–182.

Begley, S. (2009). *The plastic mind*. London: Constable.

Beitchman, J., Davidge, K.M., Kennedy, J.L., Atkinson, L., Lee, V., Shapiro, S., & Douglas, L. (2003). The serotonin transporter gene in aggressive children with and without ADHD and nonaggressive matched controls. *Annals of the New York Academy of Sciences, 1008(1)*, 248–251.

Bekoff, M., & DiMotta, M.J. (2008). *Animals at play: Rules of the game*. Philadelphia, PA: Temple University Press.

Belsky, J. (1996). Parent, infant, and social-contextual antecedents of father-son attachment security. *Developmental Psychology, 32(5)*, 905–913.

REFERENCES

Belsky, J. (2005). Differential susceptibility to rearing influence. In B. Ellis & D. Bjorklund (Eds.), *Origins of the social mind: Evolutionary psychology and child development* (pp. 139–163). New York: Guilford.

Belsky, J., Bakermans-Kranenburg, M., & van IJzendoorn, M. (2007a). For better and for worse: Differential susceptibility to environmental influences. *Current Directions in Psychological Science, 16(6)*, 300–304.

Belsky, J., & Fearon, R.M.P. (2002). Early attachment security, subsequent maternal sensitivity, and later child development: Does continuity in development depend upon continuity of caregiving? *Attachment & Human Development, 4(3)*, 361–387.

Belsky, J., Steinberg, L., & Draper, P. (1991). Childhood experience, interpersonal development, and reproductive strategy: An evolutionary theory of socialization. *Child Development, 62(4)*, 647–670.

Belsky, J., Vandell, D.L., Burchinal, M., Clarke-Stewart, K.A., McCartney, K., Owen, M.T., & NICHD Early Child Care Research Network (2007b). Are there long-term effects of early child care? *Child Development, 78(2)*, 681–701.

Bem, S.L. (1974). The measurement of psychological androgyny. *Journal of Consulting and Clinical Psychology, 42(2)*, 155–162.

Bennett, M., & Lengacher, C. (2009). Humor and laughter may influence health 4. Humor and immune function. *Evidence Based Complementary and Alternative Medicine, 6(2)*, 159–164.

Berglund, H., Lindström, P., & Savic, I. (2006). Brain response to putative pheromones in lesbian women. *Proceedings of the National Academy of Sciences, 103(21)*, 8269–8274.

Bernier, A., & Dozier, M. (2003). Bridging the attachment transmission gap: The role of maternal mind-mindedness. *International Journal of Behavioral Development, 27(4)*, 355–365.

Beši, N., & Kerr, M. (2009). Punks, Goths, and other eye-catching peer crowds: Do they fulfill a function for shy youths? *Journal of Research on Adolescence, 19(1)*, 113–121.

Bester, G. (2007). Personality development of the adolescent: peer group versus parents. *South African Journal of Education, 27(2)*, 177–190.

Beutler, L.E. (2009). Making science matter in clinical practice: Redefining psychotherapy. *Clinical Psychology: Science and Practice, 16(3)*, 301–317.

Bevins, R.A. (2001). Novelty seeking and reward: Implications for the study of high-risk behaviors. *Current Directions in Psychological Science, 10(6)*, 189–193.

Bick, E. (1968). The experience of the skin in early object relations. *International Journal of Psycho-Analysis, 49*, 484–486.

Biller, H.B. (1993). *Fathers and families: Paternal factors in child development*. Westport, CT: Greenwood.

Bion, W.R. (1977). *Second thoughts*. New York: Jason Aronson.

Birdwhistell, R.L. (1970). *Kinesics and context*. Philadelphia, PA: University of Pennsylvania Press.

Bjorklund, D.F. (2007). *Why youth is not wasted on the young: Immaturity in human development*. Oxford: Blackwell.

Black, B., & Logan, A. (1995). Links between communication patterns in mother–child, father–child, and child–peer interactions and children's social status. *Child Development, 66(1)*, 255–271.

Blakemore, S.J., & Choudhury, S. (2006). Development of the adolescent brain: Implications for executive function and social cognition. *Journal of Child Psychology and Psychiatry, 47(3–4)*, 296–312.

Block, R.W., & Krebs, N.F. (2005). Failure to thrive as a manifestation of child neglect. *Pediatrics, 116(5)*, 1234–1237.

Blum, D. (2002). *Love at Goon Park: Harry Harlow and the science of affection*. New York: Perseus Publishing.

Bock, J. (2002). Evolutionary demography and intrahousehold time allocation: Schooling and children's labor among the Okavango Delta peoples of Botswana. *American Journal of Human Biology, 14(2)*, 206–221.

Bogdan, R., & Pizzagalli, D.A. (2006). Acute stress reduces reward responsiveness: Implications for depression. *Biological Psychiatry, 60(10)*, 1147–1154.

Bokhorst, C.L., Bakermans-Kranenburg, M.J., Fearon, R.M., van IJzendoorn, M.H., Fonagy, P., & Schuengel, C. (2003). The importance of shared environment in mother–infant attachment security: A behavioral genetic study. *Child Development, 74(6)*, 1769–1782.

Bolger, K.E., Patterson, C.J., Thompson, W.E.W., & Kupersmidt, J.B. (1995). Psychosocial adjustment among children experiencing persistent and intermittent family economic hardship. *Child Development, 66(4)*, 1107–1129.

Bond, R., & Smith, P.B. (1996). Culture and conformity: A meta-analysis of studies using Asch's (1952b, 1956) line judgment task. *Psychological Bulletin, 119(1)*, 111–137.

Booth, A., Johnson, D.R., Granger, D.A., Crouter, A.C., & McHale, S. (2003). Testosterone and child and adolescent adjustment: The moderating role of parent-child relationships. *Developmental Psychology, 39(1)*, 85–98.

Bourdieu, P. (1977). *Outline of a theory of practice* (R. Nice, Trans.). New York: Cambridge University Press.

Bowie, F. (2004). *Cross-cultural approaches to adoption*. London: Routledge.

Bowlby, J. (1969). *Attachment and loss* (Vol. 1 Attachment). London: Hogarth.

Bowlby, R. (2007). Babies and toddlers in non-parental daycare can avoid stress and anxiety if they develop a lasting secondary attachment bond with one carer who is consistently accessible to them. *Attachment & Human Development, 9(4)*, 307–319.

Boyce, W.T., & Chesterman, E. (1990). Life events, social support, and cardiovascular reactivity in adolescence. *Journal of Developmental and Behavioral Pediatrics, 11(3)*, 105–111.

Bradburn, N.M., & Noll, C.E. (1969). *The structure of psychological well-being*, Chicago, IL: Aldine.

Bradley, R.M., & Mistretta, C.M. (1975). Fetal sensory receptors. *Physiology Review, 55*, 352–382.

Bradmetz, J., & Schneider, R. (1999). Is Little Red Riding Hood afraid of her grandmother? Cognitive vs. emotional response to a false belief. *British Journal of Developmental Psychology, 17(4)*, 501–514.

Brazelton, T.B., & Nugent, J.K. (1995). *Neonatal behavioral assessment scale*. London: Mac Keith Press.

Breakwell, G., Hamond, S., Fife-Schaw, C., & Smith, J. (Eds.) (2006). *Research methods in psychology* (3rd ed.). Newbury Park, CA: Sage.

Bremner, J. (2006). The relationship between cognitive and brain changes in posttraumatic stress disorder. *Annals of the New York Academy of Sciences, 1071(1)*, 80–86.

Brenneis, C.B. (2000). Evaluating the evidence: Can we find authenticated recovered memory? *Psychoanalytic Psychology, 17(1)*, 61–77.

Bronfenbrenner, U. (2004). *Making human beings human: Bioecological perspectives on human development*. Newbury Park, CA: Sage.

Bronson, P., & Merryman, A. (2009). *Nurture Shock: New thinking about children*. New York: Twelve.

Browne, J.V. (2003). New perspectives on premature infants and their parents. *Zero to Three, 24(2)*, 4–12.

Browne, K., Hamilton-Giachritsis, C., Johnson, R., & Ostergren, M. (2006). Overuse of institutional care for children in Europe. *British Medical Journal, 332(7539)*, 485–487.

Bruner, J.S. (1966). *Toward a theory of instruction*. Cambridge, MA: Harvard University Press.

Bryant, J. (2008). *Media effects: Advances in theory and research*. London: Routledge.

Bryant, W.K., & Zick, C.D. (1996). An examination of parent-child shared time. *Journal of Marriage and the Family, 58(1)*, 227–237.

Bumpass, L., & Lu, H.H. (2000). Trends in cohabitation and implications for children's family contexts in the United States. *Population Studies, 54(1)*, 29–41.

Buranasin, B. (1991). The effects of rooming-in on the success of breastfeeding and the decline in abandonment of children. *Asia-Pacific Journal of Public Health/Asia-Pacific Academic Consortium for Public Health, 5(3)*, 217.

Burck, C. (2005). *Multilingual living.* New York: Palgrave.

Burman, E. (2007). *Deconstructing developmental psychology.* London: Routledge.

Butler, J.P. (1997). *Excitable speech: A politics of the performative.* London: Routledge.

Butler, J. (1999). *Gender trouble: Feminism and the subversion of identity.* London: Routledge.

Butt, J., & Box, L. (1998). *Family centred: A study of the use of family centres by black families.* London: Race Equality Unit.

Byrnes, J.P., Miller, D.C., & Schafer, W.D. (1999). Gender differences in risk taking: A meta-analysis. *Psychological Bulletin, 125(3)*, 367–383.

Cain, M.E., Saucier, D.A., & Bardo, M.T. (2005). Novelty seeking and drug use: Contribution of an animal model. *Experimental and Clinical Psychopharmacology, 13(4)*, 367–375.

Cameron, D. (2007). *The myth of mars and venus: Do men and women really speak different languages?* New York: Oxford University Press.

Cameron, N.M., Champagne, F.A., Parent, C., Fish, E.W., Ozaki-Kuroda, K., & Meaney, M.J. (2005). The programming of individual differences in defensive responses and reproductive strategies in the rat through variations in maternal care. *Neuroscience and Biobehavioral Reviews, 29(4–5)*, 843–865.

Campbell, D.W., & Eaton, W.O. (1999). Sex differences in the activity level of infants. *Infant and Child Development, 8(1)*, 1–17.

Campbell, F.A., Wasik, B.H., Pungello, E., Burchinal, M., Barbarin, O., Kainz, K., Sparling, J.J., & Ramey, C.T. (2008). Young adult outcomes of the Abecedarian and CARE early childhood educational interventions. *Early Childhood Research Quarterly, 23(4)*, 452–466.

Campbell, R.S., & Pennebaker, J.W. (2003). The secret life of pronouns: Flexibility in writing style and physical health. *Psychological Science, 14(1)*, 60–65.

Canli, T., Zhao, Z., Desmond, J.E., Kang, E., Gross, J., & Gabrieli, J.D. (2001). An fMRI study of personality influences on brain reactivity to emotional stimuli. *Behavioral Neuroscience, 115(1)*, 33–42.

Carlson, E.A., Sroufe, L.A., & Egeland, B. (2004). The construction of experience: A longitudinal study of representation and behavior. *Child Development, 75(1)*, 66–83.

Carlson, S.M. (2009). Social origins of executive function development. *New Directions for Child and Adolescent Development, 123*, 87–98.

Carlson, V.J., & Harwood, R.L. (2003). Attachment, culture, and the caregiving system: The cultural patterning of everyday experiences among Anglo and Puerto Rican mother–infant pairs. *Infant Mental Health Journal, 24(1)*, 53–73.

Carter, C.S. (2007). Sex differences in oxytocin and vasopressin: Implications for autism spectrum disorders? *Behavioural Brain Research, 176(1)*, 170–186.

Carter, C.S., & Keverne, E.B. (2002). The neurobiology of social affiliation and pair bonding. *Hormones, Brain and Behavior, 1*, 299–337.

Carver, C.S. (1997). Adult attachment and personality: Converging evidence and a new measure. *Personality and Social Psychology Bulletin, 23(8)*, 865–883.

Carver, K., Joyner, K., & Udry, J.R. (2003). National estimates of adolescent romantic relationships. In P. Florsheim (Ed.), *Adolescent romantic relations and sexual behavior: Theory, research, and practical implications* (pp. 23–56). Hillsdale, NJ: Lawrence Erlbaum Associates, Inc.

Carver, L.J., & Vaccaro, B.G. (2007). 12-month-old infants allocate increased neural resources to stimuli associated with negative adult emotion. *Developmental Psychology, 43(1)*, 54–69.

Caspi, A., Moffitt, T.E., Morgan, J., Rutter, M., Taylor, A., Arseneault, L., Tully, L., Jacobs, C., Kim-Cohen, J., & Polo-Tomas, M. (2004). Maternal expressed emotion predicts children's antisocial behavior problems: Using MZ-twin differences to identify environmental effects on behavioral development. *Developmental Psychology, 40(2)*, 149–161.

Caspi, A., Sugden, K., Moffitt, T.E., Taylor, A., Craig, I.W., Harrington, H., McClay, J., Mill, J., Martin, J., Braithwaite, A., & Poulton, R. (2003). Influence of life stress on depression: Moderation by a polymorphism in the 5-HTT gene. *Science, 301(5631)*, 386–389.

Cassidy, J., & Mohr, J.J. (2001). Unsolvable fear, trauma, and psychopathology: Theory, research, and clinical considerations related to disorganized attachment across the life span. *Clinical Psychology: Science & Practice, 8(3)*, 275–298.

Castelli, F., Frith, C., Happé, F., & Frith, U. (2002). Autism, Asperger syndrome and brain mechanisms for the attribution of mental states to animated shapes. *Brain, 125(8)*, 1839–1849.

Catalano, R., Bruckner, T., Anderson, E., & Gould, J.B. (2005). Fetal death sex ratios: A test of the economic stress hypothesis. *International Journal of Epidemiology, 34(4)*, 944–948.

Caudill, W., & Plath, D.W. (1966). Who Sleeps by whom? Parent–child involvement in urban Japanese families. *Psychiatry, 29*, 344–366.

Caudill, W., & Weinstein, H. (1969). Maternal care and infant behaviour in Japan and America. *Psychiatry, 32*, 12–43.

Champagne, F.A., & Curley, J.P. (2009). Epigenetic mechanisms mediating the long-term effects of maternal care on development. *Neuroscience & Biobehavioral Reviews, 33(4)*, 593–600.

Champagne, F.A., & Meaney, M.J. (2007). Transgenerational effects of social environment on variations in maternal care and behavioral response to novelty. *Behavioral Neuroscience, 121(6)*, 1353–1362.

Chase, N.D. (1999). *Burdened children: Theory, research and treatment of parentification.* Cambridge, MA: Sage.

Chasiotis, A., Kiessling, F., Hofer, J., & Campos, D. (2006). Theory of mind and inhibitory control in three cultures: Conflict inhibition predicts false belief understanding in Germany, Costa Rica and Cameroon. *International Journal of Behavioral Development, 30(3)*, 249–260.

Chavajay, P., & Rogoff, B. (2002). Schooling and traditional collaborative social organization of problem solving by Mayan mothers and children. *Developmental Psychology, 38(1)*, 55–66.

Chen, C., Burton, M., Greenberger, E., & Dmitrieva, J. (1999). Population migration and the variation of dopamine D4 receptor (DRD4) allele frequencies around the globe. *Evolution and Human Behavior, 20(5)*, 309–324.

Chen, X., Hastings, P.D., Rubin, K.H., Chen, H., Cen, G., & Stewart, S.L. (1998). Child-rearing attitudes and behavioral inhibition in Chinese and Canadian toddlers: A cross-cultural study. *Developmental Psychology, 34(4)*, 677–686.

Cheng, Y., Lin, C-P., Liu, H-L., Hsu, Y-Y., Lim, K-E., Hung, D., & Decety, J. (2007). Expertise modulates the perception of pain in others. *Current Biology, 17(19)*, 1708–1713.

Chisholm, J.S. (1996). Learning 'respect for everything': Navajo images of development. In C. Hwang, M. E. Lamb, & I. Sigel (Eds.), *Images of childhood* (pp. 167–183). Hillsdale, NJ: Lawrence Erlbaum Associates, Inc.

Chugani, H.T., Behen, M.E., Muzik, O., Juhász, C., Nagy, F., & Chugani, D.C. (2001). Local brain functional activity following early deprivation: A study of postinstitutionalized Romanian orphans. *Neuroimage, 14(6)*, 1290–1301.

Cicchetti, D., & Lynch, M. (1995). Failures in the expectable environment and their impact on individual development: The case of child maltreatment. In D. Cicchetti & D. Cohen (Eds.), *Developmental psychopathology. Risk, disorder and adaptation* (pp. 32–71). New York: Wiley.

Cillessen, A.H.N., & Rose, A.J. (2005). Understanding popularity in the peer system. *Current Directions in Psychological Science, 14(2)*, 102–105.

Cirulli, F., Francia, N., Berry, A., Aloe, L., Alleva, E., & Suomi, S.J. (2009). Early life stress as a risk factor for mental health: Role of neurotrophins from rodents to non-human primates. *Neuroscience and Biobehavioral Reviews, 33(4)*, 573–585.

Clark, C.D. (2003). *In sickness and in play: Children coping with chronic illness*. New Brunswick, NJ: Rutgers University Press.

Clarke-Stewart, A., & Dunn, J. (Eds.) (2006). What have we learned. In *Families count: Effects on child and adolescent development*. New York: Cambridge University Press.

Clarke-Stewart, K.A. (1973). *Interactions between mothers and their young children: Characteristics and consequences. Monographs of the society for research in child development* (Vol. 38, pp. 1–109). Ann Abor, MI: SRCD.

Coates, J. (1993). *Women, men and language: A sociolinguistic account of gender differences in language*. London: Longman.

Cohen, M.X., Young, J., Baek, J.M., Kessler, C., & Ranganath, C. (2005). Individual differences in extraversion and dopamine genetics predict neural reward responses. *Cognitive Brain Research, 25(3)*, 851–861.

Cohen, S., Alper, C.M., Doyle, W.J., Treanor, J.J., & Turner, R.B. (2006). Positive emotional style predicts resistance to illness after experimental exposure to rhinovirus or influenza a virus. *Psychosomatic medicine, 68(6)*, 809–815.

Collishaw, S., Maughan, B., Goodman, R., & Pickles, A. (2004). Time trends in adolescent mental health. *Journal of Child Psychology and Psychiatry, 45(8)*, 1350–1362.

Connolly, J.A., & Johnson, A.M. (1996). Adolescents' romantic relationships and the structure and quality of their close interpersonal ties. *Personal Relationships, 3(2)*, 185–195.

Coolican, H. (2009). *Research methods and statistics in psychology*. London: Hodder and Stoughton.

Cooper, G., Hoffman, K., & Marvin, R.S. (2003). The circle of security intervention: Pathways to healthier attachment-caregiving bonds. In *Enhancing early attachments*: Conference of the Duke Series in Child Development and Public Policy, Durham, NC.

Cooper, M.L., Shaver, P.R., & Collins, N.L. (1998). Attachment styles, emotion regulation, and adjustment in adolescence. *Journal of Personality and Social Psychology, 74(5)*, 1380–1397.

Costello, E.J., Compton, S.N., Keeler, G., & Angold, A. (2003). Relationships between poverty and psychopathology: A natural experiment. *JAMA, 290(15)*, 2023–2029.

Cowan, P.A., & Cowan, C.P. (2003). Normative family transitions, normal family processes, and healthy child development. In F. Walsh (Ed.), *Normal family processes* (pp. 424–459). New York: Guilford.

Cowan, P.A., Cowan, C.P., Pruett, M.K., Pruett, K., & Wong, J.J. (2009). Promoting fathers' engagement with children: Preventive interventions for low-income families. *Journal of Marriage and Family, 71(3)*, 663–679.

Craig, L. (2006). Does father care mean fathers share? A comparison of how mothers and fathers in intact families spend time with children. *Gender Society, 20(2)*, 259–281.

Crews, F., He, J., & Hodge, C. (2007). Adolescent cortical development: A critical period of vulnerability for addiction. *Pharmacology, Biochemistry and Behavior, 86(2)*, 189–199.

Crittenden, P.M. (1993). Characteristics of neglectful parents: An information processing approach. *Criminal Justice and Behavior, 20(1)*, 27–48.

Crocker, W.H., & Crocker, J. (1994). *The Canela: Bonding through kinship, ritual, and sex*. Fort Worth, TX: Harcourt Brace College Publishers.

Cronk, L. (1993). Parental favoritism toward daughters. *American Scientist, 81(3)*, 272–279.

Cunningham, W.A., Johnson, M.K., Raye, C.L., Chris Gatenby, J., Gore, J.C., & Banaji, M.R. (2004). Separable neural components in the processing of black and white faces. *Psychological Science, 15(12)*, 806–813.

Curtis, W.J., & Nelson, C.A. (2003). Toward building a better brain: Neurobehavioral outcomes, mechanisms, and processes of environmental enrichment. In S. Luthar (Ed.), *Resilience and vulnerability: Adaptation in the context of childhood adversities* (pp. 463–488). New York: Cambridge University Press.

Cusson, R., & Lee, A. (1994). Parental interventions and the development of the preterm infant. *Journal of Obstetric, Gynecologic, & Neonatal Nursing, 23(1)*, 60–68.

Cutting, A., & Dunn, J. (1999). Theory of mind, emotion understanding, language, and family background: Individual differences and interrelations. *Child Development, 70(4)*, 853–865.

Dabbs, J.M.B., & Dabbs, M.G. (2000). *Heroes, rogues, and lovers: Testosterone and behavior*. New York: McGraw-Hill.

Daly, M., & Wilson, M. (1999). *The truth about Cinderella: A Darwinian view of parental love*. London: Weidenfield and Nicholson.

Damasio, A.R. (1999). *The feeling of what happens: Body, emotion and the making of consciousness*. London: Heineman.

Danner, D.D., Snowdon, D.A., & Friesen, W.V. (2001). Positive emotions in early life and longevity: Findings from the nun study. *Journal of Personality and Social Psychology, 80(5)*, 804–813.

Danner, F., & Phillips, B. (2008). Adolescent sleep, school start times, and teen motor vehicle crashes. *Journal of Clinical Sleep Medicine: JCSM: Official Publication of the American Academy of Sleep Medicine, 4(6)*, 533.

Davidson, R.J. (2000). Affective style, psychopathology, and resilience: Brain mechanisms and plasticity. *The American Psychologist, 55(11)*, 1196–1214.

Davidson, R.J. (2008). Asymmetric brain function, affective style, and psychopathology: The role of early experience and plasticity. *Development and Psychopathology, 6(04)*, 741–758.

Davidson, R.J., Kabat-Zinn, J., Schumacher, J., Rosenkranz, M., Muller, D., Santorelli, S.F., Urbanowski, F., Harrington, A., Bonus, K., & Sheridan, J.F. (2003). Alterations in brain and immune function produced by mindfulness meditation. *Psychosomatic Medicine, 65*, 564–570.

Davies, D. (1989). The effects of gender-typed labels on children's performance. *Current Psychology, 8(4)*, 267–272.

Davila, J., Steinberg, S.J., Kachadourian, L., Cobb, R., & Fincham, F. (2004). Romantic involvement and depressive symptoms in early and late adolescence: The role of a preoccupied relational style. *Personal Relationships, 11(2)*, 161–178.

Dawson, G., Carver, L., Meltzoff, A.N., Panagiotides, H., McPartland, J., & Webb, S.J. (2002). Neural correlates of face and object recognition in young children with autism spectrum disorder, developmental delay, and typical development. *Child Development, 73(3)*, 700–717.

Day, R.D., Lewis, C., O'Brien, M., & Lamb, M.E. (2005). Fatherhood and father involvement: Emerging constructs and theoretical orientations. In A. Bengston, A.C. Acock, K.R. Allen, P. Dilworth-Anderson, & D.M. Klein (Eds.), *Sourcebook of family theory and research* (pp. 341–366). Thousand Oaks, CA: Sage.

De Bellis, M.D. (2003). The neurobiology of posttraumatic stress disorder across the life cycle. In D. Moore & J. Jefferson (Eds.), *The handbook of medical psychiatry* (pp. 449–466). London: Elsevier.

De Bellis, M.D. (2005). The psychobiology of neglect. *Child Maltreatment, 10(2)*, 150.

De Casper, A., & Spence, M. (1986). Prenatal speech influences newborns perception of speech sound. *Infant Behaviour and Development, 9*, 133–150.

Deci, E.L., & Ryan, R.M. (2000). The 'what' and 'why' of goal pursuits: Human needs and the self-determination of behavior. *Psychological Inquiry, 11(4)*, 227–268.

Dehaene-Lambertz, G. (2000). Cerebral specialization for speech and non-speech stimuli in infants. *Journal of Cognitive Neuroscience, 12(3)*, 449–460.

Delobel-Ayoub, M., Arnaud, C., White-Koning, M., Casper, C., Pierrat, V., Garel, M., Burguet, A., Roze, J.C., Matis, J., Picaud, J.C., Kaminski, M., Larroque, B., & EPIPAGE Study Group (2009). Behavioral problems and cognitive performance at 5 years of age after very preterm birth: The EPIPAGE Study. *Pediatrics, 123(6)*, 1485–1492.

Demaree, H.A., Everhart, D.E., Youngstrom, E.A., & Harrison, D.W. (2005). Brain lateralization of emotional processing: Historical roots and a future incorporating dominance. *Behavioral and Cognitive Neuroscience Reviews, 4(1)*, 3–20.

Dentan, R.K. (1968). *The Semai: A nonviolent people of Malaya*. New York: Holt, Rinehart, and Winston.

de Tychey, C., Briançon, S., Lighezzolo, J., Spitz, E., Kabuth, B., de Luigi, V., Messembourg, C., Girvan, F., Rosati, A., Thockler, A., & Vincent, S. (2008). Quality of life, postnatal depression and baby gender. *Journal of Clinical Nursing, 17(3)*, 312–322.

Dex, S., & Ward, K. (2007). Parental care and employment in early childhood. *Equal Opportunities Commission Working Papers Series, 57*. London: Equal Opportunities Commission.

Diamond, J. (2003). The double puzzle of diabetes. *Nature, 423(6940)*, 599–602.

Diamond, L.M., & Lucas, S. (2004). Sexual-minority and heterosexual youths' peer relationships: Experiences, expectations, and implications for well-being. *Journal of Research on Adolescence, 14(3)*, 313–340.

Dick, D., Latendresse, S.J., Lansford, J.E., Budde, J.P., Goate, A., Dodge, K.A., Pettit, G.S., & Bates, J.E. (2009). Role of GABRA2 in trajectories of externalizing behavior across development and evidence of moderation by parental monitoring. *Archives of General Psychiatry, 66(6)*, 649–657.

Dick, D.M., Viken, R., Purcell, S., Kaprio, J., Pulkkinen, L., & Rose, R.J. (2007). Parental monitoring moderates the importance of genetic and environmental influences on adolescent smoking. *Journal of Abnormal Psychology, 116(1)*, 213–218.

Dieter, J.N.I., Field, T., Hernandez-Reif, M., Emory, E.K., & Redzepi, M. (2003). Stable preterm infants gain more weight and sleep less after five days of massage therapy. *Journal of Pediatric Psychology, 28(6)*, 403–411.

Dieter, J.N.I., Field, T., Hernandez-Reif, M., Jones, N.A., Lecanuet, J.P., Salmanm, F.A., & Redzepi, M. (2001). Maternal depression and increased fetal activity. *Journal of Obstetrics & Gynaecology, 21(5)*, 468–473.

Dittmann, R.W., Kappes, M.E., & Kappes, M.H. (1992). Sexual behavior in adolescent and adult females with congenital adrenal hyperplasia. *Psychoneuroendocrinology, 17(2–3)*, 153–170.

Dodge, K.A., Bates, J.E., & Pettit, G.S. (1990). Mechanisms in the cycle of violence. *Science, 250(4988)*, 1678–1683.

Dodge, K.A., Greenberg, M.T., & Malone, P.S. (2008). Testing an idealized dynamic cascade model of the development of serious violence in adolescence. *Child Development, 79(6)*, 1907–1927.

Doidge, N. (2008). *The brain that changes itself: Stories of personal triumph from the frontiers of brain science*. London: Penguin.

Domes, G., Heinrichs, M., Michel, A., Berger, C., & Herpertz, S.C. (2007). Oxytocin improves 'mind-reading' in humans. *Biological Psychiatry, 61(6)*, 731–733.

Dozier, M., Stovall, K.C., Albus, K.E., & Bates, B. (2001). Attachment for infants in foster care: The role of caregiver state of mind. *Child Development, 72(5)*, 1467–1477.

Dube, S.R., Anda, R.F., Whitfield, C.L., Brown, D.W., Felitti, V.J., Dong, M., & Giles, W.H. (2005). Long-term consequences of childhood sexual abuse by gender of victim. *American Journal of Preventive Medicine, 28(5)*, 430–438.

Dube, S.R., Felitti, V.J., Dong, M., Giles, W.H., & Anda, R.F. (2003). The impact of adverse childhood experiences on health problems: Evidence from four birth cohorts dating back to 1900. *Preventive Medicine, 37(3)*, 268–277.

Dubowitz, H., Black, M.M., Cox, C.E., Kerr, M.A., Litrownik, A.J., Radhakrishna, A., English, D.J., Schneider, M.W., & Runyan, D.K. (2001). Father involvement and children's functioning at age 6 years: A multisite study. *Child Maltreat, 6(4)*, 300–309.

Dunbar, R. (1998). *Grooming, gossip, and the evolution of language*. Cambridge, MA: Harvard University Press.

Dunn, J. (2004). *Children's friendships*. Oxford: Wiley-Blackwell.

Dunn, J., & Brophy, M. (2005). Communication, relationships, and individual differences in children's understanding of mind. In J. Astington (Ed.), *Why language matters for theory of mind* (pp. 50–69). Oxford: Oxford University Press.

Duyme, M., & Capron, C. (1992). Socioeconomic status and IQ: What is the meaning of the French adoption studies? *Cahiers de psychologie cognitive, 12(5–6),* 585–604.

Dwyer, C. (2000). Negotiating diasporic identities: Young British South Asian Muslim women. *Women's Studies International Forum, 23(4),* 475–486.

Egeland, B., & Hiester, M. (1995). The long-term consequences of infant day-care and mother–infant attachment. *Child Development, 66(2),* 474–485.

Einarrson, C., & Granstrom, K. (2002). Gender-biased interaction in the classroom: The influence of gender and age in the relationship between teacher and pupil. *Scandinavian Journal of Educational Research, 46(2),* 117–127.

Eisenberg, D.T.A., Campbell, B., Gray, P.B., & Sorenson, M.D. (2008). Dopamine receptor genetic polymorphisms and body composition in undernourished pastoralists: An exploration of nutrition indices among nomadic and recently settled Ariaal men of northern Kenya. *BMC Evolutionary Biology, 8(1),* 173.

Ekman, P. (1989). The argument and evidence about universals in facial expressions of emotion. In H. Wagner & A. Mansted (Eds.), *Handbook of social psychophysiology* (pp. 143–164). Chichester: Wiley.

Ekman, P., Friesen, W.V., O'Sullivan, M., Chan, A., Diacoyanni-Tarlatzis, I., Heider K., Krause, R., LeCompte, W.A., Pitcairn, T., & Ricci-Bitti, P.E. (1987). Universals and cultural differences in the judgments of facial expressions of emotion. *Journal of Personality and Social Psychology, 53(4),* 712–717.

Elfenbein, H.A., & Ambady, N. (2003). Universals and cultural differences in recognizing emotions. *Current Directions in Psychological Science, 12(5),* 159–164.

Elfer, P. (2006). Exploring children's expressions of attachment in nursery. *European Early Childhood Education Research Journal, 14(2),* 81–95.

Ellis, B., & Essex, M. (2007). Family environments, adrenarche, and sexual maturation: A longitudinal test of a life history model. *Child Development, 78(6),* 1799–1817.

Eluvathingal, T.J., Chugani, H.T., Behen, M.E., Juhász, C., Muzik, O., Maqbool, M., Chugani, D.C., & Makki, M. (2006). Abnormal brain connectivity in children after early severe socioemotional deprivation: A diffusion tensor imaging study. *Pediatrics, 117(6),* 2093–2100.

Emanuel, R. (1996). Psychotherapy with children traumatized in infancy. *Journal of Child Psychotherapy, 22(2),* 214–239.

Epstein, M.A., & Bottoms, B.L. (2002). Explaining the forgetting and recovery of abuse and trauma memories: Possible mechanisms. *Child Maltreatment, 7(3),* 210–225.

Essex, M.J., Klein, M.H., Cho, E., & Kalin, N.H. (2002). Maternal stress beginning in infancy may sensitize children to later stress exposure: Effects on cortisol and behavior. *Biological Psychiatry, 52(8),* 776–784.

Eysenck, H.J. (1971). Race, intelligence and education. *New Society, 17(455),* 1045–1047.

Eysenck, H.J. (1988). Eysenck personality questionnaire. In M. Hersen & A. Bellack (Eds.), *Dictionary of behavioral assessment techniques* (p. 207). New York: Pergamon.

Fagan, J.F., & Singer, L.T. (1983). Infant recognition memory as a measure of intelligence. In L. Lipsitt (Ed.), *Advances in infancy research* (pp. 31–78). Norwood, NJ: Ablex.

Faraone, S.V., Doyle, A.E., Mick, E., & Biederman, J. (2001). Meta-analysis of the association between the 7-repeat allele of the dopamine D4 receptor gene and attention deficit hyperactivity disorder. *American Journal of Psychiatry, 158(7),* 1052–1057.

Farber, E.A., & Egeland, B. (1987). Invulnerability among abused and neglected children. In E. Anthony & B. Cohler (Eds.), *The invulnerable child* (pp. 253–288). New York: Guilford.

Fearon, R.M., van IJzendoorn, M.H., Fonagy, P., Bakermans-Kranenburg, M.J., Schuengel, C., & Bokhorst, C.L. (2006). In search of shared and nonshared environmental factors in security of attachment: A behavior-genetic study of the association between sensitivity and attachment security. *Developmental Psychology, 42(6)*, 1026–1040.

Fein, S., & Spencer, S.J. (1997). Prejudice as self-image maintenance: Affirming the self through derogating others. *Journal of Personality and Social Psychology, 73(1)*, 31–44.

Feinberg, M.E., Button, T.M., Neiderhiser, J.M., Reiss, D., & Hetherington, E.M. (2007). Parenting and adolescent antisocial behavior and depression: Evidence of genotype x parenting environment interaction. *Archives of General Psychiatry, 64(4)*, 457–465.

Feinstein, L., Hearn, B., Renton, Z., Abrahams, C., & MacLeod, M. (2007). *Reducing inequalities: Realising the talents of all.* London: National Children's Bureau.

Feldman, R. (2003). Infant-mother and infant-father synchrony: The coregulation of positive arousal. *Infant Mental Health Journal, 24(1)*, 1–23.

Feldman, R., Eidelman, A.I., Sirota, L., & Weller, A. (2002). Comparison of skin-to-skin (kangaroo) and traditional care: Parenting outcomes and preterm infant development. *Pediatrics, 110(1)*, 16–26.

Felitti, V.J. (2002). The relation between adverse childhood experiences and adult health: Turning gold into lead. *Permanente Journal, 6(1)*, 44.

Felitti, V.J., Anda, R.F., Nordenberg, D., Williamson, D.F., Spitz, A.M., Edwards, V., Koss, M.P., & Marks, J.S. (1998). Relationship of childhood abuse and household dysfunction to many of the leading causes of death in adults. The Adverse Childhood Experiences (ACE) Study. *American Journal of Preventive Medicine, 14(4)*, 245–258.

Fergusson, D.M., Horwood, L.J., Ridder, E.M., & Beautrais, A.L. (2005). Sexual orientation and mental health in a birth cohort of young adults. *Psychological Medicine, 35(07)*, 971–981.

Fernald, A. (1985). Four-month-old infants prefer to listen to motherese. *Infant Behavior and Development, 8(2)*, 181–195.

Fernald, A. (1993). Approval and disapproval: Infant responsiveness to vocal affect in familiar and unfamiliar languages. *Child Development, 64(3)*, 657–674.

Ferreira, V.S., Bock, K., Wilson, M.P., & Cohen, N.J. (2008). Memory for syntax despite amnesia. *Psychological science: A Journal of the American Psychological Society/APS, 19(9)*, 940–946.

Feyerabend, P.K. (1993). *Against method.* London: New Left Books.

Field, T. (1981). Infant gaze aversion and heart rate during face-to-face interactions. *Infant behavior and development, 4*, 307–315.

Field, T. (2007). *The amazing infant.* London: Wiley.

Field, T., Diego, M., & Hernandez-Reif, M. (2006). Prenatal depression effects on the fetus and newborn: A review. *Infant Behavior and Development, 29(3)*, 445–455.

Field, T., Healy, B., Goldstein, S., Perry, S., Bendell, D., Schanberg, S., Zimmerman, E.A., & Kuhn, C. (1988). Infants of depressed mothers show 'depressed' behavior even with non-depressed adults. *Child Development, 59*, 1569–1579.

Field, T.M. (2002). Early interactions between infants and their postpartum depressed mothers. *Infant Behavior and Development, 25(1)*, 25–29.

Field, T.M., Cohen, C., Garcia, R., & Greenberg, R. (1984). Mother-stranger face discrimination by the newborn. *Infant Behavior and Development, 7(1)*, 19–25.

Fildes, V.A. (1988). *Wet nursing: A history from antiquity to the present.* New York: Basil Blackwell.

Finkelstein, J.W., Susman, E.J., Chinchilli, V.M., Kunselman, S.J., D'Arcangelo, M.R., Schwab, J., Demers, L.M., Liben, L.S., Lookingbill, G., & Kulin, H.E. (1997). Estrogen or testosterone increases self-reported aggressive behaviors in hypogonadal adolescents 1. *Journal of Clinical Endocrinology and Metabolism, 82(8)*, 2433–2438.

Finnegan, R.A., Hodges, E.V.E., & Perry, D.G. (1998). Victimization by peers: Associations with children's reports of mother-child interaction. *Journal of Personality and Social Psychology, 75(4)*, 1076–1086.

Fitzpatrick, K.M., Piko, B.F., Wright, D.R., & LaGory, M. (2005). Depressive symptomatology, exposure to violence, and the role of social capital among African American adolescents. *American Journal of Orthopsychiatry, 75*, 262–274.

Flouri, E. (2005). *Fathering and child outcomes*. New York: Wiley.

Foa, E.B., Molnar, C., & Cashman, L. (1995). Change in rape narratives during exposure therapy for posttraumatic stress disorder. *Journal of Traumatic Stress, 8(4)*, 675–690.

Foley, D.L., Eaves, L.J., Wormley, B., Silberg, J.L., Maes, H.H., Kuhn, J., & Riley, B. (2004). Childhood adversity, monoamine oxidase A genotype, and risk for conduct disorder. *Archives of General Psychiatry, 61(7)*, 738–744.

Fonagy, P. (2002). *Affect regulation, mentalization, and the development of the self*. New York: Other Press.

Fonagy, P., Steele, H., & Steele, M. (1991). Maternal representations of attachment during pregnancy predict the organization of infant-mother attachment at one year of age. *Child Development, 62(5)*, 891–905.

Fonagy, P., & Target, M. (1996). Playing with reality: I. Theory of mind and the normal development of psychic reality. *International Journal of Psycho-Analysis, 77(2)*, 217–233.

Fonagy, P., & Target, M. (1998). Mentalization and the changing aims of child psychoanalysis. *Psychoanalytic Dialogues, 8(1)*, 87–114.

Fonseca, C. (2004). The circulation of children in a Brazilian working-class neighborhood: A local practice in a globalized world. In F. Bowie (Ed.) *Cross-cultural approaches to adoption* (pp. 165–181). London: Routledge.

Forcada-Guex, M., Pierrehumbert, B., Borghini, A., Moessinger, A., & Muller-Nix, C. (2006). Early dyadic patterns of mother–infant interactions and outcomes of prematurity at 18 months. *Pediatrics, 118(1)*, 107–114.

Forget-Dubois, N., Boivin, M., Dionne, G., Pierce, T., Tremblay, R.E., & Pérusse, D. (2007). A longitudinal twin study of the genetic and environmental etiology of maternal hostile-reactive behavior during infancy and toddlerhood. *Infant Behavior and Development, 30(3)*, 453–465.

Foster, S., & Little, M. (1987). The vision quest: Passing from childhood to adulthood. In L. Mahdi, S. Foster, & M. Little (Eds.), *Betwixt and between: Patterns of masculine and feminine initiation* (pp. 165–81). Chicago: Open Court Publishing Company.

Fowler, J.H., Dawes, C.T., & Christakis, N.A. (2009). Model of genetic variation in human social networks. *Proceedings of the National Academy of Sciences, 106(6)*, 1720.

Fraiberg, S. (1974). Blind infants and their mothers: An examination of the sign system. In M. Lewis & L.A. Rosenblum (Eds.), *The effect of the infant on its caregiver. The origin of behavior series* (Vol. I, pp. 215–232). New York: John Wiley & Sons.

Fraiberg, S. (1982). Pathological defenses in infancy. *Psychoanalytic Quarterly, 51*, 612–635.

Francis, D., Diorio, J., Liu, D., & Meaney, M.J. (1999). Nongenomic transmission across generations of maternal behavior and stress responses in the rat. *Science, 286(5442)*, 1155–1158.

Freisthler, B., Merritt, D., & LaScala, E. (2006). Understanding the ecology of child maltreatment: A review of the literature and directions for future research. *Child Maltreat, 11(3)*, 263–280.

Freud, S. (1973). Beyond the pleasure principle. *The standard edition of the complete psychological works of Sigmund Freud*, 18. London: Vintage. (Original work published 1920)

Friedlmeier, W., Chakkarath, P., & Schwarz, B. (2005). *Culture and human development: The importance of cross-cultural research to the social sciences*. Hove: Psychology Press.

Fries, A.B.W., Ziegler, T.E., Kurian, J.R., Jacoris, S., & Pollak, S.D. (2005). Early experience in humans is associated with changes in neuropeptides critical for regulating social behavior. *Proceedings of the National Academy of Sciences, 102(47)*, 17237–17240.

Frigerio, A., Ceppi, E., Rusconi, M., Giorda, R., Raggi, M.E., & Fearon, P. (2009). The role played by the interaction between genetic factors and attachment in the stress response in infancy. *Journal of Child Psychology and Psychiatry, and Allied Disciplines, 50*, 1513–1522.

Fritz, T., Jentschke, S., Gosselin, N., Sammler, D., Peretz, I., Turner, R., Friederici, A.D., & Koelsch, S. (2009). Universal recognition of three basic emotions in music. *Current Biology, 19(7)*, 573–576.

Fromm, E., & Shor, R. (2009). *Hypnosis: Developments in research and new perspectives*. Chicago: Aldine.

Fung, W.L.A., Bhugra, D., & Jones, P.B. (2006). Ethnicity and mental health: The example of schizophrenia in migrant populations across Europe. *Psychiatry, 5(11)*, 396–401.

Furman, W., & Simon, V.A. (2004). Concordance in attachment states of mind and styles with respect to fathers and mothers. *Developmental Psychology, 40(6)*, 1239–1246.

Gaensbauer, T.J. (2002). Representations of trauma in infancy: Clinical and theoretical implications for the understanding of early memory. *Infant Mental Health Journal, 23(3)*, 259–277.

Ganong, L., & Coleman, M. (2003). *Stepfamily relationships*. New York: Springer.

Garber, J., Keiley, M.K., & Martin, C. (2002). Developmental trajectories of adolescents' depressive symptoms: Predictors of change. *Journal of Consulting and Clinical Psycholology, 70(1)*, 79–95.

Gardner, F., Johnson, A., Yudkin, P., Bowler, U., Hockley, C., Mutch, L., Wariyar, U., & Extremely Low Gestational Age Steering Group. (2004). Behavioral and emotional adjustment of teenagers in mainstream school who were born before 29 weeks' gestation. *Pediatrics, 114(3)*, 676–682.

Ge, X., Conger, R.D., Cadoret, R.J., Neiderhiser, J.M., Yates, W., Troughton, E., & Stewart, M.A. (1996a). The developmental interface between nature and nurture: A mutual influence model of child antisocial behavior and parent behaviors. *Developmental Psychology, 32(4)*, 574–589.

Ge, X., Conger, R.D., & Elder Jr, G.H. (1996b). Coming of age too early: Pubertal influences on girls' vulnerability to psychological distress. *Child Development, 67(6)*, 3386–3400.

Geertz, C. (2000). *The interpretation of cultures*. New York: Basic Books.

Geraerts, E., Schooler, J.W., Merckelbach, H., Jelicic, M., Hauer, B.J., & Ambadar, Z. (2007). The reality of recovered memories: Corroborating continuous and discontinuous memories of childhood sexual abuse. *Psychological Science, 18(7)*, 564–568.

Gergely, G., & Watson, J.S. (1996). The social biofeedback theory of parental affect-mirroring: The development of emotional self-awareness and self-control. *International Journal of Psycho-Analysis, 77*, 1181–1212.

Gergely, G., & Watson, J.S. (1999). Early socio-emotional development: Contingency perception and the social-biofeedback model. In Rochat, P. (Ed.), *Early socialization* (pp. 101–136). Hillsdale, NJ: Lawrence Erlbaum.

Gergen, K.J. (2009). *An invitation to social construction* (2nd ed.). Newbury Park, CA: Sage.

Gibson, E.J. & Walk, R.D. (1960). The visual cliff. *Scientific American, 202(4)*, 64–71.

Giedd, J.N., Blumenthal, J., Jeffries, N.O., Castellanos, F.X., Liu, H., Zijdenbos, A., Paus, T., Evans, A.C., & Rapoport, J.L. (1999). Brain development during childhood and adolescence: A longitudinal MRI study. *Nature Neuroscience, 2(10)*, 861–863.

Gilbert, R., Widom, C.S., Browne, K., Fergusson, D., Webb, E., & Janson, S. (2009). Burden and consequences of child maltreatment in high-income countries. *The Lancet, 373(9657)*, 68–81.

Gilmore, D.D. (1990). *Manhood in the making: Cultural concepts of masculinity*. New Haven, CT: Yale University Press.

Gingras, J.L., Mitchell, E.A., & Grattan, K.E. (2005). Fetal homologue of infant crying. *Archives of Diseases of Childhood (Fetal Neonatal Ed.), 90(5)*, 415–418.

Glaser, R., Kiecolt-Glaser, J.K., Marucha, P.T., MacCallum, R.C., Laskowski, B.F., & Malarkey, W.B.

(1999). Stress-related changes in proinflammatory cytokine production in wounds. *Archives of General Psychiatry, 56(5)*, 450–456.

Gleason, T.R., Gower, A.L., Hohmann, L.M., & Gleason, T.C. (2005). Temperament and friendship in preschool-aged children. *International Journal of Behavioral Development, 29(4)*, 336–344.

Glover, V., & O'Connor, T. (2002). Effects of antenatal stress and anxiety: Implications for development and psychiatry. *British Journal of Psychiatry, 180*, 389–391.

Godden, D.R., & Baddeley, A.D. (1975). Context-dependent memory in two natural environments: On land and underwater. *British Journal of Psychology, 66(3)*, 325–331.

Goethals, G.R., & Reckman, R.F. (1973). The perception of consistency in attitudes. *Journal of Experimental Social Psychology, 9(6)*, 491–501.

Golinkoff, M. (1993). When is communication a 'meeting of minds?'. *Journal of Child Language, 20(1)*, 199–207.

Golombok, S., & Badger, S. (2010). Children raised in mother-headed families from infancy: A follow-up of children of lesbian and single heterosexual mothers, at early adulthood. *Human Reproduction, 25*, 150–157.

Göncü, A., & Gaskins, S. (2007). *Play and development: Evolutionary, sociocultural, and functional perspectives*. Hillsdale, NJ: Lawrence Erlbaum Associates, Inc.

Gonzales, N.A., Cauce, A.M., Friedman, R.J., & Mason, C.A. (1996). Family, peer, and neighborhood influences on academic achievement among African-American adolescents: One-year prospective effects. *American Journal of Community Psychology, 24(3)*, 365–387.

Goodlin, R., & Schmidt, W. (1972). Human fetal arousal levels as indicated by heart rate recordings. *American Journal of Obstetetrics & Gynecology, 114(5)*, 613–621.

Gottlieb, A. (2004). *The afterlife is where we come from: The culture of infancy in West Africa*. Chicago: University of Chicago Press.

Gottman, J.M. (1994). *What predicts divorce?: The relationship between marital processes and marital outcomes*. Hillsdale, NJ: Lawrence Erlbaum Associates, Inc.

Grammer, K., Fink, B., & Neave, N. (2005). Human pheromones and sexual attraction. *European Journal of Obstetrics & Gynecology, 118(2)*, 135–142.

Greco, C., Rovee-Collier, C., Hayne, H., Griesler, P., & Earley, L. (1986). Ontogeny of early event memory. I: Forgetting and retrieval by 2- and 3-month-olds. *Infant Behavior & Development, 9(4)*, 441–460.

Green, H., McGinnity, A., Meltzer, H., Ford, T., & Goodman, R. (2005). *Mental health of children and young people in Great Britain*. London: Department of Health.

Green, J. (2006). Annotation: The therapeutic alliance – a significant but neglected variable in child mental health treatment studies. *Journal of Child Psychology and Psychiatry, 47(5)*, 425–435.

Grosser, B.I., Monti-Bloch, L., Jennings-White, C., & Berliner, D.L. (2000). Behavioral and electrophysiological effects of androstadienone, a human pheromone. *Psychoneuroendocrinology, 25(3)*, 289–299.

Grossmann, K.E., Grossmann, K., & Waters, E. (Eds.) (2005). *Attachment from infancy to adulthood: The major longitudinal studies*. New York: Guilford Press.

Grzywacz, J.G., & Bass, B.L. (2003). Work, family, and mental health: Testing different models of work-family fit. *Journal of Marriage and the Family, 65(1)*, 248–261.

Guastella, A.J., Mitchell, P.B., & Dadds, M.R. (2008). Oxytocin increases gaze to the eye region of human faces. *Biological Psychiatry, 63(1)*, 3–5.

Gunnar, M.R., Morison, S.J., Chisholm, K., & Schuder, M. (2001). Salivary cortisol levels in children adopted from Romanian orphanages. *Development and Psychopathology, 13(3)*, 611–628.

Gutek, B.A., & Gilliland, C. (2008). How much do you value your family and does it matter? The joint effects of family identity salience, family interference with work and gender. *Human Relations, 62(2)*, 189–213.

Hageman, I., Andersen, H.S., & Jorgensen, M.B. (2001). Post-traumatic stress disorder: A review of psychobiology and pharmacotherapy. *Acta Psychiatrica Scandinavica, 104(6)*, 411–422.

Hagen, E.H. (1999). The functions of postpartum depression. *Evolution and Human Behavior, 20(5)*, 325–359.

Hagenauer, M.H., Perryman, J.I., Lee, T.M., & Carskadon, M.A. (2009). Adolescent changes in the homeostatic and circadian regulation of sleep. *Developmental Neuroscience, 31(4)*, 276–284.

Haglund, M.E.M., Nestadt, P.S., Cooper, N.S., Southwick, S.M., & Charney, D.S. (2007). Psycho-biological mechanisms of resilience: Relevance to prevention and treatment of stress-related psychopathology. *Development and Psychopathology, 19(3)*, 889–920.

Haig, D. (2004). Genomic imprinting and kinship: How good is the evidence? *Annual Review of Genetics, 38*, 553–585.

Haley, D.W., & Stansbury, K. (2003). Infant stress and parent responsiveness: Regulation of physiology and behavior during still-face and reunion. *Child Development, 74(5)*, 1534–1546.

Hall, G.S. (1904). *Adolescence: Its psychology and its relations to physiology, anthropology, sociology, sex, crime, and religion.* New York: Appleton.

Hall, S.S. (2006). *Size matters: How height affects the health, happiness, and success of boys and the men they become.* Boston: Houghton Mifflin Company.

Hamarman, S., Fossella, J., Ulger, C., Brimacombe, M., & Dermody, J. (2004). Dopamine receptor 4 (DRD4) 7-repeat allele predicts methylphenidate dose response in children with attention deficit hyperactivity disorder: A pharmacogenetic study. *Journal of Child & Adolescent Psychopharmacology, 14(4)*, 564–574.

Hammer, M.F., Mendez, F.L., Cox, M.P., Woerner, A.E., & Wall, J.D. (2008). Sex-biased evolutionary forces shape genomic patterns of human diversity. *PLoS Genetics, 4(9)*, e1000202.

Hamond, N.R., & Fivush, R. (1991). Memories of Mickey Mouse: Young children recount their trip to Disneyworld. *Cognitive Development, 6(4)*, 443–448.

Han, J.J., Leichtman, M.D., & Wang, Q. (1998). Autobiographical memory in Korean, Chinese, and American children. *Developmental Psychology, 34(4)*, 701–713.

Harden, K.P., Turkheimer, E., Emery, R.E., D'Onofrio, B.M., Slutske, W.S., Heath, A.C., & Martin, N.G. (2007). Marital conflict and conduct problems in children of twins. *Child Development, 78(1)*, 1–18.

Hare, T.A., Tottenham, N., Galvan, A., Voss, H.U., Glover, G.H., & Casey, B.J. (2008). Biological substrates of emotional reactivity and regulation in adolescence during an emotional go-nogo task. *Biological Psychiatry, 63(10)*, 927–934.

Hariri, A.R., Bookheimer, S.Y., & Mazziotta, J.C. (2000). Modulating emotional responses: Effects of a neocortical network on the limbic system. *Neuroreport, 11(1)*, 43–48.

Hariri, A.R., Drabant, E.M., & Weinberger, D.R. (2006). Imaging genetics: Perspectives from studies of genetically driven variation in serotonin function and corticolimbic affective processing. *Biological Psychiatry, 59(10)*, 888–897.

Harlow, H.F., Dodsworth, R.O., & Harlow, M.K. (1965). Total social isolation in monkeys. *Proceedings of the National Academy of Sciences, 54(1)*, 90–97.

Harman, C., Rothbart, M.K., & Posner, M.I. (1997). Distress and attention interactions in early infancy. *Motivation and Emotion, 21(1)*, 27–44.

Harper, M.L., Rasolkhani-Kalhorn, T., & Drozd, J.F. (2009). On the neural basis of EMDR therapy: Insights From qEEG Studies. *Traumatology, 15(2)*, 81.

Harris, J.R. (2009). *The nurture assumption: Why children turn out the way they do, revised and updated.* New York: Free Press.

Harris, M., & Ross, E.B. (1987). *Food and evolution.* Philadelphia, PA: Temple University Press.

Harris, P.L. (2007). Hard work for the imagination. In A. Goncu & S. Gaskins (Eds.), *Play and development: Evolutionary, sociocultural, and functional perspectives* (pp. 205–226). Hove: Psychology Press.

Hart, B., & Risley, T.R. (1999). *The social world of children: Learning to talk*. Baltimore, MD: Paul H. Brookes Publishing Co.

Hart, S. (2008). *Brain Attachment personality: An introduction to neuro-affective development*. London: Karnac.

Haviland, J.M., & Lelwica, M. (1987). The induced affect response: 10-week-old infants. *Developmental Psychology, 23(1)*, 97–104.

Hawkes, K., O'Connell, J.F., & Blurton Jones, N.G. (1997). Hadza women's time allocation, offspring provisioning, and the evolution of long postmenopausal life spans. *Current Anthropology, 38(4)*, 551–577.

Hay, D.F., Payne, A., & Chadwick, A. (2004). Peer relations in childhood. *Journal of Child Psychology and Psychiatry, 45(1)*, 84–108.

Hazan, C., & Zeifman, D. (1994). Sex and the psychological tether. In K. Bartholomew & D. Perlman (Eds.), *Advances in personal relationships* (Vol. 5, p. 151). London: Jessica Kingsley.

Hazell, P. (2007). Does the treatment of mental disorders in childhood lead to a healthier adulthood? *Current Opinion in Psychiatry, 20(4)*, 315–318.

Hebb, D.O. (1949). *The organisation of behaviour*. New York: Wiley.

Helgeson, V.S., & Fritz, H.L. (1999). Unmitigated agency and unmitigated communion: Distinctions from agency and communion. *Journal of Research in Personality, 33(2)*, 131–158.

Hemenover, S.H., & Schimmack, U. (2007). That's disgusting! . . ., but very amusing: Mixed feelings of amusement and disgust. *Cognition and Emotion, 21(5)*, 1102–1113.

Hendin, H., & Haas, A.P. (2004). Wounds of war: The aftermath of combat in Vietnam. In D. Knafo (Ed.), *Living with terror, working with trauma: A clinician's handbook* (p. 155). New York: Jason Aronson.

Hendry, J. (1986). *Becoming Japanese: The world of the pre-school child*. Honolulu: University of Hawaii Press.

Henggeler, S.W., Schoemwald, S.K., Borduin, C.M., Rowland, M.D., & Cunningham, P.B. (2009). *Multisystemic therapy for antisocial behavior in children and adolescents*. New York: The Guilford Press.

Henry, G. (2004). Doubly deprived. In P. Barrows (Ed.), *Key papers from the journal of child psychotherapy* (p. 105). London: Routledge.

Herdt, G. (1994). *Guardians of the Flutes* (Vol. 1). Chicago: University of Chicago Press.

Herrenkohl, R.C., Egolf, B.P., & Herrenkohl, E.C. (1997). Preschool antecedents of adolescent assaultive behavior: A longitudinal study. *American Journal of Orthopsychiatry, 67(3)*, 422–432.

Hesse, E., & Main, M. (2000). Disorganized infant, child, and adult attachment: Collapse in behavioral and attentional strategies. *Journal of the American Psychoanalytic Association, 48(4)*, 1097–1127.

Hetherington, E.M., & Elmore, A.M. (2003). Risk and resilience in children coping with their parents' divorce and remarriage. In S. Luthar (Ed.), *Resilience and vulnerability: Adaptation in the context of childhood adversities* (pp. 182–212). New York: Cambridge University Press.

Hewlett, B.S. (1991). *Intimate fathers: The nature and context of Aka pygmy paternal infant care*. Ann Arbor: University of Michigan Press.

Hewlett, B.S., & Lamb, M.E. (Eds.) (2005). *Hunter-gatherer childhoods*. New York: Aldine.

Hewstone, M., Rubin, M., & Willis, H. (2002). Intergroup Bias. *Annual Review of Psychology, 53(1)*, 575–604.

Hinde, R.A. (1970). *Animal behaviour: A synthesis of ethology and comparative psychology*. New York: McGraw-Hill.

Hines, M., Ahmed, S.F., & Hughes, I.A. (2003). Psychological outcomes and gender-related development in complete androgen insensitivity syndrome. *Archives of Sexual Behavior, 32(2)*, 93–102.

Hines, M., & Collaer, M.L. (1993). Gonadal hormones and sexual differentiation of human behavior: Developments from research on endocrine syndromes and studies of brain structure. *Annual Review of Sex Research, 4*, 1–48.

Hobson, P. (2002). *The cradle of thought*. London: Macmillan.

Hobson, P., Patrick, M., Crandell, L., García-Pérez, R., & Lee, A. (2005). Personal relatedness and attachment in infants of mothers with borderline personality disorder. *Development and Psychopathology, 17(02)*, 329–347.

Hodges, J., Steele, M., Hillman, S., Henderson, K., & Kaniuk, J. (2003). Changes in attachment representations over the first year of adoptive placement: Narratives of maltreated children. *Clinical Child Psychology and Psychiatry, 8(3)*, 351–367.

Hodnett, E.D., Gates, S., Hofmeyr, G.J., & Sakala, C. (2005). Continuous support for women during childbirth. *Birth, 32(1)*, 72–72.

Hofferth, S.L., & Anderson, K.G. (2003). Are all dads equal? Biology versus marriage as a basis for paternal investment. *Journal of Marriage and the Family, 65(1)*, 213–232.

Hoffman, E. (1990). *Lost in translation: A Life in a new language*. London: Penguin.

Hofstede, G. (2001). *Culture's consequences: Comparing values, behaviors, institutions, and organizations across nations*. Newbury Park, CA: Sage.

Holmes, T.R., Bond, L.A., & Byrne, C. (2008). Mothers' beliefs about knowledge and mother–adolescent conflict. *Journal of Social and Personal Relationships, 25(4)*, 561.

Holowka, S., & Petitto, L.A. (2002). Left hemisphere cerebral specialization for babies while babbling. *Science, 297(5586)*, 1515–1515.

Horrocks, R. (1994). *Masculinity in crisis: Myths, fantasies and realities*. New York: Palgrave.

Horswill, M.S., Waylen, A.E., & Tofield, M.I. (2004). Drivers ratings of different components of their own driving skill: A greater illusion of superiority for skills that relate to accident involvement. *Journal of Applied Social Psychology, 34(1)*, 177–195.

Howe, D. (2005). *Child abuse and neglect: Attachment*. London: Palgrave.

Hrdy, S.B. (1999). *Mother nature: Natural selection and the female of the species*. London: Chatto & Windus.

Hsu, H.C., Fogel, A., & Messinger, D.S. (2001). Infant non-distress vocalization during mother–infant face-to-face interaction: Factors associated with quantitative and qualitative differences. *Infant Behavior and Development, 24(1)*, 107–128.

Huang, C.C., Garfinkel, I., & Waldfogel, J. (2000). *Child support and welfare caseloads*. Wisconsin, MA: Institute for Research on Poverty, University of Wisconsin-Madison.

Hubel, D.H., & Wiesel, T.N. (1970). The period of susceptibility to the physiological effects of unilateral eye closure in kittens. *Journal of Physiology, 206(2)*, 419–436.

Hulanicka, B. (1999). Acceleration of menarcheal age of girls from dysfunctional families. *Journal of Reproductive and Infant Psychology, 17(2)*, 119–132.

Hull, P., Kilbourne, B., Reece, M., & Husaini, B. (2008). Community involvement and adolescent mental health: Moderating effects of race/ethnicity and neighborhood disadvantage. *Journal of Community Psychology, 36(4)*, 534–551.

Hungerford, A., Brownwell, C., & Campbell, S. (2000). Child care in infancy: A transactional perspective. In C. H. Zeanah (Ed.), *Handbook of Infant Mental Health* (pp. 519–532). New York: Guilford.

Hungerford, A., & Cox, M.J. (2006). Family factors in child care research. *Evaluation Review, 30(5)*, 631–635.

Hyde, J.S. (2005). The gender similarities hypothesis. *American Psychologist, 60(6)*, 581–592.

Iacoboni, M. (2005). Understanding others: Imitation, language, empathy. In S. Hurley & N. Chater (Eds.), *Perspectives on imitation: From cognitive neuroscience to social science* (pp. 77–99). Cambridge, Mass: MIT Press.

Itard, J.M.G. (1802). *An historical account of the discovery and education of a savage man.* London: Richard Phillips.

Jacobs, S.E., Thomas, W., & Lang, S. (1997). *Two-spirit people: Native American gender identity, sexuality, and spirituality.* Illinois: University of Illinois Press.

Jacobson, B., & Bygdeman, M. (1998). Obstetric care and proneness of offspring to suicide as adults: Case-control study. *British Medical Journal, 317(7169),* 1346–1349.

Jacques, S., & Zelazo, P.D. (2005). Language and the development of cognitive flexibility: Implications for theory of mind. In E. Astington & J. Baird (Eds.), *Why language matters for theory of mind* (pp. 144–162). Oxford University Press.

Jaffee, S.R., Moffitt, T.E., Caspi, A., & Taylor, A. (2003). Life with (or without) father: The benefits of living with two biological parents depend on the father's antisocial behavior. *Child Development, 74(1),* 109–126.

James, O. (2008). *Affluenza.* London: Ebury.

Jetten, J., Haslam, C., Haslam, A.S., & Branscombe, N.R. (2009). The social cure. *Scientific American Mind, 20(5),* 26–33.

Ji, E.K., Pretorius, D.H., Newton, R., Uyan, K., Hull, A.D., Hollenbach, K., & Nelson, T.R. (2005). Effects of ultrasound on maternal-fetal bonding: A comparison of two- and three-dimensional imaging. *Ultrasound in Obstetrics and Gynecology, 25(5),* 473–477.

Jones, S. (2002). *Y: The descent of men.* Boston: Little Brown.

Joyner, K., & Udry, J.R. (2000). You don't bring me anything but down: Adolescent romance and depression. *Journal of Health and Social Behavior, 41(4),* 369–391.

Judd, P.H., & McGlashan, T.H. (2003). *A developmental model of borderline personality disorder: Understanding variations in course and outcome.* Arlington, Virginia, VA: American Psychiatric Publishing Inc.

Juffer, F., Bakermans-Kranenburg, M.J., & van IJzendoorn, M.H. (Eds.) (2008). *Promoting positive parenting: An attachment-based intervention.* New York: Taylor & Francis Group.

Kaitz, M., & Maytal, H. (2005). Interactions between anxious mothers and their infants: An integration of theory and research findings. *Infant Mental Health Journal, 26(6),* 570–597.

Kansaku, K., & Kitazawa, S. (2001). Imaging studies on sex differences in the lateralization of language. *Neuroscience research, 41(4),* 333–337.

Karsten, L. (2003). Children's use of public space: The gendered world of the playground. *Childhood, 10(4),* 457–473.

Kasari, C., Sigman, M., Mundy, P., & Yirmiya, N. (1990). Affective sharing in the context of joint attention interactions of normal, autistic, and mentally retarded children. *Journal of Autism and Developmental Disorders, 20(1),* 87–100.

Kazdin, A., & Weisz, J. (Eds.) (2009). *Evidence-based psychotherapies for children and adolescents.* New York: Guilford.

Keller, H. (2007). *Cultures of infancy.* Hillsdale, NJ: Lawrence Erlbaum Associates, Inc.

Keller, H., & Lamm, B. (2005). Parenting as the expression of sociohistorical time: The case of German individualisation. *International Journal of Behavioral Development, 29(3),* 238–246.

Keller, H., Yovsi, R., Borke, J., Kärtner, J., Jensen, H., & Papaligoura, Z. (2004). Developmental consequences of early parenting experiences: Self-recognition and self-regulation in three cultural communities. *Child Development, 75(6),* 1745–1760.

Kendler, K.S., & Greenspan, R.J. (2006). The nature of genetic influences on behavior: Lessons from 'simpler' organisms. *Am J Psychiatry, 163(10),* 1683–1694.

Kennedy, A., Burger, H., Ormel, J., Huisman, M., Verhulst, F.C., & Oldehinkel, A.J. (2009).

Socioeconomic position and mental health problems in pre- and early-adolescents. *Social Psychiatry and Psychiatric Epidemiology, 44(3)*, 231–238.

Kennedy, E. (2004). *Child and adolescent psychotherapy: A systematic review of psychoanalytic approaches*. London: North Central London Strategic Health Authority.

Kenrick, J., Lindsey, C., & Tollemache, L. (2006). *Creating new families: Therapeutic approaches to fostering, adoption, and kinship care*. London: Karnac Books.

Kerr, M. (2001). Culture as a context for temperament: Suggestions from the life courses of shy Swedes and Americans. In T. Wachs, G. Kohnstamm, & R. McCrae (Eds.), *Temperament in context* (pp. 139–153). London: Routledge.

Kiecolt-Glaser, J.K., Loving, T.J., Stowell, J.R., Malarkey, W.B., Lemeshow, S., Dickinson, S.L., & Glaser, R. (2005). Hostile marital interactions, proinflammatory cytokine production, and wound healing. *Archives of General Psychiatry, 62(12)*, 1377–1384.

Kiernan, K.E., & Huerta, M.C. (2008). Economic deprivation, maternal depression, parenting and children's cognitive and emotional development in early childhood 1. *British Journal of Sociology, 59(4)*, 783–806.

Kim, Y.K., & Lee, Y. (1995). Cultural differences in Korean-and Anglo-American preschoolers' social interaction and play behaviors. *Child Development, 66(4)*, 1088–1099.

Kimata, H. (2007). Laughter elevates the levels of breast-milk melatonin. *Journal of Psychosomatic Research, 62(6)*, 699–702.

Kimball, M.M. (1986). Television and sex-role attitudes. In T. Williams (Ed.), *The impact of television: A natural experiment in three communities: A developmental model of border-line personality disorder: Understanding variations in course and outcome* (pp. 265–301). Orlando, FL: Academic Press.

Kindermann, T.A. (1993). Natural peer groups as contexts for individual development: The case of children's motivation in school. *Developmental Psychology, 29(6)*, 970–977.

King, F.T. (1932). *Feeding and care of baby*. London: Macmillan.

Kirsch, P., Esslinger, C., Chen, Q., Mier, D., Lis, S., Siddhanti, S., Gruppe, H., Mattay, V.S., Gallhofer, B., & Meyer-Lindenberg, A. (2005). Oxytocin modulates neural circuitry for social cognition and fear in humans. *Journal of Neuroscience, 25(49)*, 11489–11493.

Kisilevsky, B., Hains, S.M., Brown, C.A., Lee, C.T., Cowperthwaite, B., Stutzman, S.S., Swansburg, M.L., Lee, K., Xie, X., Huang, H., Ye, H.H., Zhang, K., & Wang, Z. (2009). Fetal sensitivity to properties of maternal speech and language. *Infant Behavior and Development, 32(1)*, 59–71.

Kitayama, S., Markus, H.R., Matsumoto, H., & Norasakkunkit, V. (1997). Individual and collective processes in the construction of the self: Self-enhancement in the United States and self-criticism in Japan. *Journal of Personality and Social Psychology, 72(6)*, 1245–1267.

Klaus, M. (1998). Mother and infant: early emotional ties. *Pediatrics, 102 (Suppl 5)*, 1244–1246.

Klaus, M.H., Kennell, J.H., & Klaus, P.H. (1993). *Mothering the mother: How a doula can help you have a shorter, easier, and healthier birth*. Reading, MA: Perseus.

Klein, M. (1975). *The psycho-analysis of children*. New York: Delacorte Press.

Knickmeyer, R., Baron-Cohen, S., Raggatt, P., & Taylor, K. (2005). Foetal testosterone, social relationships, and restricted interests in children. *Journal of Child Psychology and Psychiatry, 46(2)*, 198–210.

Kosfeld, M., Heinrichs, M., Zak, P.J., Fischbacher, U., & Fehr, E. (2005). Oxytocin increases trust in humans. *Nature, 435*, 673–676.

Kosko, B. (1993). *Fuzzy thinking*. New York: Hyperion.

Kraemer, S. (2000). The fragile male. *British Medical Journal, 321*, 1609–1612.

Kramer, L., & Radey, C. (1997). Improving sibling relationships among young children: A social skills training model. *Family Relations, 46(3)*, 237–246.

Kramer, T.H., Buckhout, R., & Eugenio, P. (1990). Weapon focus, arousal, and eyewitness memory. *Law and Human Behavior, 14(2)*, 167–184.

Kratz, C.A. (1990). Sexual solidarity and the secrets of sight and sound: Shifting gender relations and their ceremonial constitution. *American Ethnologist, 17(3)*, 449–469.

Kugiumutzakis, G., Kokkinaki, T., Makrodimitraki, M., & Vitalaki, E. (2004). Emotions in early mimesis. In J. Nadel & D. Muir (Eds.), *Emotional development: Recent research advances* (pp. 161–182). New York: Oxford University Press.

Kuhl, P.K., Stevens, E., Hayashi, A., Deguchi, T., Kiritani, S., & Iverson, P. (2006). Infants show a facilitation effect for native language phonetic perception between 6 and 12 months. *Developmental Science, 9(2)*, 13–21.

Kuhn, C.M., & Schanberg, S.M. (1998). Responses to maternal separation: Mechanisms and mediators. *International Journal of Developmental Neuroscience, 16(3–4)*, 261–270.

Kuhn, T.S. (1970). *The structure of scientific revolutions*. Chicago: University of Chicago Press.

Kujawski, J.H., & Bower, T.G.R. (1993). Same-sex preferential looking during infancy as a function of abstract representation. *British Journal of Developmental Psychology, 11*, 201–209.

Ladd, C.O., Huot, R.L., Thrivikraman, K.V., Nemeroff, C.B., Meaney, M.J., & Plotsky, P.M. (2000). Long-term behavioral and neuroendocrine adaptations to adverse early experience. *Progress in Brain Research, 122*, 81–103.

Ladd, G.W. (2005). *Children's peer relations and social competence: A century of progress*. New Haven: Yale University Press.

LaFrance, M. (1979). Nonverbal synchrony and rapport: Analysis by the cross-lag panel technique. *Social Psychology Quarterly, 42*, 66–70.

Lakatos, K., Nemoda, Z., Toth, I., Ronai, Z., Ney, K., Sasvari-Szekely, M., & Gervai, J. (2002). Further evidence for the role of the dopamine D4 receptor (DRD4) gene in attachment disorganization: Interaction of the exon III 48-bp repeat and the-521 C/T promoter polymorphisms. *Molecular Psychiatry, 7(1)*, 27–31.

Lamb, M.E. (1996). Effects of nonparental child care on child development: An update. *Canadian Journal of Psychiatry, 41(6)*, 330–342.

Lamb, M.E. (2004). *The role of the father in child development*. New York: Wiley.

Lambert, L., & Hart, S. (1976). Who needs a father. *New Society, 37(718)*, 80–80.

Lambert, M.J. (2005). Early response in psychotherapy: Further evidence for the importance of common factors rather than placebo effects. *Journal of Clinical Psychology, 61(7)*, 855–869.

Laursen, B., & Collins, W.A. (2004). Parent–child communication during adolescence. In A. Vangelisti (Ed.). *Handbook of family communication* (pp. 333–348). Hillsdale, NJ: Lawrence Erlbaum Associates, Inc.

LaVelle, M. (1995). Natural selection and developmental sexual variation in the human pelvis. *American Journal of Physical Anthropology, 98(1)*, 59–72.

Lazar, S.W., Kerr, C.E., Wasserman, R.H., Gray, J.R., Greve, D.N., Treadway, M.T., McGarvey, M., Quinn, B.T., Dusek, J.A., Benson, H., Rauch, S.L., Moore, C.I., & Fischl, B. (2005). Meditation experience is associated with increased cortical thickness. *Neuroreport, 16(17)*, 1893–1897.

Leach, P. (2009). *Child care today*. Cambridge: Polity Press.

Leach, P., Barnes, J., Malmberg, L-E., Sylva, K., & Stein, A. (2008). The quality of different types of child care at 10 and 18 months: A comparison between types and factors related to quality. *Early Child Development and Care, 178(2)*, 33.

Leach, P., Barnes, J., Nichols, M., Goldin, J., Stein, A., Sylva, K., Malmberg, L-E., & the FCCC team (2006). Child care before 6 months of age: A qualitative study of mothers' decisions and feelings about employment and non-maternal care. *Infant and Child Development, 15*, 471–502.

Leckman, J.F., Goodman, W.K., North, W.G., Chappell, P.B., Price, L.H., Pauls, D.L., Anderson, G.M., Riddle, M.A., McDougle, C.J., Barr, L.C., et al. (1994). The role of central oxytocin in obsessive compulsive disorder and related normal behavior. *Psychoneuroendocrinology, 19(8)*, 723–749.

LeDoux, J. (1998). *The emotional brain*. New York: Simon & Schuster.

Lee, K. (2000). Crying patterns of Korean infants in institutions. *Child: Care, Health & Development, 26(3)*, 217–228.

Leichty, M.M. (1978). The effect of father-absence during early childhood upon the Oedipal situation as reflected in young adults. In S. Fisher & R. Greenberg (Eds.), *The scientific evaluation of Freud's theories and therapy: A book of readings* (p. 196). New York: Basic Books.

Leng, G., Meddle, S.L., & Douglas, A.J. (2008). Oxytocin and the maternal brain. *Current Opinion in Pharmacology, 8(6)*, 731–734.

Lengua, L.J., & Kovacs, E.A. (2005). Bidirectional associations between temperament and parenting and the prediction of adjustment problems in middle childhood. *Journal of Applied Developmental Psychology, 26(1)*, 21–38.

Lepper, M.R., Greene, D., & Nisbett, R.E. (1973). Undermining children's intrinsic interest with extrinsic rewards: A test of the overjustification hypothesis. *Journal of Personality and Social Psychology, 28(1)*, 129–137.

Leung, R. (2005, August 21). Sea gypsies see signs in the waves. CBN news.com. Retrieved April 3, 2010, from http://www.cbsnews.com/stories/2005/08/17/60minutes/main782658_page2.shtml

LeVine, R.A. (1994). *Child care and culture: Lessons from Africa*. Cambridge: Cambridge University Press.

Levy, K.N., Meehan, K.B, Weber, M., Reynoso, R., & Clarkin, J.F. (2005). Attachment and borderline personality disorder: Implications for psychotherapy. *Psychopathology, 38(2)*, 64–74.

Libet, B. (1985). Unconscious cerebral initiative and the role of conscious will in voluntary action. *Behavioral and Brain Sciences, 8(4)*, 529–566.

Lieberman, A.F., Padron, E., van Horn, P., & Harris, W.W. (2005). Angels in the nursery: The intergenerational transmission of benevolent parental influences. *Infant Mental Health Journal, 26(6)*, 504–520.

Lieberman, M., Doyle, A.B., & Markiewicz, D. (1999). Developmental patterns in security of attachment to mother and father in late childhood and early adolescence: Associations with peer relations. *Child Development, 70(1)*, 202–213.

Lilienfeld, S. (2007). Psychological treatments that cause harm. *Perspectives on Psychological Science, 2(1)*, 53–70.

Lilienfeld, S.O., & Arkowitz, H. (2009). Foreign afflictions. *Scientific American Mind, 20(6)*, 68–69.

Linn, M.C., & Petersen, A.C. (1986). A meta-analysis of gender differences in spatial ability: Implications for mathematics and science achievement. In J. S. Hyde & M. Linn (Eds.), *The psychology of gender: Advances through meta-analysis* (pp. 67–101). Baltimore: Johns Hopkins University Press.

Lipka, J. (1994). Schools failing minority teachers: Problems and suggestions. *Educational Foundations, 8(2)*, 57–80.

Lippa, R.A. (2005). *Gender, nature, and nurture*. Hillsdale, NJ: Lawrence Erlbaum Associates, Inc.

Lockhart, K.L., Chang, B., & Story, T. (2002). Young children's beliefs about the stability of traits: Protective optimism? *Child Development, 75(5)*, 1408–1430.

Loftus, E.F. (1997). Repressed memory accusations: Devastated families and devastated patients. *Applied Cognitive Psychology, 11(1)*, 25–30.

Loftus, E.F., & Burns, T.E. (1982). Mental shock can produce retrograde amnesia. *Memory & Cognition, 10(4)*, 318–323.

Loftus, E.F., & Palmer, J.C. (1974). Reconstruction of automobile destruction: An example of the interaction between language and memory. *Journal of Verbal Learning and Verbal Behavior, 13(5)*, 585–589.

Loney, B.R., Frick, P.J., Ellis, M., & McCoy, M.G. (1997). *Intelligence, psychopathy, and antisocial behavior*. Alabama: University of Alabama.

Lovejoy, M.C., Graczyk, P.A., O'Hare, E., & Neuman, G. (2000). Maternal depression and parenting behavior: A meta-analytic review. *Clinical Psychology Review, 20(5)*, 561–592.

Lumey, L.H., Stein, A.D., Kahn, H.S., van der Pal-de Bruin, K.M., Blauw, G.J., Zybert, P.A., & Susser, E.S. (2007). Cohort profile: The Dutch hunger winter families study. *International Journal of Epidemiology, 36(6)*, 1196–1204.

Luthar, S.S., D'Avanzo, K., & Hites, S. (2003). Parental substance abuse: Risks and resilience. In S. Luthar (Ed.), *Resilience and vulnerability. Adaptation in the context of childhood adversities* (pp. 104–129). New York: Cambridge University Press.

Lutz, A., Dunne, J.D., & Davidson, R.J. (2007). Meditation and the neuroscience of consciousness. In P.D. Zelazo, M. Moscovitch, & E. Thompson (Eds.), *Cambridge handbook of consciousness* (pp. 499–551). Cambridge, MA: Cambridge University Press.

Lyons, D.M., Parker, K.J., Katz, M., & Schatzberg, A.F. (2009). Developmental cascades linking stress inoculation, arousal regulation, and resilience. *Frontiers in Behavavioural Neuroscience, 32(3)*, 32.

Lyons-Ruth, K., Connell, D.B., Grunebaum, H.U., & Botein, S. (1990). Infants at social risk: Maternal depression and family support services as mediators of infant development and security of attachment. *Child Development, 61(1)*, 85–98.

Lyons-Ruth, K., Yellin, C., Melnick, S., & Atwood, G. (2003). Childhood experiences of trauma and loss have different relations to maternal unresolved and Hostile-Helpless states of mind on the AAI. *Attachment & Human Development, 5(4)*, 330–352.

McAlister, A., & Peterson, C.C. (2006). Mental playmates: Siblings, executive functioning and theory of mind. *British Journal of Developmental Psychology, 24(4)*, 733–751.

McAlister, A., & Peterson, C. (2007). A longitudinal study of child siblings and theory of mind development. *Cognitive Development, 22(2)*, 258–270.

Mc Auley, M.M.T., Kenny, R.A., Kirkwood, T.B., Wilkinson, D.J., Jones, J.J., & Miller, V.M. (2009). A Mathematical Model of aging-related and cortisol induced hippocampal dysfunction. *BMC Neuroscience, 10(1)*, 10–26.

Macfarlane, A. (1975). Olfaction in the development of social preferences in the human neonate. *Ciba Foundation Symposium, 33*, 103–117.

McHale, J.P., & Fivaz-Depeursinge, E. (1999). Understanding triadic and family group interactions during infancy and toddlerhood. *Clinical Child and Family Psychology Review, 2(2)*, 107–127.

Mackay, J. (2000). *The Penguin atlas of human sexual behavior*. London: Penguin.

McLaughlin, D.K., Gardner, E.L., & Lichter, D.T. (1999). Economic Restructuring and Changing Prevalence of Female-Headed Families in America. *Rural Sociology, 64(3)*, 394–416.

MacLean, K. (2003). The impact of institutionalization on child development. *Development and Psychopathology, 15(04)*, 853–884.

MacLean, P.D. (1990). *The triune brain in evolution: Role in paleocerebral functions*. Norwell, MA: Kluwer Academic Publishers.

McNally, R.J. (2003). *Remembering trauma*. Cambridge, MA: Belknap Press.

McNally, R., Brett, J., Litz, T., Prassas, A., Shin, L.M., & Weathers, F.W. (1994). Emotional priming of autobiographical memory in post-traumatic stress disorder. *Cognition and Emotion, 8(4)*, 351–367.

Maddi, S.R. (2005). On hardiness and other pathways to resilience. *American Psychology, 60(3)*, 261–262.

Madsen, S.A., & Juhl, T. (2007). Paternal depression in the postnatal period assessed with traditional and male depression scales. *Journal of Men's Health & Gender, 4(1)*, 26–31.

Maestripieri, D., Roney, J.R., Debias, N., Durante, K.M., & Spaepen, G.M. (2004). Father absence, menarche and interest in infants among adolescent girls. *Developmental Science, 7(5)*, 560–566.

Maguire, E.A., Gadian, D.G., Johnsrude, I.S., Good, C.D., Ashburner, J., Frackowiak, R.S., & Frith, C.D. (2000). Navigation-related structural change in the hippocampi of taxi drivers. *Proceedings of the National Academy of Sciences of the United States of America, 97(8)*, 4398–4403.

Magurran, A.E., & Garcia, C.M. (2000). Sex differences in behaviour as an indirect consequence of mating system. *Journal of Fish Biology, 57(4)*, 839–857.

Main, M., & George, C. (1985). Responses of abused and disadvantaged toddlers to distress in agemates: A study in the day care setting. *Developmental Psychology, 21(3)*, 407–412.

Main, M., Kaplan, N., & Cassidy, J. (1985). *Security in infancy, childhood, and adulthood: A move to the level of representation. Monographs of the society for research in child development*, (Vol. 50, pp. 66–104). Ann Abor, MI: SRCD.

Main, M., & Solomon, J. (1986). Discovery of an insecure-disorganized/disoriented attachment pattern: Procedures, findings and implications for the classification of behavior. In T. B. Brazelton & M. Yogman (Eds.), *Affective development in infancy* (pp. 95–124). Norwood, NJ: Ablex.

Mampe, B., Friederici, A.D., Christophe, A., & Wermke, K. (2009). Newborns' cry melody is shaped by their native language. *Current Biology, 19*, 1994–1997.

Marazziti, D., Akiskal, H.S., Rossi, A., & Cassano, G.B. (1999). Alteration of the platelet serotonin transporter in romantic love. *Psychological Medicine, 29(03)*, 741–745.

Markus, H.R., & Kitayama, S. (1991). Culture and the self: Implications for cognition, emotion, and motivation. *Psychological Review, 98(2)*, 224–253.

Marmot, M. (2005). *Status syndrome: How your social standing directly affects your health.* London: Bloomsbury.

Marshall, T. (1982). Infant care: A day nursery under the microscope. *Social Work Service, 32*, 15–32.

Martini, M. (1994). Peer interactions in Polynesia: A view from the Marquesas. In J. Roopnarine (Ed.), *Children's play in diverse cultures* (pp. 73–103). Ithaca, NY: State University of New York Press.

Martins, C., & Gaffan, E.A. (2000). Effects of early maternal depression on patterns of infant–mother attachment: A meta-analytic investigation. *Journal of Child Psychology and Psychiatry and Allied Disciplines, 41(6)*, 737–746.

Marvin, R.S., VanDevender, T.L., Iwanaga, M.I., LeVine, S., & LeVine, R.A. (1977). Infant-caregiver attachment among the Hausa of Nigeria. In H. McGurk (Ed.), *Ecological factors in human development* (pp. 73–103). Amsterdam, Elsevier.

Masten, A.S. (2006). Developmental psychopathology: Pathways to the future. *International Journal of Behavioral Development, 30(1)*, 47–54.

Masten, A.S., & Powell, J.L. (2003). A resilience framework for research, policy, and practice. In S. Luthar (Ed.), *Resilience and vulnerability: Adaptation in the context of childhood adversities* (pp. 1–25). New York: Cambridge University Press.

Masten, A.S., Roisman, G.I., Long, J.D., Burt, K.B., Obradovic, J., Riley, J.R., Boelcke-Stennes, K., & Tellegen, A. (2005). Developmental cascades: Linking academic achievement and externalizing and internalizing symptoms over 20 years. *Developmental Psychology, 41(5)*, 733–746.

Masuda, T., & Nisbett, R.E. (2001). Attending holistically versus analytically: Comparing the context sensitivity of Japanese and Americans. *Journal of Personality and Social Psychology, 81(5)*, 922–934.

Matsumoto, D. (2002). American-Japanese cultural differences in judgements of emotional expressions of different intensities. *Cognition & Emotion, 16(6)*, 721–747.

Matsumoto, D., & Willingham, B. (2009). Spontaneous facial expressions of emotion of congenitally and noncongenitally blind individuals. *Journal of Personality and Social Psychology, 96(1)*, 1–10.

Mayer, J.D., DiPaolo, M., & Salovey, P. (1990). Perceiving affective content in ambiguous visual stimuli: A component of emotional intelligence. *Journal of Personality Assessment, 54(3–4)*, 772–781.

Mayseless, O., & Scharf, M. (2007). Adolescents' attachment representations and their capacity for intimacy in close relationships. *Journal of Research on Adolescence, 17(1)*, 23–50.

Mead, M. (1943). *Coming of age in Samoa*. London: Penguin Books.

Medina, K.L., Schweinsburg, A.D., Cohen-Zion, M., Nagel, B.J., & Tapert, S.F. (2007). Effects of alcohol and combined marijuana and alcohol use during adolescence on hippocampal volume and asymmetry. *Neurotoxicology and Teratology, 29(1)*, 141–152.

Meeus, W., Oosterwegel, A., & Vollerbergh, W. (2002). Parental and peer attachment and identity development in adolescence. *Journal of Adolescence, 25(1)*, 93–106.

Meins, E., Fernyhough, C., Fradley, E., & Tuckey, M. (2001). Rethinking maternal sensitivity: Mothers' comments on infants' mental processes predict security of attachment at 12 months. *Journal of Child Psychology and Psychiatry and Allied Disciplines, 42(5)*, 637–648.

Meins, E., Fernyhough, C., Wainwright, R., Clark-Carter, D., Das Gupta, M., Fradley, E., & Tuckey, M. (2003). Pathways to understanding mind: Construct validity and predictive validity of maternal mind-mindedness. *Child Development, 74(4)*, 1194–1211.

Meins, E., Fernyhough, C., Wainwright, R., Das Gupta, M., Fradley, E., & Tuckey, M. (2002). Maternal mind-mindedness and attachment security as predictors of theory of mind understanding. *Child Development, 73(6)*, 1715–1726.

Meltzoff, A.N. (1988). Infant imitation and memory: Nine-month-olds in immediate and deferred tests. *Child Development, 59(1)*, 217–225.

Meltzoff, A.N. (2007). 'Like me': A foundation for social cognition. *Developmental Science, 10(1)*, 126–134.

Meltzoff, A.N., & Borton, R.W. (1979). Intermodal matching by human neonates. *Nature, 282(5737)*, 403–404.

Meltzoff, A.N., Tager-Flusberg, H., & Cohen, D.J. (Eds.) (1993). *Understanding other minds: Perspectives from autism*. New York: Oxford University Press.

Mennella, J.A., Jagnow, C.P., & Beauchamp, G.K. (2001). Prenatal and postnatal flavor learning by human infants. *Pediatrics, 107(6)*, e88.

Messer, S.B., & Wampold, B.E. (2002). Let's face facts: Common factors are more potent than specific therapy ingredients. *Clinical Psychology: Science and Practice, 9(1)*, 21–25.

Milgram, S. (1974). *Obedience to authority: An experimental view*. London: Tavistock.

Miller, G., & Chen, E. (2006). Life stress and diminished expression of genes encoding glucocorticoid receptor and β2-adrenergic receptor in children with asthma. *Proceedings of the National Academy of Sciences of the United States of America, 103(14)*, 5496–5501.

Miller, G., Tybur, J.M., & Jordan, B.D. (2007). Ovulatory cycle effects on tip earnings by lap dancers: Economic evidence for human estrus? *Evolution and Human Behavior, 28(6)*, 375–381.

Mills, C.M., & Keil, F.C. (2005). The development of cynicism. *Psychological Science, 16(5)*, 385–390.

Minde, K. (2000). Prematurity and serious medical conditions in infancy: Implications for development, behavior, and intervention. In C. Zeanah (Ed.), *Handbook of infant mental health* (pp. 176–195). New York: Guilford Press.

273

Minoura, Y. (1992). A sensitive period for the incorporation of a cultural meaning system: A study of Japanese children growing up in the United States. *Ethos, 20(3)*, 304–339.

Minzenberg, M.J., Poole, J.H., & Vinogradov, S. (2006). Adult social attachment disturbance is related to childhood maltreatment and current symptoms in borderline personality disorder. *Journal of Nervous and Mental Disease, 194(5)*, 341–348.

Mitchell, R.W. (2001). Imaginative animals, pretending children. In R. Mitchell (Ed.), *Pretending and imagination in animals and children* (pp. 3–22). Cambridge, MA: Cambridge University Press.

Mithen, S.J. (2006). *The singing Neanderthals: The origins of music, language, mind, and body.* Cambridge, MA: Harvard University Press.

Moir, A., & Jessel, D. (1992). *Brain sex: The real difference between men and women.* New York: Dell.

Monk, C., Fifer, W.P., Myers, M.M., Sloan, R.P., Trien, L., & Hurtado A. (2000). Maternal stress responses and anxiety during pregnancy: Effects on fetal heart rate. *Developmental Psychobiology, 36(1)*, 67–77.

Monk, C.S., Nelson, E.E., McClure, E.B., Mogg, K., Bradley, B.P., Leibenluft, E., Blair, R.J., Chen, G., Charney, D.S., Ernst, M., & Pine, D.S. (2006). Ventrolateral prefrontal cortex activation and attentional bias in response to angry faces in adolescents with generalized anxiety disorder. *American Journal of Psychiatry, 163(6)*, 1091–1097.

Moon, C., Cooper, R.P., & Fifer, W.P. (1993). Two-day-olds prefer their native language. *Infant Behavior & Development, 16(4)*, 495–500.

Moore, T.H.M., Zammit, S., Lingford-Hughes, A., Barnes, T.R., Jones, P.B., Burke, M., & Lewis, G. (2007). Cannabis use and risk of psychotic or affective mental health outcomes: A systematic review. *The Lancet, 370(9584)*, 319–328.

Morelli, G.A., Rogoff, B., Oppenheim, D., & Goldsmith, D. (1992). Cultural variation in infants' sleeping arrangements: Questions of independence. *Development, 2(4)*, 604–613.

Mosier, C.E., & Rogoff, B. (2003). Privileged treatment of toddlers: Cultural aspects of individual choice and responsibility. *Developmental Psychology, 39(6)*, 1047–1059.

Mundy, P., & Burnette, C. (2005). Joint attention and neurodevelopmental models of autism. In F. Volkmar & J.D. Cohen (Eds.), *Handbook of autism and pervasive developmental disorders* (pp. 650–681). New York: Wiley.

Murray, L. (1998). Contributions of experimental and clinical perturbations of mother–infant communication to the understanding of infant intersubjectivity. In S. Braten (Ed.), *Intersubjective communication and emotion in early ontogeny* (pp. 127–143). New York: Cambridge University Press.

Murray, L., & Cooper, P. (1999). *Postpartum depression and child development.* New York: Guilford Press.

Murray, L., Cooper, P., Creswell, C., Schofield, E., & Sack, C. (2007). The effects of maternal social phobia on mother–infant interactions and infant social responsiveness. *Journal of Child Psychology and Psychiatry and Allied Disciplines, 48(1)*, 45–52.

Murray, L., Halligan, S.L., Adams, G., Patterson, P., & Goodyer, I.M. (2006). Socioemotional development in adolescents at risk for depression: The role of maternal depression and attachment style. *Development and Psychopathology, 18(02)*, 489–516.

Murray, L., Kempton, C., Woolgar, M., & Hooper, R. (1993). Depressed mothers' speech to their infants and its relation to infant gender and cognitive development. *Journal of Child Psychology and Psychiatry, 34(7)*, 1083–1101.

Murray, L., Stanley, C., Hooper, R., King, F., & Fiori-Cowley, A. (1996). The role of infant factors in postnatal depression and mother–infant interactions. *Developmental Medicine & Child Neurology, 38(2)*, 109–119.

Music, G. (2001). *Affect and emotion.* Cambridge: Icon.

Music, G. (2004). The old one-two. *Journal of Child Psychotherapy, 30(1)*, 21–37.

Music, G. (2005). Surfacing the depths: Thoughts on imitation, resonance and growth. *Journal of Child Psychotherapy, 31(1)*, 72–90.

Music, G. (2009a). Neglecting neglect: Some thoughts about children who have lacked good input, and are 'undrawn' and 'unenjoyed'. *Journal of Child Psychotherapy, 35(2)*, 142–156.

Music, G. (2009b). Neuroscience and child psychotherapy. In M. Lanyado & A. Horne (Eds.), *The handbook of child and adolescent psychotherapy*. London: Routledge.

Nachmias, M., Gunnar, M., Mangelsdorf, S., Parritz, R.H., & Buss, K. (1996). Behavioral inhibition and stress reactivity: The moderating role of attachment security. *Child Development, 67(2)*, 508–522.

Nadel, J., & Muir, D. (2005). *Emotional development: Recent research advances*. Oxford: Oxford University Press.

Nash, A. (1995). Beyond attachments: Towards a general theory of the development of relationships in infancy. In K. Hood, G. Greenberg, & E. Tobach (Eds.), *Behavioral development: Concepts of approach/withdrawal and integrative levels* (pp. 287–326). London: Routledge.

National Institute of Child Health and Human Development (NICDH) (2004). Type of child care and children's development at 54 months. *Early Childhood Research Quarterly, 19(2)*, 203–230.

Neave, N., & Wolfson, S. (2003). Testosterone, territoriality, and the 'home advantage'. *Physiology and Behavior, 78(2)*, 269–276.

Neiderhiser, J.M., & Lichtenstein, P. (2008). The twin and offspring study in Sweden: Advancing our understanding of genotype-environment interplay by studying twins and their families. *Acta Psychologica Sinica, 40(10)*, 1116–1123.

Ness, C.D. (2004). Why girls fight: Female youth violence in the inner city. *Annals of the American Academy of Political and Social Science, 595(1)*, 32–48.

Newton, M. (2002). *Savage girls and wild boys: A history of feral children*. London: Faber.

Nicolopoulou, A. (1997). Children and narratives: Toward an interpretive and sociocultural approach. In M. Bamberg (Ed.), *Narrative development: Six approaches* (pp. 179–215). Hillsdale, NJ: Lawrence Erlbaum Associates, Inc.

Niedenthal, P.M., & Showers, C. (1991). The perception and processing of affective information and its influences on social judgment. In J. Forgas (Ed.), *Affect and social judgment* (pp. 125–143). Oxford: Pergamon.

Nisbett, R.E., & Cohen, D. (1996). *Culture of honor: The psychology of violence in the South*. Boulder, CO: Westview Press.

Obel, C., Hedegaard, M., Henriksen, T.B., Secher, N.J., & Olsen, J. (2003). Stressful life events in pregnancy and head circumference at birth. *Developmental Medicine and Child Neurology, 45(12)*, 802–806.

Oberman, L.M., Hubbard, E.M., McCleery, J.P., Altschuler, E.L., Ramachandran, V.S., & Pineda, J.A. (2005). EEG evidence for mirror neuron dysfunction in autism spectrum disorders. *Cognitive Brain Research, 24(2)*, 190–198.

O'Brien, M., Commission, E.O., & Britain, G. (2005). *Shared caring bringing fathers into the frame*. London: Equal Opportunities Commission.

Ochs, E., & Schieffelin, B.B. (2009). *Language socialization across cultures*. Cambridge, MA: Cambridge University Press.

O'Connor, S., Vietze, P.M., Sherrod, K.B., Sandler, H.M., & Altemeier, W.A. 3rd. (1980). Reduced incidence of parenting inadequacy following rooming-in. *Pediatrics, 66(2)*, 176–182.

O'Connor, T.G., Bredenkamp, D., & Rutter, M. (1999). Attachment disturbances and disorders in children exposed to early severe deprivation. *Infant Mental Health Journal, 20(1)*, 10–29.

O'Connor, T.G., Deater-Deckard, K., Fulker, D., Rutter, M., & Plomin, R. (1998). Genotype-environment correlations in late childhood and early adolescence: Antisocial behavioral problems and coercive parenting. *Developmental Psychology, 34(5)*, 970–981.

O'Driscoll, K., Foley, M., & MacDonald, D. (1984). Active management of labor as an alternative to cesarean section for dystocia. *Obstetrics and Gynecology, 63(4)*, 485–490.

Offer, D., Kaiz, M., Howard, K.I., & Bennett, E.S. (2000). The altering of reported experiences. *Journal of the American Academy of Child & Adolescent Psychiatry, 39(6)*, 735–742.

Olde, E., van der Hart, O., Kleber, R., & van Son, M. (2006). Posttraumatic stress following childbirth: A review. *Clinical Psychology Review, 26(1)*, 1–16.

Osofsky, J.D. (1999). The impact of violence on children. *The Future of Children, 9(3)*, 33–49.

Osofsky, J.D. (2007). *Young children and trauma: Intervention and treatment.* New York: Guilford Press.

Ostrov, J.M., & Keating, C.F. (2004). Gender differences in preschool aggression during free play and structured interactions: An observational study. *Social Development, 13(2)*, 255–277.

Owens, E.B., & Shaw, D.S. (2003). Poverty and early childhood adjustment. In S. Luthar (Ed.), *Resilience and vulnerability: Adaptation in the context of childhood adversities* (pp. 267–292). New York: Cambridge University Press.

Panksepp, J. (2007). Can play diminish ADHD and facilitate the construction of the social brain? *Journal of the Canadian Academy of Child and Adolescent Psychiatry, 16(2)*, 57–66.

Panksepp, J., Burgdorf, J., Turner, C., & Gordon, N. (2003). Modeling ADHD-type arousal with unilateral frontal cortex damage in rats and beneficial effects of play therapy. *Brain and Cognition, 52(1)*, 97–105.

Parke, R.D., McDowell, D.J., Kim, M., Killian, C., Dennis, J., Flyr, M.L., & Wild, M.N. (2002). Fathers' contributions to children's peer relationships. In C. Tamis-LeMonda & N. Cabrera (Eds.), *Handbook of father involvement: Multidisciplinary perspectives* (pp. 141–167). Hillsdale, NJ: Lawrence Erlbaum Associates, Inc.

Parker, K.J., Rainwater, K.L., Buckmaster, C.L., Schatzberg, A.F., Lindley, S.E., & Lyons, D.M. (2007). Early life stress and novelty seeking behavior in adolescent monkeys. *Psychoneuroendocrinology, 32(7)*, 785–792.

Parks, C.L., Robinson, P.S., Sibille, E., Shenk, T., & Toth, M. (1998). Increased anxiety of mice lacking the serotonin1A receptor. *Proceedings of the National Academy of Sciences of the United States of America, 95(18)*, 10734–10739.

Patterson, C.J., & Wainright, J.L. (2007). Adolescents with same-sex parents: Findings from the national longitudinal study of adolescent health. In D. Brodzinsky, A. Pertman, & D. Kunz (Eds.), *Lesbian and gay adoption: A new American reality.* New York: Oxford University Press.

Patterson, T.L., Smith, L.W., Smith, T.L., Yager, J., & Grant, I. (1992). Symptoms of illness in late adulthood are related to childhood social deprivation and misfortune in men but not in women. *Journal of Behavioral Medicine, 15(2)*, 113–125.

Pellegrini, A.D. (2007). The development and function of rough-and-tumble play in childhood and adolescence: A sexual selection theory perspective. In A. Goncu & S. Gaskins (Eds.), *Play and development: Evolutionary, sociocultural, and functional perspectives* (pp. 77–98). New York: Psychology Press.

Perani, D., Paulesu, E., Galles, N.S., Dupoux, E., Dehaene, S., Bettinardi, V., Cappa, S.F., Fazio, F., & Mehler, J. (1998). The bilingual brain. Proficiency and age of acquisition of the second language. *Brain, 121(10)*, 1841–1852.

Perry, B.D. (2002). Childhood experience and the expression of genetic potential: What childhood neglect tells us about nature and nurture. *Brain and Mind, 3(1)*, 79–100.

Perry, B.D., Pollard, R.A., Blakley, T.L., Baker, W.L., & Vigilante, D. (1995). Childhood trauma, the neurobiology of adaptation, and "Use-dependent" development of the brain: How "states" become "traits". *Infant Mental Health Journal, 16(4)*, 271–291.

Peters, W. (1987). *A class divided: Then and now*. New Haven, CT: Yale University Press.

Peterson, C., Maier, S.F., & Seligman, M.E.P. (1993). *Learned helplessness: A theory for the age of personal control*. New York: Oxford University Press.

Phillips, A., Wellman, H.M., & Spelke, E.S. (2002). Infants' ability to connect gaze and emotional expression to intentional action. *Cognition, 85(1)*, 53–78.

Phillips, D.I.W. (2007). Programming of the stress response: A fundamental mechanism underlying the long-term effects of the fetal environment? *Journal of Internal Medicine, 261(5)*, 453.

Piaget, J. (1976). *The grasp of consciousness: Action and concept in the young child*. Cambridge, MA: Harvard University Press.

Pilowsky, D.J., Wickramaratne, P., Talati, A., Tang, M., Hughes, C.W., Garber, J., Malloy, E., King, C., Cerda, G., Sood, A.B., Alpert, J.E., Trivedi, M.H., Fava, M., Rush, A.J., Wisniewski, S., & Weissman, M.M. (2008). Children of depressed mothers 1 year after the initiation of maternal treatment: Findings from the STAR* D-Child Study. *American Journal of Psychiatry, 165(9)*, 1136–1147.

Pine, D.S., Mogg, K., Bradley, B.P., Montgomery, L., Monk, C.S., McClure, E., Guyer, A.E., Ernst, M., Charney, D.S., & Kaufman, J. (2005). Attention bias to threat in maltreated children: Implications for vulnerability to stress-related psychopathology. *American Journal of Psychiatry, 162(2)*, 291–296.

Pinker, S. (2002). *The blank slate*. London: Penguin Books.

Piontelli, A. (1992). *From fetus to child: An observational and psychoanalytic study*. London: Tavistock Publications.

Pope, A. (1867). *The Odyssey of Homer*. G. Bell & sons.

Popper, K.R. (2002). *Conjectures and refutations: The growth of scientific knowledge*. London: Routledge.

Posada, G., & Jacobs, A. (2001). Child–mother attachment relationships and culture. *American Psychologist, 56(10)*, 821–822.

Povinelli, D.J., Landau, K.R., & Perilloux, H.K. (1996). Self-recognition in young children using delayed versus live feedback: Evidence of a developmental asynchrony. *Child Development, 67(4)*, 1540–1554.

Prinz, R.J., Sanders, M.R., Shapiro, C.J., Whitaker, D.J., & Lutzker, J.R. (2009). Population-based prevention of child maltreatment: The US Triple P system population trial. *Prevention Science, 10(1)*, 1–12.

Prior, V., & Glaser, D. (2006). *Understanding attachment and attachment disorders: Theory, evidence and practice*. London: Jessica Kingsley.

Pruett, K.D. (2000). *Fatherneed: Why father care is as essential as mother care for your child*. New York: Free Press.

Pryor, J., & Rodgers, B. (2001). *Children in changing families: Life after parental separation*. Oxford: Blackwell Publishers.

Putallaz, M., & Sheppard, B.H. (1992). Conflict management and social competence. In C. Shantz & W. Hartup (Eds.), *Conflict in child and adolescent development* (pp. 330–355). Cambridge, MA: Cambridge University Press.

Putnam, R.D. (2000). *Bowling alone: The collapse and revival of American community*. New York: Simon & Schuster.

Pyers, J.E., & Senghas, A. (2009). Language promotes false-belief understanding: Evidence from learners of a new sign language. *Psychological Science, 20(7)*, 805–812.

Quattrone, G.A., & Tversky, A. (1984). Causal versus diagnostic contingencies: On self-deception and on the voter's illusion. *Journal of Personality and Social Psychology, 46(2)*, 237–248.

Radke-Yarrow, M., & Zahn-Waxler, C. (1984). Roots, motives, and patterns in children's prosocial behavior. In E. Staub (Ed.), *The development and maintenance of prosocial behavior: International perspectives on positive morality* (pp. 81–99). New York: Plenum.

Rakel, D.P., Hoeft, T.J., Barrett, B.P., Chewning, B.A., Craig, B.M., & Niu, M. (2009). Practitioner empathy and the duration of the common cold. *Family Medicine, 41(7)*, 494.

Rakoczy, H., Tomasello, M., & Striano, T. (2004). Young children know that trying is not pretending: A test of the 'Behaving-As-If' construal of children's early concept of pretense. *Developmental Psychology, 40(3)*, 388–399.

Raleigh, M.J., McGuire, M.T., Brammer, G.L., Pollack, D.B., & Yuwiler, A. (1991). Serotonergic mechanisms promote dominance acquisition in adult male vervet monkeys. *Brain Research, 559(2)*, 181–190.

Ramachandran, V.S. (2000). Mirror neurons and imitation learning as the driving force behind the great leap forward'in human evolution. *Edge*. Retrieved April 2, 2010, from http://www.edge.org/3rd_culture/ramachandran/ramachandran_p1.html

Ramchandani, P., Stein, A., Evans, J., O'Connor, T.G. & ALSPAC Study Team (2005). Paternal depression in the postnatal period and child development: A prospective population study. *The Lancet, 365(9478)*, 2201–2205.

Ramey, C.T., Campbell, F.A., Burchinal, M., Skinner, M.L., Gardner, D.M., & Ramey, S.L. (2000). Persistent effects of early childhood education on high-risk children and their mothers. *Applied Developmental Science, 4(1)*, 2–14.

Ramey, C.T., & Watson, J.S. (1972). Nonsocial reinforcement of infants. *Developmental Psychology, 6(3)*, 538.

Rauch, S.L., van der Kolk, B.A., Fisler, R.E., Alpert, N.M., Orr, S.P., Savage, C.R., Fischman, A.J., Jenike, M.A., & Pitman, R.K. (1996). A symptom provocation study of posttraumatic stress disorder using positron emission tomography and script-driven imagery. *Archives of General Psychiatry, 53(5)*, 380–387.

Rebec, G.V., Christensen, J.R., Guerra, C., & Bardo, M.T. (1997). Regional and temporal differences in real-time dopamine efflux in the nucleus accumbens during free-choice novelty. *Brain research, 776(1–2)*, 61–67.

Reddy, V. (1991). Playing with others' expectations: Teasing and mucking about in the first year. In A. Whiten (Ed.), *Natural theories of mind* (pp. 143–158). Oxford: Blackwell.

Reddy, V. (2008). *How infants know minds* (1st ed.). Cambridge, MA: Harvard University Press.

Redelmeier, D.A., & Baxter, S.D. (2009). Holiday review. Rainy weather and medical school admission interviews. *CMAJ: Canadian Medical Association journal, 181(12)*, 933.

Reichman, N.E., Corman, H., & Noonan, K. (2008). Impact of child disability on the family. *Maternal and Child Health Journal, 12(6)*, 679–683.

Reiner, W.G., & Gearhart, J.P. (2004). Discordant sexual identity in some genetic males with cloacal exstrophy assigned to female sex at birth. *New England Journal of Medicine, 350(4)*, 333–341.

Reiss, D., Hetherington, E.M., Plomin, R., Howe, G.W., Simmens, S.J., Henderson, S.H., O'Connor, T.J., Bussell, D.A., Anderson, E.R., & Law, T. (1996). Genetic questions for environmental studies: Differential parenting and psychopathology in adolescence. *Archives of General Psychiatry, 52(11)*, 925–936.

Reiss, D., Neiderhiser, J., Hetherington, E.M., & Plomin, R. (2000). *The relationship code: Deciphering genetic and social influences on adolescent development.* Cambridge, MA: Harvard University Press.

Repacholi, B.M., & Gopnik, A. (1997). Early reasoning about desires: Evidence from 14-and 18-month-olds. *Developmental Psychology, 33(1)*, 12–21.

Ressler, K.J., & Mayberg, H.S. (2007). Targeting abnormal neural circuits in mood and anxiety disorders: From the laboratory to the clinic. *Nature Neuroscience, 10(9)*, 1116–1124.

Rice, F., Harold, G.T., Boivin, J., van den Bree, M., Hay, D.F., & Thapar, A. (2010). The links between prenatal stress and offspring development and psychopathology: Disentangling environmental and inherited influences. *Psychological Medicine, 40*, 335–345.

Richardson, J., & Lelliott, P. (2003). Mental health of looked after children. *Advances in Psychiatric Treatment, 9(4)*, 249–256.

Riggins-Caspers, K.M., Cadoret, R.J., Knutson, J.F., & Langbehn, D. (2003). Biology-environment interaction and evocative biology-environment correlation: Contributions of harsh discipline and parental psychopathology to problem adolescent behaviors. *Behavior Genetics, 33(3)*, 205–220.

Rizzolatti, G. (2005). The mirror neuron system and its function in humans. *Anatomy and Embryology, 210(5)*, 419–421.

Robertson, J. (1971). Young children in brief separation – A fresh look. *Psychoanalytic Study of the Child, 26*, 264–315.

Rochat, P. (2009). *Others in Mind: Social origins of self-consciousness*. Cambridge: Cambridge University Press.

Rogoff, B. (2003). *The cultural nature of human development*. New York: Oxford University Press.

Roisman, G.I., Padrón, E., Sroufe, L.A., & Egeland, B. (2002). Earned-secure attachment status in retrospect and prospect. *Child Development, 73(4)*, 1204–1219.

Romeo, R., Knapp, M., & Scott, S. (2006). Economic cost of severe antisocial behaviour in children – and who pays it. *British Journal of Psychiatry, 188(6)*, 547–553.

Rose, R.J., & Kaprio, J. (2008). Genes, environments, and adolescent substance use: Retrospect and prospect from the finntwin studies. *Acta Psychologica Sinica, 40(10)*, 1062–1072.

Rosenthal, R., & Fode, K.L. (1963). The effect of experimenter bias on the performance of the albino rat. *Behavioral Science, 8(3)*, 183–189.

Rosenthal, R., & Jacobson, L. (1968). Pygmalion in the classroom. *Urban Review, 3(1)*, 16–20.

Rosenthal, S.L., Von Ranson, K.M., Cotton, S., Biro, F.M., Mills, L., & Succop, P.A. (2001). Sexual initiation: Predictors and developmental trends. *Sexually Transmitted Diseases, 28(9)*, 527–532.

Roth, A., & Fonagy, P. (2005). *What works for whom?: A critical review of treatments for children and adolescents* (2nd ed.). New York: Guilford Press.

Rothbaum, F., & Morelli, G.F. (2005). Attachment and culture: Bridging relativism and universalism. In G. Friedlmeier, P. Chakkarath, & B. Schwarz (Eds.), *Culture and human development: The importance of cross-cultural research for the social sciences* (pp. 99–124). London: Routledge.

Rousseau, J.J. (1985). *Discourse on the origin and foundations of inequality among men*. London: Penguin.

Rubin, K.H., Burgess, K.B., Dwyer, K.M., & Hastings, P.D. (2003). Predicting preschoolers' externalizing behaviors from toddler temperament, conflict, and maternal negativity. *Developmental Psychology, 39(1)*, 164–176.

Russek, L.G., & Schwartz, G.E. (1997). Feeling of parental caring predict health status in midlife: A 35-year follow-up of the harvard mastery of stress study. *Journal of Behavioral Medicine, 20(1)*, 1–13.

Russell, A., Hart, C.H., Robinson, C.R., & Folsen, S.F. (2003). Children's sociable and aggressive behaviour with peers: A comparison of the US and Australia, and contributions of temperament and parenting styles. *International Journal of Behavioral Development, 27(1)*, 74–86.

Rust, J., Golombok, S., Hines, M., Johnston, K., Golding, J., & ALSPAC Study Team (2000). The role of brothers and sisters in the gender development of preschool children. *Journal of Experimental Child Psychology, 77(4)*, 292–303.

Rutter, M. (1998). Developmental catch-up, and deficit, following adoption after severe global early privation. *Journal of Child Psychology and Psychiatry and Allied Disciplines, 39(04)*, 465–476.

Rutter, M. (2000). Resilience reconsidered: Conceptual considerations, empirical findings, and policy implications. In J. P. Shonkoff & S. J. Meisels (Eds.), *Handbook of early childhood intervention* (pp. 651–682). Cambridge, MA: Cambridge University Press.

Rutter, M. (2005). How the environment affects mental health. *British Journal of Psychiatry, 186,* 4–6.

Rutter, M., Andersen-Wood, L., Beckett, C., Bredenkamp, D., Castle, J., Groothues, C., Kreppner, J., Keaveney, L., Lord, C., & O'Connor, T.G. (1999). Quasi-autistic patterns following severe early global privation. *Journal of Child Psychology and Psychiatry and Allied Disciplines, 40(4),* 537–549.

Rutter, M., Beckett, C., Castle, J., Colvert, E., Kreppner, J., Mehta, M., Stevens, S., & Sonuga-Barke, E. (2007). Effects of profound early institutional deprivation: An overview of findings from a UK longitudinal study of Romanian adoptees. *European Journal of Developmental Psychology, 4(3),* 332–350.

Rutter, M., & O'Connor, T.G. (1999). Implications of attachment theory for child care policies. In J. Cassidy & P.R. Shaver (Eds.), *Handbook of attachment: Theory, research, and clinical applications* (pp. 823–844). New York: Guilford Press.

Sabbagh, M.A., Xu, F., Carlson, S.M., Moses, L.J., & Lee, K. (2006). The development of executive functioning and theory of mind: A comparison of Chinese and US preschoolers. *Psychological Science, 17(1),* 74.

Saffran, J.R., & Thiessen, E.D. (2003). Pattern induction by infant language learners. *Developmental Psychology, 39(3),* 484–494.

Sagi, A., van Ijzendoora, M.H., Aviezer, O., Donnell, F., Koren-Karie, N., Joels, T., & Harel, Y. (1995). *Attachments in a multiple-caregiver and multiple-infant environment: The case of the Israeli kibbutzim. Monographs of the society for research in child development* (Vol. 60, pp. 71–91). Ann Abor, MI: SRCD.

Sahar, T., Shalev, A.Y., & Porges, S.W. (2001). Vagal modulation of responses to mental challenge in posttraumatic stress disorder. *Biological Psychiatry, 49(7),* 637–643.

Sallenbach, W.B. (1993). The intelligent prenate: Paradigms in prenatal learning and bonding. In T. Blum (Ed.), *Prenatal perception, learning, and bonding: Learning and bonding* (p. 61). Hong Kong: Leonardo.

Salomone, R.C. (2003). *Same, different, equal: Rethinking single-sex schooling.* New Haven: Yale University Press.

Salovey, P., & Grewal, D. (2005). The science of emotional intelligence. *Current Directions in Psychological Science, 14(6),* 281.

Sameroff, A. (1998). Environmental risk factors in infancy. *Pediatrics, 102(5),* 1287–1292.

Sameroff, A., Gutman, L.M., & Peck, S.C. (2003). Adaptation among youth facing multiple risks: Prospective research findings. In S. Luthar (Ed.), *Resilience and vulnerability: Adaptation in the context of childhood adversities* (pp. 364–391). New York: Cambridge University Press.

Sander, L. (2007). *Living systems, evolving consciousness, and the emerging person: A selection of papers from the life work of Louis Sander.* London: Routledge.

Sandler, I., Wolchik, S., Davis, C., Haine, R., & Ayers, T. (2003). Correlational and experimental study of resilience for children of divorce and parentally-bereaved children. In S. Luthar (Ed.), *Resilience and vulnerability: Adaptation in the context of childhood adversities* (pp. 213–243). New York: Cambridge University Press.

Sapolsky, R.M. (1998). *Why zebras don't get ulcers: An updated guide to stress, stress-related diseases, and coping.* New York: WH Freeman.

Savage-Rumbaugh, E.S., & Lewin, R. (1994). *Kanzi: The ape at the brink of the human mind.* New York: Wiley.

Savin-Williams, R.C., & Ream, G.L. (2006). Pubertal onset and sexual orientation in an adolescent national probability sample. *Archives of Sexual Behavior, 35(3),* 279–286.

Scarr, S. (1999). American child care today. In A. Slater & D. Muir (Eds.), *The Blackwell Reader in Developmental Psychology* (p. 375). Oxford: Blackwell.

Scheper-Hughes, N. (1992). *Death without weeping: The violence of everyday life in Brazil.* California: University of California Press.

Schieffelin, B.B., & Ochs, E. (1986). Language socialization. *Annual Review of Anthropology, 15(1)*, 163–191.

Schlegel, A., & Barry, H. (1991). *Adolescence: An anthropological inquiry.* New York: Free Press.

Schoppe-Sullivan, S.J., Brown, G.L., Cannon, E.A., Mangelsdorf, S.C., & Sokolowski, M.S. (2008). Maternal gatekeeping, coparenting quality, and fathering behavior in families with infants. *Journal of Family Psychology, 22(3)*, 389–398.

Schore, A.N. (1994). *Affect regulation and the origin of the self: The neurobiology of emotional development.* Hillsdale, NJ: Lawrence Erlbaum Associates, Inc.

Schore, A.N. (2005). Back to basics attachment, affect regulation, and the developing right brain: Linking developmental neuroscience to pediatrics. *Pediatrics in Review 2005, 26*, 204–217.

Schultz, R.T. (2005). Developmental deficits in social perception in autism: The role of the amygdala and fusiform face area. *International Journal of Developmental Neuroscience, 23(2–3)*, 125–141.

Schwartz, D., Dodge, K.A., Pettit, G.S., & Bates, J.E. (1997). The early socialization of aggressive victims of bullying. *Child Development, 68(4)*, 665–675.

Schwartz, J., & Begley, S. (2002). *The mind and the brain: Neuroplasticity and the power of mental force.* New York: Harper.

Schwarz, B., & Trommsdorff, G. (2005). The relationship between value orientation, child-rearing goals, and parenting: A comparison of South Korean and German mothers. In W. Friedlmeier, P. Chakkarath, & B. Schwarz (Eds.), *Culture and human development.* Hove: Psychology Press.

Schwarz, N., & Clore, G.L. (1983). Mood, misattribution, and judgments of well-being: Informative and directive functions of affective states. *Journal of Personality, 45(3)*, 513–523.

Scott, S. (2008). Parenting programmes for attachment and conduct problems. *Psychiatry, 7(9)*, 367–370.

Sear, R., & Mace, R. (2007). Who keeps children alive? A review of the effects of kin on child survival. *Evolution and human behavior, 29(1)*, 1–18.

Selby, J.M., & Bradley, B.S. (2003). Infants in groups: A paradigm for the study of early social experience. *Human Development, 46(4)*, 197–221.

Seligman, M.E.P. (2002). *Authentic happiness: Using the new positive psychology to realize your potential for lasting fulfillment.* New York: Free Press.

Seligman, M.E.P., & Nathan, E. (1998). *Learned optimism.* New York: Pocket Books.

Sexton, T.L., Ridley, C.R., & Kleiner, A.J. (2004). Beyond common factors: Multilevel-process models of therapeutic change in marriage and family therapy. *Journal of Marital and Family Therapy, 30(2)*, 131–149.

Shamir, A., & Sakowski, S. (n.d.) WikiGenes – TPH2 – tryptophan hydroxylase 2. Retrieved December 26, 2009, from http://www.wikigenes.org/e/gene/e/121278.html

Shea, M.T., Stout, R.L., Yen, S., Pagano, M.E., Skodol, A.E., Morey, L.C., Gunderson, J.G., McGlashan, T.H., Grilo, C.M., Sanislow, C.A., Bender, D.S., & Zanarini, M.C. (2004). Associations in the course of personality disorders and Axis I disorders over time. *Journal of Abnormal Psychology, 113(4)*, 499–508.

Sherif, M., Harvey, O.J., White, B.J., Hood, W.R., & Sherif, C.W. (1961). *Intergroup conflict and cooperation: The Robbers Cave experiment.* Norman. OK: University Book Exchange.

Siegel, D.J. (1999). *The developing mind: Toward a neurobiology of interpersonal experience.* New York: Guilford Press.

Siegel, D.J. (2007). *The mindful brain: Reflection and attunement in the cultivation of well-being.* New York: Norton.

Siegman, A.W., & Feldstein, S. (1987). *Nonverbal behavior and communication,* Hillsdale, NJ: Lawrence Erlbaum Associates, Inc.

Sierra, M., Senior, C., Phillips, M.L., & David, A.S. (2006). Autonomic response in the perception of disgust and happiness in depersonalization disorder. *Psychiatry Research, 145(2–3),* 225–231.

Silvén, M. (2001). Attention in very young infants predicts learning of first words. *Infant Behavior & Development, 24(2),* 229–237.

Simmonds, J. (2007). Holding children in mind or holding therapy: Developing an ethical position. *Clinical Child Psychology and Psychiatry, 12(2),* 243–251.

Simons, L., & Conger, R. (2007). Linking mother-father differences in parenting to a typology of family parenting styles and adolescent outcomes. *Journal of Family Issues, 28(2),* 212–241.

Singh, L., Morgan, J.L., & Best, C.T. (2002). Infants' listening preferences: Baby talk or happy talk? *Infancy, 3(3),* 365–394.

Sisk, C.L., & Zehr, J.L. (2005). Pubertal hormones organize the adolescent brain and behavior. *Frontiers in Neuroendocrinology, 26(3–4),* 163–174.

Slade, A. (2006). Parental reflective functioning. *Psychoanalytic Inquiry, 26,* 640–657.

Slater, A., Quinn, P.C., Hayes, R., & Brown, E. (2000). The role of facial orientation in newborn infants preference for attractive faces. *Developmental Science, 3(2),* 181–185.

Smith, A.J., & Williams, D.R. (2007). Father-friendly legislation and paternal time across Western Europe. *Journal of Comparative Policy Analysis: Research and Practice, 9(2),* 175–192.

Smith, P. (2004). Play: Types and functions in human development. In D. Bjorklund & A. Pellegrini (Eds.), *Origins of the social mind: Evolutionary psychology and child development* (pp. 271–291). New York: Guilford Press.

Smyke, A.T., Dumitrescu, A., & Zeanah, C. (2002). Attachment disturbances in young children. I: The continuum of caretaking casualty. *Journal of the American Academy of Child & Adolescent Psychiatry, 41(8),* 972–982.

Solms, M., & Kaplan-Solms, K. (2001). *Clinical studies in neuro-psychoanalysis: Introduction to a depth neuropsychology.* New York: Other Press.

Solomon, J., George, C., & De Jong, A. (1995). Children classified as controlling at age six: Evidence of disorganized representational strategies and aggression at home and at school. *Development and Psychopathology, 7,* 447–463.

Soon, C.S., Brass, M., Heinze, H.J., & Haynes, J.D. (2008). Unconscious determinants of free decisions in the human brain. *Nature Neuroscience, 11(5),* 543–545.

Sorce, J.F., Emde, R.N., Campos, J.J., & Klinnert, M.D. (1985). Maternal emotional signaling: Its effect on the visual cliff behavior of 1-year-olds. *Developmental Psychology, 21(1),* 195–200.

Sorenson, E.R. (1979). Early tactile communication and the patterning of human organization: A New Guinea case study. In M. Bullowa (Ed.), *Before speech: The beginning of interpersonal communication* (pp. 289–330). Cambridge: Cambridge University Press.

Sowell, E.R., Trauner, D.A., Gamst, A., & Jernigan, T.L. (2002). Development of cortical and subcortical brain structures in childhood and adolescence: A structural MRI study. *Developmental Medicine and Child Neurology, 44(01),* 4–16.

Spencer, N. (2005). Does material disadvantage explain the increased risk of adverse health, educational, and behavioural outcomes among children in lone parent households in Britain? *Journal of Epidemiology and Community Health, 59(2),* 152–157.

Sperry, R.W. (2001). Hemisphere deconnection and unity in conscious awareness. In B. Baars (Ed.), *Essential sources in the scientific study of consciousness.* Cambridge, MA: MIT Press.

Spinka, M., Newberry, R.C., & Bekoff, M. (2001). Mammalian play: Training for the unexpected. *Quarterly Review of Biology, 76(2),* 141–168.

Spitz, R.A. (1945). Hospitalism – An inquiry into the genesis of psychiatric conditions in early childhood. *Psychoanalytic Study of the Child*, *1*, 53–74.

Spotts, E.L., Neiderhiser, J.M., Towers, H., Hansson, K., Lichtenstein, P., Cederblad, M., Pederson, N.L., & Reiss, D. (2004). Genetic and environmental influences on marital relationships. *Journal of Family Psychology*, *18(1)*, 107–119.

Sroufe, L.A. (2005). *The development of the person: The Minnesota study of risk and adaptation from birth to adulthood.* New York: Guilford Press.

Sroufe, L.A., & Waters, E. (1977). Attachment as an organizational construct. *Child Development*, *48*, 1184–1199.

Stallings, J., Fleming, A.S., Corter, C., Worthman, C., & Steiner, M. (2001). The effects of infant cries and odors on sympathy, cortisol, and autonomic responses in new mothers and nonpostpartum women. *Parenting*, *1(1&2)*, 71–100.

Standley, J.M. (2003). The effect of music-reinforced nonnutritive sucking on feeding rate of premature infants. *Journal of Pediatric Nursing*, *18(3)*, 169–173.

Stanton, S., Beehner, J.C., Saini, E.K., Kuhn, C.M., & LaBar, K.S. (2009). Dominance, politics, and physiology: Voters' testosterone changes on the night of the 2008 United States presidential election. *Plos One*, *4(10)*, e7543.

Steele, C.M. (1997). A threat in the air: How stereotypes shape intellectual identity and performance. *American Psychologist*, *52(6)*, 613–629.

Steele, H., & Steele, M. (2005). Understanding and resolving emotional conflict. In K. Grossman, K. Grossmann, & E. Waters (Eds.), *Attachment from infancy to adulthood: The major longitudinal studies* (pp. 137–164). New York: Guilford.

Steele, H., Steele, M., & Fonagy, P. (1996). Associations among attachment classifications of mothers, fathers, and their infants. *Child Development*, *67(2)*, 541–555.

Stein, A., Gath, D.H., Bucher, J., Bond, A., Day, A., & Cooper, P.J. (1991). The relationship between post-natal depression and mother-child interaction. *British Journal of Psychiatry*, *158(1)*, 46–52.

Stein, A., Woolley, H., Senior, R., Hertzmann, L., Lovel, M., Lee, J., Cooper, S., Wheatcroft, R., Challacombe, F., Patel, P., Nicol-Harper, R., Menzes, P., Schmidt, A., Juszczak, E., & Fairburn, C.G. (2006). Treating disturbances in the relationship between mothers with bulimic eating disorders and their infants: A randomized, controlled trial of video feedback. *American Journal of Psychiatry*, *163(5)*, 899.

Steinberg, L. (2007). Risk taking in adolescence: New perspectives from brain and behavioral science. *Current Directions in Psychological Science*, *16(2)*, 55–59.

Stern, D.N. (1977). *The first relationship.* Cambridge, MA: Harvard University Press.

Stern, D.N. (2000). *The interpersonal world of the infant.* New York: Basic Books.

Stern, D.N. (2001). Face-to-face play. In Jaffe, J., Beebe, B., Feldstein, S., Crown, C. & Jasnow, M.D. (Eds.), *Rhythms of dialogue in infancy: Coordinated timing in development. Monographs of the society for research in child development* (Vol. 66). Ann Abor, MI: SRCD.

Stern, D.N. (2004). *The present moment in psychotherapy and everyday life.* New York: Norton.

Stern, K., & McClintock, M.K. (1998). Regulation of ovulation by human pheromones. *Nature*, *392(6672)*, 177–179.

Stern, M., & Karraker, K.H. (1989). Sex stereotyping of infants: A review of gender labeling studies. *Sex Roles*, *20(9)*, 501–522.

Sternberg, K.J. (1997). Fathers, the missing parents in research on family violence. In M. E. Lamb (Ed.). *The role of the father in child development* (pp. 284–308). New York: Wiley.

Stevenson, B., & Wolfers, J. (2007). Marriage and divorce: Changes and their driving forces. working paper series. San Francisco: Fedral Reserve Bank of San Francisco. Retrieved April 3, 2010, from http://www.frbsf.org/publications/economics/papers/2007/wp07-03bk.pdf

Stipek, D., & Gralinski, J.H. (1996). Children's beliefs about intelligence and school performance. *Journal of Educational Psychology, 88(3)*, 397–407.

Stone, N., & Ingham, R. (2002). Factors affecting British teenagers' contraceptive use at first intercourse: The importance of partner communication. *Perspectives on Sexual and Reproductive Health, 34(4)*, 191–197.

Storey, A.E., Walsh, C.J., Quinton, R.L., & Wynne-Edwards, K.E. (2000). Hormonal correlates of paternal responsiveness in new and expectant fathers. *Evolution and Human Behavior, 21(2)*, 79–95.

Suddendorf, T., Simcock, G., & Nielsen, M. (2007). Visual self-recognition in mirrors and live videos: Evidence for a developmental asynchrony. *Cognitive Development, 22(2)*, 185–196.

Suomi, S.J. (1997). Early determinants of behaviour: Evidence from primate studies. *British Medical Bulletin, 53(1)*, 170–184.

Suomi, S.J., Novak, M.A., & Well, A. (1996). Aging in rhesus monkeys: Different windows on behavioral continuity and change. *Developmental Psychology, 32(6)*, 1116–1128.

Sutter-Dallay, A.L., Murray, L., Glatigny-Dallay, E., & Verdoux, H. (2003). Newborn behavior and risk of postnatal depression in the mother. *Infancy, 4(4)*, 589–602.

Sylva, K. (1984). A hard-headed look at the fruits of play. *Early Child Development and Care, 15(2)*, 171–183.

Sylva, K., Stein, A., Leach, P., Barnes, J., & Malmberg, L-E. (2007). Family and child factors related to the use of non-maternal infant care: An English study. *Early Childhood Research Quarterly, 22(1)*, 118–136.

Tajfel, H., & Turner, J.C. (1979). An integrative theory of intergroup conflict. In W. Austin & S. Worschel (Eds.), *The social psychology of intergroup relations*. Monterey, California: Brooks/Cole (pp. 33–47).

Talge, N.M., Neal, C., & Glover, V. (2007). Antenatal maternal stress and long-term effects on child neurodevelopment: How and why? *Journal of Child Psychology and Psychiatry and Allied Disciplines, 48, 3(4)*, 245–261.

Tamir, M. (2005). Don't worry, be happy? Neuroticism, trait-consistent affect regulation, and performance. *Journal of Personality and Social Psychology, 89(3)*, 449.

Tamis-LeMonda, C.S., Bornstein, M.H., & Baumwell, L. (2001). Maternal responsiveness and children's achievement of language milestones. *Child Development, 72(3)*, 748–767.

Tanaka, S. (2005). Parental leave and child health across OECD countries. *Economic Journal, 115(501)*, F7–F28.

Taylor, C. (1989). *Sources of the self*. Cambridge, MA: Harvard University Press.

Taylor, S.E., & Armor, D.A. (1996). Positive illusions and coping with adversity. *Journal of Personality, 64(4)*, 873–898.

Taylor, S.E., Klein, L.C., Lewis, B.P., Gruenewald, T.L., Gurung, R.A., & Updegraff, J.A. (2000). Biobehavioral responses to stress in females: Tend-and-befriend, not fight-or-flight. *Psychological Review, 107(3)*, 411–429.

Therien, J.M., Worwa, C.T., Mattia F.R., & deRegnier, R.A. (2004). Altered pathways for auditory discrimination and recognition memory in preterm infants. *Developmental Medicine and Child Neurology, 46(12)*, 816–824.

Thomas, K.M., Drevets, W.C., Dahl, R.E., Ryan, N.D., Birmaher, B., Eccard, C.H., Axelson, D., Whalen, P.J., & Casey, B.J. (2001). Amygdala response to fearful faces in anxious and depressed children. *Archives of General Psychiatry, 58(11)*, 1057–1063.

Tizard, B., & Hodges, J. (1978). The effect of early institutional rearing on the development of eight year old children. *Journal of Child Psychology and Psychiatry, 19(2)*, 99–118.

Tomasello, M. (2003). *Constructing a language: A usage-based theory of language acquisition*. Cambridge, MA: Harvard University Press.

Tomasello, M. (2009). *Why we cooperate*. Cambridge, MA: MIT Press.

Trainor, L.J., & Desjardins, R.N. (2002). Pitch characteristics of infant-directed speech affect infants' ability to discriminate vowels. *Psychonomic Bulletin & Review, 9(2)*, 335–340.

Travis, J. (2003). Gypsy secret: Children of sea see clearly underwater. *Science news (Washington), 163(20)*, 308–309.

Trehub, S.E., Unyk, A.M., & Trainor, L.J. (1993). Maternal singing in cross-cultural perspective. *Infant Behavior & Development, 16(3)*, 285–295.

Trevarthen, C., & Aitken, K.J. (2001). Infant intersubjectivity: Research, theory, and clinical applications. *Journal of Child Psychology and Psychiatry and Allied Disciplines, 42(1)*, 3–48.

Trevarthen, C., Kokkinaki, T., & Fiamenghi Jr, G.A. (1999). What infants' imitations communicate: With mothers, with fathers and with peers. In J. Nadel (Ed.), *Imitation in infancy* (pp. 127–185). New York: Cambridge University Press.

Trivers, R. (2002). *Natural selection and social theory: Selected papers of Robert L. Trivers.* Oxford: Oxford University Press.

Tronick, E. (2007). *The neurobehavioral and social emotional development of infants and children.* New York: Norton.

Tronick, E.Z., & Brazelton, T.B. (1980). Preverbal communication between mothers and infants. In D.R. Olson (Ed.), *The social foundations of language and thought.* New York: Norton.

Tronick, E.Z., Morelli, G.A., & Ivey, P.K. (1992). The forager infant and toddler's pattern of social relationships: Multiple and simultaneous. *Developmental Psychology, 28(4)*, 568–577.

Tronick, E.Z., Morelli, G.A., & Winn, S. (1987). Multiple caretaking of Efe (Pygmy) infants. *American Anthropologist, 91(1)*, 96–106.

Trowell, J., Joffe, I., Campbell, J., Clemente, C., Almqvist, F., Soininen, M., Koskenranta-Aalto, U., Weintraub, S., Kolaitis, G., Tomaras, V., Anastasopoulos, D., Grayson, K., Barnes, J., & Tsiantis, J. (2007). Childhood depression: A place for psychotherapy. *European Child & Adolescent Psychiatry, 16(3)*, 157–167.

True, M.M.M., Pisani, L., & Oumar, F. (2001). Infant-mother attachment among the Dogon of Mali. *Child Development, 72(5)*, 1451–1466.

Tully, E.C., Iacono, W.G., & McGue, M. (2008). An adoption study of parental depression as an environmental liability for adolescent depression and childhood disruptive disorders. *American Journal of Psychiatry, 165(9)*, 1148–1154.

Twain, M. (1986). *The adventures of Tom Sawyer and the adventures of Huckleberry Finn.* London: Penguin.

Uddin, M.S. (2006). Arranged marriage: A dilemma for young British Asians. *Diversity in Health and Social Care, 3(3)*, 211–219.

Udry, J.R. (2000). Biological limits of gender construction. *American Sociological Review, 65(33)*, 443–457.

Urwin, C. (2001). Getting to know the self and others: Babies' interactions with other babies. *Infant Observation, 4(3)*, 13–28.

Uslaner, E.M. (2008). Trust as a moral value. In D. Castiglione, V. Deth, & G. Wolleb (Eds.), *The handbook of social capital* (pp. 101–121). New York: Oxford University Press.

Utami, S.S., Goossens, B., Bruford, M.W., de Ruiter, R., & van Hooff, J. (2002). Male bimaturism and reproductive success in Sumatran orang-utans. *Behavioural Ecology, 13(5)*, 643–652.

Vaillant, G.E. (2002). *Aging well.* Boston: Little, Brown.

Valdimarsdottir, H.B., & Bovbjerg, D.H. (1997). Positive and negative mood: Association with natural killer cell activity. *Psychology & Health, 12(3)*, 319–327.

van den Bergh, B.R.H., Van Calster, B., Smits, T., Van Huffel, S., & Lagae, L. (2007). Antenatal maternal anxiety is related to HPA-axis dysregulation and self-reported depressive symptoms in adolescence: A prospective study on the fetal origins of depressed mood. *Neuropsychopharmacology, 33(3)*, 536–545.

van der Kolk, B.A. (1989). The compulsion to repeat the trauma. *Psychiatric Clinics of North America, 12(2),* 384–411.

van Heteren, C.F., Boekkooi, P.F., Schiphorst, R.H., Jongsma, H.W., & Nijhuis, J.G. (2001). Fetal habituation to vibroacoustic stimulation in relation to fetal states and fetal heart rate parameters. *Early Human Development, 61(2),* 135–145.

van IJzendoorn, M.H., Moran, G., Belsky, J., Pederson, D., Bakermans-Kranenburg, M.J., & Kneppers, K. (2000). The similarity of siblings' attachments to their mother. *Child Development, 71(4),* 1086–1098.

van Zeijl, J., Van Mesman, J., Van IJzendoorn, M.H., Bakermans-Kranenburg, M.J., Juffer, F., Stolk, M.N., Koot, H.M., & Alink, L.R.A. (2006). Attachment-based intervention for enhancing sensitive discipline in mothers of 1- to 3-year-old children at risk for externalizing behavior problems: A randomized controlled trial. *Journal of Consulting and Clinical Psychology, 74(6),* 994–1005.

Viner, R. (2002). Splitting hairs. *Archives of Disease in Childhood, 86(1),* 8–10.

Volkow, N.D., & Li, T.K. (2004). Drug addiction: The neurobiology of behaviour gone awry. *Nature Reviews Neuroscience, 5(12),* 963–970.

von Baeyer, C.L., Marche, T.A., Rocha, E.M., & Salmon, K. (2004). Children's memory for pain: Overview and implications for practice. *Journal of Pain, 5(5),* 241–249.

Votruba-Drzal, E., Coley, R.L., & Chase-Lansdale, P.L. (2004). Child care and low-income children's development: Direct and moderated effects. *Child Development, 75(1),* 296–312.

Vygotsky, L.S. (1962). *Thought and language* (E. Hanfmann & G. Vakar, Trans.). Cambridge, MA: MIT Press.

Wadhwa, P.D. (2005). Psychoneuroendocrine processes in human pregnancy influence fetal development and health. *Psychoneuroendocrinology, 30(8),* 724–743.

Wagner, G., Koschke, M., Leuf, T., Schlösser, R., & Bär, K-J. (2009). Reduced heat pain thresholds after sad-mood induction are associated with changes in thalamic activity. *Neuropsychologia, 47(4),* 980–987.

Wager, T.D., Rilling, J.K., Smith, E.E., Sokolik, A., Casey, K.L., Davidson, R.J., Kosslyn, S.M., Rose, R.M., & Cohen, J.D. (2004). Placebo-induced changes in FMRI in the anticipation and experience of pain. *Science, 303(5661),* 1162–1167.

Walker, S., Berthelsen, D.C., & Irving, K.A. (2001). Temperament and peer acceptance in early childhood: Sex and social status differences. *Child Study Journal, 31(3),* 177–192.

Waller, M.R., & Swisher, R. (2006). Fathers' risk factors in fragile families: Implications for 'healthy' relationships and father involvement. *Social Problems, 53(3),* 392–420.

Wallerstein, J.S., Lewis, J.M., & Blakeslee, S. (2000). *The unexpected legacy of divorce: A twenty-five-year landmark study.* New York: Hyperion.

Walton, G.E., & Bower, T.G.R. (1993). Newborns form 'prototypes' in less than 1 minute. *Psychological Science, 4(3),* 203–205.

Walum, H., Westberg, L., Henningsson, S., Neiderhiser, J.M., Reiss, D., Igl, W., Ganiban, J.M., Spotts, E.L., Pedersen, N.L., Eriksson, E., & Lichtenstein, P. (2008). Genetic variation in the vasopressin receptor 1a gene (AVPR1A) associates with pair-bonding behavior in humans. *Proceedings of the National Academy of Sciences, 105(37),* 14153–14156.

Ward, J. (1998). Sir Cyril Burt: The continuing saga. *Educational Psychology, 18(2),* 235–241.

Webster-Stratton, C., Reid, M.J., & Hammond, M. (2004). Treating children with early-onset conduct problems: Intervention outcomes for parent, child, and teacher training. *Journal of Clinical Child and Adolescent Psychology, 33(1),* 105–124.

Weinstein, S.M., Mermelstein, R.J., Hankin, B.L., Hedeker, D., & Flay, B.R. (2007). Longitudinal patterns of daily affect and global mood during adolescence. *Journal of research on adolescence: the official journal of the Society for Research on Adolescence, 17(3),* 587–600.

Weisfeld, C.C., Weisfeld, G.E., & Callaghan, J.W. (1982). Female inhibition in mixed-sex competition among young adolescents. *Ethology and Sociobiology, 3(1)*, 29–42.

Weisfeld, G.E., & Woodward, L. (2004). Current evolutionary perspectives on adolescent romantic relations and sexuality. *Journal of the American Academy of Child & Adolescent Psychiatry, 43(1)*, 11–19.

Welch-Ross, M.K. (1997). Mother–child participation in conversation about the past: Relationships to preschoolers' theory of mind. *Developmental Psychology, 33(4)*, 618–629.

Wermke, K., & Friederici, A.D. (2005). Developmental changes of infant cries – the evolution of complex vocalizations. *Behavioral and Brain Sciences, 27(4)*, 474–475.

Werner, E.E., & Smith, R.S. (1992). *Overcoming the odds: High risk children from birth to adulthood.* New York: Cornell.

White, G.M., & Kirkpatrick, J. (1985). *Person, self, and experience: Exploring Pacific ethnopsychologies.* California: University of California Press.

Whyte, J. (1986). *Girls into science and technology: The story of a project.* London: Routledge, Kegan & Paul.

Widdowson, E.M. (1951). Mental contentment and physical growth. *The Lancet, 1(24)*, 1316–1318.

Widom, S. (2007). A prospective investigation of major depressive disorder and comorbidity in abused and neglected children grown up. *Archives of General Psychiatry, 64(1)*, 49–56.

Widström, A.M., Wahlberg, V., Matthiesen, A.S., Eneroth, P., Uvnäs-Moberg, K., Werner, S., & Winberg, J. (1990). Short-term effects of early suckling and touch of the nipple on maternal behaviour. *Early Human Development, 21(3)*, 153–163.

Wikan, U. (1991). *Behind the veil in Arabia: Women in Oman.* Chicago: University of Chicago Press.

Wikström, P.O. (2000). Do disadvantaged neighborhoods cause well-adjusted children to become adolescent delinquents? A study of male juvenile serious offending, individual risk and protective factors, and neighborhood context. *Criminology, 38(4)*, 1109–1142.

Wilkinson, R.G. (2005). *The impact of inequality: How to make sick societies healthier.* London: Routledge.

Wilkinson, R., & Pickett, K. (2009). *The spirit level: Why more equal societies almost always do better.* London: Allen Lane.

Williams, J., Jackson, S., Maddocks, C., Cheung, W-Y., Love, A., & Hutchings, H. (2001). Case-control study of the health of those looked after by local authorities. *British Medical Journal, 85(4)*, 280–285.

Wilson, M.I., Daly, M., & Weghorst, S.J. (2008). Household composition and the risk of child abuse and neglect. *Journal of Biosocial Science, 12(3)*, 333–340.

Winnicott, D.W. (1958). The capacity to be alone. *International Journal of Psycho-Analysis, 39*, 416–420.

Winnicott, D.W. (1996). *The maturational processes and the facilitating environment: Studies in the theory of emotional development.* London: Karnac.

Winnicott, D.W. (1971). *Playing and reality.* New York: Basic Books.

Winsler, A., Fernyhough, C., & Montero, I. (Eds.) (2009). *Private speech, executive functioning, and the development of verbal self-regulation.* Cambridge, MA: Cambridge University Press.

Wittgenstein, L. (1974). *Philosophical investigations.* London: Blackwell.

Wolman, W.L., Chalmers, B., Hofmeyr, G.J., & Nikodem, V.C. (1993). Postpartum depression and companionship in the clinical birth environment: A randomized, controlled study. *American Journal of Obstetrics and Gynecology, 168*, 1388–1393.

Woolfenden, S.R., Williams, K., & Peat, J. (2001). Family and parenting interventions in children and adolescents with conduct disorder and delinquency aged 10–17. *Cochrane Database of Systematic Reviews* 2001, Issue 2. Art. No: CD003015.

REFERENCES

Wynne, L., Tienari, P., Sorri, A., Lahti, I., Moring, J., & Wahlberg, K.E. (2006). Genotype-environment interaction in the schizophrenia spectrum: Genetic liability and global family ratings in the Finnish Adoption Study. *Family process, 45(4)*, 419–434.

Yehuda, R. (2004). Risk and resilience in posttraumatic stress disorder. *Journal of Clinical Psychiatry, Supplement, 65(1)*, 29–36.

Yehuda, R., Engel, S.M., Brand, S.R., Seckl, J., Marcus, S.M., & Berkowitz, G.S. (2005). Transgenerational effects of posttraumatic stress disorder in babies of mothers exposed to the World Trade Center attacks during pregnancy. *Journal of Clinical Endocrinology & Metabolism, 90(7)*, 4115–4118.

Yeung, W.J., Duncan, G.J., & Hill, M.S. (2000). Putting fathers back in the picture: Parental activities and children's adult outcomes. *Marriage and Family Review, 29(2/3)*, 97–114.

Youngblade, L.M., & Curry, L.A. (2006). The people they know: Links between interpersonal contexts and adolescent risky and health-promoting behavior. *Applied Developmental Science, 10(2)*, 96–106.

Yurgelun-Todd, D.A., & Killgore, W.D.S. (2006). Fear-related activity in the prefrontal cortex increases with age during adolescence: A preliminary fMRI study. *Neuroscience Letters, 406(3)*, 194–199.

Yussen, S.R., & Levy Jr, V.M. (1975). Developmental changes in predicting one. *Journal of Experimental Child Psychology, 19(3)*, 502–508.

Zak, P., Matzner, W., & Kurzban, R. (2008). The neurobiology of trust. *Scientific American Magazine, 298(6)*, 88–95.

Zanarini, M.C. (1997). Reported pathological childhood experiences associated with the development of borderline personality disorder. *American Journal of Psychiatry, 154*, 1101–1106.

Zanna, M.P., & Pack, S.J. (1975). On the self-fulfilling nature of apparent sex differences in behavior. *Journal of Experimental Social Psychology, 11(6)*, 583–591.

Zautra, A. (2003). *Emotions, stress, and health.* New York: Oxford University Press.

Zeanah, C.H., & Smyke, A.T. (2005). Building attachment relationships following maltreatment and severe deprivation. In L. Berlin, M. Greenberg, & L. Amaya-Jackson (Eds.), *Enhancing early attachments: Theory, research, intervention, and policy* (pp. 195–216). New York: Guilford.

Ziegler, T.E. (2000). Hormones associated with non-maternal infant care: A review of mammalian and avian studies. *Folia Primatol, 71(1)*, 6–21.

Zimbardo, P.G., Maslach, C., & Haney, C. (2000). Reflections on the Stanford prison experiment: Genesis, transformations, consequences. In T. Blass (Ed.), *Obedience to authority: Current perspectives on the Milgram paradigm* (pp. 193–237). Hillsdale, NJ: Lawrence Erlbaum Associates, Inc.

Zucker, R.A., Wong, M.M., Puttler, L.I., & Fitzgerald, H.E. (2003). Resilience and vulnerability among sons of alcoholics: Relationship to developmental outcomes between early childhood and adolescence. In S. Luthar (Ed.), *Resilience and vulnerability: Adaptation in the context of childhood adversities* (pp. 76–103). New York: Cambridge University Press.

Zweyer, K., Velker, B., & Ruch, W. (2004). Do cheerfulness, exhilaration, and humor production moderate pain tolerance? A FACS study. *Humor-International Journal of Humor Research, 17(1–2)*, 85–119.

Author index

Subject index

AAI, *see* Adult Attachment Interview
Abandonment 24, 26, 30, 153
Abecedarian Project 219
Abuse 205–206, 209–210
   children's narratives 129
   disorganised attachment 69, 208–209
   health outcomes 215
   influence on serotonin levels 145
   intergenerational cycle 168–169
   long-term effects 207–208, 236–237
   memory of 115, 118–119
   neglect distinction 202
   peer relationships 168–169, 170
   reactive attachment disorder 69
   step-fathers 180
   theory of mind, 50, *see also* Neglect;
     Trauma
ACE, *see* Adverse Childhood Experiences
   study
ADHD, *see* Attention-deficit hyperactivity
   disorder
Adolescence 8, 185–197
   brain development 95, 188–190, 196–197
   cultural factors 186–187, 196
   drug use during 20
   gender differences 140
   height and status 168
   male suicide 143
   mental health problems 194–195, 196
   peer relationships 191–192, 193–194,
     196
   rough and tumble play 127
   sex and romance 192–194
Adoption 153–154, 227, 230, 231,
   237
Adult Attachment Interview (AAI)
   16–18, 43, 64–65, 67, 69, 107,
   120, 209, 243
Adverse Childhood Experiences
   (ACE) study 207–208, 237
Affect
   definition of 243
   regulation of, 34, 46–47, 54, 55–56,
     107, 210, *see also* Emotions;
     Negative affect; Positive affect
'Affectional bonds' 25, 26, 61
Aggression
   abused children 168–169, 170
   adolescence 190
   boys 139
   fathers 178
   gender differences 144, 146–147
   impact of daycare on 155
   infant defences 38
   maltreated children 234
   rough and tumble play 127
   temperament 170
   testosterone link, 144, 145,
     see also Violence
Aka people 74, 174, 175, 182
Alcohol 17, 189, 196, 207, 220, 230
Alleles 226, 227, 228, 243